NATIVE
AMERICAN
COLLECTIBLES
IDENTIFICATION AND PRICE GUIDE

NATIVE

AMERICAN
COLLECTIBLES
IDENTIFICATION AND PRICE GUIDE

FIRST EDITION

DAWN E. RENO

The CONFIDENT COLLECTOR™

AVON BOOKS ◆ NEW YORK

THE CONFIDENT COLLECTOR: NATIVE AMERICAN COLLECTIBLES IDENTIFICATION AND PRICE GUIDE (1st edition) is an original publication of Avon Books. This work has never before appeared in book form.

AVON BOOKS
A division of
The Hearst Corporation
1350 Avenue of the Americas
New York, New York 10019

Copyright © 1994 by Dawn E. Reno
Photographs by Robert G. Reno
Interior design by Suzanne H. Holt
Produced by Publisher's Studio, Albany, New York
The Confident Collector and its logo are trademarked properties of Avon Books.
Published by arrangement with the author
Library of Congress Catalog Card Number: 94-23304
ISBN: 0-380-77069-5

Library of Congress Cataloging in Publication Data:

Reno, Dawn E.
   Native American collectibles: identification and price guide/
Dawn E. Reno. 1st ed.
      p. cm.
   1. Indians of North America—Antiquities—Collectors and collecting—United States. 2. Indians of North America—Material culture. 3. United States—Antiquities—Collectors and collecting. I. Title.
E77.9.R46 1994   94-23304
973'.0497'0074—dc20   CIP

First Avon Books Trade Printing: December 1994

AVON TRADEMARK REG. U.S. PAT. OFF. AND IN OTHER COUNTRIES, MARCA REGISTRADA, HECHO EN U.S.A.

Printed in the U.S.A.

OPM 10 9 8 7 6 5 4 3 2

Dedicated to

my assistant and friend

Jenna L. Bartlett

without whom this book

would not have been completed

Contents

❦

Acknowledgments

While I was putting this book together, I had a series of personal crises that set me back, making it almost impossible to continue. With the help of my assistant, Jenna L. Bartlett, a woman who had her own writing to attend to and who selflessly gave her time to help me, I was able to continue and to finish what I believe is a better book than my first edition. I could not have completed my work without her and I extend my utmost gratitude to her.

My husband, Robert Reno, a professional photographer, traveled with me to visit our contributors in the Southwest and took the photos included in this book of their collections. It was his first time photographing still objects (he usually does portraits), and I am grateful for his help, as well as proud of his accomplishments.

Of course, books like this one would not be possible without the contributions of auctioneers, collectors, dealers, and artisans. I am constantly amazed at how affable and congenial these people are, and I feel honored to be associated with them.

I also extend my thanks to Carrington Morris, formerly at Avon Books, who took on a tough task and was always there when I needed a question answered; to Lisa Considine of Avon Books, who took over the project and did a spectacular job finishing the editing; and to the Volusia County Library system, whose employees answered my queries promptly and efficiently.

Introduction

It has come to my attention, during the years between the publication of the first edition of this book and the completion of this one, that interest in Native American arts has not waned, but strengthened. More and more people are incorporating the southwestern look into their homes and beginning to learn more about our Native American heritage. I applaud their efforts and hope that their learning experience continues.

Personally, I am amazed at how many medicinal cures, sports, games, foods, and crafts of mainstream American culture come directly from the people who preceded the European white man on this continent. I strongly believe that the Native American view of ecology, respect for Mother Earth, and religious beliefs are philosophies that this nation as a whole can benefit by.

I count many Indian artisans among my friends and stand in awe of their talent. I also envy the quiet, humble way they deal with the genius that enables them to create extraordinarily beautiful and meaningful pieces of art. Though there is much to be learned from the past, I believe these new artists are the future—incorporating the thousands of years of their culture into what they create today.

If you are a new collector of the art of the Native American, I would suggest you read not only the collector's magazines but also historical books that detail the background of each tribe, their beliefs, their creativity, their lifestyle, and what we learned and can still learn from them. There were hundreds of indigenous tribes in the United States, some of which were decimated by exposure to diseases brought with colonial settlers from Europe. Each group is intrinsically different from its neighbors. Each produced items that they used every day, many of which we now consider art, but all had a deep reverence for the land on which they lived, often worshiping before creating a clay pot or a carved mask.

When items become as popular and valuable as some of the examples of the Native American art listed in this book, people are bound to "jump on the bandwagon." Reproductions surface and it is important for beginning collectors to watch carefully for them, as well as to buy the best-quality examples available in their price range. The contributors to this book can help. Feel free to write to them or visit their shops. They will not only share their knowledge with you, they will be happy to be your "eyes" when they meet with the Native American artisans or go on their buying trips. Making knowledgeable contacts is often worth more than the price of this book ten times over.

My last bit of advice is to buy that which appeals to you. Don't purchase an item because you think it may rise in value within a few years; make a purchase because something about that item speaks to you—and enjoy!

NATIVE AMERICAN COLLECTIBLES

IDENTIFICATION AND PRICE GUIDE

Chapter One

Art

In compiling the information for this chapter, there was much deliberation about whether to focus only on Indian artists or to also include those artists whose work includes scenes of Indian life. I have decided to include both categories because I believe collectors should be familiar with the full scope of art by (and of) the American Indian.

In the biographies section of this chapter, those artists who are Indian are denoted by tribe. Those not so noted are either not of Native American heritage, or there was no tribal information uncovered during research.

Publications such as *American Indian Art* and *Southwest Art* focus their attention on Indian art and are the best source for tracking what is happening today in the collecting world.

Since the first edition of this book was released in 1988, new galleries have opened, museums have sponsored special exhibits, and shows have sprung up all over the country. Recent developments in the art world with regard to those artists who specialized in painting the American Indian have included an exhibit titled "Alfred Jacob Miller: Watercolors of the American West" shown at the Amon Carter Museum in Fort Worth in 1992; the second annual Antique American Indian and Tribal Art Show and Auction in Santa Fe, held in June of 1993; the ninth annual Marin Antique American Indian & Ethnographic Art Show and Sale, held in February of 1993; Philip Garaway's showing entitled "Master Works of Western Indian Basketry"; the Maitland (Florida) Art Center's "The People: Art of Native Americans," held in June 1992; "Objects of Myth and Memory: American Indian Art at the Brooklyn Museum," a traveling show; the "Chiefly Feasts" exhibit, which focused on the Northwest Coast Kwakiutl Indians and was held at the American Museum of Natural History in 1991; as well as many others.

Suffice it to say, Indian art is part of the American heritage, and should you own a quality piece of work in this category, you have an investment that will continue to grow.

How to Buy a Native American Work of Art

As I've stated in all my other books on antiques and art, the first premise in beginning a collection—or even buying one piece—is that the piece of art should be something with which you are absolutely in love. This applies whether you intend to decorate your home or to accumulate works with investment potential.

Dealers of Native American art have told me that when you're considering a piece for purchase, it helps to have some understanding of the culture the artist was influenced by, as well as a general knowledge of the composition, form, and color of the work. In Indian art, colors are often symbolic, and geometric forms can spell out a whole language. (You will read more about this later in this chapter.) Education is paramount.

It helps to deal with a reputable gallery—someone who has been around awhile and whose tastes somewhat reflect your own. Research the painting you're interested in. There are several good books on the market, but the ones most often suggested are *Southwest Indian Painting*, by Clara Tanner, and *American Indian Painting*, by Dorothy Dunn. Find a guide (like this one!) that includes prices of recently sold works of art to give you an idea of the value of your artist's work. If the value has appeared to rise during the past few years, you probably will be making a good investment. Keep in mind that paintings and other works of art that have won awards at the Indian Market, the Gallup Intertribal, or other fairs will be more marketable should you decide to sell them in the future. Finally, the condition of a painting is a primary concern. Paintings that have been repaired or obviously cut down will be considered of less value than ones in their original condition and frames.

Native American Indian Women Artists

It is important to note at this juncture that the first American women artists were Indian. During the early years of our history, their art—whether it was the art of quilling, pottery, blanket weaving, beadwork, or painting scenes on walls, tepees, or clothing—expressed their sensitivity to textures and colors. That intuition produced some of the most imaginative designs the world has seen.

Native American women's art was not taught to them in a classroom, but rather passed down to them by their mothers, sisters, aunts, and grandmothers. The geometry of forms they used and the interlocking of figures and space are techniques that the American Indian women have used for centuries—techniques that some abstract painters struggle for years to master.

I have mentioned them here to give them the recognition they deserve, but also to direct your attention to the other sections of this volume in which you can discover creative works that may not be listed as "formal art."

SYMBOLS IN INDIAN ART

Amerind artists did not paint simply to produce pretty pictures. They often told stories through their art, relaying family histories, recording tales of battle, or providing directions to another location.

Though most symbols used in Native American art have a very clear, definitive meaning, that meaning can change if it is painted in a different color. A pipe tomahawk, for example, represents a peaceful council, but if painted red, could denote a war council.

Meanings of particular symbols can also vary depending on the tribe from which a piece originates. A symbol such as a triangle or a semicircle with straight lines descending from the base represents a rain cloud and rain to one of the Pueblo tribes. It can mean a mountain with streams to a Plains Indian, or a bear (or bear claw) to other tribes.

The Southwest tribes use many different, distinctive designs, as do the Pacific Coast, Northwest Coast, and Plains tribes. Southwestern Indians decorate pottery, rugs, sandpaintings, and kachinas with their symbols, while Northwest Coast tribes use them on house poles, boxes, rattles, clothing, and carvings, and the Plains Indians use them on hides, blankets, and clothing.

By learning to recognize some of these symbols and their meanings, you are learning a new language. Consequently, the work done by the Native American people will suddenly become more interesting.

The following are some of the symbols used:

Arrow = Protection

Arrowhead = Alertness

Bear tracks = Good omen

Big mountain = Abundance

Bird = Carefree

Butterfly = Beauty

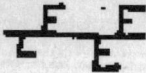

Cactus = Sign of desert

Deer tracks = Abundance of game

Enclosure = Surrounded

Hopi cloud = Prayer for snow

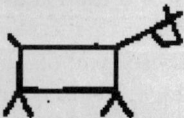

Horse = Journey

Lasso = Captivity

Lightning = Swiftness

Lightning Snake = Swiftness

Rain clouds = Good prospects

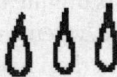

Raindrops = Food

Rattlesnake jaw = Strength

Running water = No thirst

Squash blossom = Fertility

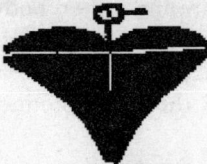

Summer bird = Prayer for warmth

Sun symbol = Happiness

Thunderbird = Bearer of happiness

Thunderbird tracks = Bright prospects

Watchful eye = Caution

PLAINS INDIAN ART OF HORSE-PAINTING

Though it's not something that can be kept on display, or that we can attribute to a particular artist, I'm fascinated by the Plains Indian art of painting their horses. The animals were painted in preparation for war—they were either camouflaged or decorated according to tribal ritual and ceremony.

Certain tribes used symbols and colors unique to that clan, but some markings were universal. For example, when a warrior had led his people into battle, a rectangle was painted on his horse. If a warrior had, in the past, been struck down by an enemy or engaged in hand-to-hand combat, a handprint was the symbol painted on the horse. The Sioux's mark of highest honor was a red handprint on the rump of a warrior's horse.

Thick circles with red centers meant a battle had been fought from behind logs or rocks and enemies had been killed. Small open circles in a row meant the warrior had been in a battle fought in trenches. Circles around the horse's nose were thought to improve the animal's smell; if circles were made around the eyes, it was believed to improve eyesight. Circles around other body parts could show that the animal had been wounded. *Coup* marks were signified by three or four short, straight lines, while arrowheads on the horse's hooves signified the surefootedness and fleetness of the horse.

As with symbolism used in other Native American art forms, each marking had a different meaning, and some markings meant different things to different tribes.

SOUTHWESTERN SANDPAINTING

Another Indian art that was not collectible until recent history is sandpainting. These works were not originally produced to create a historical record or lasting influence on spiritual forces—rather they were a spiritual remedy to an acute problem.

Though general belief is that the Pueblo Indian tribes taught the Navajos the art of sandpainting, the Navajos insist that their art was taught to them by the "Holy Ones."

Sandpainting has traditionally been used by the tribe's medicine man in an effort to maintain the delicate balance of the world. That balance can only be upset by man when he "causes" a disaster or illness. The shaman comes to the offender's *hogan*, a small igloo-shaped mud hut, designs his sandpainting on clean white sand on the hogan's dirt floor, and incorporates an opening in the painting that faces east. This opening is intended to make it difficult for evil to enter.

Only five sacred sand colors are used in sandpainting, and each detail in the process of creating a sandpainting must be perfect. The slightest deviation in this ritual is believed to cause great trouble.

The medicine man, in a deep trance, takes the design for the sandpainting from his mind, never making two alike. Once the painting is finished, the patient is brought to the center of the work, and the medicine man performs his ceremony to drive the evil away. When the ceremony is finished, the sandpainting is swept into a blanket. Before sunset, the blanket is carried outside and the sand is blown into the wind—to be returned to Mother Earth so that the evil forces trapped by the sandpainting will not escape.

The sacred sandpainting designs were not viewed by people outside the tribes until the late 1800s. By the early 1900s, historians and traders were reproducing the designs, though sandpaintings were not done in a permanent manner until a "How to Sandpaint" kit was developed by David Villasenor (ca. 1960). Today both natural and synthetic dyes are used to make sandpaintings. The sands are glued to a chipboard support so that they may be hung. Though sandpaintings have only been commercially available for about thirty-five years, one can sometimes find earlier examples.

To craft a sandpainting, only hand-ground rocks, minerals, pollen, charcoal, or sandstone are used. The work is a buildup of these materials, with the finest sands producing the highest-quality work.

Native American artists developing sandpaintings are now beginning to garner some interest in the art world. Some of these artists include Thomas and Cora Bryant, Jerald Sherman, Keith Silversmith, and Janice Charles.

BIOGRAPHIES

As you might be able to tell by reading some of the biographies included in this chapter, American Indian art was influenced by such people as Olaf Nordmark, a muralist, who taught a cross section of Native American artists; Frederick Dockstader, a former director of the Museum of the American Indian in New York City and a man who has a large collection of the finest of American Indian art; and by Dorothy Dunn, a young white woman who, in 1932, founded the first department of painting at the Santa Fe Indian School, an early and important Indian school in the United States. Dunn taught in the classical European style and instructed her students to paint without using any shadows.

At one point during the early pioneering days of the Southwest, an advertising man, W. H. Simpson, decided to use art to lure travelers to the exotic regions of Santa Fe and Taos. Indians learned to do murals and to enlarge their work to poster size. Because of the availability of work and the encouragement given, artists built colonies in the area, and those establishments flourished and gave us a rich tapestry of works.

Since the early part of the twentieth century, Native American artists are far less restricted by cultural barriers and have begun breaking with tradition to use new mediums and materials not originally associated with Indian artwork. However, they are often still not listed in the directories of American artists, and one wonders whether it is because their work is often restricted to being sold within the framework of an "Indian market" or whether it is because quite a few Native American artists have never received the formal training that is "acceptable" in the art world.

The lack of well-kept records at Indian schools and the lack of communication about Indian artists often makes it difficult to trace an artist's history. In fact, the only book this writer found that documented biographies of Indian artists is one published by the Museum of the American Indian and compiled by Jeanne Snodgrass, the former curator of American Indian art at the Philbrook Art Center.

Snodgrass's accumulated information, gathered from exhibits and competitions held by the Center since its first exhibition in 1946, was the basis for the directory when it was first published in 1968. Though plans were originally made to update the directory, the task has not been undertaken at this writing. I would like to update and continue that bibliographical listing and am currently investigating ways in which it could be done. It would be a monumental task, but one that *needs* to be done before we lose the thread of history linking today's Native American artist with yesterday's.

Snodgrass's compilation, as well as a good smattering of newspaper and magazine articles and other listings of artists, and information accumulated through other sources (primarily the artists themselves or the galleries representing them), served as the basis for the biographies in this chapter.

Along with a brief description of the artists and their work, I have tried to include an approximate range of what the artists' work is currently bringing in today's market.

THE ARTISTS
ANDY ABEITA AND ROBERTA ABEITA

This husband-and-wife team are stone sculptors and fetish carvers who travel almost a hundred thousand miles a year across the country to bring their art and heritage to the American people. Andy has lectured on Native American culture and art at his gallery appearances, is recognized by the Native American Art Council as a lecturer, is a member of the American Indian Arts & Crafts Association board of directors, serves as a consultant to the Native American Arts Council, and writes educational material about his culture.

He is a native of the Isleta Pueblo, while Roberta is a full-blood Navajo. Their specialty is creating stone-carved fetishes, accented with precious stones and their signature heart-line. The larger fetishes have medicine bundles made up of shells, feathers, carved stone shapes, antlers, and tiny pieces of stones tied to their backs. The Abeitas make pouch fetishes as well as fetish pendants, and Andy recently produced his first large carved piece, a three-hundred-pound bear, which sold almost immediately.

NARCISSO PLATERO ABEYTA (1918–)

Originally named Ascending (Ha So Deh), Abeyta was born in Gallup, New Mexico, and began his artistic career drawing on canyon walls; he was later published in *Art in America*.

He studied at the Santa Fe Indian School, graduating in 1939, and at the Somerset Academy School, graduating in 1940. Abeyta received his bachelor of arts degree in 1953 from the University of New Mexico, served in the U.S. Army during World War II, and worked for the New Mexico State Employment Commission as a job placement interviewer after returning home.

His work has been published by Tanner (1957) and others (including the aforementioned *Art in America*).

Abeyta's work was exhibited in shows such as the San Francisco World's Fair (1939–1940), and examples of his work are held at the University of Oklahoma, Museum of New Mexico, and Arizona State Museum. He has won fourteen awards, including the ITIC Grand Award.

Paintings by Narcisso Platero Abeyta sell for approximately $1,300, and drawings are averaging $500–$800.

TONY ABEYTA

The son of a Navajo father (Narcisso Abeyta) and an Anglo mother, Tony Abeyta was commissioned to paint the cover of the 1992 issue of the *Indian Market* magazine. He learned to paint from his father while the family lived in Gallup and he completed a two-year apprenticeship there. Later he studied at the Institute of American Indian Arts in Santa Fe. He went on to the Art Institute in Chicago, believing that he would be able to expand his talents by putting some distance between himself and the Southwest.

While there, he began experimenting with sand and using it in his paintings, working on a three-dimensional style. His style encompasses a wide range of colors, from black and white to bright primary colors.

He lives in Chicago with artist-wife Patricia and young son Gabriel. He looks forward to moving back to New Mexico once Patricia finishes her degree at the Art Institute.

His awards include first and third place in mixed media at the Indian Market, first place in two-dimensional painting, and second place in lithographs.

ALICE ASMAR

Asmar works in all media, but colored inks are her specialty.

She received her bachelor of arts degree and graduated magna cum laude from Lewis and Clark College in Portland, Oregon, and later earned a master of fine arts from the University of Washington.

Asmar paints Indians because she sees them as "America's real ecologists."

Solo shows of her work have been held at Galerie de Fondation des Etas-Unis, Paris; New York; Italy; the Minnesota Museum of Art; and the Western Association of Art Museums.

HARRISON BEGAY (1917–)

This well-known Navajo painter/illustrator/printmaker/muralist was born in White Cone, Arizona. His Indian name is Warrior Who Walked Up to His Enemy (Haskay Yah Ne Yah).

Begay studied at the Santa Fe Indian School (1939) under Dorothy Dunn. He later studied architecture at Black Mountain (1940–1941) and attended Phoenix Junior College (1941). He served in the U.S. Army Signal Corps in the Pacific during World War II, using his native language, which became renowned as one of the codes the Japanese could not break.

Internationally known, Begay's work has had a great influence on other Navajo artists. His works have been published by Frederick Dockstader (director of the Museum of the American Indian— 1961) and in a number of issues of *Arizona Highways* magazine, as well as many other publications.

Begay began exhibiting in 1946. His work has won many awards and has been exhibited in such shows as the First Annual American Indian Art Exhibition in 1964 at Wayne State University, the Museum of Modern Art in New York, and the Philbrook Art Center.

Begay's paintings have recently sold for approximately $1,300, and his drawings have fetched prices in the $500 range.

ALBERT BIERSTADT (1830–1902)

This landscape painter born in Düsseldorf, Germany, studied in Germany and Rome before becoming a U.S. member of ANA in 1860.

Bierstadt exhibited throughout Europe, then came to live in New Bedford, Massachusetts, in 1831. His works are held at the capitol building in Washington, D.C.; the Hermitage in Saint Petersburg; the Imperial Place in Berlin; the New York Public Library; the Academy of Fine Arts in Buffalo, New York; and Corcoran Gallery in Washington, D.C. Some of the honors he received during his lifetime include being named Chevalier of the Legion of Honor in 1867; the Order of Saint Stanislaus of Russia in 1869; and the Imperial Order of the Medjidi from the Sultan of Turkey in 1886.

His paintings of American Indians are finely done and much admired by collectors of American art. The prices average in the four- to five-figure range, although they have gone as high as $2,640,000.

ARCHIE BLACKOWL (1911–   )

Award-winning painter Blackowl was born an Apache in Weatherford, Oklahoma, a descendant of the Cheyenne Roman Nose. His Indian name is Flying Hawk (Mis Ta Moo To Va).

Blackowl studied at the Segr Indian School, as well as at the Concho Indian School, and learned various painting techniques from muralist Olaf Nordmark.

During his artistic career, Blackowl was commissioned to paint murals for quite a few institutions (including the Riverside Indian School), and also did portraits of public officials. He created illustrations for the Georgia Agricultural Extension Service and was both author and illustrator of *Charts for Visual Instruction*. His work was published by various newspapers and magazines, and exhibitions of his work have been held throughout the United States at galleries and museums such as the Agra Gallery in Washington, D.C., the Oklahoma Art Center, and various state colleges and universities.

Archie Blackowl's work is held in public and private collections throughout the United States.

ACEE BLUE EAGLE (1910–1959)

Born on the Wichita Reservation in Anadarko, Oklahoma, Blue Eagle was a Creek/Pawnee who became orphaned before he was five. Adopted by his grandparents, Blue Eagle chose to take his paternal grandfather's name, though his given name was Alex C. McIntosh and his Indian name was Laughing Boy (Che Bon Ah Bu La).

Blue Eagle spent part of his childhood at the Nuyaka Mission in Oklahoma and was educated there, as well as at Oklahoma University; Oxford University in England; Bacone College, Oklahoma; and through commercial art classes given at Oklahoma S.U./S.T. from 1951 to 1952.

His career was full and colorful, and included travel throughout the United States and Europe. Blue Eagle gave lectures and exhibits on "Life and the Character of the American Indian"; started, then became head of, the Art Department at Bacone College; and also conducted a television program in Muskogee, Oklahoma.

Acee Blue Eagle received many honors during his life, including being named "Outstanding Indian of the United States" (1958), and in 1959 being honored for service to the state through a resolution passed by the Oklahoma Legislature. He also acted as director of art at Bacone College in Oklahoma.

He was commissioned by Oklahoma public buildings (i.e., Oklahoma College for Women and the Muskogee Public Library); had works published by Jacobson and D'Ucel, as well as in *Indians of Oklahoma* (1966); exhibited at the National Exhibition of American Indian Painters at the Philbrook Art Center (1946), the Xth Olympiad at the Los Angeles Museum of History, Science and Art (1932), American Indian Expositions, the Denver Art Museum, Grand Central Art Galleries, and many others; held one-man art shows at the Young Gallery in Chicago and the Muskogee Public Library, to name just a few; won over forty awards in his lifetime; and had the honor of having his work held in major public and private art collections all over the world, such as those held by Hailie Selassie, Eleanor Roosevelt, and King Alfonso XIII of Spain.

Blue Eagle's paintings sell in the four- to five-figure range in today's market, and there are prints being made of his work on a regular basis.

PARKER BOYIDDLE, JR. (1948–   )

Boyiddle was born with a mixture of Indian blood. His mother was Wichita-Delaware-Chickasaw, and his father, Kiowa.

The artist graduated from Classen High School in Oklahoma City in 1965 and was honored with an art scholarship at the Oklahoma Science and Art Foundation.

His work has been exhibited at Riverside Museum in New York.

GEORGE CATLIN (1796–1872)

Catlin is often credited with being the most prolific painter of the American Indian, but he was also an author, ethnographer, historian, showman, and traveler.

Catlin's love of Indian lore and interest in art went hand in hand from the time he was a youngster, straight through to his death at the age of seventy-five.

His paintings of members of the various Indian tribes that existed during his lifetime are the most accurate and the most complete of any artist who took the time to record the personalities and characteristics of the Amerind.

Catlin's art education began after he sold his law books and bought artist brushes and paints with the proceeds. He moved from

Litchfield, Connecticut, to Philadelphia and, without any formal instruction, was fairly successful painting miniature portraits. In 1824 he was elected to the prestigious Pennsylvania Academy of the Fine Arts.

In 1830 he began his travels to the "Far West." Meeting with the Sauk and Fox tribes, he did portraits and wrote of his impressions of the Treaty that allied the two tribes. He went on to paint northeastern woodland tribes, such as the Shawnees, Delawares, Kickapoos, and Potawatomis.

Catlin visited the Konzas, of Kansas, later that same year and wrote about the tribe, stating that they most certainly "sprung from the Osages, as their personal appearance, language and traditions clearly prove."

Before the smallpox epidemic of 1832, Catlin painted Otoes, Missouris, Omahas, and Pawnees, and his writings give us some of the only historical information available on these tribes, about half of which were wiped out by the epidemic.

The Plains Indians visited Catlin while he was in Saint Louis in 1832 and had their portraits painted by him.

Other tribes that Catlin recorded with his brush include the Arikara, Sioux, Teton Sioux, Cheyennes, Mandan, Osage, Kiowas, Comanches, Wichitas, Choctaw, Cherokee, Creeks, Seminole, and perhaps a Nez Perce.

His attention to detail and the notes he took during his travels served as the background for his *Letters and Notes on the Manners, Customs and Conditions of the North American Indians* and for his "Indian Gallery," completed in 1837 and which included some 507 portraits, all listed in his 1840 catalog.

Exhibits were arranged to show Catlin's Indian Gallery to the public in various eastern cities including Pittsburgh, New York, Boston, Philadelphia, and Washington. He also took his gallery to the Louvre in Paris, at the invitation of King Louis Philippe, in 1845.

After his last year in London (1848), Catlin began having financial difficulties and turned to writing books, traveling, and trying to copy his works on cardboard. He had hoped to sell his collection of paintings to the government, but died before accomplishing his aim.

Today, works of Catlin's are often sold for large sums to museums and wealthy private collectors, though prints often come on the market at a fairly reasonable price. When auctioned, portraits by

Catlin are always expected to bring close to half a million dollars. His drawings bring $15,000–$75,000.

POP CHALEE (MARINA LIYAN) (1908–   )

Chalee was born of an East Indian mother and a Taos Indian father, and his childhood was one that fostered the development of art, whch became his career.

His style—a light, surrealistic fantasy world—shows the influence of both East Indian and Taos cultures.

Chalee was tutored by Dorothy Dunn at the Santa Fe Indian School during the 1930s.

ROBERT CHEE (1938–1971)

A Navajo artist, Chee attended school in Billemont, Arizona, and is one of the few lucky Indian artists who were able to devote a career entirely to art.

Chee's works have been published in many periodicals, including *New Mexico Magazine* and the *Inter-Tribal Indian Ceremonial Annual Magazine.*

His work has been exhibited at the Museum of New Mexico and the Philbrook Art Center.

Public collections of his work are held by the Museum of New Mexico, the Philbrook Art Center, the Bureau of Indian Affairs, and many others. Frederick Dockstader and Leland Wyman are just two of the private collectors who have works by Robert Chee in their possession.

His paintings sell for $150–$700, while his drawings are in the $40–$80 range.

WOODROW WILSON CRUMBO (1912–1989)

Woody Crumbo was born a Creek-Potawatomi Indian in Lexington, Oklahoma. His career as an artist began at an early age when Susie Peters encouraged him, and other Anadarko, Oklahoma, Indian boys, to paint. Though his education was temporarily halted in the third grade, he returned to formal schooling at the age of seventeen to enroll in the eighth grade at the Chilocoo Indian School. When he turned nineteen, he was given a scholarship to study at the American Indian Institute in Wichita, where he concentrated on art and anthropology. He graduated from there as valedictorian of his class, then went on to attend Wichita University from 1933 to 1936. He studied art at the American Indian Institute in Wichita, Kansas, at the University of Oklahoma, and at Wichita State University. At one point he was director of art for Bacone College in Muskogee.

His first painting, *Deer and Birds*, was given to the Philbrook Art Center in 1939. During his career, he made it a point to accurately complete a pictorial record of Indian life.

As with other Indian artists of his day, Crumbo studied under the muralist Olaf Nordmark. He also learned watercolor techniques from Clayton Henri Staples, and O. B. Jacobson trained him in painting and drawing.

Woody's career was a long and interesting one. He held a variety of arts and crafts positions and even designed aircraft for Cessna Aircraft and Douglas Aircraft. In 1944 Crumbo helped convince the Philbrook Art Center to sponsor the first national Indian art show. Crumbo was the artist-in-residence at the Gilcrease Museum, where he assembled an American Indian and western art collection in 1945, and also served as the assistant director of the El Paso Museum of Art (1962–1968).

He won many honors, including the Julius Rosenwald Fellowship, and his work has been published by many periodicals, including *Tulsa Sunday World Magazine* and *New Mexico* magazine.

Over two hundred exhibitions of Crumbo's work, many of them one-man shows, have been held all over the United States, Europe, and North and South America. He was inducted into the Oklahoma Hall of Fame in 1978.

Collections of his work are held by the Philbrook Art Center, the Gilcrease Institute, the Southeast Museum of the North American Indian, and many others.

Woody Crumbo died of a heart attack at his home in Cimarron, New Mexico, in 1989. He left his wife, Lillian, a Creek Indian whom he married in 1941, as well as a son and daughter.

Prices for his works range from the low thousands to the teens.

CHARLES DEAS (1818–1867)
Deas grew up in Philadelphia, where he was educated in the classics and art. By 1835 he moved to upstate New York with his widowed mother and began to pursue his natural affinity for art.

He, as others had before him (most notably George Catlin, whose New York Indian gallery opened in 1837), headed west to seek adventure. He lived in Saint Louis for eight years, where he continued to paint. His works were exhibited there, as well as in New York and Philadelphia.

Deas had a fascination for Indian culture and shared his view that they were a people whose way of life should be preserved with other artists such as George Catlin and John Mix Stanley.

Notable works include his painting of members of the Winnebago tribe leisurely playing checkers in 1842 after a long trip through the Wisconsin Territory, and one of members of the Sioux tribe playing ball in 1843.

Few of his paintings survived a yearlong trip that took Deas through the Wisconsin Territory, but he took advantage of that time to collect sketches of the Winnebago tribe.

Deas also painted the Sioux tribe in the summer of 1841 while he was visiting Fort Snelling. Though documented by Deas's biographer, Henry Tuckerman, who wrote about the artist for *Godey's Lady's Book* in 1846, few of these paintings exist today.

Deas was described in the unofficial journal of a Lt. J. Henry Carleton to be a "Rocky Mountains' free spirit," who was quite at home with the Indians and whose good humor helped him break the ice with whomever he was painting at the time.

His paintings have been exhibited and sold at the American Art Union in New York, as well as galleries in Saint Louis and on the East Coast.

At the height of his career in the 1840s, Deas produced now lost works such as *The Last Shot* and *The Oregon Pioneers*. His last major painting was exhibited at the 1847 Mechanics' Fair, whereupon he left Saint Louis for good.

Once back in New York City in 1848, Deas was committed to an asylum for the insane. His career had ended before he was thirty years old. His last painting, *A Vision*, now lost, was a horrific, yet delicately beautiful, depiction of despair and death.

He died of apoplexy on March 2, 1867, while hospitalized at the Bloomingdale Asylum for the Insane in New York.

WILLIAM COCHISE FOX

Though this artist has never given an interview or been photographed, forty-seven of his drawings brought $3.2 million dollars at a 1992 Christie's auction. The catalog described the drawings as "dazzling and flawlessly executed." The rarest of the group was a monotype entitled *Crossfire*, which depicted the Kennedy assassination. The group also included sketches of celebrities, including: country singer Billy Ray Cyrus, rock singer George Michael, actress Greta Garbo, and members of the Kennedy family.

Rumors persist that Fox cast a powerful Indian curse on the rock singer Jim Morrison, and that the artist also had some connection with Janis Joplin.

It is said Mr. Fox has been inactive since 1973. He is also a leading diamond expert and gemologist. He lives in Greenport, New York, and information about him was obtained from the Indian Museum in Southold, New York.

JACK GLOVER
Half-Cherokee, half-cowboy, this contemporary sculptor is also the author of fourteen books on Indian culture, as well as the creator of investment-quality bronzes, a collector of Indian artifacts, and the owner of an old West museum and trading post in Bowie, Texas.

Glover believes strongly in his Indian heritage and religion, and those beliefs come through in the beautiful bronze figurines he crafts on a regular basis.

Visitors to Glover's Museum in Bowie, Texas, will be regaled by his stories, and impressed by his collection of Indian artifacts and knowledge of the history of the American West.

R.C. GORMAN (1933–   )
Gorman is one of the best-known contemporary Native American artists, his sensuous style and large canvases well known in this market. He has had a commercial success that reaches far beyond the circle of those who collect strictly Native American art. His posters and lithographs of Navajo women are sold almost everywhere.

While living on the Navajo reservation, his father, painter Carl Nelson Gorman, inspired R.C. to paint. R.C. still insists that wherever he is, he is never far enough from home to forget the source of his inspiration.

Gorman has also written several books, including *R.C. Gorman: The Radiance of My People*, released in 1992.

Joe Grandee (1929–   )

A contemporary painter of the highest regard, Grandee was the first official Texas state artist and has won many awards (including the Franklin Mint Gold Medal 1973, 1974). He has attended White House receptions and been a special guest at many government functions, and is a television and radio personality. His work is exhibited in many American museums, including the Montana Historical Society, the El Paso Museum of Fine Art, and the United States Marine Corps Museum.

Grandee's paintings of the American West and American Indians are extremely realistic. He is such a stickler for detail that he has been known to dress models in authentic period clothing and to stage scenes he plans to paint. He is a respected authority on the historical details of the American West and houses an incredible collection of clothing, artifacts, and other items in his gallery outside of Dallas, Texas.

Works done by Grandee include a portrait of Lynda Bird Johnson's wedding and a painting of a Texas Ranger, given to President Nixon on behalf of the State of Texas.

Though Grandee's first painting only netted him $75, originals of his work now command $35,000 or more.

Helen Hardin (1943–1984)

Helen Hardin (whose Indian name was Tsa Sah Wee Eh) was the daughter of artist Pablita Velarde. Velarde, a recognized talent with Dorothy Dunn's "studio" during the 1930s, was called the "greatest woman artist in the Southwest" by Clara Lee Tanner in her second edition (1980) of *Southwest Indian Painting*.

Hardin's style was more modern and abstract than traditional Indian painting and often integrated the designs of the potters of Acoma and Mimbres. She began building that style after winning an art contest at the age of six—she wasn't intimidated by the fact that the contest was for boys only. Her subject was a fire engine.

At the University of New Mexico, Hardin studied art history and anthropology, later winning a painting scholarship to a special school for Indians at the University of Arizona.

Hardin's first art show, in Bogota, Colombia, was almost a sellout, and she continued to win prizes for her art in the following years.

Her work, by her own admission, is definitely not traditional Native American painting. Hardin used her drafting training in creating abstract and geometric works, and often her paintings have an art deco quality. During the 70s she developed a series of Kachina paintings, then went on to her "Women" series.

Helen Hardin was not only a leading Indian artist, but a television panelist and actress as well. She died of cancer in 1984.

The prices of Hardin's paintings skyrocketed after her death; however, her drawings are still available below $1,000.

Velino Shije Herrera (1902–1973)

This Zia artist, also known as Velino Shije, Ma Pe Wi, or Oriole, was born on October 22, 1902, at the Zia Pueblo in New Mexico. He continued to use the name Oriole, a pun that meant "bad egg."

In the course of his career, he owned a studio in Santa Fe, taught painting at the Albuquerque Indian School, and was a rancher. He studied in Santa Fe with E. Hewett.

Herrera was commissioned to do murals for the Albuquerque Indian School and others; illustrated books during the 1940s; and has had his work published in magazines including *School Arts, American Magazine of Art,* and *Arizona Highways,* as well as in books such as *Compton's Pictured Encyclopedia.* He was also commissioned to do work for the Amon Carter Museum, the American Museum of Natural History, the Corcoran Gallery, the Denver Art Museum, and the Museum of New Mexico.

Exhibits that included his work were held at the Heard Museum in Phoenix, the Southwest Museum, the Museum of New Mexico, and at various tribal ceremonials. Herrera's works are included in private and public collections such as the Dockstader and Rockefeller collections.

When his wife, Mary, was killed in an automobile accident in the 1950s, Herrera, who was with her, suffered lasting injuries and his art career came to an end.

His paintings bring between $400 and $1,000.

Edward Hicks (1780–1849)

Hicks's painting of William Penn's treaty with the Lenape Indians hung as a sign for Samuel West's Inn in Chester, Pennsylvania, until 1920.

In 1987 it was purchased by the Newtown Historical Association in Newtown, Pennsylvania, and now hangs in the Court Inn, near Hicks's first house in Newtown.

ALLAN C. HOUSER (1915–   )

Born "Pulling Roots" in Apache, Oklahoma, on June 30, 1915, this Chiricahua Apache's parents were part of a group held prisoner with Geronimo's band.

Houser's skills as a painter are matched by his sculpting talents, and though the artist's formal schooling ended at the eighth grade level, he had instruction from muralist Olaf Nordmark, the same painter who had taken other Indian artists under his wing. He also worked with Dorothy Dunn in Santa Fe.

Through Nordmark's tutelage, Houser's talent emerged and he won honors such as a scholarship for sculpture and painting from John Simon Guggenheim, and a Certificate of Appreciation by the IACB in 1967.

He was commissioned to paint a number of murals in Indian schools, including Fort Sill, Riverside, and Jicarilla, and he sculpted the marble war memorial entitled *Comrades in Mourning* at the Haskell Institute in 1948.

Publications such as *Arizona Highways* and *Oklahoma Today* are only two of the many magazines that chose to feature Houser's work.

His paintings and sculptures were included in the 1937 National Exhibition of Indian Art in New York, where he was the only American Indian represented; at the O'Hara Exhibition in Goose Rocks Beach, Maine, in 1937; and at the New York World's Fair in 1939. Houser also gave one-man shows at the Chicago Art Institute, the Denver Art Museum, and others.

He earned three Grand Awards as well as a trophy for outstanding work in Indian art from the Santa Fe Indian School.

Houser's work is held today in many public and private collections, including the Fort Sill Indian School in Oklahoma, the Museum of New Mexico, the Philbrook Art Center, and the Arizona State Capitol.

WILLIAM ROBINSON LEIGH (1866–1955)

William Robinson Leigh was an American artist who was born in West Virginia and studied in Maryland. After quite a few one-man shows and exhibits, he died leaving a legacy of 534 oils and 344 charcoals at the Gilcrease Institute in Oklahoma. He was the author/ illustrator of *Frontiers of Enchantment*, and contributed to *Scribner's Natural History* and *Collier's*.

CHARLES LOLOMA (1921–   )

Loloma is a multitalented Hopi Indian native of Hotevilla, Arizona.

Though he was first recognized as a painter, Loloma is better known for his pottery and silversmithing talents.

After graduating from a Phoenix high school in 1940, Loloma studied mural painting under Olaf Nordmark and ceramics at Alfred University. He served in the army in World War II, then returned home to operate an arts and crafts shop in Shungopovi, Arizona, (1955). A year later, he started another in Scottsdale, which was in operation from 1956 to 1960. Loloma also instructed special classes at the University of Arizona and Arizona State. In 1955 Loloma received a John A. Whitney Fellowship for his work in the research of raw native materials that were used in the making of pottery.

He has won awards in national and state competitions and has exhibited at the Arizona State Fair, the Museum of Modern Art in New York City, and the New Mexico State Fair.

RICHARD MARTINEZ (1904–   )

Born on the San Ildefonso Pueblo, Martinez had the Indian name Opa Mu Nu.

Martinez was one of the original students at the Santa Fe Indian School and helped paint a series of murals there in 1936.

Most of his work was completed between 1920 and 1950. His subjects were often mythological or ceremonial.

Martinez's work was exhibited with the Exposition of Indian Tribal Arts, Inc., in 1931, and collections of his work are held by the Denver Art Museum, the Museum of New Mexico, and the Chrysler Art Museum, among others.

His paintings sell for below $1,000.

GEORGIA MASAYESVA

In 1988 this Hopi artist was the first female to be selected as poster artist for the Festival of Native American Art.

She attended the University of Arizona, where she received her bachelor of arts and her masters in education.

Masayesva's photography features sepia-toned black-and-white images that are hand-tinted just as similar photos were one hundred years ago.

MARSHALL MITCHELL (1917–)

Mitchell produces old West sculptures that are compared to those of Frederic Remington. His work deals with western themes such as Indians and cowboys, and features animals associated with the area.

At the age of twelve, Mitchell was left on his own when his parents divorced. He spent his time outside of school doing a variety of odd jobs. Teachers and employers saw Mitchell's talent and helped him through the last couple of years of school by teaching him what they knew about art—sometimes even taking him home and feeding him.

Mitchell's work reflects the disgraceful treatment of Indians at the hands of white men—as does his speech.

The sculptor's work is exclusively represented by a dealer in Florida and is made in limited editions by what his representative calls "the granddaddy of contemporary western art."

DAN NAMINGHA (1950–)

Namingha was born in the Tewa village of Polaca at First Mesa. He is a member of a family with five generations of artists and potters. He attended the University of Kansas, the IAIA, and the American Academy of Art in Chicago. As a marine, he traveled the world, then returned to the Southwest in the 1970s to blend what he had learned in Europe with what he knew from his life in the village.

A contemporary artist, Namingha paints in an abstract manner, creating Hopi Kachina figures that "are the embodiment of world mythology in its universal search for spiritual wholeness" (*Santa Fe and Taos Arts*, 1991). He says, "Work is an extension of me; it's a bridge" (*Indian Market Magazine*, 1992).

NASA commissioned Namingha to interpret the three space programs in art in 1991. He also witnessed the orbiter *Discovery*'s landing when it returned from deep space.

He is currently working on a series of paintings with environmental themes. He also teaches, passing his artistic knowledge on to others.

Tonita Vigil Pena (1895–1949)

A San Ildefonso native, Pena had the Indian name Quah Ah. She was painting by the age of seven in the San Ildefonso Day School and was later encouraged by archaeologists Edgar Hewett and Kenneth Chapman to paint village scenes. Pena developed a realistic, serene, and joyful style that was truly her own. Her sense of form and design enabled her to break away from the stiff figures that had been the norm for traditional painters from the San Ildefonso Pueblo.

Later in life, Tonita married and moved to the Cochiti Pueblo, where she taught the women at the Santa Fe Indian School to paint in freer, less structured ways.

Her work was exhibited at the First National Exhibit of American Indian Painting at the Philbrook Art Center in 1946. Examples of her work are held by the American Museum of Natural History, the Saint Louis Art Museum, the Corcoran Gallery, the Denver Art Museum, the Museum of the American Indian, and the Museum of New Mexico.

Today her paintings fetch $300–$2,500.

Charles Pratt

Born on an Indian Agency in Concho, Oklahoma, Pratt is Cheyenne-Arapaho and one-quarter French. Pratt began his career in art when his grandfather taught him to make clay figures. Today he creates large-scale as well as miniature creations, in cast bronze, metal, and stone. He is also an accomplished silversmith.

A self-taught artist, he weaves colors and textures from his Native American heritage into his signature works, which include *The Blue Corn People.*

He has been listed in "Who's Who In American Art" and has won nearly four hundred awards for his work. Commissioned works included pieces for the Heard Museum, the Philbrook Art Center, the Oklahoma Science and Arts Foundation, and the A. Murrad Federal Building in Oklahoma City.

His works range in price from $300 to $50,000.

Art, Charlie Pratt, **White Buffalo,** *alabaster from El Capitan, buffalo horns are authentic horns; 19 x 19 x 9 inches; 1993; $3,500.* Courtesy of Charlie Pratt. Photo by Robert Reno.

BEN QUINTANA (1923–1944)

This young Cochiti artist (A Tee) made quite an impression on the art world during his brief career. He won first prize in a poster contest at the age of fifteen and won another, in a field of over fifty thousand entries, at seventeen years of age.

His work has been published in *Arizona Highways*, is held in public and private collections, and has been exhibited in shows such as the National Gallery of Art's "Contemporary Indian Painting" (1953).

Recently one of his paintings sold for $825.

WILLIAM RABBIT (CONTEMPORARY)

Bill Rabbit, of Cherokee ancestry, worked as a silversmith in the early years of his career, before turning to painting. Today it is his award-winning paintings for which he is well known.

He paints, he says, with the influence of Solomon McCombs, Fred Beaver, Blackbear Bosin, and Jerome Tiger, combining their styles to please himself.

Rabbit fought in the Vietnam war and claims the experience "taught me to appreciate the commonplace and to appreciate every day."

Awards won by this contemporary artist are many and include first place at the Five Civilized Tribes Museum in Muskogee, Oklahoma (1981), and a number of prizes at the 1982 61st Annual Gallup Ceremonial. Rabbit was chosen as the poster artist for the 1985 "Trail of Tears" art show and for an exhibit at the Smithsonian Institution.

Collections of his work are held all over the world and he is represented in galleries throughout the Southwest.

JAIME TAWODI REASON (1947–   )

Reason is a self-taught artist who began carving in 1976. He is keeping alive the Cherokee art of carving cedar boxes that were used to hold sacred items such as gourd rattles and fans. He focuses on nature, using the eagle feather as a recurring theme in his work. Reason's work can be found in galleries throughout the United States and Great Britain. He has won many awards for his work, and his boxes are currently being priced from $300 to $3,000 each.

ROBERT REDBIRD (APPROXIMATELY 1940–   )

Redbird is a Southern Plains Indian who was raised in Gotebo, Oklahoma, where he later married and had two children. Redbird is an associate pastor at the Tabernacle of Deliverance Church in Anadarko, Oklahoma.

He won best of class in theme and first place in painting at the Colorado Indian Market in Denver, Colorado, during the summer of 1987, and in the same year was named to the top five of "Best Investments in Indian Art under $1000 for 1987" by the Colorado Indian Market.

Collections of his work are held by Carnegie High School and private collectors. The Susan Peters Gallery of Anadarko, Oklahoma, represents him.

KEVIN RED STAR (1943–   )

Red Star is a Crow Indian born in Montana. The Museum of New Mexico gave him a special award in 1965, and Red Star was exhibited at that museum as well as at the "First Annual Invitational Exhibition of American Indian Paintings" in 1965 and in the 1966 exhibit at the Riverside Museum (New York City) entitled "Young American Indian Artists."

The Indian Arts and Crafts Board holds a collection of his work.

FREDERIC REMINGTON (1861–1909)

Remington was born in Canton, New York. His father owned the local newspaper and his mother's family ran the local hardware business. He was an only child.

Raised in upstate New York, he went to school at the Highland Military Academy in Worcester, Massachusetts, and the Vermont Episcopal Institute in Burlington, Vermont, where he had his first formal art lessons.

He also attended Yale University, where, it is said, he played a good game of football. Large and muscular, he was built perfectly for the game.

At twenty-one Remington married Eva Caten and they took off for Kansas. She left him there, after which he promptly went farther west.

In a little over a year, the artist established himself as a New York illustrator with *Harper's Weekly*. He also illustrated for *St. Nicholas, Outing, Country Illustrated Magazine,* and others. His oils began bringing in good money during the late 1880s, and the money brought his wife, Eva, back to his side.

Remington's artistic style developed so rapidly during this period that it is hard to believe his early and turn-of-the-century pieces were created by the same artist.

Though never a real cowboy, and often uncomfortable with western life, Remington painted Indians and the life of the old West as though he had been a part of it all.

Illustrations that depict Indians include: *A Dash for the Timber* (1889); *The Outlier* (1909); *The Scout—Friends or Enemies?* (1890); *Downing the Night Leader* (1907); and *Apache Scouts Listening* (1908).

Remington's paintings are held in private collections and museums all over the world; recently an example of his work sold for almost $5 million. His drawings sell from $2,000 to $200,000, and his sculptures from below a thousand to over $4 million.

KENNETH RILEY (CONTEMPORARY)

Born and raised in the Midwest, Riley later pursued a career as an illustrator when he lived in the East as an adult. He studied at the Kansas City Art Institute and was a combat artist in World War II. During the 1950s his illustrations appeared in *National Geographic, Life,* and *Saturday Evening Post.*

His paintings of American Indians have won him various awards such as the Stetson Award at the 1987 Cowboy Artists of

America show at the Phoenix Art Museum; a purchase award from Phoenix Art Museum for Bodmer in 1986; and a gold medal and Best of Show award at CAA in 1984.

Riley works in oil on fairly large canvases and has moved away from realistic painting to a more impressionistic style.

BERT D. SEABOURN (1931–   )

Seabourn was born in Iraan, Texas. His father, James, was a Cherokee. Seabourn married Bonnie Jo Tompkins in 1950 and together they had two children.

The artist received a certificate of art from Oklahoma C.U. in 1960 and studied on his own with the Famous Artists Correspondence Art School.

Seabourn has participated in exhibitions throughout the Southwest, including one-man shows at Henson Gallery in Yukon, Oklahoma, and Chandler Galleries in Oklahoma.

His awards include three from Inter-Tribal Indian Ceremonies (ITIC). The Oklahoma Art Center holds a collection of Seabourn's work.

LOIS SMOKY (1907–   )

Born Bou Ge Tah, this Kiowa was encouraged to pursue her talent by Susan Peters, a field-worker at the Anadarko Indian Agency in Oklahoma.

Smoky was the only female of a group of five Kiowa Indians who became world-renowned for their bold, broad style and knowledge of American Indian tribes and traditions during the 1920s when they studied at the University of Oklahoma. She stopped painting by the end of that period, but her work is in Jacobson's *Kiowa Indian Art* and *American Indian Painters.* Examples of her work are held by the Museum of the American Indian and McNay Art Institute in San Antonio.

JOHN MIX STANLEY (1814–1872)

One of the most important painters of Indian and western life, Stanley visited the Blackfoot Indians in 1850 while on a railroad survey.

Today his paintings sell between $6,000 and $50,000.

CARL SWEEZY (1879–1953)

Born an Arapaho on a Cheyenne-Arapaho reservation near Darlington, Oklahoma, Sweezy had the Indian name Wattan (Black). He did not become Carl Sweezy until his older brother took the name of Sweezy and subsequently named his siblings likewise.

Sweezy was given a box of paints in school at the age of fourteen and learned to use them well. He continued to work in watercolors or oils during the rest of his career. Collectors should note that much of his work is unsigned. He worked for James Mooney, a Smithsonian Institution anthropologist, and learned to paint in what Sweezy called "the Mooney Way."

Sweezy's work history was varied and included stints as an Indian police officer, a farmer, a professional baseball player, and, as mentioned above, a position as assistant to James Mooney.

Sweezy's work has been exhibited in a number of shows, including: The American Indian Exhibition (annual), the Inter-Tribal Indian Ceremonies, and the Museum of the Plains Indian.

Collections of Sweezy's work are held by the Gilcrease Museum, the Museum of the American Indian, and the Philbrook Art Center, among others.

MONROE TSATOKE (1904–1937)

Tsatoke, or Hunting Horse, was a Kiowa who had had no art instruction until a woman named Susie Peters organized a Fine Arts Club and began to teach those children who showed a talent for drawing and other native art forms. He studied with her, Mrs. Willie Baze Lane, and Miss Mahier (at the University of Oklahoma). While at the university, he became one of the "Five Kiowas" who won international acclaim in the late 1920s.

Tsatoke's creative ability sustained him through a bout with tuberculosis, and his association with the Peyote faith and the Native American Church helped him to express his religious feelings through art.

The University of Oklahoma Press honored Tsatoke in *Indians of Today*, and his work was commissioned for the Anadarko Federal Building, among others. Tsatoke's work was exhibited at the United Nations Conference in 1945, and at many other shows. Examples of his work are held in public and private collections, such as the

Museum of the American Indian, the Museum of New Mexico, and the Philbrook Art Center.

Today his paintings sell in the vicinity of $1,500 and up.

PABLITA VELARDE (1918–)

Velarde, a well-known artist, painted accurate portraits of Indian life and culture in the "traditional" style of Santa Fe. Clara Tanner called her the "greatest woman artist in the Southwest." Her daughter, Helen Hardin, also became quite well known. (See Hardin's biography earlier in this chapter.)

Among other works, she painted murals for the Bandelier National Monument in New Mexico (1939–1948). Her paintings sell below $1,000.

PAUL VIGIL

A Tesuque Pueblo native, Vigil painted during his teenage years in the 1950s, but turned to carpentry while in the army and later used those skills on the Navajo Reservation. His father was a painter, and one of Paul's nine children (a son) is now learning to carry on the tradition.

Vigil paints traditional Tewa dancers in the style of the early Pueblo artists, using delicate brushwork and geometric designs, as well as traditional motifs like corn, water, and Pueblo architecture.

He won a first-place ribbon at the 1991 Indian Market in Santa Fe.

DAVID WILLIAMS (1933–1985)

Williams was born in Oklahoma, and given his Indian name, "Tosque," or Apache Man, by his Kiowa mother and Tonkawa-Apache father. He is descended from the famous Kiowa chief Sitting Bear.

Williams studied art at Bacone College and he made his career as a painter with exhibits at places like the Sporting Gallery in Williamsburg, Virginia, and Stouffer's Manor Gate House in Pittsburgh, Pennsylvania.

Today his paintings sell in the $1,000–$1,500 range.

PRICES

Acrylic: Dan Namingha (Hopi); *Parrot Deity*; very good condition; $145–$200.

Acrylic: Jackie Tobaahe Gene (Navajo); *Gathering of the Medicine Men*; framed, dated 1983, and signed; very good condition; $130–$190.

Acrylic on canvas: Ben Wright; *Peace Indian I*; 48 x 60 inches; very good condition; $3,600–$5,600.

Acrylic on canvas: Ben Wright; *Youth With a Bow*, #12/86; very good condition; $3,250–$3,650.

Acrylic on canvas: Ben Wright; *Man from the East;* very good condition; $3,000–$3,500.

Acrylic on canvas: Ben Wright; *Return of the Buffalo*; 48 x 60 inches; very good condition; $3,480–$3,880.

Acrylic on canvas: Davis Ramos; 35 x 47 inches; very good condition; $3,600–$5,600.

Acrylic on canvas: John Nieto (Comanche); *Quanah Parker*; 48 x 60 inches; very good condition; $14,000–$16,000.

Acrylic on canvas: Nelson Begay (Navajo); *Hatathli* (Navajo for "chanter/sandpainting chanter"), 18 x 24 inches; depicts male Hatathli performing Shooting Chant; dated '78 and signed; very good condition; $145–$215.

Acrylic on rice paper: Jean Bales (1946–   ) (Iowa); *Dancer*; 13 x 10 inches; depicts a male Indian facing left, body painted yellow, holding fur-wrapped lance in extended hand, round ring/circle in other; framed and signed; very good condition; $350–$450.

Brass sculpture: Charlie Pratt; *Gift of the Gods*; 40 x 24 inches; fabricated brass, blue corn and chili peppers, color is patina, corn has coral, turquoise, lapis, serpentine, garnets, freshwater pearls, Pacific clam; 1993; $6,500.

Brass sculpture: Charlie Pratt; *Harvest Time*; 36 x 15 inches; fabricated brass with amethyst base, corn is coral, turquoise, serpentine, garnet, freshwater pearls, Pacific clam; 1993; $3,800.

Brass sculpture: Charlie Pratt; *Medicine Feather*; 36 x 9 inches; fabricated brass, lapidary work (turquoise and lapis); 1993; $1,500.

Brass sculpture: Charlie Pratt; *Offering to the Gods*; 15 x 10 inches; fabricated brass, color is patina, corn of coral, turquoise, lapis, serpentine, garnets, freshwater pearls, Pacific clam; 1993; $2,600.

Brass sculpture: Charlie Pratt; *Summer Storm*; 35 x 24 inches; fabricated brass, terra-cotta mask in light blue, beige, corn yellow, and terra-cotta; cornelia stones; 1993; $1,200.

Art, Charlie Pratt, **Gift of the Gods,** *fabricated brass, blue corn and chili peppers, color is patina, corn has coral, turquoise, lapis, serpentine, garnets, freshwater pearls, Pacific clam; 40 x 24 inches; 1993;* $6,500. Courtesy of Charlie Pratt. Photo by Robert Reno.

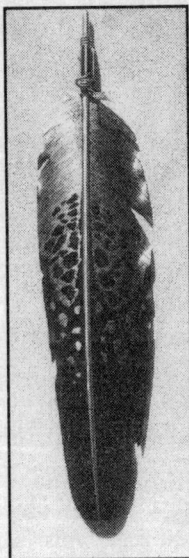

Art, Charlie Pratt, **Medicine Feather,** *fabricated brass, lapidary work (turquoise and lapis); 36 x 9 inches; 1993;* $1,500. Courtesy of Charlie Pratt. Photo by Robert Reno.

Art, Charlie Pratt, **Summer Storm,** *fabricated brass, terra-cotta mask in light blue, beige, corn yellow, and terra-cotta; cornelia stones; 35 x 24 inches; 1993;* $1,200. Courtesy of Charlie Pratt. Photo by Robert Reno.

Brass sculpture: Charlie Pratt; *Desert Dwellers*; 32 x 20 inches; fabricated brass with lava rock base, depicting cactus with hummingbirds; 1993, $3,800.

Brass sculpture: 9 x 7 inches; depicting an Indian on a horse spearing a buffalo; ca. 1980; $100–$150.

Bronze: Bob Scriver, CAA (1914–   ); *Piegan Brave*, #34/35; 11 x 11 inches; mounted on a walnut base; depicts an Indian warrior from the Horn Society mounted on a war pony; sculpture is titled, dated, numbered, and signed; very good condition; $1,550–$2,250.

Bronze: Carl Kauba (American/Austrian, 1865–1922); seated Indian Chief on horseback; 13 x 12½ inches; very good condition; $1,400–$1,650.

Bronze: Charlie Pratt; bronze shield with turquoise bear paw; 32 x 18 inches; very good condition; $3,000–$3,500.

Bronze: Ernest Berke (1921–   ); *Rallying his Warriors*; #59/200; 11½ inches high; signed and dated 1979; very good condition; $2,000–$3,500.

Bronze: Jim Pasma; *Prophecy of Sweet Medicine*; very good condition; $10,000–$11,500.

Bronze sculpture: Jake Livingston; *Nas Bah*; 17½ inches high x 10 inches wide; bust of girl with necklace, turquoise inset, wears different pairs of earrings; combination of the faces of his sister-in-law and wife; 1987; $3,200.

Bronze sculpture: Bob Scriver, CAA (1914–   ); *Paul's Bull*; #38/1000; 2 ⅜ x 5 inches; mounted on walnut base; shows buffalo lying down; dated 1968 and signed; very good condition; $180–$255.

Bronze sculpture: Bob Scriver, CAA (1914–   ); *Piegan Brave*; #34/35; 11 x 11 inches; mounted on a walnut base; depicts an Indian warrior from the Horn Society mounted on a war pony; dated and signed; very good condition; $2,350–$3,100.

Bronze sculpture: David Bradley (1954–   ) (Chippewa); *Little Big Woman;* very good condition; $220–$310.

Bronze sculpture: Joe Halko, NWA, SAA (1940–   ); *Chipmunk*; very good condition; $475–$650.

Bronze: Y. E. Cheno; *A-Gi-Du-Da* ("grandfather"); very good condition; $6,000–$8,500.

Bust: 18 x 6 x 12 inches; classic plaster bust of elegant Indian warrior; ca. 1910; very good condition; $60–$85.

Carving: 18 x 5 inches; Tlingit; old fully carved mountain sheep horn with many human and animal figures; ca. 1870; very good condition; $500–$730.

Carving, turquoise: 3½ x 2 inches; solid turquoise carving of a Pony Express rider on a horse; ca. 1980; very good condition; $155–$200.

Cast bronze sculpture: Charlie Pratt; 9 inches each; prayer feathers; 1993; $175 each.

Cast bronze sculpture: Charlie Pratt; 1¾ x 3½ inches each; cast bronze horned toad and cast sterling silver horned toad; 1993; $595 (silver), $250 (bronze).

Cast bronze sculptures: Charlie Pratt; *Wolf Step* and *Buffalo Step*; 5½ x 4 inches each; 1993; $550 each.

Cast bronze sculpture: Charlie Pratt; *Tuffy*; 9 x 11 inches; Mohawk Indian with tortoise; limited edition; cast in 1982; $2,400.

Cast bronze statue: Charlie Pratt; *Night Hawk*; 6 feet x 26 inches x 21 inches; 280 pounds; life-size warrior with hawk on shoulder; stones in center of robe are yellow lip shell, and red is man-made stone; 1993; $28,000.

Cast silver and bronze sculpture: Charlie Pratt; horny toads, both silver and bronze; bellies are semiprecious stones—for example, turquoise, malachite, azurite, mother-of-pearl (each is different); $595 (silver), $250 (bronze).

Drawing: Andy Tsinajinnie; 9 x 6 inches; unusual picture of man on a horse; ca. 1975; very good condition; $25–$45.

Art, Charlie Pratt, prayer feathers, cast bronze, 9 inches each; 1993; $175 each.
Courtesy of Charlie Pratt. Photo by Robert Reno.

Drawing: Cherokee; 12 x 18 inches; chalk drawing; still life with crystals; ca. 1992; very good condition; $40–$110.

Drawing: Ernest Miles Rost; *American*; 14 x 20 inches; pen and ink drawing of Chief Jack Sioux; ca. 1924; very good condition; $50–$125.

Charcoal drawings: Forsyth (Sioux); *Red Cloud* and *High Bear* (both show tears); on brown paper, signed Forsyth; very good condition; $50–$70.

Drawing: *Warrior*; 15 x 10 inches; colored "warrior" drawing showing several Indians on horses; very good condition; $30–$50.

Engraving: after Karl Bodmer (1809–1893); *The Interior of the Hut of a Mandan Chief*; plate 19; 16⅜ x 21¼ inches; engraving and aquatint with hand-coloring; printed by Bougeard; published by Ackermann & Co., London; very good condition; $300–$500. Note that this engraving is "after Bodmer."

Engraving: Albert Bierstadt (1830–1902); *The Rocky Mountains*; 16¾ x 28 inches; engraving and roulette; engraved by James Smillie; published by Edward Bierstadt; signed by the artist and engraver in pencil; proof before letters; 1866; very good condition; $1,500–$3,000.

Engraving: Karl Bodmer (1809–1893); *Bison Dance*; 12 x 17 inches; hand-colored engraving; very good condition; $500–$1,000.

Etching: Ace Powell (1912–1978); framed limited edition #81/100 Northwest Coast etching; 7 x 5 inches; ca. 1975; very good condition; $100–$150.

Etching: Edward Borien (1872–1945); matted and framed etching from Borien estate depicting two mounted riders; ca. 1910; very good condition; $150–$300.

Gouache on board: William Robinson Leigh (1866–1955); *At the Loom*; 29¹³⁄₁₆ x 21⅜ inches; very good condition; $125,000–$150,000.

Graphic: Richard Skyhawk; *Hoop Dancer*; signed; ca. 1986; very good condition; $30–$60.

Ledger drawing: Cheyenne; ca. 1870; (C0043–05022); very good condition; $4,000–$5,200.

Ledger drawing: Kiowa; ca. 1880; (C0021–02138); very good condition; $5,750–$6,900.

Ledger drawing: Sioux; Short Bull; ca. 1880; (04288); very good condition; $4,500–$4,850.

Ledger drawings: two colored ledger drawings showing Indians riding horseback; ca. 1885; very good condition; $115–$230.

Lithographs (set of four): Kevin Red Star (1943–   ) (Crow); *Crow Res Cop I, II, III* and *IV*; #10 of 60; depicts four different male Indians dressed in traditional Indian and non-Indian garments and accessories, all wearing a star (law enforcement) badge; matted, numbered, titled, and signed; $750–$1,250/set.

Lithograph: *Catlin's Indian No. 11*; 20½ x 26½ inches; hand-colored hunter stalking buffalo; mounting board titled in pencil; framed; very good condition; $75–$150.

Lithograph: Comanche; 19 x 3½ inches; Monument Valley in 13 colors, hand-signed by Diane O'Leary; ca. 1986; very good condition; $15–$185.

Lithograph: 20 lithograph prints; *Indians of the Southwest*; published by Fred Harvey; colored; very good condition; $60–$80.

Lithograph: McKenney and Hall; *Spring Frog*; hand-tinted, very good condition; $175–$300.

Lithograph: McKenney and Hall; *O Che-Finceco*; hand tinted; very good condition; $175–$300.

Lithograph: McKenney and Hall; *A Chippeway-Widow*; hand-tinted; very good condition; $175–$300.

Lithograph: McKenney and Hall; *Ledagie*; hand-tinted; very good condition; $175–$300.

Lithograph: McKenney and Hall; *Red Jacket;* hand-tinted; very good condition; $175–$300.

Art, McKenney and Hall, lithograph; **Okee-Makee-Quid,** *a Chippewa chief; 21 x 15 inches; $500-$600.* Courtesy Jack Sellner, CAI.

Lithograph: McKenney and Hall; *Okee-Makee Quid*; hand-tinted; very good condition; $500–$600.

Lithograph: McKenney and Hall; *Se-Loc-Ta*; hand-tinted; very good condition; $175–$300.

Lithograph: McKenney and Hall; *Ca-Ta-He-Cas-Sa-Black Hoof*; hand-tinted; very good condition; $175–$300.

Lithographs: *Kish-Ke-Kosh, Fox,* etc.; (four) 10¼ x 7 inches; published by J. T. Bowen, Philadelphia; ca. 1830; very good condition; $90–$120.

Metal sculpture: *Stealing Sugar*; 6 x 11 inches; one-of-a-kind; 1992; $650.

Oil on board: Blakelock; 7 x 10 inches; with frame, 11¾ x 14½ inches; Indian encampment with tepees and moon; attributed to Blakelock; artwork in very good condition; frame in good condition; $900–$1,500.

Oil on paper: four matted pictures of kachinas; very good condition; $170–$220/set.

Oil painting: Ace Powell (Blackfoot); *Old Ways and New Ways*; 24 x 48 inches; modern Blackfoot on horseback watching oil-paved highway on the reservation; excellent condition; $8,000–$15,000.

Oil painting: M. Wold; *Sioux Indian Leaders*; 9 x 12 inches; on board, no frames ca. 1907; very good condition; $500–$700.

Oil painting: Tex Moore; 9 x 22 inches; mountain scene with Indian camp; on board, with copy of book of life story of Tex Moore, Official Artist of Texas in 1935; early work; very good condition; $550–$750.

Painting: Cherokee; 12 x 18 inches; ram's skull; contemporary; very good condition; $75–$110.

Painting: Sti Mone Justino Herrera (Cochiti); 3 x 6 inches; two deer; ca. 1950; very good condition; $100–$200.

Painting: David Namoki (Hopi); 12 x 20 inches; three separate panels, one kachina and two still lifes; ca. 1982; very good condition; $50–$150/set.

Painting: Hopi; 16 x 20 inches; oil on canvas; corn stalk and Yei figures; contemporary; very good condition; $20–$75.

Painting: Lee Joshua (1937–   ) (Creek-Seminole); *Coming on a Long Winter*; 20 x 16 inches; shows blanketed warrior standing in snow; double-matted, titled, dated 1982, and signed; very good condition; $200–$350.

Art, J. Reinhart, painting; portrait of Chief Frozen Dog; painted on hide with depiction of Plains warrior in feathered headdress with ermine drops; 37½ x 53½ inches; ca. 1930; excellent condition; $800–$1,200. Courtesy of W. E. Channing & Co., Inc.

Painting: Lee Monette Tsa Toke (1929–   ) (Kiowa); *Shield Dancer* and *Eagle Dancer;* dated 10/15/59 and signed; very good condition; $350–$450/set.

Painting: Robert Chee (Navajo); 8 x 10 inches; pastel of rearing horse and rabbit; ca. 1950; very good condition; $80–$200.

Painting: Sandy Percy, aka Kaisa (Zuni); *The Buck and Doe on the Open Field;* matted and framed, 12 x 14 inches; ca. 1940; very good condition; $200–$400.

Pen-and-ink illustrations of making stone tools; 10 x 14 inches; ca. 1940; very good condition; $40–$100.

Picture: Wess; *The Weaver;* 12 x 16 inches; stamped and painted work; contemporary; very good condition; $40–$80.

Limited edition print: Jean Bales (1946–   ) (Iowa); *Bear Mystery;* #19/60; shows bear in large proportions, with Zuni-like heartline; matted, numbered, titled, and signed; $50–$100.

Print: Ace Powell (1912–1978); *Evening Prayer;* limited edition #99; 4 x 8 x 4 inches; imbricated geometric designs; ca. 1910; very good condition; $260–$315.

Print; Austin Deuel, AICA, WAI (1939–   ); *The Deer Slayer;* #198/375; 23¾ x 17½ inches; depicts Indian hunter on a rock, snow-covered scene, holding bow with arrow at ready; numbered lower left, signed lower right; $30–$60.

Print: Howard Terpning, CAA, NAWA (1927–   ); *Crossing Medicine Lodge Creek;* signed limited edition print; very good condition; $300–$500.

Art, Antoine Tzapoff, painting; acrylic on canvas; **A Tlinglit Shaman;** *depicts a shaman clad in a Chilkat blanket and wearing a headdress, seated in a canoe heading into a bay with a schooner in the background; signed and dated 1981; 21 x 21 inches; Tzapoff is known as Europe's great scholar-painter of American Indian and Eskimo art and culture; excellent condition; $2,000-$3,000.* Courtesy of W. E. Channing & Co., Inc.

Print: Jane Mauldin; limited edition #28/100; 9 x 7 inches; colored print of an Indian; ca. 1985; $20–$30.

Print: Parker Boyiddle (1947–   ) (Kiowa-Delaware); *Kiowa Warrior*, $25–$50.

Print: Parker Boyiddle (1947–   ) (Kiowa-Delaware); *Peyote Vision: Buffalo Skull*; 33 x 24½ inches; depicts head of snarling grizzly bear superimposed over face of male Indian, over feathered buffalo skull; $35–$50.

Print: Quincy Tahoma; *The Last Struggle*; limited edition #421/1000; 30 x 18 inches; ca 1945; $75–$100.

Print: Ron Stewart (contemporary); *Unknown Destiny*; #116/250; 18 x 24 inches; remarqued signed limited edition print; depicts tepees in a snow-covered scene with four mounted Indian riders preparing to cross a stream; numbered, titled, signed, and remarqued (small original sketch); $125–$175.

Print: Winold Reiss; set of six colored Blackfoot prints; ca. 1915; $50–$75.

Print: Woody Crumbo; peyote bird; $30–$50.

Sandpainting: Eugene "Baatsoslanii" Joe; this artist signed his pieces E. B. Joe up until 1974, then changed his signature to Baatsoslanii; 1988; $4,000–$5,000.

Sandpainting: Eugene "Baatsoslanii" Joe (Navajo); image 18 x 23 inches, complete painting 27 x 32½ inches; mint condition; $1,695–$1,795.

Sandpainting: Francis Miller (Navajo); *House of Many Paints*; $100–$150.

Sandpainting: Judy Lewis (Navajo); means "good luck"; by artist from Window Rock, Arizona; $150–$300.

Sand sculpture: Jim Jackson; $1,500–$2,000.

Sculpture: Charlie Pratt; *Birdwoman*; 5 feet 4 inches high; portrait of Laura Birdwoman, a Cheyenne. Called Aunt Laura, this small-boned, hunched-over woman never married but is known as a bighearted, giving person. The white feather down the back of this life-size figure is a symbol of her virginity; $23,000.

Sculpture: Charlie Pratt; *Blue Sky*; 17 x 10 inches; turquoise nugget out of Senora mine in Mexico, feathers are fabricated brass, and medallion is turqoise, coral, and Pacific clam; 1993; $2,600.

Sculpture: Charlie Pratt; *White Buffalo*; 19 x 19 x 9 inches; made of alabaster from El Capitan, buffalo horns are authentic; 1993; $3,500.

Art, sandpainting, Navajo; artist is Eugene "Baatsoslanii" Joe. The image size is 18 x 23 inches and overall size is 27 x 32½ inches; mint condition; $1,695–$1,795. Courtesy of Wanda Campbell/Indian Art Unlimited.

Sculpture: Charlie Pratt; brass corn sculptures; large piece (12 inches) is blue corn, and the smaller is Indian corn; lapis, turquoise, brass, and coral beads; 1993; $1,200 and $650 respectively.

Sculpture: Charlie Pratt; sculpted brass; *Harvest Time*; 50 inches; Indian corn, 30 inches; blue corn, 36 inches; squaw corn, 63 inches; $3,000, $1,600, $1,900, and $2,800 respectively.

Sculpture: Dennis Silvertooth; *Beneath a Dream Robe*; Silvertooth was 18 when he won a gold medal at Philbrook; $4,000–$5,000.

Sculpture: E. Ashley (Zuni); 12 x 7 inches; stone sculpture with three Zuni stone bear fetishes mounted on a lava rock and wood; signed E. Ashley; ca. 1985; $175–$275.

Sculpture: Frank Tenney Johnson; Indian bust; unsigned; very good condition; $300–$500.

Sculpture: Ken Camel (Flathead); 25 x 9 inches; large Indian bust; ca. 1982; $50–$75.

Sculpture: Northwest Coast; 11 x 5 inches; Northwest Coast head wearing a potlatch hat; ca. 1930; $75–$100.

Serigraph: Kevin Red Star (1943–   ) (Crow); *Tranquility*, matted, framed, numbered, titled, and signed; $300–$500.

Signed limited edition print: Ace Powell (1912–1978); *Buffalo Hunt*; depicts two mounted Indian hunters on each side of the herd; numbered, titled, and signed; $75–$125.

Signed limited edition print: Harvey W. Johnson, (1921–   ); *Whitewater Keelboat*; #1/1000; 15 x 26 inches; depicts the boat of the title with a total of eight hunters and trappers aboard; double-matted, framed, numbered, and signed; $100–$175.

Signed limited edition print: Howard Rees (1941–   ); *Winter Sun*; #41/750; 17¼ x 24 inches; depicts three Indian hunters mounted on horseback crossing snow-covered ground; numbered and signed; $50–$100.

Signed limited edition print: William Acheff (1947–   ); *Tewa Lady*; #70/325; 11 x 8 inches; depicts a historical period Southwest Indian pottery jar placed upon a banded Pueblo Indian weaving with a photograph of a Tewa-Hopi maiden in the background; matted, framed, numbered, and signed; $125–$175.

Signed limited edition print: Jack Hines (1923–   ); *Fort Laramie . . . the Gathering of the Tribes*; #31/1000; 20 x 30 inches; depicts seven Indians on horseback; matted, framed, numbered, and signed; $100–$175.

Signed limited edition print: Bert D. Seabourn (1931–)
(Cherokee); *In the Beginning*, numbered and signed; $50–$75.

Signed limited edition print: Joe Beeler—founding member of CAA
(1931–)(Cherokee); *The Warning*, matted, framed, numbered, and signed; $100–$200.

Silk-screen prints (three): Woody Big Bow (1914–)(Kiowa); *Flute
Player*, *Eagle Dancer*, and *Feather Dancer*, $50–$75/set.

Silk screen: Woody Crumbo (Creek-Potawatomi); *Baby with Fawn*,
Birds and Animals, 16 x 12 inches, matted and framed;
$150–$250.

Silver sculpture: Charlie Pratt; approximately 2–3 inches; cast sterling silver snakes with rubies, sapphires, and emeralds; $95.

Stone carving: Andy Abeita; *Spirit Stone*, 2 feet x 20 inches; made of
white alabaster with brass rainbow kachina in paw; weighs over
300 pounds; to be cast bronze in an edition of ten; $6,800.

Stone carving: Andy Abeita, (Pueblo); taupe alabaster fetish bobcat
with medicine bundle; 2½ x 1¾ inches; $45.

Stone carving: Andy Abeita (Pueblo); taupe alabaster fetish wolf
with medicine bundle; 5½ x 2¾ inches; 1993; $135.

Stone carving: Andy Abeita (Pueblo); taupe alabaster bear fetish
with medicine bundle; 2 inches x 1 inch; $27.

Stone carving: Andy Abeita (Pueblo); taupe alabaster fetish bear
with medicine bundle; 8 x 5 inches; 1993; $690.

Stone carving: Andy Abeita (Pueblo); Tibetan turquoise bighorn
pouch fetish; 1¾ inches x 1 inch; $54.

Stone carving: Andy Abeita (Pueblo); serpentine mole pouch fetish;
1⅛ x ⅝ inch; $21.

*Art, Andy Abeita, Pueblo,
taupe alabaster fetish bobcat
with medicine bundle; 2½ x
1¾ inches; $45.* Courtesy of
Andy Abeita and Silver
Sun Gallery, Santa Fe.
Photo by Robert Reno.

Stone carving: Andy Abeita (Pueblo); taupe alabaster heart-line fetish wolf with medicine bundle; 14 x 6 inches; $720.

Stone carving: Andy Abeita (Pueblo); steatite (black soapstone) heart-line deer with medicine bundle; 11 x 8 inches; $525.

Stone carving: Andy Abeita (Pueblo); white alabaster fetish action bear with medicine bundle; amethyst, ruby, turquoise, diamonds, and garnet decorated; 7 x 4½ inches; $300.

Stone carving: Andy Abeita (Pueblo); zebra alabaster heart-line fetish eagle with medicine bundle; 14 x 13 inches; $1,350.

Stone carving: Andy Abeita (Pueblo); white alabaster action bear carving; multi-inlay; 7½ x 4½ inches; $450.

Stone carving: Andy Abeita (Pueblo); zebra marble bear pouch fetish; 1½ x ¾ inch; $39.

Stone carving: Andy Abeita (Pueblo); serpentine eagle pouch fetish; 1⅛ x 1 inch; $36.

Stone carving: Andy Abeita (Pueblo); white alabaster action bear carving; multi-inlay; 8 x 5 inches; $425.

Stone carving: Andy Abeita (Pueblo); white alabaster fetish bear with medicine bundle; 5½ x 3½ inches; $240.

Stone carving: Andy Abeita (Pueblo); white alabaster fetish bear with medicine bundle; 6½ x 4½ inches; 1993; $270.

Stone carving: Andy Abeita (Pueblo); pipestone bear pouch fetish; ⅝ x 1¼ inches; $27.

Stone carving: Andy Abeita (Pueblo); Utah orange alabaster rabbit carving; 5 x 2¾ inches; 1993; $135.

Art, Andy Abeita, Pueblo, white alabaster fetish action bear with medicine bundle; amethyst, ruby, turquoise, diamonds, and garnet decorated; 7 x 4½ inches; $300. Courtesy of Andy Abeita and Silver Sun Gallery, Santa Fe. Photo by Robert Reno.

Art, Andy Abeita, Pueblo, Italian translucent alabaster fetish eagle with medicine bundle; 2½ x 2 inches; $54. Courtesy of Andy Abeita and Silver Sun Gallery, Santa Fe. Photo by Robert Reno.

Stone carving: Andy Abeita (Pueblo); gray alabaster heart-line fetish wolf with medicine bundle; 14 x 7½ inches; $900.

Stone carving: Andy Abeita (Pueblo); gray Colorado translucent alabaster fetish bighorn sheep with medicine bundle; 2 x 3 inches; $60.

Stone carving: Andy Abeita (Pueblo); green serpentine eagle pouch fetish; 1⅛ x ⅞ inch; $27.

Stone carving: Andy Abeita (Pueblo); gray dendritic alabaster fetish bobcat with medicine bundle; 3¼ x 1½ inches; $69.

Stone carving: Andy Abeita (Pueblo); brown alabaster fetish mountain lion with medicine bundle; 3 x 1½ inches; $45.

Stone carving: Andy Abeita (Pueblo); brown alabaster bear fetish with medicine bundle; 2 x 1¼ inches; $30.

Stone carving: Andy Abeita (Pueblo); alabaster action bear carving, decorated with amethyst, sugilite, diamonds, rubies, coral, garnet; 7 x 4¼ inches; $300.

Stone carving: Andy Abeita (Pueblo); serpentine bighorn sheep pouch fetish; 1¼ x ¾ inch; $27.

Stone carving: Andy Abeita (Pueblo); golden serpentine action bear pouch fetish; 1¾ x 1⅛ inches; $54.

Stone carving: Andy Abeita (Pueblo); gray alabaster heart-line mountain lion with medicine bundle; 13½ x 8 inches; $990.

Stone carving: Andy Abeita (Pueblo); fetish elk of Picasso marble with mother-of-pearl antlers; ¾ x ¾ inch; $36.

Stone carving: Andy Abeita (Pueblo); rose alabaster fetish mountain lion with medicine bundle; 8 x 4½ inches; 1993; $390.

Stone carving: Andy Abeita (Pueblo); Italian translucent alabaster fetish wolf with medicine bundle; 2¼ x 1 inch; $24.

Stone carving: Andy Abeita (Pueblo); mother-of-pearl pouch fetish bear; 1½ x ¾ inch; $36.

Stone carving: Andy Abeita (Pueblo); Italian translucent alabaster fetish mountain lion with medicine bundle; 4 x 2½ inches; $105.

Stone carving: Andy Abeita (Pueblo); Italian translucent alabaster fetish eagle with medicine bundle; 2½ x 2 inches; $54.

Stone carving: Andy Abeita (Pueblo); jet bear pouch fetish; 1 x ½ inch; $21.

Stone sculpture: Charlie Pratt; *White Bear;* 7 x 12 inches; white alabaster polar bear with spearpoint and lapis stone on back; 1992; $1,000.

Tempera painting: Archie Blackowl (1911–deceased) (Cheyenne); *The Cheyenne Brave;* $100–$250.

Tempera painting: Ed Joshua, Jr. (Kiowa-South Plains);*Wolf Man;* 14½ x 9 inches; left profile of two Indian men, one wearing wolf headdress, with large full moon in the background; Dated 1984 and signed; $50–$75.

Tempera painting: Robert Montoya (San Juan Pueblo); depicts a single kachina dancer; signed "Soe-Kuwa-Pin '75"; $200–$300.

Art, Richard Martinez, tempera painting, from San Ildefonso; depicts two eagle dancers; 10½ x 12¾ inches; $400-$600. Courtesy Robert W. Skinner, Inc., Bolton/Boston, Massachusetts.

Tempera painting: Justino Herrera (1920–?) (Southwestern); Cochiti Pueblo, depicting five male dancers and two female drummers under a stylized sky; $500–$750.

Tempera painting: Richard Martinez (Southwestern Pueblo); 10½ x 12¾ inches; San Ildefonso, depicting two eagle dancers; signed; $500–$750.

Watercolor: Acee Blue Eagle (1907–1959); *Indian Maiden*; matted and signed; $1300–$1,500.

Watercolor: Andy Tsinajinni; depicting a group of Indians dancing around a fire; ca. 1980; $50–$75.

Watercolor: Beatien Yazz—Jimmy Toddy (1928–)(Navajo); *Yeibichai Dancers*; $250–$350.

Art, Spencer Asah (Kiowa), **Buffalo Hunter;** *watercolor; artist lived 1905–1954; 13 x 17 inches; triple-matted, framed, and signed;* $1,000–$1,300. Courtesy Jack Sellner, CAI.

Art, Rafael Medina (Zia), **Buffalo Dancer;** *watercolor; artist was born in 1929; 14 x 10 inches; matted, framed, signed, and dated 1963;* $550–$800. Courtesy Jack Sellner, CAI.

Art, Joe Beeler, watercolor, (CAA 1931–), Mandan; 8 x 6½ inches; double-matted, framed, titled LC; signed UC; $950–$1,000. Courtesy Jack Sellner, CAI.

Watercolor: Bert D. Seabourn (1931–   ); *Cheyenne Girl*, 4 x 3 inches; left profile of subject; matted and titled on reverse, signed LC and dated '73; $75–$150.

Watercolor: David Stephens-Yona (Cherokee); *Grannie's Stories*; depicts white-haired Indian woman, seated with needle and thread and blanket in her lap, Indian youth beside her chair; dated 1984 and signed; $75–$150.

Watercolor: David Stephens-Yona (Cherokee); *Apache*; titled, dated, and signed; $75–$125.

Watercolor: David Stephens-Yona (Cherokee); *I Offer you Peace*, 12 x 6 inches; showing spiritual Indian warrior extending peace pipe to realistic Indian warrior; dated 1984 and signed; $100–$175.

Watercolor: David Stephens-Yona (Cherokee); *Little People of the Cherokees*; dated 1984 and signed; $50–$100.

Watercolor: Doc Tate Nevaquaya (1932–   )(Comanche); *Black Legging Dancer*; double-matted, framed, dated, and signed; $225–$325.

Watercolor: Duke W. Sine (Apache); *Elder Statesman*, 15 x 12 inches; bust portrait of white-haired Indian man with shawl around shoulders; triple-matted, signed, and dated 1981; $100–$200.

Watercolor: Ed Joshua, Jr. (Kiowa-South Plains); *Warriors*; matted, dated, and signed; $50–$100.

Watercolor: Ed Joshua, Jr. (Kiowa-South Plains); *Kiowa Warrior*; 14 x 18 inches; matted, dated 1984, and signed; $50–$100.

Watercolor: Hubert Wackerman (1945–   ); *Sac and Fox—Minnesota 1815*; 18½ x 14 inches; matted, framed, titled LC, signed, and dated 1974; from the Biltmore Galleries Collection, Biltmore Hotel, Los Angeles, California; $350–$500.

Watercolor: Jerry Lee-Hosteen Nez (1944–   )(Navajo); *Fox Dance Yeibichai Dancer*; 10½ x 7½ inches; matted, framed and signed; $150–$250.

Watercolor: Joe Beeler (CAA 1931–   ); *Mandan*; 8 x 6½ inches; double-matted, framed, titled LC; signed UC; $900–$1,300.

Watercolor: John Hauser; *In the Enemy's Country*; 10 x 18 inches; $5,000–$7,500.

Watercolor: José (J.) D. Roybal (1922–deceased)(San Ildefonso); *Deer Dancer*; 5 x 4 inches; $200–$400.

Watercolor: Ken Longmore (contemporary); *A Hard Watch*; 14 x 18 inches; Plains Indian campsite containing tepees, meat-drying racks, and Indians against a high rock mesa background; matted, framed, dated, and signed; $450–$550.

Watercolor: M. Sandy (Pueblo); 10 x 14 inches; two magpies, ca. 1960; signed; very good condition; $30–$90.

Watercolor: Michael Chiago-Tho-Hono (1946–   )(Papago); *Still Life with Pottery, Basket Corn and Sash*; double-matted, dated 1982, and signed; $125–$225.

Watercolor: Mirac Creepingbear (1947–   ) (Kiowa-Pawnee-Arapaho); *Yesterday*; 19 x 14 inches; depicts face of male Indian with eyes closed superimposed over another of the same, Indian in left profile view with two riderless horses above; matted, framed, and signed; $125–$225.

Watercolor: Paul Vigil (Tesuque); *Tesuque Eagle Dancer*; matted, dated 1967, and signed; $275–$375.

Watercolor: Quincy Tahoma (1921–1956) (Navajo); *Grazing Horses–Monument Valley*; double-matted, framed, dated 1949, signed, and remarqued; $275–$375.

Watercolor: Rafael Medina (1929–   )(Zia); *Buffalo Dancer*; 14 x 10 inches; matted, framed, signed, and dated 1963 LR; $700–$1,000.

Watercolor: Robert Redbird (1939–   )(Kiowa); *Horse Thief*; titled and signed; $75–$115.

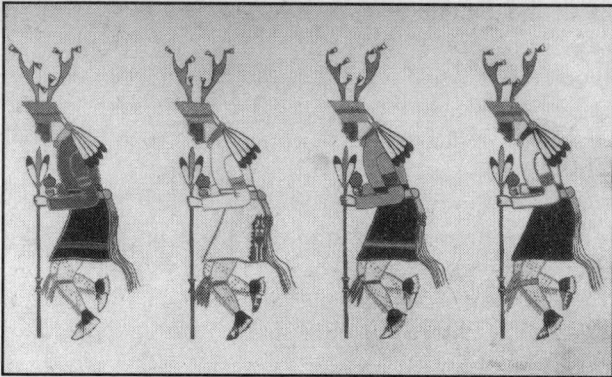

Art, Nana-Tside, Pueblo, watercolor; on paper; depicts ceremonial deer dancers in full costume; ca. 1930; 10 x 16½ inches; excellent condition; $300–$500.
Courtesy of W. E. Channing & Co., Inc.

Watercolor: Jose Encarnacion Pena (1902–1984) (San Ildefonso Pueblo); *Koshare Dancer, Soqueen*; $350–$500.

Watercolor: 15 x 11 inches; shows Indian looking at the moon; ca. 1980; $50–$75.

Watercolor: Spencer Asah (1905–1954) (Kiowa); *Buffalo Hunter*; 13 x 17 inches; triple-matted, framed, and signed LC. $1,000–$1,500.

Watercolor: Tony Atencio (San Ildefonso Pueblo); 18 x 17 inches; of a pinto pony; matted and framed; very good condition; $35–$65.

Watercolors (pair): Tonita Pena, Quah Ah (1895–1949); *Male Cochiti Corn Dancer* and *Female Cochiti Corn Dancer*; matted, framed, and signed; $1,000–1,500/set.

Watercolors (pair): David Stephens-Yona (Cherokee); *Apache* and *Society of the Ten Bravest*; both depicting warriors standing beside their horses; both signed and dated 1984; $150–$300/set.

Signed limited edition wood-block print: Benjamin Harjo, Jr. (South Plains Indian); *Many Beings Within the Four Seasons*; #3/32; 12 x 10 inches; depicts surrealistic blanketed figures in right profile on views with five dark suns/moons overhead; matted, numbered, titled, and signed; $75–$150.

Wood-block limited edition print: Benjamin Harjo, Jr. (South Plains Indian); *Earth Mother*; #2/32; 11 x 9 inches; Indian woman, completely covered with shawl except for her face and one hand; matted, numbered, titled, dated 1982, and signed; $50–$75.

Wood-block print: Benjamin Harjo, Jr. (South Plains Indian); *As long as*; #8/32; 14½ x 9½ inches; depicts the right profile bust of a male Indian; matted, numbered, dated, and signed; $50–$75.

Wood, painted boxes: Jamie Tawodi Reason (1947–) (Cherokee); group of three award-winning carved and painted cedar boxes; $500–$1,500 each.

Wood carving: Seri; 13 inches long; wood carving depicting a bear; "#1–8445" written on the base; very good condition; $90–$130.

Wood: Sigsah; two oils on wood; deer and buffalo hunting scenes; signed; very good condition; $90–$130.

Wood carvings (three): Abner Johnson (Tlingit); depicting shark, grizzly bear, and whale; signed; $100–150.

Wood: totem pole; Haida; 9½ x 2 inches; black argillite totem pole depicting a female shaman with an eagle on top; ca. 1920; $500–$750.

Chapter Two

Artifacts

    Since the publication of the first edition of this book, there have been some major "finds" in the world of Indian artifacts. Some are simply the contents of a forgotten storage warehouse or items uncovered in a museum; others have been the result of archaeological digs. In 1991 nearly one million American Indian artifacts that were stored in an East Bronx building were uncovered and were a part of the 1993 inaugural exhibition of a new Indian museum at the Old Customs House on Bowling Green in Lower Manhattan. This building is now a branch of the National Museum of the American Indian, part of the Smithsonian Institution. W. Richard West, Jr., a Cheyenne-Arapaho, has been director of the National Museum since May 1990 and will oversee the tagging of this collection, assembled by the late George Gustav Heye. The artifact collection includes objects from the earliest Paleolithic period to modern times and from all of North and South America. Edgar Perry, one of the people chosen to select the items that will be displayed, has been director of the White Mountain Cultural Center in Fort Apache, Arizona, for more than twenty years. He is most interested in preserving Native American languages and is trying to figure out how best to do so.

    In 1992, when the museum opened in the Alexander Hamilton Custom House, nine hundred of the more than one million objects were chosen to make up the permanent displays, dating from thirteenth-century objects to contemporary pieces. They were chosen as objects of "cultural, aesthetic, and spiritual power" (Rick Hill, a Tuscarora Indian and assistant director of public programs at the museum).

    Beyond the rediscovery of objects held by museum collections, there has been a lot of concern in recent years regarding the sale of what are considered sacred artifacts. In May 1992 the *Maine Antiques Digest* newspaper published an article discussing the uncovering and ultimate sale of some Native American artifacts. Certain dealers were upset at the resistance from members of Native American tribes who did not believe dealers had any right to sell artifacts the tribespeople considered sacred. The only legislation that protects Native American artifacts is Public Law 101–601, the Native American Grave Protection and Repatriation Act, signed into law by President Bush on November 16, 1990. The act protects funerary objects and objects of cultural patrimony (inherited objects and those items deemed particularly important to native cultures). Such remains are to be returned to the tribes or people from whose lands the objects were taken. My opinion is that Native American peoples (including Native Hawaiians) have a right to recover any objects that they consider sacred, and I have done my best to monitor items included in this book. Should any of them be offensive to members of any American tribes, I will make every effort to remove such material in future editions of this book.

Another important museum collection, considered a survey of American Indian art, was organized in 1991 and traveled around the country in 1991–1992. The show was the result of a collection accumulated by R. Stewart Culin, the Smithsonian Institution's first curator of ethnology, and included 250 of the 9,000 artifacts in the collection. Culin often commissioned Native Americans to create objects that he could not obtain because they were sacred or simply rare.

OVERVIEW

Though the field of Native American collectibles is a large and varied one, it's clear that artifacts are the oldest form of collectibles in this category. Some arrowheads or lanceheads found in northern America are believed to be more than twenty thousand years old, yet such pieces of antiquity often sell for much less than more recent objects made by the Amerind.

The categories listed in this chapter are only the tip of the iceberg. More than five hundred types of projectile points exist, and there are almost as many different kinds of knives. For the novice, the field is vast and there is a lot to learn. For the professional, years of collecting may net only a few truly wonderful discoveries, for knowledge is sometimes more crippling than uplifting. In my research, I have found the best book on the subject to be another of The Confident Collector series, namely *The Overstreet Indian*

Arrowhead Identification and Price Guide (Third Edition) by Robert M. Overstreet and Howard Peake. It is chock-full of photos, as well as excellent information on identification which I cannot possibly provide in one chapter. If you are serious about collecting arrowheads, pick up Overstreet's book.

Because the artifacts described herein are the product of ancient cultures from which North American Indians, as we know them, I thought it best to give an overview of a couple of different ancient cultures before beginning our exploration of the types of artifacts found in North America.

THE ANASAZI TRIBE

These early North American Indians lived in the southwestern United States, growing corn, around the same time Jesus was living in the arid areas of Bethlehem and Nazareth.

The buildings the Anasazi constructed were multifamily dwellings linked by well-constructed roads and served by advanced water-control devices and sewer systems.

New Mexico holds twenty-five thousand such Anasazi sites, and many more are located in Arizona, Colorado, and Utah. Though there are thousands more waiting to be discovered, it is more likely that modern man will pillage the land and dig under ancient ruins in order to find the riches of coal, natural gas, and uranium that are plentiful throughout the region where the Anasazi once roamed, rather than protect the area as archaeological sites.

Scholars call these early people "Anasazi the Basket Makers" because archaeologists have discovered that these early settlers did not produce pottery. Their water vessels were tightly woven basketry ollas. Pottery arrived around A.D. 500, about the same time they began to use the bow and arrow. The hafted ax developed during the same era.

After A.D. 700, the Anasazi began living above ground within the walls of hillsides, and the *kiva*, or ceremonial room, became the center for ceremonial life. Another important sociological change came as adults began strapping their young to wooden cradleboards, causing the back of the baby's head to flatten.

Because the land they lived on was dry, and drought a constant companion, the Anasazi people were always on the move, looking for wetter lands and a more even temperature. Their main crop, corn, called for warm temperatures, but the vegetable also needed moisture in order to grow. After dealing with a fickle environment for another one hundred or so years, the Anasazi discovered a way to beat the system and, by A.D. 900, had learned to channel water to better suit their purposes. They then began to build pueblos from sandstone. One of the finest examples of such architecture is Pueblo Bonito in Chaco Canyon. The area boomed and other communities blossomed in Chaco Canyon over the next 130 years. The main Pueblo—Pueblo Bonito—contained some 650 rooms and was the largest building of its kind. Eleven other such structures in the canyon held another 2,000 rooms.

Craftspeople in this pueblo worked with turquoise, and various metals; laborers were kept busy enlarging the various buildings, which required the loading and moving of thousands of pounds of stone and timber—it was a thriving community.

The construction of roads to and from the outlying pueblos was a marvel of engineering ability. These roads were still visible from the air as late as 1927, when Lindbergh made his famous flight. Even now, some roads are still identifiable.

During the early years when the Anasazi were building their community, they developed and constructed a most sophisticated astronomical device, the Chacoan "sun dagger."

Around 1150, a drought began that eventually brought a halt to the Anasazi community, and Chaco Canyon became a monument of sorts, void of any living civilization. The Anasazi abandoned the area. While the Chaco community was dying, the Anasazi culture on Mesa Verde was flourishing. By the end of the thirteenth century, the cliff dwellers began constructing an enormous temple to the gods, but it was never completed, for they, too, gave up and abandoned their homeland.

The richness of this society, their tools, way of life, and talent for constructing large buildings are still being explored by anthropologists and archaeologists today.

THE MOGOLLON CULTURE

Located in the southern sections of New Mexico and Arizona, peoples of the Mogollon culture were largely farmers. Their early period, dating from 10,000 B.C., is referred to as the Desert Culture; and a later period, dating from 5000 B.C., is called the Cochise Culture. The society that existed between 300 B.C. and 1000 A.D., is called the Mogollon Culture.

The Mogollons are credited as the peoples who made the first pottery in the Southwest.

Five developmental periods have been named after representative sites by scholars: Pine Lawn period—200 B.C.–A.D. 500; Georgetown period, 500–700; San Francisco period, 700–900; Three Circle period, 900–1050; and Mimbres period, 1050–1200.

During the Pine Lawn period, these people built small villages populated by circular pole-and-mud-covered pit houses. No arrow or spearpoints have been found from this period; hence experts believe that these people did not hunt.

Hunting was prominent during the Georgetown period, and the people living during that time also made more pottery than their ancestors. Both activities became more common during the San Francisco period.

The Three Circle period was an age of developmental advances. Separate ceremonial houses were built, and there were also some rectangular pit houses made with masonry products. Their pottery became more sophisticated.

During the Mimbres period, pit houses were replaced by one- to three-story apartment houses, some containing forty to fifty rooms that encircled a plaza.

The Mogollon culture came to an end in the thirteenth century, though no one, to this day, knows exactly why.

THE MOUND BUILDERS

Mound Builders were people who, just as their name implies, erected mounds in and around the central and southern states. They were the ancestors of Creeks, Cherokees, Natchez, and other tribes—the same tribes who first greeted the arrival of the white man.

Archaeological research has uncovered stone pipes in Oklahoma that are believed to have been used in rituals by southern cult temple mound builders. Evidence of this culture has been found in Tennessee, Ohio, and Illinois as well.

Twelfth-century **Cahohia** (north of the Rio Grande) was a community that supported thirty thousand people. Farmers grew beans, squash, and corn; hunters found plenty of game; and craftsmen made ceramics and baskets, which were carried by canoe for trade with other establishments. Today Monk's Mound, part of Cahohia, remains in Saint Louis, and its base surpasses that of Egypt's Great Pyramid.

Mounds arose all over the Midwest. One, in southern Wisconsin, resembles a bird; in Ohio a dumbbell-shaped hilltop still exists. The Newark Earthworks is the largest Hopewell mound complex in Ohio. Fig Island Shell Ring, one of the oldest mounds in North America, is located in South Carolina, and Louisiana is the site of a three-thousand-year-old complex called the Poverty Point Mound. Huvasee Island in Tennessee is now partially submerged, but originally temples were built on twin mounds.

Through the study of these mounds, archaeologists discovered that the dead were honored with material goods (Archaic period burial grounds, Indian Knoll, Kentucky). They also established that no pottery was made in the Illinois Valley by 1100 B.C. Digs substantiate the conclusion that the first pottery made in North America was made of clay strengthened by vegetable fiber (Stalling's Island, Georgia; Port Royal, South Carolina; and Saint Johns River, Florida).

The purpose of these mounds, whether made of shells, dirt, or rocks, is unknown, but they have enabled archaeologists to assemble a history of the area, its arts and crafts, and early Indian peoples.

At Poverty Point, a mound site in Louisiana, early artisans made ornaments of hard stone, such as red jasper and hematite. Some pieces resemble those made by the Olmeco, a people who lived across the Gulf of Mexico.

The Hopewell Cult, appearing in the Ohio Valley by the second century B.C., left behind vestiges of its culture, such as embossed breastplates, ear ornaments, ritual weapons, and scenes of the culture cut into silhouettes of hands, bird claws, animals, and headless men. It is thought that this culture was abandoned for fortified hilltop sites, though archaeologists are not quite sure why.

Mounds became smaller, less distinct around A.D. 700, and corn-growing communities seemed the mainstay of the Indian culture along the Mississippi. Monk's Mound, in Saint Louis, represents one of these communities and today is the largest ancient structure in the United States. By 1500 the mound-making communities along the Mississippi began to die. When the DeSoto expedition traveled through the area between 1539 and 1542, they chronicled painfully little of the society.

Today archaeologists still struggle to piece together this part of the North American Indian's past.

FINDING ARTIFACTS

The *Overstreet Indian Arrowhead Identification and Price Guide* suggests that large, flat areas close to old river or creek beds are a good place to start looking for points or arrowheads, because often they represent locations where an Indian tribe could have safely located their small community. Hunting for relics after a hard rain could raise your chances of finding objects since the rain will make them easier to spot. Plowed fields "next to springs and cave openings have also produced relics" (Overstreet, third edition), and sandbars often produce relics after winter storms ravage the area.

GRADING POINTS

The factors to consider when collecting points are condition, size, form, symmetry, flaking, thinness, material, and color. You should also consider the point's provenance, rarity, popularity, and fire damage.

TYPES OF INDIAN ARTIFACTS

ABRADERS   Made from almost any type of stone or antler, abraders were used for polishing, grinding, and abrasion. They may be shaped for fine or delicate abrasion work. Slabs were used for small abrading jobs, stones (sometimes called whetstones) were used to sharpen tools or weapons.

ANVILS   Many cultures used anvils or grooved handstones in the production of pottery. They were made from almost any stone. Most are round, but rectangular and square examples have been found. For easy handling, the peripheral edge contains a full groove.

ARROWS   Arrows were usually longer versions of atlatl darts. The main shaft was made of a hollow reed, while the foreshaft was made of hardwood. The two pieces were spliced together with animal guts or cactus fibers. Three feathers were usually attached to one end to aid the arrow in straight flight, and the point was attached to the other.

ATLATL   A weapon that added greater length and propulsion to a spear or dart, enabling the thrower to throw the spear or arrow harder and longer. An atlatl is a long wooden shaft with a finger-grip (two loops) at one end and a hook or spur at the other.

The atlatl dart's main shaft was made of hardwood, and was separate from the pointed end. It was a reusable piece of the weapon which contained the feathered end. An atlatl dart blunt was used to stun rather than to kill its target. It was a stubby foreshaft inserted into the shaft's end.

Atlatl weights are like bannerstones, only they do not have a large central hole as bannerstones do, and atlatl weights are generally flat or concave on the bottom. Most are long and narrow with square or round sides and tops.

Weights were functional as well as ornamental. Their function was to add weight to the lance, giving added impetus to the thrower. When well made, the atlatl could be ornamental, and some were even recognized as effigy forms.

The atlatl was used for approximately eight thousand years—from prehistory until A.D. 500—throughout North America.

AWLS Used to make the holes in skins, weaving materials, and basketry pieces, awls were made from deer, sheep, or antelope knee or fetlock bones. They usually measure from 2 to 9 inches long, and some are perforated at the butt end so that the user might wear them on a cord until needed.

AXES Axes were first made six thousand years ago out of stone. Instead of chipping at the stone, which created projectile points, Indians learned to pound, grind, and polish larger stones in order to make the axes that became an integral part of their lives.

Grooves in the ax were used to secure the handle, and they can be used to determine the age of an ax. The oldest examples were fully grooved, while later axes were three-quarter or one-half grooved. The most recent examples are known as celts (which came about after the arrival of the white man).

A celt was longer and narrower than the older axes and did not have a groove, but was instead mounted on a thick handle through a socket.

The Lakes area Indians made a fluted ax, while perforated mauls were unique to the Northwest Coast. The southeastern Indians and Northwest Coast tribes made ceremonial monolithic axes. The Northwest Coast variety often had stonework shaped in the form of birds or other animals.

As with points, the value of an ax is determined by symmetry, workmanship, and balance. Damage to the ax should be slight or nonexistent if it is to retain a high value for the collector.

Ax sharpeners were usually made from large rectangular chunks of vesicular basalt or another type of abrasive stone. Some measure almost a foot by half a foot and might weigh up to ten pounds.

BANNERSTONES   The function of *bannerstones* is still a puzzle to many collectors. They were drilled from edge to edge with a hollow drill and are double-sided. They appear to be some sort of projectile (spear) point, yet experts surmised that they were used as weights on early spears.

Some bannerstones are sharp-edged, others are curved, and still others have an upward curve on each end.

BOWS   The first bows were made during the mid-fourteenth century, from a single stave of wood. Very few whole bows have been found intact, perhaps because they were made of wood, which tends to disintegrate quite easily.

CELTS   Ungrooved axes or *celts* were found in early Southeast cultures. Celts with gouges in them were only found in the early cultures of Maine, while the Northwest Coast celts were long and double-edged (see information on axes).

CEREMONIAL OBJECTS   Objects of this type usually have some religious or cultural significance. Some items that fall into this category are: ceremonial axes, bells, fetishes, flutes, koshare symbols, medicine boxes, painted shells and stones, pipes, prayer sticks, smoking tubes, effigy statues, whistles, and charms.

CHISELS   Used to split or shape wood when making various wooden artifacts. Most were two to six inches long and made from bone, slender stones, or sheets of laminated stone.

CHOPPERS   Often used to pound material that needed to be softened, choppers were usually rough-chipped, blunt on one side, and weighed less than half a pound.

COOKING STONES   Small, smooth stones used to quickly boil foods cooked in water. The stones would be heated over a fire, then placed into the pot in which the food was cooked.

DISCS   Discs served many purposes. Some were used to make spindle whorls or disc beads. Some had a center perforation and were worn in a necklace to separate shells, stone, and beads. Large granite discs were used for games, thrown much like a discus is at a track and field meet. Multiperforated discs were used as ceremonial pieces or noisemakers, while shell discs were probably used as ornaments. Thick vesicular basalt discs were also used in a game that resembles today's shuffleboard.

DRILLS A drill can be almost any length, but most have symmetrical bases. They were designed for making holes and are usually between one and three inches long.

Some drills were used in the making of clothing or working with leatherlike materials. The drill was the tool used to poke a hole in the material so that a sewing tool or awl could follow through with some sinew to hold the pieces together. Other, stronger drills were used to make holes in bannerstones or other mineral tools.

Due to function strains, drills were made of very strong rock materials or fossilized limestones, sometimes even of shells.

FETISHES Fetishes were held sacred by prehistoric Indians and are still held sacred by some tribes today. They are often carved figures made from clay or minerals, often in the shape of bears, lions, coyotes, wolves, birds, and other animals. Early fetishes are crude figures, hand-molded from clay. A few examples were made from potsherds, though these are quite scarce.

GORGETS These are small breastplates that were worn as necklaces by certain members of the tribe, usually to distinguish their rank as medicine man, chief, or other leader. Examples made of mica and potsherds have been found.

KNIVES Knives made in prehistoric times have been found in many archaeological sites throughout the United States. Some experts will tell you that it is often difficult to determine the difference between a point and a knife when collecting Indian artifacts. There are names for over five hundred different kinds of chipped artifacts in this country, so this field of collecting requires serious study in order for the collector to be able to identify the origin of a knife, blade, or point.

For example, an Ashtabula knife, distinguished by wide notches, its knifelike appearance, and offset tip, originated in Oneida County, New York, while a cream-white chert-type knife with basal strength, and large, wide notches is typical of Pike County, Missouri, and is called a *godar*.

As scientists study artifacts, they determine the type names and the region from which they came. It is a wonder that they can come to a decision about where these items originated when so many Indian tribes were nomadic, carrying their spears, knives, and arrowheads with them to use along the way. How confusing it must be for these geologists and historians when they find a Castroville knife made of dark gray flint with white incisions, and indigenous to Stone County, Missouri, in Taney County, Missouri, where the Stanlee knife, an off-white chert, is said to have originated.

I certainly admire the collectors who are able to pick up a knife and immediately identify its age, origin, and name. I must reiterate something that holds true in the antiques business —if you are around a kind of collectible long enough, touch examples, study them, and buy and sell them on a regular basis, you cannot help but learn about them—more than you are aware.

The first and most important point to remember about knives is that prehistoric Indians used them for more than just cutting up game for food. A good knife was the most important tool an Indian could own. Of course, different size knives were made for different purposes, and the shape of a knife's blade can often tell you its intended use.

Knives are generally split into three categories: scrapers, shapers, and drills. (Each category is described in greater detail under its own heading in this chapter.)

Knives, such as Folsom points, have been found north of Fort Collins, Colorado, at the Lindenmeir site. Microlithic flint blades have been found on Santa Rosa Island, off the coast of California. Both are examples of bladelets and are thought to have been used to drill shell beads.

Paleo knife forms, found at the Williamson site in Virginia, were larger than fluted points and lacked grinding of the base bottom and lower sides.

In Illinois, at the Koster site, a four-thousand-year-old temporary hunting camp, it was proved that knives were part of the Indian's hunting tool kit as the hunters dressed the slain animal on site instead of bringing it back to the camp.

Even in Vermont, at the Reagan site just south of the Canadian border, knives have been found that resembled projectile points.

To determine the value of prehistoric blades, collectors should keep in mind the symmetry of the knife, material (glossy, fine-grained flint is more desirable than dull, large-grained chert), the type of knife, its configuration, the workmanship, and, above all, its condition.

MAULS   Mauls were heavy, mallet-type tools that were generally used to reduce or to pound larger, softer stones.

Ceremonial mauls are made from light or soft material, impractical in pounding larger rocks.

NEEDLES   Made of bone or shell, prehistoric needles used by Native Americans were quite fragile, thus are rarely found today. They resemble darning needles used today.

They were used to sew leather garments or to work with basketry materials.

PADDLES (See Wooden Items Chapter Thirteen)

PETROGLYPHS   Prehistoric carvings or paintings are called *petroglyphs*. They are usually found on walls of rock and were made by picking at the wall or rock surface with a hammerstone or chopper. These carvings are usually of animals, reptiles, or geometric patterns that had meaning for that particular tribe. Some of them will tell a story.

PLANTING STICKS   Usually made of a thin piece of wood approximately a yard long, *planting sticks* were used to make holes the desired depth in which to drop seeds for crops. A uniform depth was set by attaching a circular ring weight to the stick.

POLISHING STONES   *Polishing stones* are worn, almost polished, stones that are used by potters to smooth and polish wet ceramic surfaces before the pots are fired. This method of working pottery is still used by contemporary Native American potters today.

PROJECTILE POINTS   This category includes both arrowheads and lanceheads, and it is often difficult to tell the difference between the two.

The easiest guide is size. The average length of a lancehead is about two inches, while the space between basal notches is approximately one half inch. Arrowheads are between one and one and one half inches long, and the space between basal notches approximately one quarter inch. Arrowheads are also thinner and lighter in weight.

Atlatls (covered elsewhere in this chapter), the most widely used North American weapon before A.D. 500, was a hand-held lance thrower. Examples are very rare today. The atlatl had a feather-vaned main shaft, which was retrieved, while the thin, short foreshaft was left in the animal.

These points were made by chipping processes, and the makers of such points were held in high regard by their tribes.

The skill required to make a fine-grade point is recognized today and reflected in the value of such a point in the collectibles market. Workmanship and quality are determined by the thinness of the point, the regularity of pressure-chipping scars, the point's size (larger pieces are more valuable), and the grade of material.

There should be visual "balance" in a point, meaning both sides should be symmetrical. Though collectors may choose such a point because it is more pleasing to the eye, one must keep in mind the original purpose for such symmetry was that a blade would fly straighter and farther if it was made as evenly as possible.

Each tribe had a different style of point. Some arrowheads are jagged-edged, while others have sharp tips and rather rounded bodies. Hopewell points (ca. 300 B.C. to A.D. 300) are rather curved, the point itself showing artistically rounded edges. Hohokam points (600–1400 A.D.) are tall and thin with jagged edges. The two points, though used for basically the same purpose, look nothing alike.

It's incredible to think that no two tribes made exactly the same *type* of point, yet they were all making points at the same time.

The different parts of a projectile point are as illustrated below:

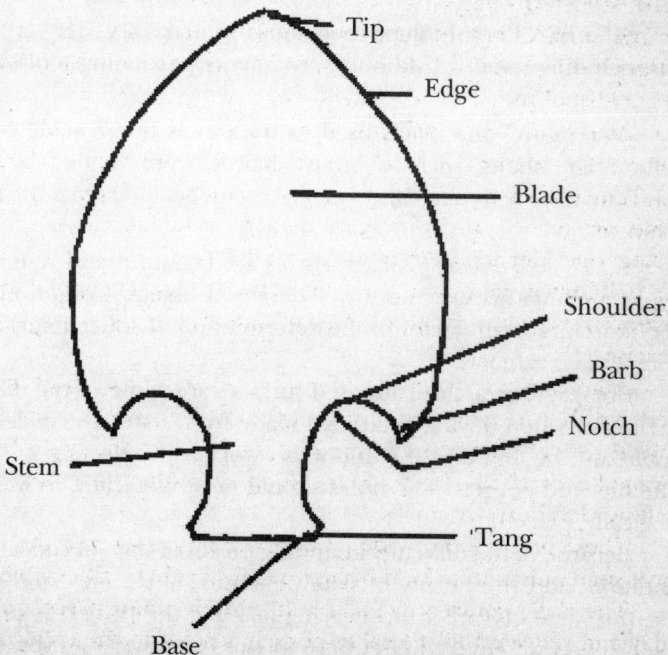

Blades were set into a slot to fit the size of the blade and were then tied onto the wood with wet sinew, which tightened as it dried.

Some cultures, as was the case in some Northern California tribes, judged personal wealth by the number of obsidian blades in an individual's possession. Such blades were used in ceremonies, such as the White Deer Dance.

SCRAPERS Scrapers of prehistoric age are less interesting and much cruder than later examples, which tribes such as the Plains Indians used to scrape and prepare animal hides for tanning.

The Yurok tribe used scrapers or adzes with stone handles.

Because the short, strong edges of scrapers would often have to be repolished, they show heavy wear.

Though prices are low for these artifacts (usually under five dollars each), there are not many collectors who hunt for these items.

SHAPERS A hafted shaper will have a base that remains mostly intact and either a single or double working edge. Shapers are not chipped, but rather ground down, giving the edge a smooth face and a sharp cut.

SHELLS Early Indians used shells to make a variety of artifacts including jewelry, fishhooks, ornaments, gardening tools, dippers, and spoons.

"Wampum," the beads used in trade, was often made from shells. Some shells, such as bivalve halves, were treated by the Hohokam tribe with pitch and saguaro cactus acid to create the first etchings.

SLATE ARTIFACTS Slate articles are beautiful and required simple methods to execute a well-designed object. Condition, as ever, is an important factor in the determintion of collectibility and value of slate artifacts.

Breakage, scratches, and dull surfaces are some of the things to consider when buying an artifact made from slate. The collector should also be aware of the importance of proper drilling in slate pendants and gorgets. The holes should be strategically, as well as artistically, placed.

Because of the difficulty in finding pieces of slate in collectible condition, and the beauty of slate pendants, birdstones, and gorgets, the value of slate artifacts is higher than the projectile point-type artifacts we covered elsewhere in this chapter. However, with diligence and a little luck, it is still possible to put together a collection of pieces for $50 (or less) each.

SPADES   Spades are usually heavier than a digging blade, with a squared and blunted bottom edge.

The better the polish on the blade edge (a sign of use), the more valuable the spade to a collector.

WEAVING PINS   Made in varying lengths, these pins were made from bone, mesquite, or wood, and used to beat down the *weft* (yarn) of a piece of fabric being woven.

WHISTLES   Whistles were used during ceremonies, and as tools to attract animals during the hunt. They were often made of one piece of hollowed bone with a hole in the center. The sound was produced when the blower held his thumb and index finger over the opposite ends of the whistle while blowing across the hole.

PRICES

Adze: 3½ inches; rare old Columbia River jade adze; prehistoric; very good condition; $55–$85.

Arrowhead coffee table: 18 x 16 x 39 inches; two-tiered wooden coffee table with over 600 arrowheads and spearpoints mounted under glass; very good condition; $575–$800.

Arrowhead: excavated iron trade point arrowhead; very good condition; $50–$75.

Arrowheads (11) and one spearhead: flint; very good condition; $90–$130.

Arrowheads: copper; five old native copper (cleaned) hunting arrow tips from Alaska; ca. 1700; very good condition; $40–$60.

Arrowheads: Riker mount containing three choice Oregon gem points; prehistoric; very good condition; $85–$115.

Arrowheads: two large choice Columbia River arrowheads; prehistoric; very good condition; $40–$60.

Arrows, Plains: two feathered Plains arrows with stone points; ca. 1870; very good condition; $115–$175.

Atlatl carved stone pieces: three pieces; fish line weight and two flat polished stones, one with stylized carved face; very good condition; $80–$100.

Axhead: 4 x 3 inches; ¾ groove with collection number; from Ohio; ca. prehistoric; very good condition; $30–$90.

Axhead: excavated iron trade axhead; very good condition; $100–$150.

Axhead: Mound Builder; 3 x 5 inches; ¾ groove with wedge slot; ca. prehistoric; very good condition; $40–$85.

Axhead: Mound Builder; 3 x 5 inches; ¾ groove; ca. prehistoric; very good condition; $35–$90.

Axhead: 7 x 4½ inches; large mottled black ¾ grooved axhead; prehistoric; very good condition; $115–$140.

Axheads (two): Midwest; 3 x 5 inches; both with ¾ groove, from O. L. Houser collection; ca. prehistoric; very good condition; $30–$80.

Ax: 6 x 3 inches; fully grooved black stone axhead from the Columbia River; prehistoric; very good condition; $50–$70.

Ax: Hohokam; stone; 4½ x 2 inches; ¾ grooved stone axhead; prehistoric; very good condition; $50–$85.

Ax: Midwest; 4 x 7 inches; full groove, from O. L. Houser collection; ca. prehistoric; very good condition; $25–$80.

Ax: Hohokam; stone; 7 x 3½ inches; large brown stone axhead from Arizona; prehistoric; very good condition; $25–$60.

Ax: Stone; choice greenish ¾ grooved jadite axhead; prehistoric; very good condition; $175–$230.

Ax: Stone; gray ¾ grooved stone axhead; prehistoric; very good condition; $75–$95.

Ax: 22 x 7 inches; used for war; heavy iron head with tacks, file marks, and with bead and wire-wrapped handle; ca. 1880; very good condition; $520–$635.

Bow: Northwest Coast; 52 x 1 inch; carved wooden bow with rawhide handhold; ca. 1870; very good condition; $230–$285.

Bow: Northwest Coast; 53 x 2 inches; wide carved wooden game bow; ca. 1910; very good condition; $40–$60.

Bow: Northwest Coast; 50 x 1½ inches; large wooden bow with sinew string and sealskin wrap; ca. 1890; very good condition; $85–$115.

Bow: Plains; 32 x 1½ inches; beautiful old recurved wooden short bow; ca. 1860; very good condition; $115–$175.

Bow: Plains; 55 x 1 inch; classic narrow wooden Northern Plains bow; ca. 1870; very good condition; $55–$80.

Bow: Plains; 60 x 1½ inches; very early long red and yellow ochre painted Plains bow; ca. 1870; very good condition; $85–$115.

Bow: Sioux; 48 x 1½ inches; recurved wooden bow with a sinew string; ca. 1900; very good condition; $175–$230.

Bowl: Mound Builder; 6 x 4 inches; rare and incised Mound Builder owl effigy stone bowl; prehistoric; $55–$85.

Carving: Wasco; 3 x 3 inches; rare small carved basalt mortar with owl face from the Columbia River; prehistoric; very good condition; $260–$290.

Carving: Wasco; 7 x 4 inches; rare carved basalt mortar in turtle form from the Columbia River; prehistoric; very good condition; $700–$800.

Celt: prehistoric, highly polished, finely worked jade celt from the Columbia River; Provenance: Charles Miles collection; very good condition; $155–$200.

Celt: prehistoric, large, finely worked jade celt from the Columbia River; Provenance: Charles Miles collection; very good condition; $230–$350.

Celts and plumb bob: 3 inches long; carved stone; very good condition; $50–$175.

Celts: 6 inches long; large, with collection number; from Ohio; ca. prehistoric; very good condition; $40–$90.

Ceremonial wand: Northern Plains; 29 x 1 inch; buffalo horn dance wand with fully beaded handle; very good condition; $350–$460.

Club: Northern Plains; 29 x 1 inch; "flop knob" war club with fully beaded handle and horsehair suspensions; very good condition; $350–$460.

Club: Sioux; 18 x 2 inches; egg-shaped brown stone head on a fully beaded wooden handle; ca. 1860; very good condition; $115–$175.

Club: Sioux; 19 x 2 inches; egg-shaped stone club with beaded handle; ca. 1890; very good condition; $115–$150.

Club: Sioux; 28 x 5 inches; red stone egg-shaped club on long, fully beaded handle; very good condition; $290–$400.

Club: Sioux; 30 x 5 inches; large gray egg-shaped stone head attached to a hide-covered wooden handle; ca. 1870; very good condition; $130–$200.

Club: Sioux; 31 x 5 inches; painted wooden war club with metal blades with hair suspensions; ca. 1870; very good condition; $205–$260.

Collection in large frame: excavated Columbia River artifacts including points, fossils, beads, etc.; prehistoric; very good condition; $115–$230/set.

Collection of arrowheads and scrapers in Riker mount: prehistoric; very good condition; $40–$100/set.

Collection of arrowheads mounted on board: 16 x 24 inches; triangle points; Texas; very good condition; $100–$250/set.

Collection of arrowheads: 2 inches long; 11 spearpoints from Illinois, Missouri, Tennessee, and Kentucky; ca. 7500 B.C.–A.D. 500; very good condition; $40–$100/set.

Collection of 25 stone weights, tablets, etc.: 22 x 18 inches, prehistoric; very good condition; $115–$230/set.

Collection: approximately 600 pieces including points, blades, celts, and adze blades; very good condition; $300–$350.

Collection: arrowheads; 31 pieces, including bird points, gouges, two Clovis points, etc.; very good condition; $90–$110/set.

Collection: 48 x 53 inches; fantastic glassed frame containing 1,500 points laid in the form of two deer and the sun; very good condition; $700–$1,150/set.

Collection: four stone pieces; two pipes, one chelum, and one flat with a fox; two birdstones; very good condition; $90–$130/set.

Collection: frame containing 13 large points and beads from Missouri; prehistoric; very good condition; $65–$85/set.

Collection: frame containing 15 assorted arrow and spearpoints; prehistoric; very good condition; $35–$60/set.

Collection: frame containing 40 white stone points; prehistoric; very good condition; $45–$70/set.

Collection: frame containing nine stone salmon-cleaning knives; prehistoric; $20–$45/set.

Collection: 11 x 9 inches; frame containing over 50 choice arrowheads; prehistoric; very good condition; $85–$175/set.

Collection: frame of 25 large points and beads from Missouri; prehistoric; very good condition; $40–$65/set.

Collection: framed box of 30 flint and quartz arrowheads; very good condition; $55–$85/set.

Collection: 12 x 10 inches; glass frame containing 55 Columbian River points; prehistoric; very good condition; $70–$100/set.

Collection: glassed frame containing 37 Columbia River cogs, pestles, balls, and sinkers; prehistoric; very good condition; $435–$500/set.

Collection: glassed frame containing 52 arrowheads and points; pre-historic; very good condition; $100–$115/set.

Collection: 23 x 18 inches; glassed frame containing 39 pipes, net sinkers, and other artifacts; prehistoric; very good condition; $90–$115/set.

Collection: glassed frame containing 50 very unusual choice pink arrowpoints; prehistoric; very good condition; $30–$60/set.

Collection: 11 x 9 inches; glassed frame containing 53 Oregon points; prehistoric; very good condition; $70–$95/set.

Collection: 12 x 10 inches; glassed frame containing 61 Oregon arrowheads; prehistoric; very good condition; $70–$95/set.

Collection: 12 x 10 inches; glassed frame containing 54 Columbia River points and some trade beads; prehistoric; very good condition; $140–$195/set.

Collection: 12 x 10 inches; glassed frame containing 56 Oregon arrowheads; prehistoric; very good condition; $60–$190/set.

Collection: 10 x 12 inches; glassed frame containing 50 very unusual and ornate projectile points; prehistoric; very good condition; $200–$260/set.

Collection: 12 x 9 inches; glassed frame containing 51 choice arrows and spearpoints; prehistoric; very good condition; $175–$210/set.

Collection: 12 x 10 inches; glassed frame containing 54 Columbia River points and some trade beads; prehistoric; very good condition; $145–$200/set.

Collection: 12 x 10 inches; glassed frame containing four rare Phoenix buttons, old Chinese coins, beads, etc., from the Columbia River; ca. 1840; very good condition; $200–$260/set.

Collection: 11 x 9 inches; glassed frame containing nine arrowheads and many rare trade beads; ca. 1900; very good condition; $110–$160/set.

Collection: 12 x 10 inches; glassed frame containing 60 Oregon points; prehistoric; very good condition; $60–$190/set.

Collection: glassed frame containing 75 black and brown obsidian arrow and spearpoints; very good condition; $230–$400.

Collection: 11 x 9 inches; glassed frame containing seven arrow-heads and many rare trade beads; ca. 1870; very good condition; $100–$115/set.

Collection: 11 x 9 inches; glassed frame containing rare Columbia River gem points, trade beads, and an old coin; ca. 1820; very good condition; $85–$115/set.

Collection: 12 x 10 inches; glassed frame containing 66 fine Columbia River arrowheads; prehistoric; very good condition; $40–$60/set.

Collection: group, Southern Plains; including a beaded hide awl case and a "strike-a-light" pouch, each trimmed with tin cones, a beaded hide belt pouch, a woven beadwork strap with pouch, a bone hair-pipe necklace with brass and translucent red glass beads, and a doll with model cradleboard, wearing a cloth costume, red painted details; provenance: "Captured from Apaches in 1878 by Mrs. R. Der. Hoyle"; very good condition; $2,000–$2,500.

Collection: Hohokam; large bone awl, ten points, and three beads; ca. A.D. 1200; very good condition; $30–$70.

Collection: 48 x 52 inches; huge frame containing 1,500 choice points mounted in Northwest Coast bear design; prehistoric; very good condition; $700–$1,150/set.

Collection: 53 x 48 inches; huge glassed frame containing 1,500 projectile points inlaid in prehistoric animal designs; very good condition; $800–$1,150/set.

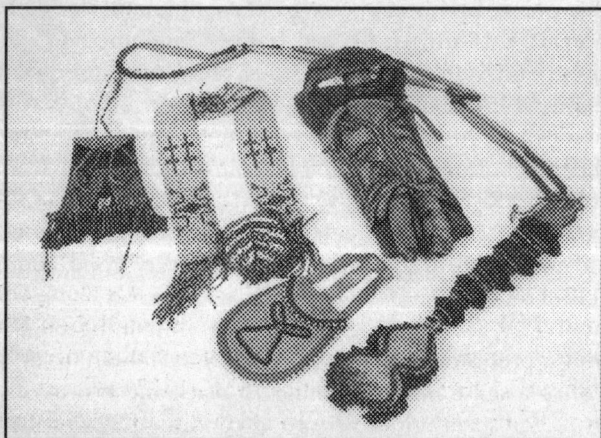

Artifacts, group, Southern Plains; including a beaded hide awl case and a "strike-a-light" pouch, each trimmed with tin cones, a beaded hide belt pouch, a woven beadwork strap with pouch, a bone "hair-pipe" necklace with brass and translucent red glass beads, and a doll with model cradleboard, wearing a cloth costume, red painted details; "Captured from Apaches in 1878 by Mrs. R. Der. Hoyle"; $2,000–$2,500. William R. Nash Collection. Photo by Donald Vogt.

Collection: 23 x 18 inches; large glassed frame containing over 55 bone artifacts from the Columbia River; prehistoric; very good condition; $185–$230/set.

Collection: large glassed frame containing 268 similar points; prehistoric; very good condition; $100–$115/set.

Collection: Midwest; 12 points and celt in Riker mount, 2 inches long; from Illinois, Arkansas, Missouri and Ohio; ca. A.D. 500; very good condition; $45–$80/set.

Collection: Midwest; 13 points, 3 inches long; Riker-mounted; from Illinois, Tennessee, and Missouri; ca. 1000 B.C.; very good condition; $60–$125/set.

Collection: Midwest; 14 spearpoints and drills from Tennessee, Mississippi, Illinois, and Missouri; ca. 3000 B.C.–A.D. 500; very good condition; $75–$150/set.

Collection: Midwest; 36 x 30 inches; framed points including scrapers and spearpoints; ca. prehistoric; very good condition; $200–$400/set.

Collection: Midwest; nine spearpoints and scrapers in Riker mount; ca. prehistoric; very good condition; $45–$100/set.

Collection: Midwest; flint blades, 8 inches long; two shaped as hoes; one large blade; ca. prehistoric; very good condition; $50–$110/set.

Collection: Nootka; lot of two teeth and trinket box; one tooth Nootka with cedar basketry, quid box with scrimshaw of fish and bird, and a wooden puffin stopper; very good condition; $100–$150.

Collection: Riker mount containing three Oregon gem points, all three having serrated edges; prehistoric; very good condition; $155–$200/set.

Collection: Riker mount containing 24 arrowheads along with an elk antler hide scraper; very good condition; $135–$150/set.

Collection: Riker mount containing 21 choice stone arrowheads; prehistoric; very good condition; $115–$175/set.

Collection: Riker mount containing 22 stone arrowheads; prehistoric; very good condition; $25–$50/set.

Collection: Riker mount containing 22 large stone arrowheads; very good condition; $85–$140/set.

Collection: Riker mount containing 16 pieces including arrowheads, bones, and beads; prehistoric; very good condition; $40–$60/set.

Collection: Riker mount containing 15 pieces of Mimbres material; prehistoric; very good condition; $55–$85/set.

Collection: Riker mount containing seven prehistoric pottery pieces; very good condition; $30–$60/set.

Collection: Riker mount containing 43 pieces of material excavated from the Columbia River; prehistoric; very good condition; $40–$60/set.

Collection: Riker mount containing four choice Rogue River points; prehistoric; very good condition; $85–$145/set.

Collection: Southwest; arrowheads and crescents in Riker mount; prehistoric; very good condition; $45–$100/set.

Collection: stone items; five assorted arrowheads, eccentrics, etc; prehistoric; very good condition; $40–$60.

Collection: 21 arrowheads, framed, from different areas of the country; very good condition; $120–$160.

Collection: two mounts containing eight choice Oregon and Washington gem mounts; prehistoric; very good condition; $70–$90/set.

Collection: two Riker mounts containing a total of 21 arrowheads and spearheads; prehistoric; very good condition; $55–$80/set.

Collection: two small Riker mounts each containing five gem arrowheads; prehistoric; very good condition; $70–$100/set.

Collection: wooden frame containing nine rare ceremonial and effigy points; prehistoric; very good condition; $85–$115/set.

Deity: Hopi; 3 inches high; bear; ca. 1940; very good condition; $100–$200.

Effigy pot: Mound Builder; 3 x 4 inches; in the shape of a human head; very good condition; $30–$110.

Fetish pot: Zuni; 7 x 9 inches; crushed turquoise exterior with stone bear fetishes; ca. 1960; very good condition; $80–$200.

Fetish: Sioux; 4 x 2 inches; small beaded hide umbilical cord fetish in lizard form; very good condition; $65–$95.

Fetish: Zuni; 12½ inches long; antler, shell, hide, and feathered fetish; serpent/dragon/horned sea monster with two protruding (v-shaped) horns and tongue; very good condition; $300–$520.

Fetish: Zuni; 2 inches long; bear carved of amber with turquoise heart-line inlay; contemporary; very good condition; $25–$80.

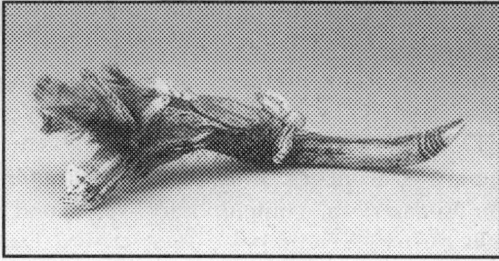

Artifacts, fetish, Zuni; antler, shell, hide, and feathered fetish; 12½ inches long; serpent/dragon/horned sea monster with two protruding (v-shaped) horns and tongue; $300–$520. Courtesy Jack Sellner, CAI.

Artifacts, fetish, Zuni; snake fetish carved from elk antler; the fetish is adorned with tin mudheads and is signed "J. Boone—Zuni"; the Boone family is noted for jewelry and other works; ca. 1950s; $800–$1,000. Collection of Donna McMenamin. Photo by Donald Vogt.

Fetish: Zuni; 3 inches long; carved turquoise by Lena Boone; badger with arrowhead on back; ca. contemporary; very good condition; $25–$50.

Fetish: Zuni; snake fetish carved from elk antler; the fetish is adorned with tin mudheads and is signed "J. Boone—Zuni"; the Boone family is noted for jewelry and other works; ca. 1950s; very good condition; $800–$1,000.

Fetishes and sack of raw turquoise: Navajo; ca. 1960; very good condition; $20–$85.

Fetishes: bird fetishes; made of black pottery; contemporary; $35–$100.

Fetishes: Crow and Plains; average 5 inches long; three beaded umbilical cord pieces in the form of lizards; very good condition; $175–$275/set.

Fetishes: Zuni; 1 x 2 inches; stone badger, turquoise bear, by Vernon Lunaser; ca. contemporary; very good condition; $35–$90.

Fetishes: Zuni; 2 inches high; stone bear, standing bear, horny toad; ca. 1985; very good condition; $70–$150.

Head: Mound Builder; 6½ x 3½ inches; rare round builder stone head from Barstow County, Georgia; prehistoric; very good condition; $195–$230.

Knife and case: 18 x 3½ inches; large knife case with paint and tacks and containing an old knife; very good condition; $95–$115.

Knife case: Plains; 11½ x 3½ inches; hide sheath with geometric beadwork and containing an old knife; ca. 1910; good condition; $115–$175.

Knife sheath: Plains; lazy stitch knife sheath; made ca. 1880s–1890s; very good condition; $175–$290.

Knife: 10 inches x 1 inch; unusual carved bone knife or awl; ca. 1900; very good condition; $20–$35.

Knife: Yurok; 11 x 1½ inches; long double-pointed black obsidian ceremonial knife; prehistoric; very good condition; $115–$175.

Knife: 14 x 4 inches; choice dark gray stone ceremonial knife from the Columbia River; prehistoric; very good condition; $290–$350.

Knife: Northwest Coast; 15 x 4 inches; choice handmade knife with carved animal head handle and painted wooden sheath; ca. 1975; very good condition; $110–$145.

Knife: Plains; old handmade knife and painted rawhide sheath; ca. 1880; very good condition; $65–$95.

Knives: Midwest; 7 inches long; chipped flint; two from Boone County, Missouri, one from Cooper County, Missouri; ca. prehistoric; very good condition; $50–$160.

Medicine items: five old Navajo sacred medicine items in a box; ca. 1880; very good condition; $75–$100.

Mortar and pestle: 10 x 9 inches; gray stone mortar and pestle from the Columbia River; prehistoric; very good condition; $40–$80.

Mortar and pestle: 14 x 7 inches; choice gray stone mortar and matching bell pestle from the Columbia River; prehistoric; very good condition; $175–$200.

Mortar and pestle: 7-inch pestle; hard stone; ca. prehistoric; very good condition; $100–$200/set.

Mortar and pestle: Casas Grandes; 4 x 8 inches; hard stone, camp mortar; prehistoric; very good condition; $70–$125.

Mortar and pestle: Wasco; 11 x 4¾ inches; rare stone mortar and pestle excavated near Celilo Falls on the Columbia River; ca. 1700; very good condition; $130–$170.

Pestle: 8 x 3 inches; black stone phallic pestle found on the Columbia River in 1960; prehistoric; very good condition; $115–$175.

Pestle: Casas Grandes; 3 x 2 inches; effigy pestle, dog's head pecked out of stone; prehistoric; very good condition; $55–$85.

Pestle: 4½ x 7 inches; choice black stone bell pestle from the Columbia River; prehistoric; very good condition; $140–$185.

Pipe Bowl: approximately 4 inches high, 3 inches wide, 3½ inches deep; with figural carvings including what appears to be a human face form, animal with long antler, another dog form; marked on base "Heike 998" with another human face carved into the bottom; $80–$200.

Pipe Head: 3½ inches tall; carved sandstone with fish and other mountain totemics; uncovered in Fulton, Illinois, excavations; marked "Heike 999" on base; $60–$120.

Artifacts, stone pipe bowl; with figural carvings including what appears to be a human face form, animal with long antler, another dog form; approximately 4 inches high, 3 inches wide, 3½ inches deep; marked on base "Heike 998" with another human face carved into the bottom; $80–$200.
Courtesy of C. E. Guarino Auction Gallery, Denmark, Maine.

Artifacts, sandstone pipe head; carved with fish and other mountain totemics; uncovered in Fulton, Illinois, excavations; 3½ inches tall; marked "Heike 999" on base; $60–$120. Courtesy of C. E. Guarino Auction Gallery, Denmark, Maine.

Pipe: Hopewell; 8 x 6½ inches; very large and unusual human sacrificial idol pipe from Illinois; prehistoric; very good condition; $315–$435.

Pipe: Mound Builder; 10½ x 3½ inches; long black Mound Builder bird effigy pipe; prehistoric; very good condition; $195–$230.

Pipe: Mound Builder; 3 inches x 1 inch; mottled black stone pipe in rabbit shape; prehistoric; very good condition; $125–$225.

Pipe: Mound Builder; 7 x 1½ inches; beautiful black Mound Builder effigy pipe; prehistoric; very good condition; $155–$175.

Pipe: Sioux, eastern; catlinite pipestone with file burned stem, round stem with nice old patina; mid-1800s; very good condition; $350–$550.

Pipe: Sioux; 19 x 2 inches; small fine red catlinite "T" bowl with carved wooden stem; ca. 1890; very good condition; $155–$175.

Pipe: Sioux; 21 x 2 x 7 inches; black stone "T" bowl with red stone and pewter inlay, dated 1888; very good condition; $140–$200.

Pipe: Sioux; 28 x 2 x 6 inches; black stone "T" bowl with red stone and pewter inlay and long beaded stem; very good condition; $350–$460.

Pipe: Sioux; 40 x 2 x 6 inches; huge black stone "T" bowl with pewter and red stone inlays and with a huge beaded and tacked stem; very good condition; $315–$400.

Pipe: Sioux; large; catlinite pipe (red pipestone) with long, quilled ash stem, ring design around bowl; old; very good condition; $1,300–$1,700.

Pipe: stone; 2 x 5 inches; in shape of an axhead; very good condition; $45–$110.

Pipe: Tlingit; 3¼ inches long x 2 inches high; very rare Northwest Coast pipe carved for Indian's own use. Beautifully carved and polychromed figure of seal, raven, eagle, and whale, brass bowl, hole in end for reed stem; good condition; $1,000–$2,000.

Pipe: tube; 2 x 5 inches; stone with flared sides; very good condition; $15–$100.

Pipe: Wasco; 6½ x 1 inch; rare excavated green stone "Cloud Blower" pipe with lizard effigy (could be lower Klamath River); prehistoric; very good condition; $350–$460.

Point: Yuma; 4½ x ¾ inch; fine large Yuma (Paleo) point from Texas; prehistoric; very good condition; $155–$160.

Point: classic chipped stone Folsom point in Riker mount; prehistoric; very good condition; $40–$60.

Point: Oregon; fantastic, large, finely chipped Oregon agate point; prehistoric; very good condition; $75–$110.

Points: bird points; bag containing approximately 50 tiny points for bird hunting; prehistoric; very good condition; $50–$75.

Points: 9 x 5½ inches; one large tan notched spearpoint and one smaller gray fluted spearpoint; prehistoric; very good condition; $95–$115.

Quiver and arrows: 24 x 3 inches; pitched covered wooden quiver with seven old arrows; ca. 1870; very good condition; $400–$460.

Scraper: Sioux; elk horn hide with steel bit; old; good condition; $250–$450.

Shaman's rattle: 6 inches long; made from buffalo vertebra, with hoof rattles, top of feathers, and red horsehair; very good condition; $150–$250.

Spearhead: black obsidian spearpoint; prehistoric; very good condition; $25–$50.

Spearhead: 16 x 2½ inches; huge gray spearhead in a large Riker mount; prehistoric; very good condition; $145–$230.

Spearpoints (two): 9 x 5½ inches; one large tan notched spearpoint and one smaller gray fluted spearpoint; prehistoric; very good condition; $100–$115.

Stone discoidal: round flecked gray stone Mound Builder discoidal; prehistoric; very good condition; $60–$85.

Tipi Rest: Cheyenne; 86 x 35 inches; willow tepee rest all put together in the old style; ca. 1930; very good condition; $250–$315.

Artifacts, decoy; prehistoric fish decoy of petrified ivory with four hand-drilled holes for varied suspension underwater; $400–$600. Collection of Gene and Linda Kangas. Photo by Gene Kangas.

Tipi Rest: Northern Plains; 78 x 40 inches; old willow tepee rest with canvas trim; ca. 1900; very good condition; $275–$350.

Tomahawk: Crow; 22 x 11 x 5 inches; original iron head with cross cutout and bead-wrapped handle, which was added later; ca. 1870; very good condition; $230–$350.

Tomahawk: pipe; 17½ x 8 inches; all original Plains pipe tomahawk with traces of paint and with file burned handle; ca. 1870; very good condition; $230–$310.

Tomahawk: pipe; 21 x 8 inches; narrow pipe head with tacked and file burned wooden handle; ca. 1870; very good condition; $175–$230.

Tomahawk: Plains; 22 x 6½ inches; iron head with heart cutout and with tacked and decorated handle; ca. 1880; very good condition; $90–$140.

Tool: Hopewell; bonded gray slate tool from a mound; prehistoric; very good condition; $30–$55.

Tool: Mound Builder; 13 x 3 inches; choice black carved stone tool; prehistoric; very good condition; $175–$230.

Trade Beads: 24 inches; strand of large cobalt blue trade beads; ca. 1890; very good condition; $85–$115.

Chapter Three

Baskets

〰️

Indian baskets were made for a variety of uses. Some, like the Apache water jars *(ollas)*, were made to carry liquids, while others were woven to carry a much more precious cargo: babies.

Baskets were used to carry loads of fruit, corn, or wheat. Some were made as bowls for eating, shelling beans, or mixing herbs. Trays and plaques were created for ceremonial or even gambling purposes; others held trinkets, clothes, and a variety of belongings. Depending on their needs, Indians wore baskets for a great variety of uses. Those Indians who grew wheat or oat made sifters to separate the chaff from the grain. Indian fishermen wove fish weirs in a basketry fashion, while those owning horses wove saddlebags.

While most baskets filled some kind of working role in everyday Indian life, some were made as gifts or for the tourist trade, such as the miniature baskets made by the Pomo Indians of California. They are considered some of the finest baskets in the world, woven so tightly that there are sixty stitches to the inch. ·

Before trade with the white man, most basket makers remained anonymous; later, as trade became more established, some weavers became recognized as prominent basketmaking artists, such as Mary Benson (Pomo), Mrs. Hickox (Karok), and Dat So La Lee (Great Basin), whose biography appears later in this chapter.

Baskets have long been part of the Native American's ceremonies, and in each tribe the basket has its place and uses. Navajo medicine men use baskets in their healing rites, as part of the wedding ceremony, and in religious ceremonies. Apaches have used baskets for gambling purposes, while Hopis use baskets in wedding ceremonies.

All baskets made by Native Americans fall into one of five major periods: early, classic, transitional, hiatus, and contemporary. The Early Period refers to the first archaeological specimens of basketry to come from the Native American's first contact with European influences. Classic baskets were made during the early period of contact with Europeans, but before the European influence is seen in Native American arts. Transitional baskets were made between 1775 and 1875, while hiatus period baskets were created during the late nineteenth and early twentieth century, when traditional basketmaking techniques began to degenerate. Contemporary baskets include those made from the early twentieth century to today.

There are many legends that surround the art of basketry. The Navajos have a myth about the Bat Woman and the strength of her baskets. The Pueblo Indians tell a story of a young man being lowered over a cliff in a basket—in an effort to obtain eagle feathers—and how he learned the eagle's secrets and lived with them. The Hopis tell the legend of Tiyo, the mythical snake hero.

Geometric designs on baskets have evolved as many other designs have. Simple and square-edged at first, Greek key designs evolved into scrollwork that was eventually integrated into pottery designs. Other geometric designs mean different things to different tribes. For one tribe an hourglass shape represents a bird, while another tribe may use two opposite triangles to signify the same animal. To the Thompson Indians the cross depicts the intersection of trails. To the Yokuts, it represents a battle, and the Wallapais and Havasupais see the cross as a phallic symbol.

Each tribe uses the materials available to them, and each has a different style of weaving and uses different colors and different symbols in their basketmaking. We will discuss a variety of tribes and their basketry later in the chapter.

As with other types of collectibles, condition is of the utmost importance in choosing a Native American basket. If the edges are broken or there are holes in any portion of the basket, you're not looking at a piece in which to invest. Look for broken reeds, weak weavings, holes, or dryness, telltale signs of baskets that may be beyond repair—and certainly not worth a high price.

Once you have decided on the condition of your basket, you should pay attention to the tightness of the weave. Fifteen stitches to the inch is considered a fine weave, twenty-eight stitches to the inch is an art. Collectors should know the three basic types of basketmaking: coiling, twining, and plaiting. Coiled baskets are sewed or stitched, twined basketry interweaves two or more flexible weft materials with vertical warp elements, and plaited baskets are those in which the warp and weft elements are interwoven at right angles. Once a collector understands these basic types, the rest of the factors that influence a decision to purchase will fall into place. They include the originality of design, the colors, the workmanship/weave/ornamentation, the basket's function, age, size, rarity, aesthetic appeal, unusual features, and documention.

The collector should be aware that a basket could have been made by one tribe and used by another. Also note that some baskets were more appealing to Europeans (for trade) than to the Native American. Unusual baskets are more often the work of contemporary weavers than the classical. Realize that baskets made in other countries or by other peoples may resemble Native American styles/techniques, so do your homework carefully.

For a more in-depth examination of the types of basketmaking and discussions of style, form, and design, see some of the books on basketry mentioned in the Bibliography.

For names and addresses of contemporary basket makers, write the Indian Arts and Crafts Board, U.S. Department of the Interior, Washington, D.C., and ask for the current *Source Directory*.

MATERIALS USED IN BASKETMAKING

Tribe	Material
Cayuses, Umatillas, Nez Perces, and Wascos	Split corn husks and wild hemp
Hopi	Yucca and fine grass
Klickitat	Roots of young spruce and cedar trees, squaw grass
Mono	Tender shoots, roots, and fibres
Nootka	Tough spruce roots, inner bark of red and yellow cedar, cattail or tule stems, wild cherry tree bark, mountain goat wool, duck down, dog wool, and various grasses, fern stems, and other native plants for decoration

Tribe	Material
Panamint	Young shoots of tough willow, sumac shoots, horns on pods of unicorn plants, and yucca roots
Paiute and Havasupai	Martynia (cat's claw), yucca, and amole
Pima and Maricopa	Sisal willow, squaw weed, skunk weed, tule root, and martynia
Pomo	Roots of slough grass
Salish	Same bark and plant fibers as Nootka, but especially prized mountain goat and dog wool
Southern California	Tule root and squaw weed
Tlingit	Spruce root, split and soaked in water

COLORS USED IN BASKETRY

The use of colors in basketry is symbolic to the Native American weaver. For instance, the Cherokees believe that red is synonymous with success or triumph, blue signifies defeat or trouble, black is death, and white represents (what else?) peace and happiness. Red is considered sacred to almost all tribes.

Tribe	Use of Colors
Cahuilla	Exclusively used yellow, white, black, and brown. The only one of these colors that is not natural is black. It was made by taking a pot of mud from the nearby sulur springs, boiling it, and stirring the mud and water together. Once the mud settled, the liquid was poured off and used to color the splints.
Havasupai	Used the peeled pod of the martynia, which is black, but did not dye the willow they use in baketweaving.

Tribe	Use of Colors
Hopi	Use plants, flowers, and roots as dyes, though much of their modern basketry uses aniline dyes.
Klickitat	The natural color of squaw grass, used in Klickitat basketry, is white. When soaked in water, it becomes yellow, and if soaked in hot water, it becomes brown.
Navajo	Use a variety of colors. The order of color appearance has great significance in basketmaking, as in planting corn (i.e., the white goes first because it is the color of the East and has most importance; blue, the color of the South, goes next; yellow, the next color in the sun wise movement, is planted after blue; and black is last).
Pomo	Dyed their basketry materials by a process that involved charcoal paste, willow ashes, and dirt. The process took nearly eighty hours to produce what the Pomos considered a perfect dye.
Potawatomi	Produce baskets the color of gold sunset clouds.
Shasta	Dye the white grass they use brown by adding an extract of alder bark. Maidenhair fern stem is used for black detailing.
Southeast	Used plaited techniques, with glossy cane splints. Reddish orange, black, neutral shades, and other colors, such as yellow and dark purple, occasionally used.
Yakima	Use white, blue, and yellow as spiritual colors.
Zuni	Colors represent directions: Yellow is north, blue is west, red is south, and white is east.

Basket Makers

The most famous North American basket maker, *Dat So La Lee* (or Mrs. Louisa Kayser), lived from approximately 1850 to 1924. Kayser was born into the Washo tribe, which lived around Lake Tahoe, and she learned to make baskets with her people.

After her tribe's land was stolen by settlers and polluted by miners, Dat So La Lee worked doing odd jobs as a domestic maid and laundress.

When she was sixty, her talent was recognized by Abe Cohn, who owned an emporium in Carson City, Nevada. He became her business agent, providing her and her husband with a home, food, clothing, and payment for medical bills in exchange for her baskets.

Dat So La Lee's weaving was tight and even, and her baskets are considered classics by the experts. Her triangular and flame-shaped motifs are perfectly spaced to the field on which they are placed. Some of her baskets incorporate symbols that represent sunrise, or the midday ascending heat waves.

Though she could not sign her name, she used a handprint as her signature. Cohn listed, numbered, and titled Dat So La Lee's baskets based on conversations with her, and his efforts make it easier to study her development as an artist.

When Dat So La Lee brought her work to the Saint Louis Exposition in 1919, she was one of its stars.

Clara Dardin

Dardin was a Chitimacha basket maker who lived in Bayou Teche, Louisiana. She wove in the style of the Southeast culture, using the double twill plaited technique with splints of river cane. Particularly talented in manipulating weaving elements, she incorporated different colors into her designs such as "bottom of basket" (k^axt-ma'xta), "cross marks" (nakc-apcta'nk^in^ic), "eyes of cattle" (wa'ct^ik-ka'ni), and "something around" (hakc-koksko'kšn).

She worked during the late 1800s to early 1900s, and at least one of her designs is held by the Peabody Museum at Harvard University.

Maria Antonia

Antonia, a Diegueño, is credited with designing the first rattlesnake basket in 1898, although others before her may have made cruder versions of the same design.

MARY SNYDER

Snyder, a Chemeheuvi Indian, was well-known throughout Arizona for making the same type of basket and design, using a unique combination of Chemeheuvi and Cahuilla materials. Though her baskets look like those made by Southern California Indians, different materials were most likely used. Chemeheuvi basket makers almost always used willow for white stitches and devil's claw for black details. True Mission weavers never used these materials.

There were and are many other basket makers; though biographies of them are rare. It is not common for basket makers to put their signatures on their work, thus the work of the researcher is a challenging one.

It is my hope that there will someday be biographies of these artisans. Perhaps it can begin with those who have won awards with their work. It is important to document the antiques you buy and to be certain that you obtain as much information about the maker of your Indian pieces as possible. Good documentation could lead to an easier sale of your collection in the future—you may own pieces by a not-yet-acknowledged expert that would obviously add to the value of your collection.

VARIOUS TRIBES AND THEIR BASKETMAKING

ALEUT

Aleut baskets are among the finest examples of all woven North American Indian baskets. The weaving done to form these baskets is extremely delicate, and though they stand the test of time well, they always give the impression that they will fall apart the moment you touch them.

The Aleut basket makers often decorated their lidded baskets with silk embroidery flosses or wool, grass embroidery, or bird feathers.

ANASAZI

This prehistoric tribe, ancestors of the modern-day Pueblo tribes, made twined bag-type baskets, some of which are today held in museum collections.

APACHE

Since this tribe is split into numerous groups, I will give the general information first, then a few details on the different branches of this southwestern tribe.

Apache basketry's staples are water jugs *(tuus)* and burden baskets. The jugs are made of sumac or strawberry twigs that are twined and woven over each other. Juniper leaves and red ocher are used to fill in the cracks, and the jar is waterproofed with piñon pitch, applied with a brush made of cow's hair.

The Apache burden basket is made of willow, cottonwood, or wild mulberry and decorated with strips of buckskin ended in tin cones that "tinkle" when the baskets move. These pendants are typical of Apache work. Other tribes, including some in California, may hang bits of shells or beads or even feathers as decorative accents on their baskets.

The swastika design, also called "whirling logs," is one common to Apache (as well as Pima) basketry. It was said to represent water, an important life-giving commodity to most Indian tribes. The "swirling" line represents the source of the water supply, and the geometric lines leading away from the center of the design depict winding streams.

The *Jicarilla Apaches* are located in the northwestern part of New Mexico. They used a five-rod coiling method in basketmaking and sewed their coils together with gold sumac. Note that no plaited work has been identified as Jicarilla.

The *Mescalero Apaches* of south central New Mexico used a three-rod stacked coiling method to weave their baskets. Early attempts at basketry produced exclusively utilitarian objects. Their weaving was coarse, their colors and designs rather boring. Once the Mescalero Apache began to make commercial baskets, their style improved, though their weaving, in general, is still not as fine as that of other tribes.

The *San Carlos* and *White Mountain Apaches* are expert weavers who incorporate intricate designs in their work. Most of their basketry work is coiled, and they use willow or twigs in weaving. Their work includes water bottles *(ollas)*, bowls, saucers, trinket baskets, and cradles.

Southern Apaches used a finishing that was simple coiling around the splint.

CALIFORNIA MISSION TRIBES

The California Indians came under the control of Spanish religious leaders when the Spaniards forcibly took the land from the Indians, built missions, and proceeded to convert the Indians to Christianity. The Spanish military bought some Indians and forced them to work as slaves. Eventually the Indians took Spanish names, learned how to speak the language, and thus began communicating with the Mission fathers. Normally more peaceful than their Southwestern Indian brothers, California tribes such as the *Modoks*, *Karoks*, and *Yuroks* wove fine baskets from the indigenous reeds and vegetation.

The basketry acknowledged as that of the Mission Indians is a broad category that includes the weaving of the many tribes and subtribes that were under the control of the Spanish missions (beginning in 1769). The basketmaking has a similar structure and style, though many of the creators spoke different languages.

The Mission Indians used three main types of vegetation in weaving their baskets, though other suitable varieties were available throughout the regions where they lived, some of which would have been easier to use. Juncus grass, which grows beneath mountain oak trees, allowed a variety of color combinations in design because of its variegated stem. Sumac provided a white color for backgrounds and for outlining dark patterns. The Indians often dyed juncus a dark brown to accent patterns woven into their baskets. Deer grass, found commonly in Southern California, was the grass-bundle foundation material.

Geometric patterns, as well as pictures of animals, such as doves, burros, camels, fish, rats, mice, butterflies, lizards, and rattlesnakes, decorate baskets made by Mission Indians. Though designs were similar, no weaver ever copied another's design exactly (except for the rattlesnake pattern, and even then, the maker took special care to add distinctive identifying features).

Their baskets were closely stitched and fine, some comparable to the intricate Pomo baskets. Eighteen to thirty wrappings per inch is the average stitch count for most Mission Indian baskets, and one can find all sizes, shapes, and designs. Their baskets were never decorated with beads and only occasionally with feathers. Thus, the decorating done during the weaving itself is where the weaver expressed his or her art.

Other materials used included sedge root, willow, bulrush root, and redbud bark.

The most common design in all California basketry is the rattlesnake design mentioned above. Also commonly used among these Indians is the "quail" design—distinctive because of its plume, which resembles an upside-down golf club. They also incorporated flower and fern designs into their basketry.

Mission Indian rattlesnake baskets were rare during the late 1800s because they bore a stigma of evil. When the baskets were made for the tourist trade, there were two distinct types of rattlesnake baskets. One was an abstract design found in the *Chumash, Monache, Panamint, Shoshone, Tejon, Kawaiisu, Yokut,* and *Tubatalabal* territories. In the late nineteenth century, the Mission groups produced a realistic version of the reptile, and these later baskets were the ones made "for sale." Indians always respected the rattlesnake and its power and believed that blindness, untimely death, and other misfortunes that plagued the weavers of rattlesnake baskets were directly associated with the power of the snake. Because of this belief, production of the baskets came to a halt around 1920.

CHEMEHEUVI
Basketry by this Indian tribe is not as commonly available as others because the tribe is a small Shoshone band which was originally Californian. They "moved in" with the much larger Mohave tribe when their own reservation proved uninhabitable.

Chemeheuvi basketry is refined, yet sprightly. Their designs—animals, butterflies, or animal tracks—are considered the property of the weaver and are not supposed to be copied by other artisans.

See also California Mission Tribes.

CHEROKEE
Indians of the Cherokee nation in North Carolina used the plaiting technique to weave baskets, bending their warps over a hoop to make a rim. The rims are usually bound with hickory bark. They used plain plaiting with oak splints, river cane twill plaiting, and some double twill plaiting. The Oklahoma Cherokees use wicker plaiting.

Cherokee basket makers developed many basket forms such as melon baskets, gathering and processing baskets, storage baskets, fish baskets, sieves, trays, bottleneck, miniatures, and nesting baskets.

The North Carolina Cherokee use twill plaited geometric patterns in decorating their baskets; diamond patterns are the most common. The Oklahoma Cherokees use wicker elements that are brilliantly colored with aniline dyes.

Materials used by the North Carolina Cherokee include white oak splints, river cane, and sugar maple. Both the North Carolina and Oklahoma Cherokee use honeysuckle vine in wicker plaiting and hickory bark in binding hoops of rim finishes.

The Cherokee people are still producing baskets today.

CHICKASAW

The Chickasaw Indians used a twill plaiting style and often made winnowing and wall baskets. They produced twilled geometric patterns and often incorporated dyed splints in their work. They took advantage of natural and aniline dyes, especially red and black, in decoration.

Chicasaw baskets are still made in Oklahoma.

CHITIMACHA

The Chitimacha Indians use twill plaiting (both single and double twill weave), and their characteristic rim finish is compound binding, doubled twined, or braided selvage. During the contemporary period, they used bundle coiling of pine needles with spaced thread stitching or cane splints. They use narrow river cane stem splints in plaiting their baskets and long leaf pine needles in coiling.

Chitimacha baskets usually have square bases with rounded sides and rims. They also make flat trays with low sides, sieves and winnowing baskets, lidded "cigarette case" basketry, and coiled trinket baskets with knobbed lids.

Decorative designs seen on Chitimacha baskets include zigzag and geometric patterns, and the colors include black, red, yellow, dark purple, and orange. They also use colored thread in stitching the coiled examples of their baskets.

CHOCTAW

The Choctaw basket makers in Mississippi and Oklahoma make baskets that are twill and double twill plaited. The most common forms are the double-mouth "elbow," triangular "cownose," winnowing, and wall baskets. Other types of baskets include egg, laundry, miniature, and storage baskets, as well as rimmed burden baskets used for harvesting.

The Choctaw baskets follow some of the Chitimacha patterns, although Choctaw decorations are less complex than the Chitimacha. They use dyed red and black splints for decoration on a natural-dyed cane background.

Narrow cane stem splints are used to make the baskets, as well as some oak splints (mainly used by the Mississippi Choctaw).

CREEK

The Creek's technique of plaiting was to twist the ends of the warp into a false braid. Though winnowing and wall baskets are the most common, the Creek also make "elbow," "cownose," trays, and sieves.

Creek Indians use twill plaited geometric designs in decoration, especially zigzag patterns, and dyed splints (black) are also used.

Materials used in manufacturing baskets include split cane stem splints and hickory splints. Oranges and browns are common colors in a Creek basket.

HAIDAS

As with everything else they make, the Haida Indians cover their basketry with totemic symbols and drawings. Their basketry forms include twined hats, plaited bags and mats, and wallets.

All their basketry is twined, sometimes with reinforcement (on hats' crowns), and sometimes they use open wrap twining. Sitka spruce is used for twining, and western red cedar bark for plaiting. Common colors include black, red, and some green. Bear grass was used in false embroidery.

HAVASUPAI

Havasupai baskets are masterful and were made most frequently during the period from 1900 to 1925. The Havasupai Indians made about the same amount of money for their best baskets as they did for the most poorly made. In the early 1970s the art was dying out, and fewer than half a dozen weavers remained.

The basket makers used three-rod coiling with a fine closed plan and diagonal twining to make their baskets. They utilized a starting knot of four warp elements. Some of their coiled rims are stitched with light overcasting, while others are black. Rims might consist of "herringbone" false-braid borders that are common to Apache, Paiute, and Navajo basketry.

Basket types common to the Havasupai include trays, bowls, bottle jars, and burden baskets. The trays and bowls are made in the coiling style, while bottle jars and burden baskets are made in the twining style. The bottles have woven or horsehair handles and are waterproofed with piñon gum or pitch.

Designs are less complex than the Apache designs, but Havasupai use black boldly, though they are likely to favor concentric circles or simple geometric patterns. Frequently life forms were used on 1930s contemporary baskets.

They used willow, black devil's claw, acacia, shrub strawberry, or sumac in making the basket, and devil's claw to make their patterns, as well as dyes of red, gold, yellow, and black (contemporary period).

Many ethnologists believe that pottery and basketry share much of the same history. Early reports of life among the Havasupai of Arizona (there is a portion of the tribe left, living on the floor of the Grand Canyon) showed that the base of a basket would be lined with clay and the pottery piece would be formed within the basket before being removed to stand on its own as a vessel. Baskets, or basketry vessels, had originally been used to transport water. The talent of those early basket makers must have been great to weave so tightly that the basket could hold water!

Today's basket makers use coiling to make the small number of baskets that they sell.

HIDATSA

The Hidatsa Indians wove their baskets from box elder and willow bark, using willow splints for coiling, and twill plaiting with black willow and box elder for weaving. Four ash saplings formed the U-shaped framework for their twill burden baskets. The pieces would be dyed before being woven together to form these geometrically patterned baskets.

Their work included coiled gambling trays and burden baskets.

HOPI

The Hopi Indians are considered the greatest basket producers of the Pueblo Indians. They practiced all three types of weaving and are characterized by the great variety in their basket shapes and designs. Because baskets were used in trade, occasionally a Navajo design will show up on a Hopi basket, or vice versa.

Supposedly Hopi basketry degenerated when they began to use aniline dyes in the late 1800s and early 1900s. By 1906, the Hopis had shifted from Old Oraibi to Hotevilla and had gone back to using natural dyes. At that time, they were also still using large coils. By the late 1920s and 1930s, they reduced the size of their coils and improved their designs. By the early 1960s, their work had much improved overall. Hopi basketry continues to reach higher and higher peaks of artistic perfection, partially through more elaborate designs.

Traditionally Hopi baskets have been made only on the Second Mesa of the Hopi Reservation in Arizona; however, Third Mesa women also make baskets. Each Mesa has distinct ways of making different items.

The materials generally used by Hopi basket weavers are galleta grass and yucca. Designs were less generalized and coordinated in earlier baskets than they are now. Patterns were basically geometric or in a sunburst style with rays extending to the edge of the basket, though themes (including clouds with or without rain and kachinas) have been used.

Between 1930 and 1960, patterns became more elaborate and structured; wedding trays became an established form, and the pattern would not necessarily reach the rim of the basket as it had earlier. Between 1960 and 1980, Hopi baskets were serving the needs of those interested in Indian crafts, and their values climbed to a new high.

Plaques are the most abundant form of Hopi basketry, and designs have changed in the past one hundred years. These plaques are made by the mother of a bride and often given away for years before the daughter is married, and serve to build up credit once the marriage is announced. Sometimes women hold "plaque parties," with the guests working all day to create a plaque, somewhat like the quilters who got together to create wedding quilts. A variety of different designs are used on the plaques, although kachinas and mudheads have often been incorporated into the new designs. The plaques that are given away are usually displayed by the family for a while, but often are sold when the family needs cash and the sale does not offend the maker.

Plaques are also used ceremonially by the Hopi when a husband dies and needs a safe passage to the Underworld—he uses the plaque given to him at the wedding. The family will bring the plaque to the man's burial, then it is taken back to the village to be kept by the man's mother or sister. She must keep it safe for his journeying spirit.

Other plaques are made and given to newborn babies, both male and female, during a ritual held in February or July (whichever date comes soonest after the child's birth). An adolescent girl will also receive a plaque piled high with corn seeds. Plaques are also used as elements in the ceremonial cycle for raising various crops and praying for rain.

There is symbolism in the way Hopi women weave plaques. If the inner grass is left to "flow out," having an unfinished appearance, its maker was an unmarried virgin (this is called the "flowing gate"). Married women of childbearing age leave the ends of the grass flowing, but the grass is cut off approximately one inch from the last stitch (called the "open gate"). Widows, or women who are incapable of bearing children, finish off their work completely (the "closed gate").

It is important to be familiar with the types of material the Indians use in their basketry. The Hopis use sumac for warps and several types of rabbit brush for wefts. They also use more color in their basketry than any other southwestern tribe. Hopi designs are geometric and extremely colorful—sometimes incorporating seven to nine colors in a single piece of basketry. The most common designs in Hopi basketry are the lightning symbol and the rain clouds, as well as mountain and valley symbols. Butterflies, eagles, and kachinas may be woven into basketry pieces, making the overall effect even more striking.

The difference between a Hopi wicker bowl and tray goes further than just the depth of the piece. The bowl has straighter sides and a larger, flatter bottom than a tray. Most Hopi bowls are decorated in bands.

A piki tray is flat and rectangular and used for serving piki—cornmeal bread served for ceremonial purposes. The main area of the piki tray is plaited by weaving bundles of split elements over other bundles of the same. The trays are used by Hopis in ceremonies and are usually made of wrapped coils. Some of these trays are wonderfully decorative and colorful, incorporating such patterns as the spiderweb.

Hopi burden baskets have often been called peach-gathering baskets (as opposed to peach *trays*). These baskets were used by the men to gather peaches and corn and were woven by the women. It is the same type of basket used in the Bean Dance.

Peach trays are not as flat as piki trays, nor as deep as peach-gathering baskets, and they are always woven in plain wicker weave.

The Hopis made snake charm liquid in a basket. This ritual began with the medicine man pouring liquid into the basket from the six sacred directions of the Hopi (north, south, east, west, up and down). He went through some incantations, and the ceremony ended with the medicine man mixing white paint from the earth with the liquid in the basket, then rubbing the paint on the body of the chief priest.

The Hopis also wove a basket that imitates a spiderweb and used this basket in dances and offerings in honor of the Spider Woman (Ko-kyan-wuh-ti). Sacred meal trays also often bear this spiderweb design.

Baskets are so intrinsic to the Hopi culture that they even have basket dances. (Owakult and Kohonino are two of the basket dances.) In the Kohonino dance, only baskets made by the Havasupai Indians (who traded regularly with the Hopis) are used.

Hopi basket weavers' use of plaiting is distinctive because they tie the yucca splints of ring baskets over a sumac withe.

The art of Hopi basketweaving is alive and well. Hopi baskets often win first prize at ceremonials and markets throughout the Southwest, and there are new weavers, some as young as twelve or thirteen, competing for first place every year.

HUPA

This tribe used open and closed plain twining in manufacturing their baskets. Baskets common to the Hupa include open-work cradles and utility baskets, wood baskets, dippers, cooking and storage and serving baskets, fish baskets, burden baskets, sifts, mats, and caps.

Their decoration consisted of half-twist overlays in yellow, red, white, and black, plus geometric designs that relied on a horizontal dividing line through the center of the main pattern. They also used horizontal bands of triangles at the base or rim of caps.

Materials used include hazel, alder, willow, cottonwood, wild grape, and sometimes digger and yellow pine, or lowland spruce roots imported from the coastal Yuroks. In the late 1800s they used willow to make smaller, finer baskets.

The Hupa basket makers are still creating baskets today.

IROQUOIS

The basket makers of the Iroquois tribe used the plaiting technique in making baskets, usually using two black ash splints to make a double hoop; the hoop held the upper ends of the warps.

Iroquoian basket styles often resemble those of other tribes, such as the Cherokee melon and storage baskets. The Iroquois basket makers also made sieves similar to those of the eastern Algonquian people.

Most distinctive of all Iroquoian basketry are their corn-husk pieces. With this material they made ceremonial masks and small bottles to hold salt and tobacco. Mask-making techniques may date back to the classic period.

Occasionally the Iroquois basket makers used bark to make ladles and bowls. The transitional period Hurons also used birch bark to make baskets which they embroidered with moose hair. Their designs, taught to them by French nuns, were primarily naturalistic and floral.

JEMEZ

The Jemez Pueblo is one of the only Rio Grande pueblos still active in the art of basketmaking. Both men and women have pursued this art and still produce plaited baskets. They make shallow ring baskets used for winnowing, as well as twill plaited mats and rings for carrying water jars on one's head. Jemez baskets were made for winnowing, washing wheat, shelling corn, and other purposes. One weaver might make three to five baskets per week.

Jemez weavers use yucca as their main material because it is readily available and can be harvested at any time during the year. Sumac is also used for the rim of the ring basket. Most Jemez baskets are round because almost all of the mats are woven in squares. They don't use anything other than yucca to decorate their basketry.

NAVAJO

Basketry of the Navajo tribe serves a purpose, whether it be utilitarian or ceremonial. The Navajo basketry water bottle *(tus jeh)* was an ingenious way of carrying water across great distances. It could be easily fastened to a saddle or a belt by a rawhide thong, and if dropped, kicked, or bumped, it would not break or empty the precious fluid it carried.

The basket used in the Navajo wedding ceremony is a highly collectible piece. The bride's family prepares a cornmeal porridge, which is transferred to the basket. Then a male relative sprinkles pollen in a design over the meal. When the bridegroom enters the bride's hogan, the basket of porridge is placed between them. With great ceremony, the bride and groom perform small services for each other, then he takes a pinch of porridge from where the lines of the pollen design meet. Once his bride matches his actions, the bowl is passed to the other (younger) guests while the elders give the wedding couple sage advice.

NORTHWEST COAST

Northwest Coast tribes often wove their twined baskets upside down and depicted fish in their basketmaking.

The *Coast Salish* groups especially prized mountain goat wool or dog wool in their weaving. They picked out the long, coarse guard hairs from the wool and discarded them; then the wool was collected in loose hanks, and a core of yellow cedar bark string added for strength. The wool was spun into two-ply yarn. Sometimes they used bird down or the soft cotton pappus of certain plants in their baskets as well.

The most common weaving technique was twining—the warps caught by pairs of transverse strands (wefts), which crossed and twisted about them. They used plain twining to make spruce-root basketry containers, hats, and capes, as well as robes and capes of red and yellow cedar bark yarn.

The baskets woven by this technique were so fine that they were watertight and used as containers for liquids or even for cooking. The hats made with the twining technique were waterproof, and decoration was applied with bleached or dyed grasses and splints of black fern stems to produce geometric designs.

Some Coast Salish tribes (i.e., *Pentlatch, Sanetch, Cowichan*) made baskets with twined openwork that incorporated crossed or zigzag warp elements. When creating a basketry cradle for an infant, the cradle was treated with magical techniques to protect the infant.

Coiled basketry (sewn rather than woven) was made by a few Northwest Coast groups, but is thought to have been introduced to these tribes by the Plateau tribes.

PAIUTES

The Paiute tribe has three distinct styles of basketmaking. They use aromatic sumac, yucca, and martynia in creating their baskets.

The Paiute bowls, known as "Navajo wedding baskets" or "Apache medicine baskets," are the most sought after of all Paiute baskets. The border is woven in a diagonal whip stitch, often called the "herringbone"—the stitch is the distinguishing mark of Paiute, Navajo, and Havasupai weaving.

The Navajos, however, claim this stitch to be their own and even tell a legend of how a Navajo basket-weaving woman was given the idea for the stitch from the god Qastceyelci. It is said that Qastceyelci tore a piece of juniper off a tree and threw it into the woman's half-made basket, causing her to imitate the juniper leaves' peculiar folds in her work. Since then, if the margin of a basket is broken through or torn, it is considered unfit for sacred use and must be given away.

The Paiutes incorporate into their basket design the belief that the Paiute came from an underworld (or "lower" world) that corresponds to the hills and valleys of the upper world. The communication link between the two (Shipapu) is represented by the basket's opening. If the opening is closed, the basket maker would make it impossible for any more of her people to be born into the upper world.

PAPAGO

Early Papago baskets, sturdy black trays of martynia (devil's claw), were used for parching corn with live coals. Modern baskets are made of yucca leaves, coiled over bear grass or yule stem foundations.

Their baskets are made by the bundle-coiling technique with closed, spaced, or split stitching. Determining the age of a Papago basket is fairly easy since spaced stitching was used until 1900, while split stitching was used after 1934.

Papago basket varieties include shallow coiled bowls, twill plaited mats, head rings, baskets with and without lids, jars, trays, storage baskets, trinket baskets, and miniature baskets (made of horsehair or yucca).

They generally used black devil's claw designs or geometric horizontal figures to decorate their baskets. Natural green and red colors were used to decorate coiled wares, while aniline dyes were used between 1920 and 1943.

The baskets today's Papago weaver makes are in tune with commercial needs (i.e., wastebaskets, hampers, and covered baskets). These weavers are considered the most prolific contemporary basket makers.

PIMA/MARICOPA

The Pima and Maricopa baskets are similar to the Paiute, Havasupai, and Apache, though their work is coarser.

The border stitch these tribes use is a distinctive forward and backward kind of stitch, and their designs incorporate the Greek fret and the circular swastika forms.

The Pima tribe makes shallow, medium-size bowls, closely woven of cattail, over which the basket maker will sew strips of willow shoots and devil's claw. The Pima bowls are made with such well-known designs as fret, star, butterfly, squash blossom, swastika, and whirlwind. They also make miniatures of their creations, some of which are held in museums. A good example of a Pima miniature basket might take as long as three months to make.

POMO

According to early experts, the Pomós used nine distinct weaves in their basketry between 1880 and 1920, and there were five other weaves found in earlier baskets. The weaves are described in detail in many books on basketry.

The first weave to produce patterns was the "bam-tush." The weave process, a one-rod coiling method, was an increasing spiral, and the basket would eventually show spaces that required extra ribs. These were filled in with stitches made by a bone awl. A change of thread would be required to make the pattern, and we often find rings of "ti" stitches worked into the pattern. ("Ti" in the Pomo language means ponderous, stable, and unyielding, and describes the Pomo double weave, which is actually twined weaving.)

The weave of the basket can also tell us its purpose. Seed baskets were of a fine weave, while water baskets were finer still. Gathering baskets could be a looser weave depending on whether the basket was being used to gather acorns or larger items.

The shape of the basket also indicates its use. For example, ovoid baskets held sugar, trinkets, or clothing, while conical baskets were used to transport items—they were hung by a headband that was placed over the carrier's brow. Plain baskets held food, while fanciful ones were given as gifts.

SKOKOMISH

This tribe uses an open and closed plain and wrap twining. In the late classic period, some of the baskets made by the Skokomish were coiled.

Skokomish baskets include cylindrical bags or berry baskets with looped rims. To decorate such baskets, they use an all-over half-twist overlay in vertical geometric patterns. If the tails turn up on the four-legged figures, they are dogs; if down, they're wolves.

TLINGIT

Tlingit baskets are made using twining and plain plating, and forms include hats, cradles, trays, and shaman's double baskets with looped leather handles.

The Tlingits decorate their baskets with stylized animals in native pigments such as the black of sulphur spring mud, hemlock bark, and iron scrapings; the red of alder bark or sea urchin juice; the yellow of lichen or wolf moss; the green-blue of hemlock bark with copper oxide; the purple color made by huckleberries; the blackish purple of maidenhair fern, the brown of undyed Sitka spruce root; and the white of undyed grasses. Animal representations such as the raven or wolf are symbolic of the basket maker's clan.

Tlingits continue to make fashion basketry today.

YAVAPAI

There is much discussion about whether the Yavapai taught the Apaches to weave or vice versa. Whatever the case, Yavapai baskets are strong and fine enough so that food can be boiled in them.

Burden baskets were made in abundance because the Yavapai did not have horses.

The materials used by the Yavapai in making baskets today include willow twigs (for coiling), split willow, and devil's claw for sewing. They used the three-rod coiling method of manufacture to create bowls, plaques, trays, and deep jars.

Yavapai designs are interesting combinations of geometric designs with animal and human figures. Designs are infrequently used more than once. Common colors used are black, and sometimes, red.

ZUNI

Baskets were made by the Zuni people for everyday use as well as ceremonial purposes. They made plaited and wicker baskets, but are *not* known for making coiled baskets. It is noted that plaited baskets were made by the Zuni at the turn of the century and were still being made during the 1930s; however, wicker baskets are more readily available. The Zuni weavers made coiled water bottles, twill plaited shallow ring baskets, and fancy openwork wicker bowls.

They used a willow or sumac rod with a yucca bundle as the foundation to make their baskets, incorporating wick and twill plating in their decoration.

Zuni workmanship is not as good as Hopi; the finish is not as tight and the sewing not as regular. Little decoration was done on Zuni baskets, and it appears that they were made more often to fulfill a purpose than to serve as decoration.

PRICES

Baskets are arranged according to tribal origin.

ALEUT

Aleut: carrying basket; large, finely twined, with native cord and rim loops; red and blue geometric designs; 10 x 5 inches; ca. 1880; $200–$275.

Aleut: classic fine twined basket with lid and with red wool floral designs; ca. 1890; $350–$450.

Aleut: open basket; twined wild rye grass with seven bands of green, blue, and red wool in a diamond pattern, braided rim; 7½ inches high x 10½ inches diameter; very good condition; $125–$175.

APACHE

Apache: dark arrowpoint designs woven into sides; 9 inches; good condition; $375–$475.

Baskets, Apache—from left to right: Apache basketry tray with cross, chevrons, and quadripeds separated into six distinct designs by stacked triangles and intersecting lines, ca. 1890–1910, 3¾ inches high x 15⅝ inches diameter, excellent condition, $2,100–$2,500; Apache basketry tray, multiple star pattern, quadripeds, human figures, and coyote tracks, 2½ inches high x 15¼ inches diameter, excellent condition, $1,400–$1,800; western Apache basketry tray with negative and positive design elements with crosses, coyote tracks, and horses around the upper section, 19th century hook, ca. 1880–1910, 3 inches high, 17¾ inches diameter, excellent condition, $1,300–$1,600. Courtesy of Willis Henry Auctions, Inc.

Apache: basketry tray with cross, chevrons, and quadripeds separated into six distinct designs by stacked triangles and intersecting lines; 3¾ inches high x 15⅝ inches diameter; ca. 1890–1910; excellent condition; $2,100–$2,500.

Apache: basket; Greek key and four dogs design with stepped arrows at rim; 2¼ inches high x 2¾ inches diameter; excellent condition; $300–$475.

Apache: basket, wedding; polychrome design; 11¼ inches diameter; very good condition; $75–$90.

Apache: basketry water bottle; old; very good condition; $300–$425.

Apache: basketry bowl; spiral geometric design; 10 inches diameter; excellent condition; $250–$300.

Apache: basketry bowl; eight human and five animal figures with central snowflake design; 11½ inches diameter; excellent condition; $550–$750.

Apache: basketry bowl; five-point star design encircled by five animal figures and geometric designs; 11½ inches diameter; very good condition; $650–$850.

Apache: basketry tray; two bands of geometric alternating chain design; 15½ inches diameter; excellent condition; $900–$1,100.

Apache: basketry tray; multiple star pattern, quadripeds, human figures, and coyote tracks; 2½ inches high x 15¼ inches diameter; excellent condition, $1,400–$1,800.

Apache: bowl; three-rod construction with devil's claw forming five human female figures; 2¾ inches high x 7½ inches diameter; good condition; $200–$300.

Apache: fine-weave bowl decorated with figures of men; 12 inches; $2,500–$3,000.

Apache: bowl; belonged to a woman whose cousin sent it back to her from the Southwest; 13 inches diameter, 4 inches deep; ca. 1900; $2,000–$2,500.

Apache: burden basket; San Carlos; 21 x 3 inches; ca. 1920; excellent condition; $2,500–$3,000.

Apache: burden basket; twined basket, flaring cylindrical form decorated with panels of fringed hide; $1,000–$1,250.

Apache: burden basket; woven with the "ti" band upright warps with three bands of dark brown designs, the bottom with rawhide support skin and hide bands stretched at the top rim, other rawhide fringe at sides, the top with rawhide binding rubbed with "sacred" yellow pigment; 18 inches diameter opening, 14 inches high; originally purchased at San Carlos Reservation in 1926 by Frank Potts, who worked on the reservation; ca. 1900s; $1,000–$1,300.

Apache: coiled basketry tray; woven in willow and devil's claw with concentric geometric bands; 19 inches diameter; $1,000–$1,250.

Apache: coiled polychrome, with positive (natural), negative (black), and red (light rose) five-pointed star-flower designs; 3½ x 12¾ inches; ca. 1900; $750–$1,000.

Apache: coiled basketry bowl; with tapering sides, woven in willow and devil's claw with bands of checkered designs; 9 inches diameter; $500–$750.

Apache: coiled basketry olla; with rounded neck, woven in willow and devil's claw with human figures, tepee-type structures, and geometric devices; 20½ inches high; rim and stitch damage; $975–$1,100.

Apache: coiled basketry olla; woven in "bottleneck" form, slightly flaring body, well-shouldered, bands of concentric meandering linear motif; 9 inches high; $1,000–$1,250.

Apache: two coiled trays; one Apache, finely woven in willow and black devil's claw with a whorling pattern interlocking near rim with a band of triangular motifs, 14½ inches diameter; the other, a Jicarilla, 15 inches diameter; excellent condition; $500–$600/set.

Apache: coiled basketry tray; woven in willow and devil's claw with standing human figures and dogs contained by elongated "dagger" devices; 10¼ inches diameter; $1,000–$1,300.

Apache: coiled basketry tray; with flat base and low flaring sides, woven in willow and black devil's claw with radiating rosette pattern enclosing horses, deer, and human figures; 16¼ inches diameter; $2,800–$3,400.

Apache: coiled basketry tray; woven with flat base, flaring sides, in willow and dark brown devil's claw, spoked pattern radiating from the solid tondo, radiating joined diamond motif; 16¾ inches diameter; $2,500–$3,500 each.

Apache: figural; figures around perimeter; 10 inches diameter, 3½ inches deep; ca. 1900; $1600–2000.

Apache: gathering basket; made of split bark and bound with deerskin; deerskin fringe around base; 9 x 12 inches; fine condition; $125–$175.

Apache: large basket; traces of pine resin; human hair carrying loops; 15 x 13 inches; complete and in good condition; $225–$300.

Baskets, Apache, pair of coiled basketry trays; left—flat base, low flaring sides, woven in willow and black devil's claw with radiating rosette pattern enclosing horses, deer, and human figures, 16¼ inches; right—woven with flat base, flaring sides, in willow and dark brown devil's claw, spoked pattern radiating from the solid tondo, radiating joined diamond motif; 16¾ inches diameter; $2,500–$3,500 each. Courtesy Robert W. Skinner, Inc., Bolton/Boston, Massachusetts.

Apache: large coiled basket; with black three-petal star-flower design radiating from the tondo to rim, interspersed with alternating men (nine) and cross (three) designs; 5 x 16 inches; ca. 1900; $2,250–$2,750.

Apache: miniature burden basket; excellent condition; $35–$50.

Apache: miniature contemporary tray made by "Tu"; excellent condition; $200–$250.

Apache: old coiled basket; decorated with alternating cross and dog designs near the rim and a six-pointed star-flower radiating from the black tondo; 3 x 10 inches; ca. 1900; mint condition; $750–$1,000.

Apache: coiled olla; with small, slightly indented base, squat body, and flaring rim, woven in willow and devil's claw with meander bands flanking a row of human figures, alternating with crosses, geometric devices in the fields above and below; an old label attached reading "Dan R. Williamson Collection"; 11 inches high; $2,000–$2,500.

Apache: olla; with flaring body rounding at the shoulder, tapering to a cylindrical neck, woven in willow and devil's claw, with concentric interlocking step-terraced diamonds which enclose piggybacked triangle design motifs; 21 inches wide, 21½ inches high; excellent condition; $2,500–$3,000.

Apache: plaque; coiled, with twelve dogs and radiating star pattern; 9½ inches wide; very good condition; $125–$225.

Apache: storage basket; woven willow with carved wooden lugs woven into the sides, traces of pitch; 10 inches high x 13 inches diameter; $140–$180.

Apache: tall coiled basket with striking dogs, birds, swastikas, and arrowheads; 10 x 7 inches; ca. 1935; excellent condition; $1,000–$1,500.

Apache: basketry tray with geometric star design; 8 inches diameter; very good condition; $100–$200.

Apache: miniature tray; woven horsehair, black and white with figures; 2½ inches diameter; very good condition; $75–$175.

Apache: round coiled basketry tray; with simple black line design; 12 x 1½ inches; ca. 1920; excellent condition; $250–$350.

Apache: pair of coiled basketry trays; one with flat base, low flaring sides, woven in willow and black devil's claw with radiating rosette pattern enclosing horses, deer, and human figures, 16¼ inches; the other woven with flat base, flaring sides, in willow and dark brown devil's claw, spoked pattern radiating from the solid tondo, radiating joined diamond motif, 16¾ inches diameter; excellent condition; $2,500–$3,500 each.

Apache: water jar; bought from Creek Council House Museum; 10 x 8 inches diameter; ca. 1900; excellent condition; $700–$900.

Apache: large pitched water basket (or tus); 12 x 8 inches; ca. 1890; very good condition; $500–$800.

ATHABASCAN

Athabascan: oval birch bark basket with imbricated rim; 6 x 2 inches; ca. 1910; excellent condition; $45–$75.

California Mission: coiled polychrome basketry bowl; deep flaring form; woven with expanding columns flanked by triangles; 16¼ inches diameter; very good condition; $700–$800.

California Mission: coiled; polychrome with gold, tan, and natural colors; 2½ x 10½ inches; ca. 1900–1940; very good condition; $325–$400.

California Mission: basketry bowl; bundle construction, letter and geometric design; 17¾ inches diameter; very good condition; $850–$1,050.

California Mission: basketry tray; two-tone geometric design; 5 inches diameter; very good condition; $50–$100.

California Mission: large round coiled bowl; with line and geometric designs; 13 x 5 inches; ca. 1890; excellent condition; $150–$200.

California Mission: round coiled basketry bowl; with yellowish star designs all around; 7 x 4 inches; ca. 1920; very good condition; $225–$275.

California Mission: coiled storage basket; the banded flaring body woven in dark brown triangular motif, with faded yellowish brown designs near rim; 15 inches deep, 6½ inches high; very good condition; $400–$500.

California Mission/Maidu: coiled basketry bowl; woven with black and red winged design motifs; 6½ inches wide; very good condition; $175–$275.

California Mission: round coiled basketry bowl; with connecting square designs; 5 x 3 inches; ca. 1900; very good condition; $200–$275.

California Mission: miniature coiled basketry tray; 3 inches diameter; ca. 1940; very good condition; $30–$45.

California Mission: round deep coiled bowl; with unusual stair design; 11 x 4 inches; ca. 1920; very good condition; $150–$200.

CHEHALIS
Chehalis: large oval lidded basket; with green and black geometric design; 8 x 7 inches; ca. 1920; excellent condition; $75–$150.
Chehalis: round twined basket; with rim loops and green line design; 6 x 3 inches; ca. 1920; excellent condition; $75–$125.
Chehalis: twined; fish-type; has braided drawstringlike rim; 14½ x 14 inches; ca. turn of the century; excellent condition; $500–$750.

CHEMEHEUVI
Chemeheuvi: spitoon shape; 10½ x 9 inches; ca. 1900; very good condition; $500–$750.

CHEROKEE
Cherokee: storage; North Carolina Cherokee museum-quality splint basket; 12½ inches diameter x 16 inches; excellent condition; $700–$1,000.
Cherokee: contemporary basket; by Diana Scott; 9 x 9½ inches; ca. 1970; excellent condition; $300–$350.

Basket, Chehalis, twined; 14½ x 14 inches; fish-type; braided drawstringlike rim; ca. 1900; $500–$750. Courtesy Jack Sellner, CAI.

CHILKOTIN

Chilkotin: rare, smaller, rectangular imbricated storage basket; 13 x 7 inches; ca. 1880; very good condition; $350–$500.

Chilkotin: very large, rare, imbricated storage basket with classic wire reinforcement top; 25 x 12 x 12 inches; ca. 1880; very good condition; $500–$750.

CHIPPEWA

Chippewa: older coiled grass and birch bark; sweet grass with yellow, green, and white porcupine quill–decorated lid in a leaf design; 3½ (including lid) x 6 inches; very good condition; $100–$150.

CHOCTAW

Choctaw: typical group of baskets with handles; ca. 1900–1910; excellent condition; $200–$250 each.

Choctaw/Chitimacha: three twill plaited baskets; of blown-out square form; in natural, yellow, black, and red; 2½, 4, and 5 square inches; very good condition; $425–$500/set.

Choctaw: double-weave river cane; rare; 5½ inches; ca. 1900s; excellent condition; $300–$400.

Basket, Choctaw, handles; typical group of baskets with handles; ca. 1900–1910; $200–$250 each. Collection of Joyce Williams. Photo by Donald Vogt.

Basket, coiled, Yucca; done by Mary Duwyeme (14 years old when it was made) and entered in 1984 SWAIA Annual Indian Market. Courtesy of Miniatures at the Kiva/Steve Cowgill. Photo by Donald Vogt.

COWLITZ

Cowlitz: imbricated conical hard berry basket with fine weave; 9 x 7½ inches; ca. 1860; very good condition; $150–$250.

Cowlitz: huge, hard coiled basket; with polychrome geometric designs; 14 x 10 inches; ca. 1920; very good condition; $800–$1,000.

Cowlitz: rectangular, imbricated basket; with rim loops and lines of cross design; 10 x 5¼ x 8 inches; ca. 1900; very good condition; $325–$425.

Cowlitz: round, hard coiled basket; with rim loops and imbricated design; by Mary Kioma; 8 x 3½ inches; ca. 1920; excellent condition; $250–$350.

Cowlitz: huge, classic, imbricated basket; with finger-woven trump line from "Abe" Lincoln personal collection; 18½ x 18 inches; ca. 1860; very good condition; $3,500–$4,500.

CREE

Cree: lidded basket; porcupine quill decorations; 3¼ inches wide x 2 inches deep; ca. 1980; excellent condition; $200–$300.

GREAT LAKES

Great Lakes: older birch bark basket; oval with connecting diamond designs; 4 x 8¼ x 9¼ inches; very good condition; $80–$125.

Baskets, Cree, lidded; porcupine quill decorations; 3¼ inches wide x 2 inches deep; ca. 1980; excellent condition; $200–$300. Courtesy of, and photo by, Joyce Williams.

HAIDA

Haida: brown spruce fiber basket; with rolling log crosses in brown, two salmon red bands; 6 inches wide, 3 inches tall; very fine condition; $100–$200.

Haida: rare, round twined bowl; with openwork and with a shoulder; 6 x 4 inches; ca. 1920; very good condition; $200–$300.

Haida: twined basket; made of deep brown spruce fiber with rolling log crosses in dark brown and two salmon red bands; 6 inches wide, 3 inches tall; very fine condition; $150–$300.

Basket, Tlingit; tightly woven with natural brown fiber body and deep mahogany, light brown, and salmon-colored geometrics; 5 inches wide at top opening, 4¼ inches high; perfect condition and tone; still retains exhibition tab and number inside; $450–$750. Courtesy of C. E. Guarino Auction Gallery, Denmark, Maine.

Basket, Haida, twined; made of deep brown spruce fiber with rolling log crosses in dark brown and two salmon red bands; 6 inches wide, 3 inches tall; very fine condition; $150–$300. Courtesy of C. E. Guarino Auction Gallery, Denmark, Maine.

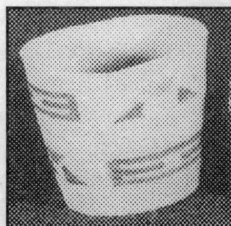

Basket, Nootka, polychrome; dome lid; basket woven with natural fiber body and killer whales in purple, green, and red; hunters in dugout canoe after a whale; the lid woven with porpoises or whale designs; approximately 5¼ inches wide, 4 inches deep; good visual piece in excellent condition; $450–$700. Courtesy of C. E. Guarino Auction Gallery, Denmark, Maine.

Haida: two baskets; one Yana, made of willow or hazel, conifer, maidenhair fern, and bear grass with full-twist overlay, 2½ inches high x 4 inches diameter; the other Northwest Coast Haida, made of spruce root and maidenhair fern woven around a bottle, 2½ inches high; both excellent condition; $100–$200 each.

HAVASUPAI

Havasupai: double bowl; 15½ x 8 inches; ca. 1920s; excellent condition; $1,500–$2,000.

HOPI

Hopi: coiled basketry storage bowl; decorated overall with "smiling" dark red and brown deer on a natural ground, coiled loop handles; 16 inches diameter; fair condition (minor stitch damage); $300–$400.

Hopi: coiled basket; polychrome with black, brown, yellow, and natural colors in terraced cross within large rectangular panels designs; 6 x 10¾ inches; ca. 1930–1940; very good condition; $325–$425.

Hopi: coiled basket; done by Mary Jane Batala for the New Mexico State Fair in 1978; won second prize; excellent condition; $300–$500.

Hopi: coiled, woven, circular dish; 11¼ inches diameter; excellent condition; $100–$200.

Hopi: fancy coiled tray; polychrome with black, sienna, yellow, green, and white in a kachina maiden design by Ramona Lenahema; 12 inches diameter; excellent condition; $250–$350.

Hopi: handled coiled basket; 17½ x 11½ x 5 inches; ca. 1910; excellent condition; $2,000–$2,500.

Hopi: plaited sifting or winnowing basket; excellent condition; $60–$80.

Hopi: plaited basket; unusual shape; in yellow and natural colors; 11¼ inches square; excellent condition; $70–$100.

Hopi: plaque; Crow Mother Kachina (proper name is Angwusnasomtaka), purchased at Hope town of Mishongnoui, Second Mesa; 18 inches diameter; very good condition; $125–$225.

Hopi: wicker basketry plaque; polychrome; 12 inches diameter; 1920s; good condition (faded colors); $55–$125.

Hopi: group of five wicker plaques from different mesas; there are some contemporary-looking ones in the group that are actually old and very colorful; one in back is coiled, other four are wicker weave; ca. 1900–1910; excellent condition; $300–$500 each.

Hopi: coiled storage basket; 12 x 12 inches; excellent condition; $1,500–$2,000.

Hopi: wicker basketry plaque; polychrome with orange, red, black, green, and white; 10¾ inches diameter; excellent condition; $100–$175.

Hopi: wicker basket; polychrome; 12 x 14½ inches diameter; ca. 1900–1930; excellent condition; $300–$400.

Basket, Hopi, plaque; two plaques by 1982 SWAIA 61st Annual Indian Market winner Remalda Markio Lomayestevea; on left is a coiled plaque in design called Shalako Kachina; and right is Butterfly Maiden. Courtesy of Miniatures at the Kiva/Steve Cowgill. Photo by Donald Vogt.

HUPA

Hupa: basketry bowl; a twined half-twist overlay basket with decoration of maidenhair fern; 5 inches high x 6½ inches diameter; good condition; $250–$350.

Hupa: basketry hat; twined half-twist overlay basket with maidenhair fern; 3¼ inches high x 7 inches; good condition; $225–$325.

Hupa: miniature twined basketry bowl; slanted brown geometric designs; 3 x 2 inches; ca. 1940; very good condition; $85–$125.

Hupa: large twined mesh cooking basket with unusual fret design; 9 x 4½ inches; ca. 1890; very good condition; $100–$175.

Hupa: hat; fairly common; 7½ inches diameter, 3 inches high; ca. 1930; excellent condition; $350–$500.

Hupa: classic twined woman's basketry hat with geometric designs; 6 x 3 inches; ca. 1910; excellent condition; $275–$375.

Hupa: miniature woven basket; excellent condition; $75–$125.

Hupa/Karok/Klamath: three twined bowl forms with dark brown geometric designs over a yellow field; 3½ inches, 8¾ inches, and 12 inches; fair condition(roughness to group); Northern California; $400–$500.

Hupa-Karok: large, old Hupa-Karok twined burden basket; 15 x 13 inches diameter at rim; excellent condition; $500–$700.

HURON

Huron: quilled birch-bark basket; with bird design on lid; about 4½ inches diameter; very good condition; $50–$100.

Huron (Canadian Woodland): three baskets, two in colored floral design, one with star design, beige; average 4 inches diameter; very good condition; $150–$200.

IROQUOIS

Iroquois: old plaited basket; ash splint construction with sweet grass handles and remnants of blue dye color on certain strips used for contrast; 22½ inches; ca. 1910–1915; very good condition; $250–$350.

JEMEZ

Jemez, plaited winnowing and sifting basket; 5 x 12½ inches; excellent condition; $50–$100.

JICARILLA APACHE

Jicarilla Apache: 10 inches diameter x 12¼ inches high; good condition; $75–$135.

Jicarilla Apache: basket with dog figures; 12½inches diameter x 3¾ inches high; good condition; $35–$75.

Jicarilla Apache: basket with polychrome zigzag designs; 11½ inches diameter x 14¼ inches high; good condition; $75–$125.

Jicarilla Apache: dish shape; orange and brown decorations on mustard color background; three v-type decorations on outside edge and orange crosses; acorn-shaped decorations veer out from center; near mint condition; ca. 1930; $250–$350.

KAROK

Karok: basketry bowl; twined half-twist overlay basket with bear grass and maindenhair design; 4 inches high x 6½ inches diameter; excellent condition; $400–$550.

Karok: gambling or flour tray; made of pine and spruce root with overlay of bear grass and maidenhair fern in circular and geometric designs; 3 inches high x 14 inches diameter; good condition; $175–$225.

Karok: early twined basketry hat; woven with dark and lighter shades of brown in stepped geometrics; 7 inches wide at top; very good condition; $200–$400.

KLAMATH

Klamath: basket bowl; two bands of geometric designs in bear grass and yellow quill; 4¼ inches high x 6 inches diameter; good condition; $125–$175.

Klamath: round twined bowl; with brown and yellow porcupine quill design; 8½ x 4 inches; ca. 1910; excellent condition; $150–$200.

Klamath: classic fine twined basketry hat; with diagonal stair-step design; ca. 1910; very good condition; $225–$325.

Klamath: rare old twined Klamath gambling tray; 9 inches; ca. 1870; very good condition; $50–$75.

Klamath: unusual twined seed basket with geometric design; 6 x 5 inches; ca. 1900; very good condition; $50–$75.

Klamath: twined basket; polychrome with red, yellow, and natural colors in banded designs; 5 x 8½ inches; ca. 1900–1930; very good condition; $150–$200.

Klamath: extremely fine twined basket; with yellow porcupine quill and brown hourglass motif; 8 x 4 inches; ca. 1900; very good condition; $225–$325.

Klamath: fine small polychrome twined basket; with green arrows and beaded top; 4 x 2½ inches; ca. 1900; very good condition; $100–$175.

Klamath: unusual large round twined basket with lid and carrying handle; 11 x 7½ inches; ca. 1910; excellent condition; $225–$300.

KLICKITAT

Klickitat: basket; black and red vertical overlapping design with original braided leather handles; 6 inches high, 13¾ inches wide, 7½ inches deep; very good condition; $160–$220.

Klickitat: classic conical hard basket with rim loops and geometric imbrication; 9 x 7½ inches; ca. 1890; very good condition; $200–$300.

Klickitat: rare small imbricated Klickitat basket with rim loops; 6 x 5½ inches; ca. 1890; very good condition; $150–$200.

Klickitat: miniature basket; classic design, hard coiled; 1 x 1 inch; ca. 1970; excellent condition; $50–$100.

Klickitat: unusual miniature figured coiled basket; ca. 1970; 1½ x 1 inch; excellent condition; $50–$75.

Klickitat: Old figure imbricated basket with animal and human figures; 14½ x 12 inches; ca. 1870; good condition (top damage); $150–$250.

Klickitat: small conical imbricated hard basket with rim loops; 6 x 5 inches; ca. 1890; very good condition; $100–$150.

Klickitat: tiny imbricated basket; with rim loops and polychrome geometric design; by Nettie Kunecki; 1½ x 1 inch; ca. 1980; excellent condition; $75–$100.

Klickitat: hard coiled and imbricated huckleberry basket; 8 x 7½ inches; ca. 1870; very good condition; $75–$100.

Klickitat: large rectangular imbricated storage basket; with rim loops and geometric designs; 16 x 10 inches; ca. 1890; very good condition (some damage); $250–$350.

Klickitat: basket; quail feather design; polychrome decorated with reticulated rim; 10½ inches high x 9½ inches diameter; excellent condition; $1,200–$1,600.

Klickitat: storage basket; 12¾ inches high x 14½ inches diameter; very good condition; $900–$1,100.

MAIDU

Maidu: basket; coiled three-rod construction in redbud and willow forming the "bush" motif; 2½ inches high x 4¼ inches diameter; good condition; $300–$500.

Maidu: coiled basketry tray; decorated with plumed triangular motifs in reddish brown on a golden ground; provenance: collected by a teacher in the service of the Department of the Interior, Office of Indian Affairs, stationed at Carson, Nevada, Indian School from 1895 to 1910; diameter 16 inches; very good condition (rim damage); $350–$500.

Maidu: coiled basketry bowl; flaring form, decorated with band of joined elongated triangles in dark red-brown on dark golden field; diameter 11 inches; good condition (rim damage); California; $500–$750.

Maidu: coiled basketry utility bowl; deep open form, decorated with radiating concentric step devices in reddish brown on a golden field; provenance: collected by a teacher in the service of the Department of the Interior, Office of Indian Affairs, stationed at Carson, Nevada, Indian School from 1895 to 1910; 13½ inches diameter; very good condition (rim damage); $500–$600.

Maidu and Pomo: four coiled basketry bowls and tray; provenance: collected by a teacher in the service of the Department of the Interior, Office of Indian Affairs, stationed at Carson, Nevada, Indian School from 1895 to 1910; 6½, 7, 10¼, and 14½ inches diameter; good condition (rim damage to group); California; $800–$1,000/set.

Maidu: bowl; three-rod construction with stepped triangular designs in redbud at neck; 7 inches high x 7 inches diameter; excellent condition; California; $250–$450.

Maidu: basket; made from dark redbud; ca. 1900; excellent condition; $200–$275.

MAKAH

Makah: lidded basket; polychrome bird design; 4 inches diameter x 2½ inches high; very good condition; $25–$75.

Makah: large basket; twined, woven in a deep square form with natural fiber background, with flying birds in deep purple and red, top rim bound with fibers around bundle core; old; 8½ inches wide, 5 inches deep, 6½ inches high; overall condition good; $35–$60.

Makah: superfine basketry-covered bottle decorated with figures; 5 x 2 inches; ca. 1890; excellent condition; $100–$150.

Makah: basketry bottle; woven geometric design with bands in purple, red, brown, blue, and beige; 8½ inches high; very good condition; $100–$150.

Makah: miniature twined carrying basket; with a whale on each side; 2 x 2 inches; ca. 1980; excellent condition; $40–$60.

Makah: rectangular carrying basket; with unusual pictorial schoolhouse design; 12 x 8 x 3 inches; ca. 1920; very good condition; $100–$150.

Makah: finely twined large lidded basket; with birds and geometrics; 6 x 5 inches; ca. 1920; excellent condition; $225–$300.

Makah: finely woven miniature lidded basket; with a boat, a whale, and a duck; ca. 1986; excellent condition; $50–$75.

Makah: large basketry-covered abalone shell; 6 x 5 x 2 inches; ca. 1920; excellent condition; $75–$115.

Makah: miniature lidded circular woven basket; excellent condition; $100–$125.

Makah: lidded woven basket; excellent condition; $75–$110.

Makah: lidded basket; simple line decorations; 4 inches wide, 2 inches deep; ca. 1920; excellent condition; $150–$200.

Makah: fine little lidded twined basket with ducks all around; 2¾ x 2 inches; ca. 1980; excellent condition; $40–$60.

Makah: large round lidded basket with multicolored sea monsters all around; 7 x 4 inches; ca. 1930; excellent condition; $200–$300.

Makah: large round twined lidded basket with whales, boats, and ducks all around; 7 x 5 inches; ca. 1935; excellent condition; $50–$100.

Makah: oval twined lidded basket with a row of geometric designs; 4 x 3 inches; ca. 1900; very good condition; $50–$75.

Makah: round fine twined lidded basket with swastikas all around; 5 x 2½ inches; ca. 1910; very good condition; $45–$75.

Makah: round twined lidded basket with birds all around; 4½ x 3 inches; ca. 1940; excellent condition; $85–$145.

Makah: small twined lidded basket with birds and boats all around; 3 x 2 inches; ca. 1940; excellent condition; $75–$125.

Makah: miniature lidded basket; polychrome bird and whale design; 2¼ inches diameter x 2⅛ inches high; very good condition; $50–$150.

Makah: oblong twined basket with lid and a band of bear grass figures all around it; 4 x 2½ inches; ca. 1930; very good condition; $50–$75.

Makah: old bottle and lid covered with twined basketry; 9 x 3 inches; ca. 1920; very good condition; $85–$125.

Makah: round twined and plaited basket with whaling boats and ducks all around; 8 x 7 inches; ca. 1920; very good condition; $80–$120.

Makah: round twined basket with a whaling boat and ducks all around; 5 x 3 inches; ca. 1920; very good condition; $40–$75.

Makah: round twined basket with lid and steamboat designs; 3½ x 2½ inches; ca. 1910; very good condition; $75–$100.

Makah: very fine twined basket with lid and with arrows and ducks as designs; 3 x 2 inches; ca. 1920; very good condition; $60–$90.

Makah: large twined basket; woven in a deep square form with natural fiber background, with flying birds in deep purple and wine red; one side with some fading of the purple; the other side with deep and original hues; top rim bound with fiber around bundle core; some indication of a rope or fiber handle; 8½ inches wide, 5 inches deep, 6½ inches high; overall good condition with no internal losses; $45–$100.

Makah: unusual basketry-covered shell with whale figures all around; 4 x 3 inches; ca. 1986; excellent condition; $80–$100.

Makah: small twined basket with lid and a boat and whale decoration; 3 x 3 inches; ca. 1986; excellent condition; $50–$75.

Makah: small twined basket with lid and with eagle design; 2½ x 2¼ inches; ca. 1986; excellent condition; $50–$75.

MESCALERO APACHE

Mescalero Apache: water jar or storage basket; braided hair tumpline loops, very tightly woven; once may have had pine pitch covering; good condition; $75–$100.

Mescalero Apache: typical design; ca. 1920–1930; very good condition; $300–$400.

Mescalero Apache: tray; shallow bowl; 22 inches diameter; ca. 1870; $800–$1,250.

MICMAC
Micmac: round basket with lid and quilled top; 4 x 3 inches; ca. 1910; excellent condition; $75–$125.

MODOC
Modoc: finely twined miniature Modoc basket; 4 x 2½ inches; ca. 1920; very good condition; $100–$140.

MONO
Monache (Western Mono): bottlenecked gift basket; fine quality bracken fern and sedge; 9 inches diameter x 4¾ inches high; ca. 1900; very good condition; $2,000–$3,200.

Western Mono(probably): tray; two-tone geometric design; 9¼ x 13¾ inches; good condition; California; $85–$185.

Mono: basket woven on rods in natural-fiber body with mahogany brown "rattlesnake" bands below a series of diamond triangle shapes under the top rim band; old; 10 inches wide at top, 5½ inches deep; very good condition; $100–$300.

(Mono) Western Mono: coiled flared bowl with striking black arrow and stair-step design; 9 x 5 inches; ca. 1840; very good condition; $500–$600.

Mono or Yucca(possibly): burden basket; very good condition; Western California; $700–$900.

Mono: large old twined basket; woven on rods in natural-fiber body with deep mahogany brown "rattlesnake" bands below a series of diamond triangle shapes under the top rim band; break in one of the top rim rods; 10 inches wide at top, 5½ inches deep; fine condition and excellent tonal quality; $200–$400.

Mono (possibly): jar with geometric design; ca. 1870s; very good condition; Northern California; $600–$800.

Mono: coiled utility basket; 20¼ x 8¾ inches; excellent condition; $2,500–$3,500.

NAVAJO
Navajo: coiled basket (rare); polychrome with black, dark green, brown, and natural colors; 3¾ x 14 inches; ca. 1900–1940; very good condition; $400–$500.

Navajo: coiled dish; 13½ inches diameter; very good condition; $85–$115.

Navajo: double saddle; pictorial with stars in corners, gray, orange, green, brown, red, and natural; 2 feet 5 inches x 4 feet 11 inches; good condition; $200–$300.

Navajo: rare old coiled basket; with black and natural colors in concentric circle and triangle designs; 3 x 14½ inches; ca. 1930s; very good condition; $350–$450.

Navajo: shallow bowl; basket is decorated with figures and lightning designs; $5,000–$5,500.

Navajo/Ute: coiled wedding basket; polychrome with black, red, and natural colors; 2½ x 12½ inches; very good condition; $60–$80.

Navajo/Ute: coiled wedding basket; polychrome with black, red, and natural colors; shows use and age; 3½ x 15 inches; fair condition; $65–$100.

Navajo/Ute: coiled wedding basket; polychrome with black, red, and natural colors; 3½ x 14¼ inches; very good condition; $100–$150.

Navajo/Ute: coiled wedding basket; polychrome with black, sienna, and natural colors, 3 x 15½ inches; ca. 1940s; very good condition; $100–$150.

Navajo/Ute: coiled wedding basket; polychrome with black, sienna, and natural colors; 2 x 13¾ inches diameter; $125–$175.

Navajo: classic coiled Navajo wedding basket with spirit release line; 11 x 3 inches; ca. 1935; very good condition; $200–$250.

Navajo: wedding basket; thick coiled construction with deep color design in black, red, and brown on a natural reed base; 12 inches width; ca. 1940; very good condition; $50–$70.

Navajo: coiled wedding basket; sumac splints over three-ring construction; finish is herringbone weave; 13 inches diameter; ca. 1920; excellent condition; $400–$500.

Navajo: contemporary wedding basket given to medicine men for performing the ceremony; excellent condition; $35–$50.

Navajo: wedding basket; thick coiled construction with deep color design in black, wine red, and brown on the natural reed base; 12 inches wide; ca. 1940; very good condition; $60–$150.

Navajo/Ute: coiled basketry wedding tray; polychrome; 3¼ x 17 inches diameter; excellent condition; $185–$245.

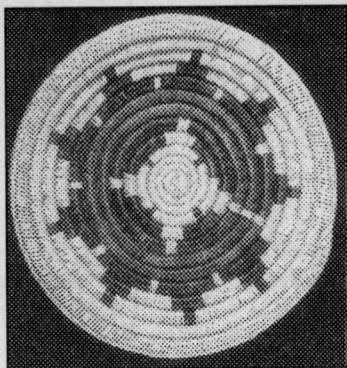

Basket, Navajo, wedding; thick coiled construction with deep color design in black, wine red, and brown on the natural reed base; 12 inches wide; ca. 1940; very good condition; $60–$150. Courtesy of C. E. Guarino Auction Gallery, Denmark, Maine.

Navajo/Ute: coiled wedding basket; polychrome with natural, black, and red; 3 inches diameter; very good condition; $75–$125.

NOOTKA

Nootka: basket; polychrome with dome lid, woven with natural-fiber body and killer whales in purple, green, and red; hunters in a dugout canoe after a whale; the lid with porpoises or whales; old; approximately 5¼ inches wide, 4 inches deep; excellent condition; $300–$500.

Nootka: unusual basketry-covered bottle; 8½ x 3 inches; ca. 1920; very good condition; $65–$110.

Nootka/Makah: twined lidded basket; polychrome with dark red, dark brown, and natural colors; 2 x 3½ inches; ca. 1900; very good condition; $60–$90.

Nootka/Northwest Coast: twined and plaited basket; Nootka polychrome with red, natural, brown, and tan; 5 x 5½ inches; ca. 1925; very good condition; $60–$90.

Nootka: polychrome basket with dome lid; woven with natural-fiber body and killer whales in purple, green, and red; hunters in dugout canoe after a whale; the lid woven with porpoises or whale designs; approximately 5¼ inches wide, 4 inches deep; good visual piece in excellent condition; $450–$700.

Nootka: round twined basket with rim loops and colored line designs; 7 x 4 inches; ca. 1935; very good condition; $100–$150.

Nootka: large lidded basket with colorful whaling scenes all around; 11 x 9 inches; ca. 1910; very good condition; $300–$400.

Nootka: two lidded baskets with wolf and geometric motifs, one lidded Alaskan basket with woven wool; very good condition; $125–$225/set.

Nootka: finely woven basket with whale and dragon design; abou 4½ inches diameter; very good condition; $75–$150.

ONEIDA

Oneida: covered splint basket with black water-base paint decoration; accompanying period note: "Mary (Hopkins) Cornell when she lived at Eaton, NY or near there, on about 1824"; 15¼ inches high x 14 inches diameter; fair condition (hole on one bottom corner); $200–$275.

PAIUTE

Paiute: basketry bowl; blue, green, and white applied geometric design, beaded; 5¾ inches diameter; very good condition; $350–$450.

Paiute: basketry bowl; green, red, and blue zigzag bead design; 5 inches diameter; good condition; $300–$400.

Paiute: rare openwork twined conical burden basket with red line design; 12 x 10 inches ; ca. 1900; very good condition; $300–$375.

Paiute: basketwork cradleboard with original strappings; is decorated in the zigzag pattern, which indicates that the baby it was made for was male; 27 x 12 inches; excellent condition; $1,000–$1,500.

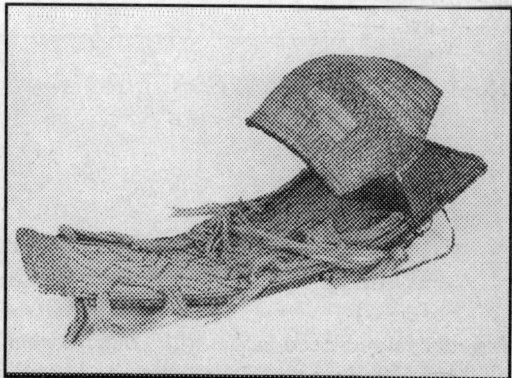

Basket, cradleboard, Paiute; basketwork cradleboard, with original strappings; decorated in zigzag pattern, which indicates the baby it was made for was male; 27 x 12 inches; $1,000– $1,500. Collection of Joyce Williams. Photo by Donald Vogt.

Paiute: medicine jar with horsehair handle; sealed with piñon pitch; rare; 4¾ inches tall; ca. late 1800s; very good condition; $300–$500.

Paiute: miniature basket; full beaded exterior with design in yellow, red, green, and blue; 3 inches diameter x 1⅝ inches high; good condition; $90–$140.

Paiute: polychrome coiled basketry tray; Navajo wedding basket; 14 inches diameter; very good condition; $150–$200.

Paiute: twined seed jar; 8 x 11 inches; ca. 1890; very good condition; $300–$400.

Paiute: woven utility basket; 9 inches diameter; very good condition; $75–$100.

PANAMINT

Panamint: woven wicker basket; cylindrical with recessed flaring neck, woven with a frieze of vertical lizard images in dark brown on light ground beneath a frieze of opposed birds in light brown, and a dark brown bottom treatment of triple-spoked wheel; 14½ inches high; excellent condition; $425–$575.

Panamint: wrapped and coiled basket; designed with geometrics; 10½ inches long, 4½ inches wide, 2½ inches deep; ca. 1920; excellent condition; $2,000–$2,500.

PAPAGO

Papago: basket; martynia and willow; 12 inches diameter x 9½ inches high; good condition; $360–$600.

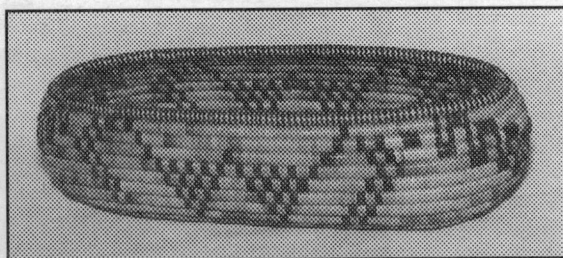

Baskets, Panamint; wrapped and coiled, designed with geometrics; 10½ inches long, 4½ inches wide, 2½ inches deep; ca. 1920; excellent condition; $2,000–$2,500. Courtesy of, and photo by, Joyce Williams.

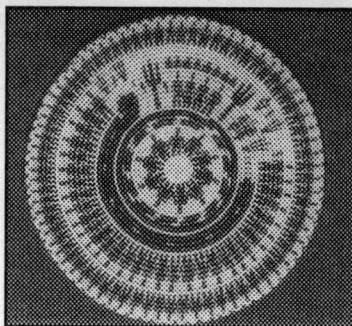

Papago: basket; bold figural designs, rim handles, flared rim; 18 inches diameter x 12½ inches high; good condition; $550–750.

Papago: lidded basket; two-tone geometric design; 2¾ inches diameter x 2⅛ inches high; very good condition; $15–$50.

Papago: lidded basket; two-tone geometric design; 3½ inches diameter x 3 inches high; good condition; $50–$100.

Papago: basket; 5¾ inches diameter x 2½ inches high; good condition; $28–$50.

Papago: basket; 9 inches diameter x 3¾ inches high; good condition; $28–$50.

Papago: basketry plaque; green and natural-colored yucca with "Man in the Maze" design; 11 inches diameter; very good condition; $85–$135.

Papago: basketry plaque; star design in middle, stick figures hand to hand in first circle, pyramid design outside edge; 16½ inches; mint condition; $900–$1,200.

Papago: round coiled basketry bowl with slanted stairstep design; 5½ x 3¾ inches; ca. 1935; very good condition; $50–$85.

Papago: coiled oval basketry tray; of bear grass, devil's claw, and yucca; 1½ x 10 x 11½ inches; very good condition; $50–$75.

Papago: coiled basketry tray with large black five-pointed star-flower and triangle designs; 13¼ inches diameter; mint condition; $150–$250.

Papago: coiled bear grass basket; bowl-shaped; 1½ x 4¾ inches; excellent condition; $25–$45.

Papago: coiled novelty basket; cup with handle, 2 inches high; ca. mid-20th century; excellent condition; $40–$60.

Papago: coiled tray with buffalo headlike designs; 1¼ x 7¼ inches; excellent condition; $45–$75.

Papago: coiled bear grass and yucca tray with green terraced designs; 1⅜ x 8 inches; excellent condition; $45–$85.

Papago: coiled bowl shape with handles; 2¾ x 7¼ inches; excellent condition; $25–$45.

Papago: coiled tray with Pima-like fret designs; 2 x 11 inches; excellent condition; $110–$160.

Papago: coiled lidded basket; bear grass and yucca construction; 3½ inches (including lid) x 3½ inches; excellent condition; $45–$85.

Papago: coiled oval basket with handles and black "Coyote Track" designs; 3¾ x 7¾ x 11¼ inches; excellent condition; $80–$125.

Papago: coiled oval basket with horizontal connected terraced design; 3 x 5½ x 6¾ inches; excellent condition; $55–$80.

Papago: coiled basket; with black rectangular designs; 3 x 6¾ inches; excellent condition; $50–$75.

Papago: coiled basket; tapering sides in bowl shape; 4 x 8 inches; very good condition; $25–$45.

Papago: coiled oval basket; with black terraced designs; 5 inches (including handle) x 6 x 8 inches; excellent condition; $60–$80.

Papago: coiled basket; with bear grass and yucca construction; 6 inches (including lid) x 6½ inches; excellent condition; $65–$85.

Papago: coiled basket; with two horizontal parallel lines of black serrated designs; 6 x 9¼ inches; excellent condition; $90–$145.

Papago: coiled basket; polychrome with green, black, and natural colors; excellent condition; $65–$110.

Papago: coiled tray with black rectangular designs; 1½ x 9½ inches; excellent condition; $35–$50.

Papago: coiled tray with black rectangular designs; 1½ x 9½ inches; excellent condition; $45–$75.

Papago: coiled basket; polychrome with black, green, and natural colors; 1½ x 8½ inches; excellent condition; $30–$60.

Papago: coiled oval tray with connected rectangular designs; 1¼ x 12 x 16 inches; ca. 1940s; excellent condition; $75–$100.

Papago: coiled basket; polychrome with black, green, and natural colors in a five-pointed star-flower design; 2½ x 11½ inches; excellent condition; $95–$135.

Papago: coiled basket with double horizontal row of terraced designs; 6¼ x 9 inches; excellent condition; $65–$115.

Papago: round coiled basketry dish with handle; 6¾ x 6 inches; ca. 1945; excellent condition; $40–$60.

Papago: pair of rare coiled basketry figures; one woman with removable hat holding mandolin, one woman with removable hat carrying purse; excellent condition; $300–$400 each.

Papago: four basketry bowls; geometric designs in brown, gold, and beige; 7-inch to 11-inch diameters; very good condition; $75–$125.

Papago: large coiled basket with black rectangular terraced designs; by Sophie Sara Ficio; 3½ x 13½ inches; excellent condition; $125–$225.

Papago: miniature coiled "wheat stitch" whirlwind bowl; 2¼ inches diameter; ca. 1970; excellent condition; $30–$60.

Papago: old coiled basket polychrome with black, yellow, and natural colors in rectangular vertical designs; 3⅜ x 6¾ inches; ca. 1940s; very good condition; $60–$90.

Papago: older coiled basket; 5 x 10½ inches; excellent condition; $90–$130.

Papago/Pima: coiled basket; with connected black slanted triangle designs; 3 x 9 inches; ca. 1900; excellent condition; $60–$110.

Papago: three basketry bowls; geometric designs in brown and gold; 7-inch, 9-inch, and 11-inch diameters; very good condition; $85–$135.

Papago: three baskets; geometric designs in beige and dark brown; average 6 inches diameter; very good condition; $90–$190.

Papago: coiled tray; ⅞ x 4½ inches; excellent condition; $25–$40.

Papago: two coiled baskets; a bowl, 8 inches tall, and an eagle-decorated tray, 12 inches diameter; very good condition; $200–$275 each.

PIMA

Pima: large coiled basket woven with a circular center in deep brown with four spiral emanations, a series of meandering and zigzag lines to the rim of the basket; other triangular forms issue from the rim with cross design in the center in deep brown bear-claw fiber on the natural willow grass field; 18½ inches wide at top; approximately 7¾ inches deep; good tone and condition; $1,600–$2,000.

Pima: coiled basket; with a circular center in brown with four spiral emanations, a series of meandering and zigzag lines to the rim of the basket, other triangular forms issuing from the rim, with cross design in the center in deep brown bear-claw fiber on the natural willow grass field; 18½ inches wide at top, approximately 7¾ inches deep; good tone and condition; $1,600–$3,000.

Pima: basket; martynia and willow, finely woven; 3½ inches diameter x 2⅜ inches high; good condition; $175–$275.

Pima: basket; finely woven, martynia and willow; 4¼ inches diameter x 2¾ inches high; very good condition; $100–$200.

Basket, Pima; large coiled basket woven with a circular center in deep brown with four spiral emanations, a series of meandering and zigzag lines to the rim of the basket. Other triangular forms issue from the rim with cross design in the center in deep brown bear-claw fiber on the natural willow grass field; 18½ inches wide at top, approximately 7¾ inches deep; good tone and condition; $1,600–$2,000.
Courtesy of C. E. Guarino Auction Gallery, Denmark, Maine.

Pima: basket, willow and martynia; 9¼ inches diameter x 4½ inches high; good condition; $145–$225.

Pima: basketry bowl; radiating step designs with dark center and rim; 14 inches diameter; very good condition; $300–$400.

Pima: basketry bowl; ten figures descending to the Underworld, with 23 cross designs; 18 inches diameter; excellent condition; $1,500–$1,900.

Pima: basketry olla; stepped geometric design in dark brown and red, rod construction, braided rim; 11 inches high; very good condition; $1,100–$1,300.

Pima: basketry tray; very fine weave (20 stitches per inch) with design of a human figure descending into the center of the earth in devil's claw; original label of Vaughn's Indian and Jewelry Store, Phoenix, Arizona; 7¼ inches diameter; excellent condition; $800–$1,200.

Pima: basketry tray; central turtle design encircled with radiating star and stepped pyramids in devil's claw; 7½ inches diameter; excellent condition; $175–$225.

Pima: bowl; bundle construction, whorl design of black devil's claw; 3 inches high x 9½ inches diameter; perfect condition; $350–$450.

Pima: round coiled bowl with classic Pima fret design; 8 x 2 inches; ca. 1935; very good condition; $115–$140.

Pima: coiled basketry tray; small flat base with flaring sides, solid tondo with radiating linear devices and human figures; 14¼ inches diameter; $500–$1,000.

Pima: coiled tray; of deep circular form, woven in willow and devil's claw with a spiraling pattern of step-terraced lines; 19 inches diameter; excellent condition; $800–$1,000.

Pima: coiled basketry tray; shallow form, woven with flaring sides, solid tondo with rabbit ears meander pattern; 10¼ inches diameter; very good condition; $500–$600.

Pima: coiled tray; 3½ x 11¼ inches; ca. 1900; very good condition; $250–$300.

Pima: coiled bowl with radiating black terraced designs from the center; 3½ x 9 inches; ca. 1920; very good condition; $200–$300.

Pima: coiled tray; 3½ x 11¼ inches; ca. 1900; very good condition; $250–$350.

Pima: coiled basket with black "coyote track" designs; 3 x 7½ inches; ca. 1900; very good condition; $100–$150.

*Baskets, Pima, group of six; squash blossom design, pre–1900, $800–$1,000;
8 inches, ca. 1940s, $350–$500; 7½ inches, lightning design, ca. 1890–1900,
$650–$850; 1930s, Greek key design, $550–$650; contemporary, $500–$600;
twirling logs, 1930s–1940s, $300–$500.* Courtesy of Two Star Collection,
Houston, Texas. Photo by Donald Vogt.

Pima: coiled basket with three horizontal rows of black terraced
    designs; 4⅜ x 7½ inches; ca. 1900; $350–$450.

Pima: miniature coiled horsehair basket; 2 inches diameter; ca.
    1940; excellent condition; $75–$100.

Pima: large old coiled tray with black fret designs; 4 x 19½ inches;
    ca. 1900; very good condition; $500–$700.

Pima: large basket with twirling logs design, 22 inches; ca.
    1910–1920; excellent condition; $2,000–$2,500.

Pima: miniature coiled basket with whirlwind design; 2 inches
    diameter; ca. 1940; very good condition; $30–$50.

Pima: extremely fine coiled miniature horsehair basket with lid; 2 x
    1 inch; ca. 1970; very good condition; $30–$50.

Pima: miniature horsehair basket with lid; 2 x 1 inch; ca. 1920; very
    good condition; $30–$50.

Pima: old coiled basket with black tondo and two horizontal rows of
    "winged" whirling logs/swastikalike designs; 3¼ x 9½ inches;
    ca. 1900; very good condition; $200–$300.

Pima: olla; willow and martynia with braid rim; 9 inches diameter x
    7 inches high; ca. 1910; good condition; $900–$1,900.

Pima: very finely coiled oval tray with two rows of rattlesnake design; 7 x 4½ inches; ca. 1930; very good condition; $175–$225.

Pima/Papago: horsehair basket; black and white with black stitches; ¼ x 1 inch diameter; very good condition; $25–$50.

Pima/Papago, horsehair animal; black mouse with white bead eyes, ears, tail, and whiskers; ⅞ x 2¼ inches; very good condition; $50–$75.

Pima/Papago: horsehair plaque; white with black fret designs and stitches; 1¼ inches diameter; excellent condition; $40–$60.

Pima/Papago: horsehair basket; white with brown stitches; ½ x ½ inch; very good condition; $25–$50.

Pima/Papago: horsehair basket; white with black stitches; ½ x 1 inch; excellent condition; $30–$50.

Pima/Papago: horsehair basket; black with black stitches; ⅜ x 1½ inches; excellent condition; $25–$45.

Pima/Papago: horsehair basket; black with white stitches; ⅜ x 1 inch; very good condition; $30–$50.

Pima/Papago: horsehair basket; black with white stitches; ⁵⁄₁₆ x 1¹⁄₁₆ inches; excellent condition; $25–$45.

Pima: tray; martynia and willow; 7¼ inches diameter; very good condition; $100–$185.

Pima: rare wheat straw basket; 10 inches diameter and 8 inches high, with a 6-inch neck opening and 3¼-inch base; ca. 1900; excellent condition; $500–$750.

Pima: woven coiled basket; 15 inches diameter; ca. 1900; very good condition; $225–$325.

Pima: basket; classic example; came from Arizona at turn of the century; 17 inches diameter, 5 inches deep; very good condition; $1,000–$1,250.

Pima: basket with fine weave; 9 inches diameter; ca. 1920; excellent condition; $400–$600.

Pima: basket decorated with human figures; 3½ x 9 inches; excellent condition; $450–$600.

Pima: large old coiled basketry bowl; used for native wine/cooking/food; 6½ x 15 inches; ca. 1900; very good condition; $500–$600.

Pima: small horsehair basketry olla; ½ x ½ inch; ca. 1960; very good condition; $35–$50.

Pima: woven coiled basket; 15 inches diameter; ca. 1900; very good condition; $225–$275.

PIT RIVER

Pit River: lidded basket; made from willow, pine root, and bear grass and twined with a full-twist overlay; 6 inches high; excellent condition; $100–$175.

Pit River: basketry-covered brown whiskey bottle; 10 x 4 inches; ca. 1900; very good condition; $125–$175.

Pit River: rare miniature twined Pit River basketry bowl; 4 x 8 x 4 inches; ca. 1910; very good condition; $275–$325.

Pit River: twined bowl with striking red graduated connecting arrowhead designs; 7 x 4 inches, ca. 1890; very good condition; $185–$235.

POMO

Pomo: basketry bowl; 5 inches high, 12½ inches diameter; $4,000–$4,400.

Pomo: coiled basketry bowl; of tapering globular form, woven in bracked fern root and willow with joined wedge and other geometric devices; 6¼ inches diameter; very good condition; California; $475–$575.

Pomo: coiled basketry gift basket; shallow bowl form, decorated in radiating step terrace pattern motif, with attached quail's top-knots and red feather decoration; 3 inches; excellent condition; $225–$275.

Pomo: gift basket; three-rod coiled of sedge root, fern root, and willow, with woodpecker and quail feathers; 6¾ inches diameter; good condition; $200–$300.

Pomo: miniature basket; boat-shaped with single-rod construction and geometric designs in fern root with attached pony beads in blue, white, and cobalt; 1 inch high x 4½ inches long; good condition; $200–$300.

Pomo: miniature coiled basket; 1 inch diameter; ca. 1930; excellent condition; $45–$60.

Pomo: three miniature coiled gift baskets; of squat globular form, each decorated on exterior surface with multicolored bird feathers; 2¾-inch, 1½-inch, and ¾-inch diameters; excellent condition (minor feather loss to group); $650–$800.

POWHATAN

Powhatan: large plaited ash splint utility basket with painted designs; 19 x 11 inches; ca. 1910; very good condition; $80–$110.

QUEETS

Queets: round twined basketry bowl with line design; 7 x 4½ inches; ca. 1935; excellent condition; $50–$75.

QUINAULT

Quinault: basket; overlapping designs in black, light tan, and red; leather-hinged lid with original handles; 8 inches high x 16 inches wide by 9 inches deep; good condition; $125–$175.

Quinault: large coiled basket with handles and with red and green geometric design; 17 x 8 inches; ca. 1920; excellent condition; $125–$225.

Quinault: oval coiled raffia basket with handle and geometric designs; 16 x 12 inches; ca. 1930; very good condition; $50–$75.

Quinault: round twined basket with simple line design; 8 x 5 inches; ca. 1920; very good condition; $80–$120.

SALISH

Salish: rectangular imbricated basket with rim loops and geometric designs; 8 x 4 inches; ca. 1900; very good condition; $120–$150.

Salish: miniature woven basket; excellent condition; $125–$150.

Salish: rectangular imbricated basket with geometric designs; ca. 1890; very good condition; $175–$225.

Salish: round imbricated basket with lid; ca. 1910; very good condition; $175–$225.

Salish: huge round imbricated tray with handles and polychrome star design; 20 x 2 inches; ca. 1910; very good condition; $300–$400.

Salish: rectangular imbricated tray with handles and geometric designs; 21 x 2 inches; ca. 1910; very good condition; $200–$300.

Salish: large imbricated storage trunk with lid and polychromed diamond designs; 18 x 12 inches; ca. 1910; very good condition; $200–$300.

Salish: very fine small rectangular lidded trunk with imbricated geometric designs; 4 x 8 x 4 inches; ca. 1910; very good condition; $275–$350.

Salish: rectangular lidded basket with handles and with imbricated six-point star designs; 9½ x 4 inches; ca. 1935; excellent condition; $200–$250.

SEMINOLE
Seminole: pine needle and raffia turtle basket; made by Leia Battise; excellent condition; $25–$50.

SERI
Seri: large coiled basket with brown and natural colors in an eleven-pointed terraced star-flower design; 4½ x 16½ inches; excellent condition; $250–$400.

SILETZ
Siletz: large old openwork clamming basket; 22 x 12 inches; ca. 1900; very good condition; $75–$100.

Siletz: round twined carrying basket with handle; 7 x 5 inches; ca. 1920; very good condition; $75–$100.

Siletz: large twined storage basket with simple brown line design; 14 x 11 inches; ca. 1930; very good condition; $100–$130.

SKOKOMISH
Skokomish: classic twined bowl with rim loops and a row of dogs around the top; 10 x 7½ inches; ca. 1920; very good condition; $100–$300.

Skokomish: choice twined basket with gold zigzag design; 18 x ½ inch; ca. 1890; $225–$300.

Skokomish: unusual oblong basket with imbricated quail plume design; 13 x 7 x 3 inches; ca. 1910; very good condition; $75–$150.

Skokomish: rectangular imbricated semihard basket with purple and yellow original designs; 7 x 7 x 10 inches; ca. 1930; very good condition; $120–$200.

Skokomish: classic twined basket with brown and black triangular designs and a row of dogs all around the top; 5 x 4 inches; ca. 1910; excellent condition; $100–$125.

Skokomish: huge cedar bark plaited utility basket with rim loops; 15 x 12 inches; ca. 1900; very good condition; $200–$250.

SOUTHEAST

Southeast: large older coiled basket tray; oval sweet grass tray with handles; 1½ x 13½ x 17 inches; excellent condition; $125–$200.

SOUTHWESTERN

Southwestern: coiled basketry olla; with rounded body, tapering to a small cylindrical neck, woven in willow and devil's claw with a pattern of longitudinal zigzags; 11¾ inches high; good condition (minor stitch damage); $600–$800.

Southwestern: coiled polychrome basketry tray; of shallow flaring form, woven in willow, devil's claw, and red-dyed willow with whirling and linear geometric devices, waving human figures, and dogs; 15½ inches diameter; excellent condition; $550–$750.

THOMPSON RIVER

Thompson River: basket; imbricated design, polychrome decorated in beige and shades of brown; 11½ inches high x 11½ inches diameter; excellent condition; $650–$850.

Thompson River: Salish harvest basket; woven with polychrome vertical imbricated design in beige, brown, red, maroon, and black; 8½ x 12¾ inches diameter; very good condition; $500–$700.

TILLAMOOK

Tillamook: round twined basketry jar with banded designs; 6 x 5 inches; ca. 1930; excellent condition; $90–$150.

Tillamook: rare Tillamook basket made after the tribe moved to Grande Ronde; 8 x 7 inches; ca. 1880; very good condition; $150–$200.

TLINGIT

Tlingit: basket; made from bear grass and spruce root in brown, dark brown, red, green, and gold in an open-twined cross-warped weave called "eye hole"; 4½ inches high; very good condition; $50–$100.

Tlingit: berry basket; made from bear grass and spruce root with diamond design (signifying waves) in brown and dark brown, red, white, and gold; 3½ inches high x 4½ inches diameter; excellent condition; $225–$375.

Tlingit (Northwest Coast): twined spruce root basket; very good condition; $50–$100.

Tlingit: basket; tightly woven with natural brown fiber and deep mahogany body, brown and salmon-colored geometrics; exhibition tab and number inside; 5 inches wide at top opening, 4¼ inches high; perfect condition and tone; $250–$500.

Tlingit: finely woven basket with rattle top; polychrome design in bracken fern and grass on cedar background; 7½ inches diameter x 4½ inches high; good condition; $500–$700.

Tlingit: round twined basketry bowl with striking brown, gold, and orange designs; 10 x 3½ inches; ca. 1910; very good condition; $300–$400.

Tlingit: large and unusual oblong carrying basket with handle and geometric designs; 13½ x 6 inches; ca. 1910; very good condition; $80–$150.

Tlingit: glass bottle covered with twined basketry; 4½ inches; ca. 1920; very good condition; $200–$275.

Tlingit: rattle top basketry lid or disc; 5½ x 1¼ inches; ca. 1910; very good condition; $75–$125.

Tlingit: oval basketry mat with circular designs; 11 x 8 inches; ca. 1890; very good condition; $150–$200.

Tlingit: oval twined basketry mat; 10 x 6 inches; ca. 1910; very good condition; $125–$175.

Tlingit: large old Tlingit basket with polychrome geometrics; 11½ x 16½ inches; ca. 1900; very good condition; $150–$200.

Tlingit: rattle top; polychromed cylindrical body and top decorated in polychrome twined false embroidery designs of linear and concentric wedge motifs; attached old label on lid: "rare tlingit, 1859 or earlier, British Columbia"; 6⅝ inches diameter; very good condition; $600–$800.

Tlingit: superfine twined rattle top basket with outstanding brown and orange geometric motif; 6 x 5½ inches; ca. 1920; very good condition; $400–$600.

Tlingit: rattle; ca. 1900; very good condition; $400–$600.

Tlingit: choice finely twined rattle top basket with outstanding brown fret design; 5 x 3½ inches; ca. 1910; very good condition; $375–$425.

Tlingit: brown terraced spruce root basket with lid and with gold geometric design; 12 x 1½ inches; ca. 1910; very good condition; $50–$75.

Tlingit: round brown spruce root basket with gold chevron designs; 7 x 4 inches; ca. 1910; $225–$300.

Tlingit: old straight-sided basket with striking orange and black fret designs; 6 x 4 inches; ca. 1880; very good condition; $150–$200.

Tlingit: superfine small twined basket with bright pink and brown diamond edges; 4 x 3 inches; ca. 1910; very good condition; $325–$400.

Tlingit (Northwest Coast): twined spruce root basket; very good condition; $50–$100.

Tlingit: very finely woven Tlingit pedestal basket with colorful floral and geometric motif; 4 x 4 inches; ca. 1910; very good condition; $300–$350.

Tlingit: large unusual twined storage basket with lid and with gold geometric designs; 8 x 6 inches; ca. 1910; very good condition; $350–$450.

Tlingit: tightly woven with the natural brown fiber body and deep mahogany, light brown, and salmon-colored geometrics; still retains exhibition tab and number inside; 5 inches wide at top opening, 4¼ inches high; perfect condition and tone; $450–$750.

TSIMSHIAN

Tsimshian: basket; finely woven with orange and natural design on a brown ground; very fragile; wear, rim damage, and splits; 8½ inches diameter x 7½ inches high; very good condition; $25–$65.

Tsimshian: very fine and rare plaited basket; 4 x 4½ inches; ca. 1910; very good condition; $175–$250.

TULARE

Tulare: fine coiled shoulder basket with bands of rattlesnake designs; rare; 8 x 5½ inches; ca. 1920; very good condition; $700–$900.

Tulare/Yokut: basket; 6½ x 11¾ inches; ca. 1920; excellent condition; $1,000–$1,500.

WASHO

Washo: single-rod coiled bowl with red butterflies all around; 8 x 4 inches; ca. 1920; $175–$250.

Washo: coiled basketry bowl; squat globular body decorated in bracken fern and willow; 5⅝ inches diameter, 3 inches high; very good condition; $500–$600.

Washo: old coiled basket; polychrome (painted) with dark green, red, and natural colors in terraced vertical and diamond designs, 4¼ x 6 inches; ca. 1920s; very good condition; $100–$200.

Washo: California Great Basin miniature basket with two-tone geometric design; 5½ inches diameter x 6 inches high; good condition; $50–$85.

Washo: basketry bowl; willow, redbud, and bracken fern root in triangular designs; 4 inches high x 6½ inches diameter; excellent condition; $250–$350.

Washo or Paiute: California Great Basin conical carrying basket; geometric two-tone design; 10 inches diameter x 11 inches high; good condition; $50–$85.

WESTERN APACHE

Western Apache: basketry tray with negative and positive design elements with crosses, coyote tracks, and horses around the upper section, 19th-century hook; 3 inches high, 17¾ inches diameter; ca. 1880–1910; excellent condition, $1,300–$1,600.

Basket, Western Apache, storage basket; design is Apache Mountain Spirit with Scottish Terrier dogs; ca. 1890–1910; 17¼ inches diameter by 19½ inches high, $20,000.
Courtesy of Alexander Anthony/Adobe Gallery. Photo by Robert Reno.

Western Apache: storage basket; design is Apache Mountain Spirit with Scottish terrier dogs; 17¼ inches diameter x 19½ inches high; ca. 1890–1910; $20,000.

Western Apache: devil's claw basket; 9½ inches tall; ca. 1880–1890; excellent condition; $700–$800.

WHITE MOUNTAIN APACHE

White Mountain Apache: basketry tray; six-point design encircled by six animals and six human forms; 15½ inches diameter; excellent condition; $2,600–$3,000.

White Mountain Apache: tray; bought in 1875 from trader on Gila River; 15½ inches diameter; excellent condition; $1000–$1,500.

YOKUT

Yokut: two baskets; basketry cradle, 27 inches; and basketry winowwing tray with redbud, 17 inches; very good condition; California; $200–$250 each.

Yokut: coiled basketry bowl; of squat shouldered form, woven in yellow willow with finely woven dark brown square, circle, triangle and "bowtie" design motifs; 7½ inches diameter; very good condition; $400–$500.

Yokut: tray; bundle construction to single rod, with stepped rectangular designs in rosebud; 16 inches diameter; good condition; $400–$500.

YUROK

Yurok: rare large conical burden basket with brown designs all around; 7 x 4 inches; ca. 1890; mint condition; $675–$800.

Yurok: fine miniature basketry bowl with brown and black designs; 3 x 2 inches; ca. 1920; very good condition; $150–$200.

Yurok: openwork twined basket with bands of cross design; ca. 1910; very good condition; $400–$500.

Yurok: tall openwork twined basketry-covered glass; 11 x 9 inches; ca. 1920; very good condition; $150–$200.

Chapter Four

Blankets and Rugs

≈

Keeping warm and dry was a matter of survival for Native American cultures, as it has been and is for every other. Native Americans learned to make blankets and coverings to keep themselves warm, but what began as a skill developed of necessity evolved into an art form in its own right.

Some New England and northeast tribes wore cloaks and blankets of plant and tree materials. Other tribes simply protected themselves with the skins of the animals common in their area, and still others learned to weave the feathers of local birds into capes and blankets. Then there were the tribes who learned to weave with natural fibers like wool and cotton, and it is those Native Americans we are most particularly interested in in this chapter.

I have chosen to blend two subjects, blankets and rugs, into one chapter and will attempt to keep as much of the information categorized as possible. That, however, is a bit difficult when speaking of Navajo weavers, because so many collectors have used the early blankets as rugs. Keeping that in mind, remember also that the Navajo tribe, though the most accomplished at the art of weaving, was not the only tribe to make decorative and warm blankets and rugs. The creation of Navajo blankets is in the domain of women; today they are recognized as masterpieces of abstract art.

Early blankets, dating from 1800, were simple and came in dull colors of natural wool—such as brown and white. Later *chief blankets* used bold colors and strong designs. Boxes and diamonds were common elements; red bayeta wool and indigo blue were used more freely. Later still came *eye dazzlers,* which used many colors and complex designs, resulting in wonderful optic effects.

Different patterns and styles of blankets are distinctive of different periods. By learning about characteristic elements of particular eras, it is possible to date a prospective purchase. For instance, shoulder blankets with stripes running across the width were made from 1875 to 1890; women's shoulder blankets that have three bands of repeated designs, but are smaller than men's blankets, were made around 1885; while the men's versions were made approximately twenty years earlier. Navajo Indian weavings for the tourist trade were considered garish until weavers were encouraged to go back to vegetal dyes (around 1920). A staple in Indian blanket and rug making was trade cloth or Stroudcloth, so named because it came from Stroud, England. It was introduced in the seventeenth century, and its use spread rapidly because of its appearance and warmth. It was used by almost all Indian tribes.

The tribes in the Southwest used trade cloth less than other North American tribes, possibly because these tribes already made their own fabrics. Trade cloth was available in red, black, navy blue, and green and was made into shawls, blankets, and other garments. Because of its availability and prevalent use, much of the other weaving done by the Amerinds (other than those in the Southwest) became outdated.

Well-known rug dealer Andrew Nagen notes: The old Navajo textile market is moving along briskly. Prices are firm and collectors come into our gallery often, eager to purchase quality. Weavings from all time periods and regional styles are in demand. Collectibility is relative to quality and condition.

In my eighteen years of buying, selling, and appraising Navajo weavings, we have not, as an industry, experienced any price decline. Occasionally, due to periods of furiously paced sales, the market will level out and pause to catch its breath.

I would recommend to anyone interested in purchasing Navajo weavings to learn as much as possible about the subject matter before purchasing. Buy the best quality you can afford. It is far more desirable to purchase a ten-on-a-ten-scale $1,200 rug than a six- or seven-on-a-ten-scale $12,000 weaving. Please do not allow the price alone to determine whether you make any particular purchase. Afford yourself the luxury of listening to your internal response. That response might be the one most worth listening to. Feel free to consult with me or my partner, Ray Dewey, at any time. For those interested in learning more, I recommend the following readings: *Navajo Weaving*, by Charles Amsden; *Walk in Beauty*, by Mary Kahlenberg and Anthony Berlant; *Navajo Textiles*, by Kate Peck Kent; *Navajo Weaving Tradition*, by Selser/Kaufman; any or all books by Marian Rodee; *Navajo Pictoral Weaving*, by Tyrone Campbell and Joel and Kate Kopp.

TRIBES AND THEIR BLANKETS

ACOMA

The Acoma, though not well known for their weaving, made blankets that were used as squaw dresses. The body of the blanket was often black and decorated with embroidered border designs.

CHUMASH

The Chumash Indians of California made blankets out of feathers. Narrow pieces of bird skin were entwined with a cord to strengthen them, then they were woven using a warp and woof technique.

HOPI

Pueblo blankets are traditionally woven by men. The blankets may be white or cream-colored wool with blue, brown, or black horizontal stripes, although the "Moki" blanket (one of the oldest Hopi styles) is woven with dark blue or black stripes. Shoulder blankets often have checkered or tartan patterns.

All blankets woven by the Hopi have a looser weave than those textiles woven by Navajos. Embroidery weaving is routinely used by the Pueblo weavers to decorate their textiles.

MAIDU

Maidu blankets are made of the skins of rabbits which are common animals in California. Strips of skin were left uncured, then knotted into one long piece. The strips were wound back and forth between two stakes horizontally, then the same type of strips were twined up and down—making a blanket that was thick, incredibly soft, and warm.

NAVAJO

Navajo Indians have been weaving rugs and blankets for more than three hundred years, ever since the Pueblo dwellers sought refuge from the Spanish during the Pueblo Revolt of 1680. The dwellers fled to their western neighbors, the Navajo, and introduced their weaving skills. From the 1680s to the late 1880s, the Navajo people learned weaving, then took advantage of the supply of cloth, yarn, and dye that came to their area via the Santa Fe Trail.

Historians have separated Navajo rug making into different periods defined as:

The Classic Period (1700–1850) Examples from this period are identified by the use of upright looms and simple patterns; they primarily consisted of narrow stripes and bands of white, gray, brown, tan, and black. The Spanish introduced indigo blue to the Navajo, and it was widely used. Late in this period, the Mexican-Saltillo serapes that found their way into the upper Rio Grande area began to influence the Navajo weavers and they adapted their designs to include diamonds and broad, wavy band motifs.

The Late Classic Period (1850–1863) Pieces from these years are identified by the broad black, indigo, and white horizontal bands used to make chief's blankets. Later blankets would incorporate red bayeta threads, and designs would include diamonds, boxes, crosses, and stripes.

The serape and poncho serape were also popular during this period. They were made to be worn over the head and cover the wearer's body (both front and back).

As weavers became more highly skilled during this period, they began to experiment. They traded for English material called baize (bayeta) and unraveled the fabric so that they could reweave it into their own designs.

Unfortunately, the period of experimentation died when the Navajo people were captured and forced into imprisoned living.

The Transition Period (1868–1890) These twenty-eight years were a time when the Navajo tribe began to rebuild their flocks of sheep and started to use more commercial yarns; indeed, they used almost any color they could find. The Germantown yarns were introduced in the early 1870s, and the height of Germantown rugs came in the 1890s when crazy designs and gaudy colors became the norm.

As the twentieth century approached, two main changes helped the weaving industry regain its balance—the shift from blanket to rug trading, and the development of regional weaving styles.

The Rug Period (1890–1930) This period marks the era when commercial dyes were beginning to be commonly used among reservation weavers. They experimented with new styles, including a rug with a border.

By 1900, rug weaving was a highly successful trade, and markets, fairs, ceremonies, trading posts, railroads, and publications all helped the Navajo sell their work. Traders such as Juan Hubbell and John B. Moore helped the craft attain higher standards by demanding that the Native American weavers use better dyes and more tightly woven fabrics. Juan Hubbell encouraged a return to the Late Classic Period designs, while John B. Moore ordered rugs that now are identified as the Two Gray Hills style—a bordered rug of natural wool tones of black, brown, and white, patterned with carded blends of beige, tan, and gray with commercially dyed blue and red.

The Revival Period (1930–1940) This era is distinguished by the work of Inja and Leon H. McSparron of Chinle, Arizona, and Mary C. Wheelwright, a Navajo patron. They encouraged weavers in the area to experiment with old vegetal-dye methods. Ultimately they developed terraced and squash blossom patterns in pastel browns, golds, and greens in simple stripes and bands on a borderless fabric—the Chinle regional style. The Chinle style eventually used dyes made by the DuPont Chemical Company and the Diamond Dye Company.

The Wild Ruins style was also the result of native plant dyes. The style was encouraged by Bill and Sallie Lippincott of Wide Ruins Trading Post in the 1930s. Gray and white are used sparingly; combinations may result in soft pastels. The weaver uses the Classic Period stripes and bands on a borderless background. Simplicity is a word often used when describing Wide Ruins rugs.

After the Wide Ruins and Chinle styles were developed, experiments carried out by Nonabah G. Bryan and Stella Young over a period of six years developed eighty-four shades of color dyes. Their research contributed one of the most important changes in Navajo weaving.

During the mid-1930s, the U.S. government implemented a stock reduction program that virtually wiped out the smaller sheepherders of the Navajo nation. Because herds were smaller, less mutton was produced for food, and fewer hides and less wool for rugs. The poverty this program imposed on the tribe was devastating.

The Regional Style Period (1940–present) This was the beginning of six new styles of rugs in the 1950s: Shiprock, Lukachukai, Teec Nos Pos, the new Crystal, Two Gray Hills, and

Ganado. Each is distinguished by style, color, dye, and design so that a collector can identify them at a glance.

The Shiprock rug, called a *Yei*, was developed from stylized sandpaintings and is often small to medium size, with bright, slender, front-facing figures. The background color is usually white or light tan and is finely woven with commercial yarn.

The *Lukachukai* rug is a larger Yei rug of hand-spun wool and synthetic dyes of gray, red, black, or brown. Examples usually have a darker border, and the Yei figures tend to take on a more human appearance.

Teec Nos Pos rugs are tightly woven, with a Persian flair; they are intricately designed with flamboyant colors of bright greens, oranges, reds, and blues. Typically they have a large border that incorporates a design, usually *H*, *T*, or *L* arrangements.

The *Crystal* rug pattern was designed by the owner of the trading post, J. B. Moore. It incorporates numerous crosses, diamonds, terraces, hook and fork patterns, swastikas, and arrows. The Crystal design is borderless and generously embellished with aniline red and outlines of blue. Usually examples are composed of all-vegetal earth-toned colors such as brown, orange, beige, gold, with subtle hints of green, blue, and maroon, in the basic classic pattern.

Two Grey Hills rugs are bordered (usually in black) and made with natural wool tones of black, brown, and white. Other than black, no dyes are used. These rugs are some of the most expensive contemporary Navajo rugs and are characterized by their light weight, careful carding and spinning, and high thread count, sometimes in excess of 120 wefts to the inch.

Ganado rugs are boldly designed, usually a diamond or cross in the middle, sometimes outlined in another color. Deep red is the dominant color, although more contemporary designs have switched to a burgundy. They are larger than the other rugs, sometimes measuring as much as twenty-four by thirty-six feet.

Red Turkish woolen cloth called "balleta" (or bayeta) was first acquired by the Navajo from Mexicans, and later from trading posts that sold it by the bolt. Indians would buy the cloth and unravel it to use the thread for their blankets.

From the time the Navajo first began making bayeta blankets, they were noted for their durability, warmth, and the quality of their weaving. Prices were high for a fine bayeta blanket ($200 in the early 1900s), and have risen. The work on these blankets takes a

Navajo woman many months to complete; the weaving is so fine that these blankets can literally hold water.

Most of the early blankets were made to be worn on the chief's shoulders and might have had a slit in the center for the head, allowing the blanket to be worn as a poncho or serape. The finest examples of these blankets were worn only on festive occasions or at ceremonies.

The Navajo learned about dying wool from Mexicans and Pueblo Indians, whose skills were limited; thus, the color selection seen in Navajo blankets of the time is limited as well. Blue was made from indigo; the bayeta wool was made in reds, black, blues, greens, pinks, oranges, and yellows.

One can tell a bayeta blanket by examining a single thread. Threads from bayeta blankets are single strand, while a triple strand indicates the yarn is Germantown. Other experts argue, though, that one can only tell a true bayeta when it's burned or by its distinctive rough and fuzzy texture.

I believe the best way to hone your identification skills is to attend auctions, go to shows, and visit shops that specialize in Indian material. You will be afforded the opportunity to place your hands on old Indian blankets, to learn their names, and how they feel, from the experts. Pretty soon you, too, will become an expert with the ability to tell a blanket by the feel of it under your fingers—even with your eyes closed!

CHIEF'S BLANKETS Blankets that are woven crosswise instead of lengthwise are called chief's blankets. The Navajo term for these blankets is *Honal-Kladi* or *Honal-Chodi*. Chief's blankets were meant to be wrapped broadside around the body to better display the stripes.

Chief's blankets have gone through three phases. During the first phase these blankets were a favored trade item among the Ute and Sioux. This version had a black "streak" or belt in the center.

Blankets of the second phase had small red rectangles woven into the ends and middles of the blue stripes. This created a twelve-block pattern.

In the 1860s the third-phase chief's blanket pattern emerged with a full diamond in the middle, quarter diamonds on each corner, and half diamonds in the center of each edge.

During the 1880s, weavers began incorporating pictorial elements and cross motifs into their textiles.

Though originally noted that chief's blankets were the property of men of high standing in the tribe, there is much documentation of women wearing the blankets (i.e., Brule Sioux women wore them on special occasions).

When it is almost impossible to stretch the stitches of the weft so that you may see the warp, the blanket would likely hold water. Blankets of this quality are the most collectible and are the ones that bring the highest auction prices. Such blankets are few and far between now, though the quality of today's Navajo blankets is of the highest order and unchallenged by blankets woven any other way.

Perhaps that is the most amazing thing about Navajo weaving—the work is still woven by hand, and their products are far superior to anything that is machine-made.

Germantown yarns were introduced to the Navajo by 1850, and the Indians, not satisfied with the texture, twisted it to make it firmer and tighter. These yarns were dyed with vegetable dye, which made the colors reliable and resistant. Though some feel the introduction of Germantown yarns produced a deterioration in the Navajo blankets, certain weavers did their best work with these yarns and continued to produce weavings that could hold water.

Certain trade posts, such as Hubbell's in Ganado, Arizona, began to offer these blankets for sale. The first Navajo blankets Juan Hubbell put up for sale were marked to sell at $2 each. Little by little, Hubbell and his partner, C. N. Cotton, urged Navajo blanket weavers to produce more of their weavings. The Indians saw a growth in their income and were pleased. Hubbell and Cotton saw a way to make money, and they were pleased. A viable commercial industry was born.

More trading posts got on the bandwagon. Soon, aniline dyes were introduced to the Navajo women who lived around Fort Defiance. Later, cotton warp was sold at low prices to Indian weavers, consequently creating a market for cheap blankets.

The Navajo women were urged to make more blankets in less time, and they began to take less care in cleaning their wool. The result was wool that did not take a proper dye and produced uneven colors. All these factors combined to make a blanket of lesser quality, looser weave, and harsher fabric. Ultimately this resulted in lower pay for the weaver. The art of weaving deteriorated quickly. Thankfully, there were those in the business determined to build weaving back into the art form it once was.

Dealers who understood what was happening—that poor-quality articles could only result in little or no sales—decided to take it upon themselves to refuse to trade any blanket that was not of the highest quality.

J. B. Moore, whose trading post was near what is now Crystal, New Mexico, took it upon himself to take the raw wool the Navajos produced and ship it east for cleaning. After cleaning, the wool was shipped back to New Mexico and the Indians were free to card, spin, and dye the yarn in the manner they chose.

The weavers who had proven themselves proficient were given specific amounts of wool—enough for a particular size blanket—and only given more when the first supplies were returned as a finished work. As a result, Moore's mail-order business was successful, and the quality of the rugs produced by the people working for him was much higher, thank to his innovative methods. Through Moore's efforts, the Navajo improved their weaving skills, and the quality of their work soon rose to a standard close to what it had been in years past.

As demand for blankets and rugs made from the wool of their sheep grew, the Navajo had to be taught more advanced methods of raising their sheep to maximize wool production. In 1911 the U.S. government put together a plan for Navajo sheep breeding and taught them what to do to increase the size of their animals, and the quality of mutton and wool. These suggestions were carried out, and by 1912, blanket production quadrupled.

The Navajos have used colors as symbols in their weaving since the advent of the art. Green is the color that symbolizes youth, while yellow, blue, orange, and red represent maturity or harvesttime. Brown and gray represent death and decay, and black is symbolic of mourning. Nature is the basis of Indian color symbolism. If one takes the time to research their history, the reasoning behind the symbolism is easy to understand. Red, for instance, the color associated with the life-giving sun, is the favorite of the Navajo weavers.

The dyes to make the colors for Navajo rugs were made from natural ingredients. Sumac, yellow ocher, and piñon gum were boiled together to make black dye; yellow dye came from the flowering tops of *Bigelowia graveolens*; red from the bark of *Alnus incana var. virescens* (black alder) and juniper twigs mixed with a few other ingredients; and blue came from a native blue clay which was boiled with sumac leaves.

As there is symbolism connected with the colors that are used in Navajo blankets and rugs, so is there symbolism in the design elements incorporated into the weaving. Each weaver infuses some of her own thoughts and interpretations of designs into her weaving, but the origin of the designs reaches far back into the Navajo's history. Designs were borrowed from the Mexicans, the Pueblo tribes, the sacred sandpaintings of the medicine man, and from nature itself. An "escape hatch" of sorts is built into each design— an exit for the weaver's spirit so it does not get trapped in her work. It is an intentional error to declare their knowledge of the small place a human holds in this universe.

Some of the designs medicine men used, which were later copied by weavers, featured the Navajo gods—the *Yei.* Divine characters, the Yei were both male and female and are shown in these depictions as extremely long and thin beings wearing masks.

A male Yei wears a helmetlike mask, and is known by the eagle plumes or owl feathers attached to the mask. He is also identified by the spruce twig he holds in his left hand and the gourd in his right. The female, usually dressed in white, is indicated by her rectangular mask, yellow arms and chest (females were created of yellow corn, males of white), and by the spruce wand held in each hand. Each Yei figure represents a different god. There are Ganaskidi, which are mountain sheep or bighorn gods; Hastseyalti or the Talking God; and Hastsehogan. The Rainbow Goddess usually borders the depiction.

Corn is one of the most important foods to the Navajo, and represents a vital part of their ceremonies. Its symbol is used everywhere in paintings, on masks, and in the designs for rugs and blankets.

Sunbeams are made of parallel straight lines in scarlet and are often depicted in sandpaintings or on masks and in designs on blankets and rugs.

The queue symbol, representing the scalps of enemies, is painted on depictions of the god Tobadzistsini or Child of the Water.

Lightning is represented by zigzag lines, which Navajo myths say gods use as ropes. When painted in white on a black background, they represent lightning on the face of a cloud.

Geometric designs used by weavers incorporate parallel lines, zigzags, triangles, spurs, quadrilaterals, hourglass figures, rectangles, double triangles, terraced edges, S-forms, crooks, feathers, stars, key patterns, bird forms, mosaic patterns, and any combination of the above.

The trading post owner Juan Hubbell had a group of blanket designs painted in oil and hung them on his office walls. "Modern" Navajo blankets appeared with designs that had names such as Tsin alnazoid (Roman cross), Kos yischin (cloud image), Be 'ndastlago noltizh (cornered zigzag), and Nahokhos (swastika cross). They were used in conjuction with the old designs or on their own, according to the weaver's preference.

When weavers first began interpreting Yei figures or kachina figures in their blankets and rugs, it upset the Indian population greatly, and a dealer who had such a piece for sale in his trading post considered his life in jeopardy. After the initial arguments, dissension was still strong and the tribe still believed the sacred Yei figure should not be represented on something more lasting than a sandpainting. However, the weavers continued to make a few here and there, and today the figures are commonly seen as part of rug and blanket designs. Older versions, however, are still rare and considered highly collectible.

NORTHWEST COAST

Though Chilkat women, like the Navajo women, wove the blankets of the tribe, the blanket patterns were designed by the men of the tribe, and deviation from those designs was forbidden. Aristocratic leaders wore the Chilkat robes displaying the animal totem of the clan in tribal ceremonies.

Chilkat blankets were made of mountain goat wool, which was tightly woven with yellow cedar bark. The Tlingit tribe (of which the Chilkat was a division) produced most of them, and they are considered the robes of Northwest Coast Indian nobility.

Their abstract representations of crest animals were woven into the fabric, and three edges of the blanket have thick fringe. Ravens, salmon, and whale's heads are commonly depicted on these nineteenth-century blankets. The "diving whale" blankets are the most common and, at first glance, examples appear identical.

Actually, the fineness of yarn and quality of weave differ in each blanket. Early and mid-nineteenth-century examples are finer than later ones.

The blankets are woven on a bar loom, which resembles the letter *H*. The horizontal bar on this loom could be set at a level that was comfortable for the weaver. The warp was suspended from the loom in lengths that followed the form of the blanket—this is known as the "warp-weighted loom" technique.

The threads that were yet unwoven were kept wrapped in bags to protect them from soiling since it took six months to a year to make a blanket.

The actual weaving was done in a tapestry-twined technique, and the long fringed sections were filled in with goat wool when the weaving was completed. Though these blankets could be as large as seventy-two by thirty-eight inches, more commonly a dance apron was eighteen by thirty-eight inches.

Button blankets evolved when the Northwest Coast tribes began trading with the white Europeans and colonists who visited them during the latter part of the eighteenth century.

These blankets were usually made from blue Hudson Bay Company blankets, which were bordered on three sides with red trade material. An appliqué crest would be sewn to the blanket and outlined with mother-of-pearl buttons.

Because mountain goat wool was highly prized, often the only blankets in a Nootka tribe belonged to the chiefs of the tribe, who wore them only on ceremonial occasions. The blankets were decorated with bold designs of the region.

Haida, Tlingit, and Kwakiutl tribes all made blankets in the late nineteenth and early twentieth centuries.

SALISH

Salish blankets were sometimes finger-woven, as the Tlingit blankets were, but often they were twill-plaited, and usually white. The materials they used included mountain goat wool, down, cattail fluff, and hair from white dogs.

The mountain goat wool was cleaned and the coarser outer hairs removed. The finer hairs were beaten to straighten them, and other fibers may have been added (i.e., bear, raccoon, squirrel fur) to increase the thickness of the weave. The fibers were worked onto spindles with rods that were often three to four feet long.

A small, white-haired, domesticated dog was bred by these people for its wool, and some have proposed that the animal may have been in the Pomeranian or spitz family.

Designs used in these early blankets were complicated and colorful. We do not know the actual colors they used because no examples have survived. Sketches show us there were three types of blankets: a plain diagonal weave; a twined-weave "nobility blanket"; and the decorative twined weave.

The white blankets were brightened with clay and were cleaned with beating. Many were used as shrouds and buried with the bodies of tribe members, leaving us few examples of this type of weaving.

In more modern times, the Salish used commercial yarns and a weaving frame, which produce finer, more decorative textiles.

ZUNI

The Zuni style of weaving differs from the Navajo mainly in quality. The Navajo are the superior weavers. Also, Zuni work is characteristically black or dark blue wool woven in a diagonal style.

Squaw dresses were basically blankets woven diagonally and worn wrapped around the wearer under the right arm and fastened over the left shoulder.

RUGS

At an exhibit held at the Museum of Our National Heritage in Lexington, Massachusetts (February–July 1988), anthropologists explored the symbolism of Navajo rug designs. Through this exhibition, anthropologists showed that three Navajo deities—Changing Woman, Born for the Water, and Monster Slayer—show up in nearly every Navajo rug ever woven. The symbols are also evident in other areas of Navajo culture (e.g., on petroglyphs and certain ceremonial objects).

The idea that weaving patterns have cultural meanings has ruffled a few feathers among historians and anthropologists. Up until this exhibit, the theory had not been so thoroughly researched.

Navajo appear to be the last of the rug-making Indians in North America, and their work sells for very high prices because the common assumption is that if it was woven by a Navajo, it will last forever. Navajo rugs, as their blankets, are woven completely by hand and may take the weaver many months to complete.

The Chilkat weavers of the Northwest Coast have almost become extinct. There are fewer women alive who retain this knowledge with each passing year, and the eastern weavers have been even less interested in preserving what rug-weaving skills they once had.

The finest Navajo rugs are woven in Two Grey Hills, New Mexico, an area between Shiprock and Gallup, New Mexico, but rugs from Crystal, Wide Ruin, Teec Nos Pos, and Ganado are also well known. (The typical black, gray, and red Navajo rugs are representative of the ones made in Klagetoh and Ganado.) Wide Ruins rugs were made of subtler colors, in beiges, light pinks, and whites, and designs were often simple geometric figures separated by stripes of varying widths. The deep red background and simple designs of Ganado rugs are often revivals of earlier patterns.

Navajo are weaving fewer rugs than they once did, and because they are scarce, the prices are affected. A three-by-five foot rug could take the maker four hundred hours to weave. The Navajo women weave the fibers of their rugs so tightly that some rugs will hold water. A good rug may have thirty threads to the inch; the better ones have ninety, some even more.

Navajo eye dazzler rugs, made with commercial Germantown yarns from Pennsylvania, were made from 1880 to 1910. The sand-painting rugs, which depict the sacred Yei figures, always have a conscious mistake incorporated into their design, and their borders are never closed because the weaver does not want to trap his spirit in the piece. Perhaps one of the most difficult designs for a weaver to accomplish is two-faced weaving—wherein each side of the rug has a different design. Zigzags and rectangles are the basic patterns of storm design rugs, which have been made since 1900 in the area near Tuba City, Arizona.

Contemporary New Lands weavers are being encouraged to switch from aniline-dyed wool to vegetal-dyed wool. The design they use is still Teec Nos Pos, but the rugs have a three-dimensional look. The new style has given weavers a boost because the soft pastel colors of the rugs, combined with their visual impact, has opened up a new retail market for them. The colors and styles of these new weavings are adaptable to styles beyond the traditional southwestern style into which they have, heretofore, been incorporated.

PRICES

CHIMAYO

Chimayo: woven wool in blue, gray, red, and white; 7 x 12 inches (including fringe); very good condition; $20–$30.

Chimayo sampler: red, gray, aqua, and white in large Thunderbird and banded designs; ca. early 20th century; 14½ x 15 inches; very good condition; $20–$25.

Chimayo wall hanging: heavy yarn in green, red, and tan design with red fringe at bottom; two small soil spots; 30 x 72 inches; very good condition; $50–$75.

Chimayo weaving: woven fringed wool in blue, red, green, and white; 14 x 17 inches (including fringe); very good condition; $20–$30.

Chimayo: woven wool in gray, black, red, and white; 14 x 16 inches (including fringe); very good condition; $20–$25.

Chimayo: tightly hand-woven with 100 percent wool yarns with a gray field, large stylized diamond pattern in black and white, with broad and narrow bands in a deep wine red; ca. 1900; 4 x 7 feet; very good condition; $230–$300.

Chimayo: central bird design with storm design interior, stripes, and whirling log design; multicolors on gray background; minute amount of color bleeding; ca. 1930; 47 x 84 inches; very good condition; $150–$200.

Chimayo: woven, fringed, in black, white, blue, aqua, green, and red; 7 x 11 inches; very good condition; $25–$40.

Chimayo: woven wool in blue, gray, red, black, and white; 9½ x 23 inches (including fringe); very good condition; $20–$30.

Classic Mexican Saltillo serape: hand-spun wool, natural dyes of red, green, blue, gold, purple, white; fringed trim; ca. 1750–1800; approximately 51 x 94 inches; excellent condition; $16,000–$22,000.

HAIDA

Haida button: fine blanket with large bear and trim in old pearl buttons; ca. 1920; 56 x 56 inches; very good condition; $700–$920.

Haida button: blue trade cloth button blanket with killer whale design; pearl buttons and red trade cloth trim; 65 x 6 inches; very good condition; $850–$1,150.

HUDSON BAY

Hudson Bay: four points; 66 x 81 inches; very good condition; $50–$100.

Hudson Bay: striped unusual color Hudson Bay Indian blanket; ca. 1920; 84 x 69 inches; very good condition; $60–$115.

KWAKIUTL

Kwakiutl button: trade cloth blanket with beautiful white pearl button designs; ca. 1920; very good condition; $515–$750.

NAVAJO

Navajo: hand-spun wool; white, brown, gray, red, taupe; red and taupe are synthetic-dyed, others no dye; excellent condition; 1920s; 50 x 77 inches; $2,500–$3,200.

Navajo: hand-spun wool; red, brown, gray, tan, white; the red is synthetic-dyed, other colors no dye; 1920s; 57 x 41½ inches; very good condition; $1,200–$1,800.

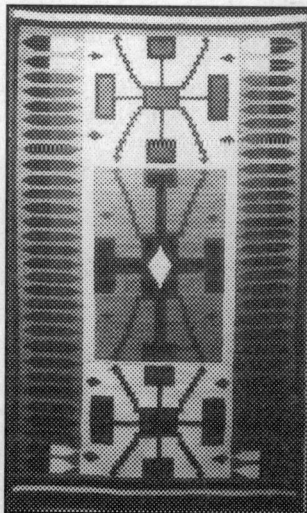

Blankets/Rugs, Navjo rug, 1920s, hand-spun wool; white, brown, gray, red, taupe; red and taupe are synthetic-dyed, others no dye; excellent condition; 50 x 77 inches; $2,500–$3,200. Courtesy of Dewey Galleries, Ltd., Andrew Nagen. Photo by Robert Reno.

Blankets/Rugs, Navajo rug, 1920s, hand-spun wool; red, bown, gray, tan, white; the red is synthetic-dyed, other colors no dye; 57 x 41½ inches; very good condition; $1,200–1,800. Courtexy of Dewey Galleries, Ltd., Andrew Nagen. Photo by Robert Reno.

Navajo: serrated diamond cross design in red, orange, gray, natural, and brown; 2 feet 2 inches x 4 feet 3 inches; very good condition; $75–$160.

Navajo: red, white, and natural with red and white stripes, gray diamond clouds, wool; 3 feet 5 inches x 4 feet 10 inches; very good condition; $550–$750.

Navajo: stepped geometric design in shades of brown, beige, and red; 3 feet 8½ inches x 5 feet 8½ inches; good condition; $450–$650.

Navajo: triangular design in brown, cream, and gold wools; 3 feet 3 inches x 5 feet 6 inches; very good condition; $175–$275.

Navajo: hourglass design, red with brown, beige, and white steps on natural background; 3 feet 7 inches x 4 feet 11 inches; good condition; $200–$300.

Navajo: Pueblo design with diamonds in light and dark brown; 4 feet 1 inch x 5 feet 5 inches; very good condition; $500–$700.

Navajo: sawtooth diamonds with brown, red, and white on gray; 4 feet x 3 feet; very good condition; $200–$400.

Navajo: jagged diamond center with two crosses and rosy openwork in shades of brown, natural, and rose; 4 feet x 5 feet; very good condition; $400–$500.

Navajo: geometric designs with stepped feather pattern in shades of brown, beige, and red; 4 feet 2 inches x 5 feet 10½ inches; good condition; $700–$900.

Navajo: geometric design with arrows and stars in shades of brown and beige; 4 feet 2 inches x 5 feet 10½ inches; very good condition; $750–$950.

Navajo: striped in natural and aniline red, natural, yellow, black, and gray; 4 feet 4 inches x 5 feet 10 inches; excellent condition; $600–$800.

Navajo: American flag design in red, white, and blue; 4 feet 7 inches x 2 feet 3 inches; very good condition; $400–$600.

Navajo: natural wools with a stepped block design; 4 feet 7 inches x 3 feet; good condition; $100–$200.

Navajo: serrated diamonds with dark brown, beige, natural, and light blue; 4 feet 8 inches x 3 feet 2 inches; very good condition; $250–$350.

Navajo: red center with connecting brown crosses, double border of arrowheads; 5 feet x 3 feet 5 inches; very good condition; $400–$600.

Navajo: center of double diamond design surmounted by one large diamond in white, with stepped pattern in black and red and a T-shape in red and white; 5 feet 2 inches x 6 feet 6 inches; excellent condition; $1,500–$2,200.

Navajo: red, brown, and white cornstalk design on natural; five feet 3 inches x 3 feet; excellent condition; $275–$375.

Navajo: striped design with blue middle stripe, brown, red, natural, yellow-beige; 5 feet 5 inches x 3 feet 11 inches; very good condition; $400–$600.

Navajo: sawtooth diamond pattern in red, natural, beige, and brown with a dark brown sawtooth border; 5 feet 7 inches x 3 feet 3 inches; very good condition; $400–$600.

Navajo: small central cross with serrated diamond and rolling blocks with a diamond border, in gray, brown, beige, and natural; 6 feet x 10 feet 10 inches; very good condition; $1,200–$1,600.

Navajo: rectangles in red, black, natural, maroon, and orange, hand-carded and spun wool; 6 feet x 8 feet 3 inches; good condition; $1,000–$3,000.

Navajo: three central crosses placed vertically, fine geometric patterns in red, shades of brown, beige, and gray, with brown border; 6 feet 10 inches x 3 feet 11 inches; overall good condition; $900–$1,200.

Navajo: central cross and keys surrounded by hooks with four hourglass designs in gold, rose, gray, and brown; 6 feet 6 inches x 4 feet 2 inches; very good condition; $700–$900.

Navajo: central cross design with four corner crosses in red, tan, and dark brown; 6 feet 1 inch x 3 feet 3½ inches; very good condition; $275–$400.

Navajo: double-hooked medallions, Greek key, and red diamonds in shades of brown, beige, and gray; 7 feet 10 inches x 4 feet 7 inches; good condition; $500–$700.

Navajo: white, red, brown, and natural in five-diamond design with T border, eight feathers; 8 feet 1 inch x 3 feet 4 inches; good condition; $350–$450.

Navajo: central cross motif with four gray crosses; diagonal brown stripe with red feathers; 9 feet 7 inches x 5 feet 1 inch; very good condition; $1,500–$1,900.

Navajo: Greek key pattern with interwoven brown and red, with double lightning strike in center; 9 feet 8 inches x 5 feet 8 inches; very good condition; $1,500–$1,900.

Navajo: bayeta man's serape; red, white, and blue; red is cochineal-dyed raveled cloth; blue is dyed with indigo; ca. 1870–1875; 52 x 66 inches; mint condition; $40,000–$50,000.

Navajo: old classic with bayeta; recarded and hand-spun wool in indigo blue, lilac, and bayeta red, vegetal green, recarded pink, gray-brown, and white; ca. 1865–1875; 45 x 66½ inches; very good condition; $7,500–$9,500.

Navajo: hand-spun wool; red, dark brown, walnut, white; red is synthetic-dyed, others no dye; ca. 1915–1925; 66 x 35 inches; excellent condition; $1,800–$2,400.

Navajo: hand-spun wool; red, gray, brown, white; ca. 1935–1945; 37 x 60 inches; excellent condition; $1,000–$1,500.

Navajo: red, white, black, peach, gold; colors are synthetic-dyed; hand-spun wool; natural white color; ca. 1935–1945; 70 x 40 inches; excellent condition; $750–$1,200.

Blankets/Rugs, Navajo rug, ca. 1915–1925, hand-spun wool; red, dark brown, walnut, white; red is synthetic-dyed, others no dye; excellent condition; 66 x 35 inches; $1,800–$2,400. Courtesy of Dewey Galleries, Ltd., Andrew Nagen. Photo by Robert Reno.

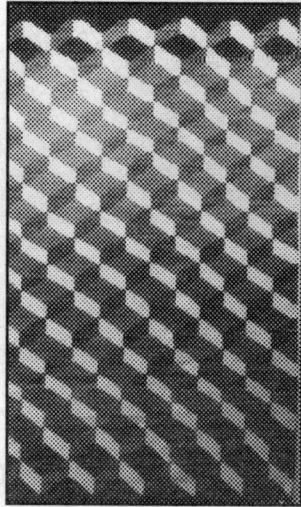

Blankets/Rugs, Navajo rug, ca. 1935–1945, hand-spun wool; red, gray, brown, white; excellent condition; 37 x 60 inches; $1,000–$1,500. Courtesy of Dewey Galleries, Ltd., Andrew Nagen. Photo by Robert Reno.

Navajo, chief's: third-phase chief's style, transitional, dark brown, beige, red, and blue-gray; 4 feet 10 inches x 6 feet; very good condition; $3,500–$4,500.

Navajo, chief's; third phase; hand-spun wool on wool warp; red, dark brown, faded indigo blue, and natural; ca. 1880; 50 x 67 inches; very good condition; $6,000–$6,700.

Navajo, chief's: third-phase chief's blanket; bayeta and indigo weave; one of the finest 19th-century blankets ever handled by dealers in the Southwest; ca. 1875; 53 x 76 inches; very good condition; $28,750–$40,250.

Navajo, child's: hand-spun wool, raveled and recarded reds, indigo blue, and natural white, and delicate green with serrated dia-

Blankets/Rugs, Navajo rug, ca. 1935–1945; red, white, black, peach, gold; colors are synthetic-dyed; hand-spun wool; white is no dye; excellent condition; 70 x 40 inches; $750–$1,200. Courtesy of Dewey Galleries, Ltd., Andrew Nagen. Photo by Robert Reno.

mond pattern; ca. 1870–1880; 30 x 48 inches; condition good to better; $1,000–$2,000.

Navajo, child's blanket: transitional with red background and arrowhead design in black, white, and yellow with a center stripe in black and yellow; 31 x 50 inches; very good condition; $2,000–$2,800.

Navajo, child's: classic; ca. 1860; 31 x 52 inches; very good condition; $34,500–$40,250.

Navajo, child's: classic child's blanket; ca. 1860; 31 x 52 inches; very good condition; $34,500–$40,250.

Navajo, child's: classic child's blanket; ca. 1865; 32 x 47 inches; very good condition; $10,950–$11,500.

Navajo, child's: classic; ca. 1865; 32 x 47 inches; very good condition; $11,000–11,500.

Navajo, child's: classic child's blanket, ca. 1860; very good condition; $24,150–$26,450.

Navajo, child's: classic; ca. 1860; very good condition; $24,150–$26,450.

Navajo, child's classic wearing blanket: native yarn and bayeta with cochineal, indigo, and green dye; ca. 1860–1870; 38½ x 60 inches; very good condition; $50,000–$59,000.

Navajo, Chinle rug: hand-spun wool; red, gray, black, white, turquoise, walnut; ca. 1935–1940; 36 x 61 inches; excellent condition; $900–$1,200.

Navajo contemporary tapestry: woven by Salina Yazzie; hand-spun wool; woven of 15 soft-shaded natural colors; "Dewey Galleries does not regularly sell contemporary weaving. We felt this example was worthy for our gallery. The best we've seen in a decade. This contemporary weaving is stylistically reminiscent of late Classic period weavings dating 1865–75" (Andrew Nagen); 72 x 53 inches; $10,000–$12,000.

Navajo, Crystal area: hand-carded, red, gray, tan, brown, and natural; 2 feet 5 inches x 4 feet 2 inches; good condition; $90–$200.

Navajo, Crystal area: vegetal dye with dark brown, gold, light gray-brown, white, and medium brown in narrow and wide banded arrowhead and hourglass designs; ca. 1950s; 60 x 105 inches; very good condition; $975–$1,550.

Navajo, weaving; choice Crystal weaving with central lozenge and fishhook motif; ca. 1930; 81 x 53 inches; very good condition; $700–$900.

Navajo, Crystal area pictoral rug: hand-spun wool; brown, gray, white, red, burgundy, gold, salmon; ca. 1915–25; 41 x 64 inches; excellent condition; $7,500–$9,000.

Blankets/Rugs, Navajo Chinle rug, ca. 1935–1940; hand-spun wool; red, gray, black, white, turquoise, walnut; excellent condition, 36 x 61 inches; $900–$1,200. Courtesy of Dewey Galleries, Ltd., Andrew Nagen. Photo by Robert Reno.

Navajo, Crystal rug: hand-spun wool; light brown, dark brown, white (no dyes); ca. 1925–1935; 51 x 77 inches; excellent condition; $6,500–$8,500.

Navajo eye dazzler: 100 percent wool hand-spun in red, black, and natural white serrated design with no borders, tasseled corners; ca. 1900s; 60 x 31 inches; generally good condition; $200–$400.

Navajo eye dazzler: red background with beige and brown; 5 feet 5 inches x 2 feet 8 inches; good condition; $125–$200.

Navajo eye dazzler: in turquoise, black, red, tan, and white; 4 feet 1 inch x 2 feet 11 inches; very good condition; $150–$250.

Navajo eye dazzler: dazzler serrated pattern in black, red, white, mustard, and gray; 7 feet 6 inches x 18 feet; fine condition; $6,000–$8,000.

Navajo eye dazzler bureau scarf: in mauve, blue, cranberry, and red-orange; 21 x 46 inches; very good condition; $1,700–$2,300.

Navajo eye dazzler: 100 percent wool in red, black, brown, and natural white in a series of connected triangles in a borderless pattern; ca. 1940–1950; 61 x 28 inches; very good condition; $185–$385.

Navajo eye dazzler rugs (two): in reds, blacks, browns, cream, and gold; 3 feet 8 inches x 2 feet 8½ inches and 4 feet 10½ inches x 2 feet 9 inches; very good condition; $150–$250 each.

Blankets/Rugs, Navajo Crystal rug, ca. 1925–1935, hand-spun wool; light brown, dark brown, white (no dyes); excellent condition; 51 x 77 inches; $6,500–$8,500. Courtesy of Dewey Galleries, Ltd., Andrew Nagen. Photo by Robert Reno.

Navajo, figural: wool hand-spun, serrated center pattern in red with borders of natural white and deep brown serrations; in the middle are two birdlike forms with wings and tails; beige background with terraced geometric shapes within terraced border; ca. 1920s; 67 x 44 inches; good condition; $800–$1,100.

Navajo figural: with twelve Yei heads, bows, arrows, and feathers in red, black, cream, natural, and brown; 4 x 6 feet; very good condition; $2,000–$2,400.

Navajo, Gallup throw: red, white, and black; 1 foot 7 inches x 1 foot 8 inches; good condition; $20–$50.

Navajo, Ganado: 100 percent wool hand-spun in red, brown, ocher, and natural white, with two serrated and terraced diamond forms in the center, with diamonds in the middle, beige background, brown border design; ca. 1920–1940; 43 x 32½ inches; generally good condition; $185–$385.

Navajo, Ganado area rug: stepped central design with log design, in red, gray, tan, and brown, hand-carded and spun wool; 4 feet 1 inch x 7 feet 2 inches; good condition; $700–$1,000.

Navajo, Germantown; fragmentary Germantown weaving; ca. 1880; 62 x 43 inches; very good condition; $235–$300.

Navajo, Germantown; tight-weave Germantown rug with red background and indigo, white, and yellow design; 24 x 31 inches; good condition; $475–$675.

Navajo, Germantown: choice, fringed, with geometric and cross designs; ca. 1900; 40 x 22 inches; very good condition; $150–$200.

Navajo, Germantown: Germantown chief-pattern blanket, finely woven in dark green, red, and natural, corner tassels; 4 feet 8 inches x 5 feet 10 inches; near mint condition; $8,000–$11,000.

Navajo, Germantown blanket: cotton warp, red, green, yellow, orange, purple, black, white, burgundy; ca. 1885–1895; 83 x 69 inches; excellent condition; $18,000–$24,000.

Navajo, Germantown double saddle blanket: finely woven in shades of green, light brown, beige, and gray, fringed with twill design in red, lavender, and green diamonds; 37 x 52 inches; condition overall good; $1,600–$2,000.

Navajo, Germantown fringed: fancy; aqua, red, gray, black, and white; ca. 1900; 36 x 39 inches (including fringe); very good condition; $525–$750.

Navajo, Germantown sampler: red, white, green, and black; ca. 1900; 19 x 20 inches; very good condition; $85–$150.

Navajo, Germantown transitional: bold black, red-orange, and white; ca. 1900; 65 x 84 inches; very good condition; $2,875–$4,000.

Navajo, Germantown weaving: woven in celery, red, gold, white, black, dark green, and light pink with an eye dazzler pattern composed of rows of serrated wedges and diamonds, remnant wool fringe on both ends; 38 x 59 inches; very good condition; $975–$1,100.

Navajo, Germantown: maroon, green, and white; ca. 1900; 19 x 20¾ inches; mint condition; $100–$150.

Navajo, Germantown: woven on a bright red ground with natural white, teal green, and lavender gray Germantown yarns in a pattern of zigzag chevrons in counterpoint; tightly woven; 30 x 50 inches; fine condition; $1,900–$2,300.

Navajo, Germantown: dark blue, gray, yellow, orange, red-orange, and white in diamonds within a large, serrated diamond design; ca. 1900; 56 x 84 inches; very good condition; $1,400–$2,100.

Navajo, Germantown: woven on a red ground in mustard, gold, olive, rust, and dark red, with serrated joined diamonds, bound at top with dark red wool, fringed at bottom; 58 x 33 inches; good/very good condition (minor roughness); $375–$575.

Navajo, Germantown: storm pattern with red, yellow, blue-gray, maroon, white, purple, and light gray; ca. 1900s; 64 x 85 inches; very good condition; $4,275–$6,000.

Navajo, Klagatoh rug: classic design with stepped terrace border in red, gray, black, and natural, hand-carded and spun wool; 6 feet x 9 feet; good condition; $775–$950.

Navajo mat: white and red geometrics on black ground; 18 x 18½ inches; very good condition; $65–$85.

Navajo miniature rug and loom: containing a partially finished weaving in black, orange, yellow, and white; 13¾ x 11 inches; very good condition; $25–$45.

Navajo pictorial: woven on a cream ground with a gray, red, and dark brown border encompassing a central design of turquoise, red, dark brown, black, khaki, and pumpkin; chickens, horses, cattle, ant-people figures, buckets, feathers, and cowboys holding branding irons; 52 x 84 inches; good/very good condition (minor dye runs and edge roughness); $4,150–$4,600.

Navajo regional: 100 percent wool in a series of serrated zigzag bands in natural white, deep red, black, and neutral brownish gray, with a border of black and white crook or key forms; ca. 1920–1940s; 48 x 80 inches; very good condition; $650–$900.

Navajo rug—fringed pillow sampler: dark brown, red, white, and gray-brown in diamond designs; ca. 1960s; 15½ x 17½ inches (including fringe); very good condition; $40–$60.

Navajo runner: red background with two winged figures, in black, brown, orange, and natural; excellent condition; $900–$1,200.

Navajo saddle blanket: very early vegetable dye chief's pattern; ca. 1910; 33 x 26 inches; very good condition; $115–$175.

Navajo saddle blanket: transitional Greek key design in red, gray, and dark gray; 33 x 33 inches; good condition; $250–$450.

Navajo saddle blanket/rug: red, brown, gray, and white diamonds; very good condition; $75–$150.

Navajo saddle blanket/child's blanket: red, white, light blue, dark blue, green; hand-spun wool and raveled cloth; colors are natural-dyed, white no dye; twill-woven; ca. 1860s; 31 x 51 inches; good condition; $7,000–$9,000.

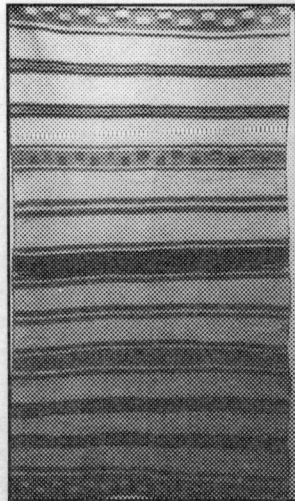

Blankets/Rugs, Navajo saddle blanket/child's blanket, 1860s; red, white, light blue, dark blue, green; hand-spun wool and raveled cloth; colors are natural-dyed, white no dye; 31 x 51 inches; twill-woven; good condition; $7,000–$9,000. Courtesy of Dewey Galleries, Ltd., Andrew Nagen. Photo by Robert Reno.

Navajo saddle blanket: rare chief's-style, striped; ca. 1890; 30 x 30 inches; very good condition; $125–$175.

Navajo saddle blanket: Germantown; diamond design with red, blue, gray, white, and green; 21 x 21 inches; very good condition; $160–$230.

Navajo saddle blanket: Germantown; "Sunday saddle" type with black, white, and green in banded and vertical zigzag (serrated) columns; ca. 1900; 27½ x 35 inches; very good condition; $1,325–$1,600.

Navajo saddle blanket: hand-woven with stars in the corners; ca. 1940; 23 x 22 inches; very good condition; $40–$60.

Navajo saddle blanket: hand-woven natural wool; ca. 1920; 28 x 15 inches; very good condition; $35–$60.

Navajo saddle blanket: natural wool, hand-woven; ca. 1940; 29 x 27 inches; very good condition; $40–$60.

Navajo saddle blanket: classic, hand-woven, striped; ca. 1940; 30 x 30 inches; very good condition; $25–$45.

Navajo saddle blanket: rare chief's style, striped; ca. 1890; 30 x 30 inches; very good condition; $125–$175.

Navajo saddle blanket: extralong staple wool with marvelous sheen; ca. 19th century; 30 x 48 inches; good condition (wear at ends and selvage); $100–$155.

Navajo saddle blanket: woven with 100 percent hand-spun wool and some Germantown yarns, in bright crimson red, deep and pale Germantown violet yarns, beige, natural gray, with three groups of stripes; ca. 1880s; 32 x 53 inches; good condition (embattled edges, some soiling and yarn pull); $300–$400.

Navajo saddle blanket: Ganado double-dyed red, gray, black, and natural diamond design; 33 x 61 inches; very good condition; $110–$175.

Navajo saddle blanket: rare "pulled warp" diagonal weave; ca. 1900; 46 x 30 inches; very good condition; $55–$85.

Navajo sampler: transitional interlocking cube design in black, gray, and yellow with red background; 21 x 33 inches; very good condition; $300–$400.

Navajo sampler: serrated diamonds with central cross design in red and black, with orange diamond and white outline; 22 x 27 inches; very good condition; $350–$450.

Navajo sampler: Germantown; on loom; 1910; 13 inches diameter x 19 inches high; very good condition; $300–$400.

Navajo sampler: Germantown; orange, burgundy, red, white, and green; ca. 1900–1910; 14 x 21 inches; very good condition; $75–$110.

Navajo sampler: Germantown; red, yellow, gray, maroon, and white; ca. 1900; 17½ x 18 inches; very good condition; $55–$100.

Navajo sampler: dark brown, white, and orange in serrated diamond and half-cross designs; ca. early to mid 20th century; 18 x 20½ inches; very good condition; $30–$50.

Navajo sampler: orange, black, and white in serrated designs; ca. 1940s; 19½ x 20½ inches; very good condition; $40–$75.

Navajo sampler: black, white, red, and gray in a large, serrated diamond design; ca. 1930s–1940s; 19½ x 20½ inches; very good condition; $25–$50.

Navajo storm pattern rug: hand-spun wool; red, gray, black, white, rust; red and rust are synthetic colors, others no dye; ca. 1920s; 66 x 41 inches; excellent condition; $1,200–$1,800.

Navajo, Teec Nos Pos: hand-spun wool; light blue, dark blue, black, orange, yellow, green, red, white, gray, walnut; note the suggestion of landscape scenery in field; ca. 1925–1935; 68 x 44 inches; excellent condition; $4,500–$6,500.

Blankets/Rugs, Navajo storm pattern rug, ca. 1920s, hand-spun wool; red, gray, black, white, rust; red and rust are synthetic colors, others no dye; 66 x 41 inches; excellent condition; $1,200–$1,800. Courtesy of Dewey Galleries, Ltd., Andrew Nagen. Photo by Robert Reno.

Navajo, Teec Nos Pos rug: storm pattern in black, gray, tan, red, dark green, orange, and natural; well-defined border, finely carded and woven wool; 5 feet x 8 feet 2 inches; good condition; $3,100–$5,100.

Navajo, Teec Nos Pos: all hand-spun and natural dyes; ca. 1910; very good condition; $2,750–$3,000.

Navajo, Teec Nos Pos eye dazzler: all native hand-spun wool with use of aniline dyes and natural wool colors; the blue is from blue jean dyes; ca. 1920s; 43 x 85 inches; very good condition; $10,350–$11,000.

Navajo, Teec Nos Pos: transitional; Circle of Cottonwoods; natural and aniline dyes; hand-spun typical design of transitional period; ca. 1900–1910; very good condition; $1,600–$1,850.

Navajo, Teec Nos Pos: by Gloria Cambridge; 20 x 28½ inches; very good condition; $900–$1,150.

Navajo, Teec Nos Pos: outline with black, dark gray, white, green, light gray, cocoa, medium brown, and gold; 42 x 50 inches; very good condition; $350–$460.

Navajo, Teec Nos Pos: fancy old Teec Nos Pos/Red Mesa outline with red, maroon, orange, green, yellow, blue, black, gray, tan, and white; ca. 1925; 51½ x 65 inches; excellent condition; $2,900–$3,075.

Navajo throw: mottled gray, yellow, brown, white, and orange in banded and serrated designs; ca. mid to late 20th century; 16½ x 36 inches; very good condition; $30–$45.

Navajo throw: dark brown, gray, red, white, orange, and blue in serrated diamond designs; 16 x 34 inches; very good condition; $30–$60.

Navajo throw: black, red, white, and mottled green in serrated designs; 18½ x 35 inches; very good condition; $30–$60.

Navajo throw: Gallup throw with red, gray, black, and white in serrated diamond design; ca. 1960s; 19¾ x 38 inches; very good condition; $45–$90.

Navajo throw: black, white, gold, and gray in serrated diamond designs; 21½ x 42 inches; very good condition; $50–$85.

Navajo throw: colorful Gallup throw; ca. 1950; 37 x 19 inches; very good condition; $25–$45.

Navajo, Toadlena (possibly) rug: gray, natural, gold, and brown, hand-carded and spun wool; 2 feet 9 inches x 4 feet 2 inches; good condition; $225–$325.

Navajo, transitional: hand-spun 100 percent wool, red background with serrated black, natural white overall zigzag pattern; ca. 1890; 74 x 54 inches; good condition; $500–$850.

Navajo, transitional wearing blanket, large: 100 percent hand-spun wool in vegetal and aniline-dyed colors, red background, stepped diamond pattern overall, "spirit" escape lines at corners; ca. 1890 to 1900s; good condition; $700–$1,000.

Navajo, transitional rug/blanket: hand-spun wool warp and weft; red, orange, green (two shades), yellow, walnut, white, burgundy; all synthetic dyes; excellent condition; ca. 1890–1900; 84 x 61½ inches; $4,500–$7,500.

Navajo, transitional serape: ca. 1800; 75 x 52 inches; very good condition; $10,000–$11,500.

Navajo, transitional serape: woven on a shaded red hand-spun ground with a pattern of crosses and terraced lozenges in blue, green, yellow, and pale pink commercial yarn, and natural white hand-spun; 69 x 54½ inches; very good condition; $9,200–$9,800.

Navajo, transitional serape: woven on an orange-red ground in white and two shades of indigo blue and blue-green with a pattern of terraced zigzags centering a row of crosses down the back, parallel bars and short serrated columns on the sides; very good condition; $10,350–$11,300.

Navajo, transitional: twill weave; red background, black and orange stripes; ca. 1900; 34 x 44 inches; very good condition; $900–$1,150.

Navajo, transitional: Northeastern Reservation area pound blanket with dark brown, gray-brown, and white in a large serrated X and whirling logs/swastikalike designs; ca. 1900; 43 x 86 inches; very good condition; $650–$850.

Navajo, transitional: Northeastern Reservation area; black, dark brown, dark gray, and white; ca. 1900; 54 x 100 inches; near mint condition; $920–$1,400.

Navajo, transitional: dark gray, red-orange, white, and gray-brown; ca. 1900s; 56 x 83 inches; very good condition; $850–$1,100.

Navajo, transitional: dark brown, red-orange, mottled brown, and white; ca. 1900; 57½ x 77 inches; excellent condition; $975–$1,150.

Navajo, transitional: dark brown, red-orange, mottled brown, and white; 1925; 57 x 84 inches; very good condition; $1,150–$1,725.

Navajo, transitional: Northeastern Reservation area with dark brown, mottled brown, gray-brown, and white in banded designs; ca. 1900; 60 x 80 inches; mint condition; $600–$850.

Navajo, transitional: dark brown, cream, and medium brown in "floating" trapezoidal designs; ca. 1900; 60 x 86 inches; very good condition; $430–$675.

Navajo rugs (two): one with diamond designs in orange, red, and natural, 4 feet x 2 feet 8 inches, other with lightning design in black, red, and shades of gray, 4 feet 3 inches x 2 feet 3 inches, repaired; $150–$225 each.

Navajo, Two Grey Hills: woven in red, white, and shades of brown on a gray field, bordered central geometric devices; ca. 1930s; 48 x 82 inches; excellent condition; $800–$1,050.

Navajo, Two Grey Hills: older tapestry quality, in black, gray, white, brown, taupe, and white; ca. 1950s–1960s; 37½ x 62½ inches; very good condition; $950–$1,275.

Navajo, Two Grey Hills: black, brown, gray, light brown, and white; ca. 1930–1950; 43½ x 71 inches; very good condition; $800–$1,150.

Navajo, Two Grey Hills: typical style in natural wool; tan, gray, and black; ca. 1930; very good condition; $4,600–$5,750.

Navajo, Two Grey Hills: classic, natural wool weaving; ca. 1950; 58 x 38 inches; very good condition; $600–$800.

Navajo weavings (two): one with central serrated hourglass design in black, tan, beige, and red, 2 feet 5½ inches x 4 feet 1½ inches; the other in an hourglass design in tan, black, rust, beige, and red, 1 foot 10 inches x 3 feet 4½ inches; very good condition; $200–$300 each.

Navajo weaving: choice, double-faced, with Yei figures on one side and stripes on the other; ca. 1970; 22 x 17 inches; very good condition; $90–$150.

Navajo weaving: fine-gap storm pattern in soft brown shades; ca. 1965; 36 x 22 inches; very good condition; $45–$90.

Navajo weaving; woman's wearing blanket style weaving, woven on shaded brownish black ground with three red panels, two with stepped zigzag and cross motifs, twill woven on one side; 48 x 70 inches; very good condition; $1,150–$1,400.

Navajo weaving: choice Crystal weaving with central lozenge and fishhook motif; ca. 1930; 81 x 53 inches; very good condition; $700–$900.

Navajo weaving (two): woven in red, black, white, and shaded brown; 32 x 52 inches and 24 x 60 inches; very good condition; $500–$630/set.

Navajo weaving: in dark brown, white, and purple crosses and serrated sawtoothed designs on a shaded red ground; 31 x 46 inches; good condition (edge damage); $700–$920.

Navajo, Wide Ruins area: tan, burgundy, white, orange, gold, gray, and dark green in banded, terraced, and serrated diamond designs; 24½ x 34½ inches; very good condition; $250–$425.

Navajo, woman's handwoven vest: woven of Germantown yarn, excellent condition, silver buttons; violet, black, orange, green, white, red; ca. 1910–1925; $600–$1,000.

Navajo, woman's manta: twill woven with a natural-shaded dark brown center flanked by two rows of terraced diamonds in indigo blue against broad raveled red bands, the long borders in indigo blue; 55½ x 36¾ inches; very good condition; $5,750–$6,300.

Navajo, woman's manta: twill woven in commercial yarn with a central dark brown panel flanked by two rows of terraced crosses against red bands, the blue side borders each with a zigzag pattern; 55 x 48 inches; very good condition; $5,750–$6,300.

Navajo, woman's second-phase wearing blanket: hand-spun wool and raveled cloth; red, blue, green, white, brown; blue,

Blankets/Rugs, Navajo woman's handwoven vest, woven of Germantown yarn, 1910–1925, excellent condition, silver buttons; violet, black, orange, green, white, red; $600–$1,000. Courtesy of Dewey Galleries, Ltd., Andrew Nagen. Photo by Robert Reno.

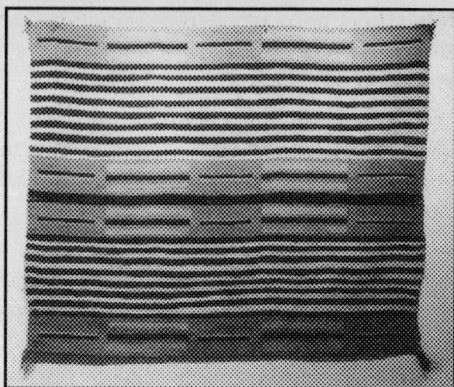

Blankets/Rugs, Navajo woman's second-phase wearing blanket, ca. 1865–1875; hand-spun wool and raveled cloth; red, blue, green, white, brown; blue, green, and red are natural dyes, brown and white no dye; excellent condition; 54 x 66 inches; $18,000–$24,000. Courtesy of Dewey Galleries, Ltd., Andrew Nagen. Photo by Robert Reno.

green, and red are natural dyes, brown and white no dye; ca. 1865–1875; 54 x 66 inches; excellent condition; $18,000–$24,000.

Navajo, Yei rug: multicolored on gray background; contemporary; 20 x 40 inches; very good condition; $55–$100.

Navajo, Yei rug: woven in red, white, black, yellow, maroon, orange, and turquoise; 35 x 44 inches; very good condition; $350–$450.

Navajo, Yei: woven with a row of skirted Yeibichai figures, with numerous feathers interspersed, brownish black and red encompassing border woven in violet, teal, red, orange, white, yellow, dark brown, and pale green; 43 x 69 inches; very good condition; $700–$800.

Navajo, Yei: fancy, six-figured Yei with three Yeis, two cornstalk symbols, and a rainbow god/guardian in red, green, white, black, blue, yellow, and cocoa; 35 x 37 inches; very good condition; $110–$150.

Navajo, Yei: woven with 100 percent wool yarns in multicolors on a mottled gray background, the border in a rich brown with an elaborate serrated pattern in black, teal blue, and white; five Yei figures dominate the design, with the end two wearing headpieces with three feathers in contrast to the central three with four feathers and different pendants; 7 feet x 4 feet 3 inches; very good condition; $2,400–$2,900.

Navajo, Yeibichai rug: hand-spun wool and commercial yarn; red, black, yellow, tangerine, orange, green, gold, carrot, brown, tan, purple, white, gray; all colors synthetic dyes; ca. 1920s; 39 x 86 inches; excellent condition; $6,500–$8,500.

Navajo two-faced Yeibichai: by Harriet Smiley; won second place in 1987 Navajo Nation Fair; 21½ x 33½ inches; very good condition; $460–$525.

Navajo, weaving: woven in brown, cream, pumpkin, tan, and gray diamond arrow design; 5 feet 1 inch x 3 feet 8 inches; very good condition; $450–$500.

Navajo, weaving: woven in brown, tan, cream, and red geometric square and rectangle design; 5 feet 3 inches x 3 feet 3 inches; very good condition; $300–$375.

Navajo, weaving: woven in light brown, dark brown, cream, jagged diamond pattern; 7 feet x 4 feet 3 inches; very good condition; $440–$475.

Navajo, weaving: woven in brown, tan, red, and cream diamond and cross design; 7 feet 8 inches x 4 feet 2 inches; very good condition; $475–$500.

Navajo, Yeibichai: different color skirts on the women is unusual; contemporary; 20 x 29 inches; very good condition; $350–$460.

Navajo: natural-dyed wool; mustard, white, tan, black, and brown; contemporary; 19 x 40 inches; very good condition; $115–$175.

Navajo: fancy older "American flag" in red, white, and purple; has fifty "stars"; 24½ x 34 inches; very good condition; $260–$400.

Navajo: woven in dark brown, white, sand, and red geometric motifs, on a shaded gray ground; 29 x 52 inches; very good condition; $350–$500.

Navajo: Defiance area Klagetoh-like with black, red, and gray, by Louise Yazzie; 3 feet ¾ inches x 4 feet ⅜ inches; very good condition; $115–$175.

Navajo: red, grey, black, and white in three vertical rows of serrated diamonds; 30 x 50 inches; very good condition; $65–$85.

Navajo: Western Reservation; geometric hand-woven; ca. 1950; 36 x 64 inches; very good condition; $75–$130.

Navajo: *Male Shooting Chant,* by Zonnie Gilmore; hand-spun, vegetal dyes; 1980; 38 x 40 inches; very good condition; $4,000–$4,600.

Navajo: Klagetoh area rug with red, gray, black, and white; ca. 1930s; 38 x 53 inches; very good condition; $230–$350.

Navajo: small rug with "waterbird" design; ca. 1965; 39 x 18 inches; very good condition; $60–$85.

Navajo: *Hail Way/Night Sky,* by Albert Jackson; 41½ x 59¾ inches; very good condition; $4,000–$4,600.

Navajo: Eastern Reservation; dark brown, rust, gray-brown, and white, in vertically connected serrated diamond designs; ca. 1940s; 42½ x 70 inches; excellent condition; $350–$575.

Navajo: *Storm with Rainbow Yei,* by Marita Gould; 42½ x 62 inches; very good condition; $1,750–$2,000.

Navajo: red, black, light gray, and white, in vertical rows of connected, serrated diamonds and zipperlike designs; old; 43½ x 66½ inches; excellent condition; $220–$320.

Navajo: old pictorial; Eastern Reservation area; dark brown, mottled brown, and white, in whirling log/swastiklike, large terraced diamond, and man with hat designs; ca. 1920s; 43 x 86 inches; very good condition; $700–$850.

Navajo: woven on a red ground in pink, light blue, white, brown, and black with large central double-hooked motif bordered by concentric stepped rectangles; 44 x 76 inches; good condition (minor staining); $375–$575.

Navajo: woven in black, cream, and mustard geometric motifs, with meandering sawtooth-line border around a shaded brownish gray field; 45 x 72 inches; very good condition; $500–$700.

Navajo: natural wool floor rug with brown, gray, and white geometric designs; ca. 1935; 50 x 26 inches; very good condition; $80–$115.

Navajo: red and black with terraced designs; ca. 1935; 50 x 28 inches; very good condition; $200–$275.

Navajo: fancy whirling logs/Tsil-Ol-Ni sandpainting with gray, chili red, yellow, black, green, raspberry, aqua, gold, blue, and white; 52½ x 54½ inches; mint condition; $1,400–$1,850.

Navajo: Northeastern Reservation area; dark brown, red, light brown, and white in serrated diamond designs; ca. 1930s; 52 x 89 inches; very good condition; $725–$900.

Navajo: woven in red, black, and white on a shaded gray field, bordered central design of stepped lozenge motif; 53 x 77 inches; very good condition; $500–$600.

Navajo: fancy Klagetoh Teec Nos Pos influence with black, taupe, gray, gold, white, and rust; ca. 1950s–1960s; 54½ x 87½ inches; very good condition; $975–$1,275.

Navajo: woven in black, shaded brown, red, and white; 54 x 69 inches; very good condition; $400–$575.

Navajo: Western Reservation; floor rug in red, white, black, and gray; ca. 1935; 60 x 30 inches; very good condition; $80–$115.

Navajo: Western Reservation; floor rug with multicolored sawtooth motif; ca. 1935; 65 x 62 inches; very good condition; $100–$115.

Navajo: woven in black, red, and white serrated diamond motifs on a shaded gray ground; 67½ x 45½ inches; very good condition; $300–$350.

Navajo: woven in black, sand, red, and white geometric devices on a shaded gray field; 69½ x 42 inches; very good condition; $425–$500.

Navajo: fine old Ganado red with "railroad track" lozenge and diamond motif; ca. 1930; 76 x 42 inches; very good condition; $300–$400.

Navajo: with dark brown, red, gray-brown, and white; ca. 1930–1950; 77 x 120 inches; very good condition; $2,600–$3,700.

Navajo: floor-type rug; Eastern Reservation; dark brown, gray-brown, and white; ca. 1930s; 82 x 126 inches; excellent condition; $1,400–$1,850.

Navajo: woven on shaded gray ground in red, black, white, and dark brown with elaborate geometric and pictorial motifs; 88 x 54 inches; good/very good condition (minor edge roughness and staining); $625–$750.

Navajo: choice early storm pattern with crisp colors in the geometric design; ca. 1930; 96 x 58 inches; very good condition; $1,000–$1,400.

Navajo: *Beauty Way/Water Creatures*, done in 1974 by Desbah Tutt Nez; hand-spun, vegetal and aniline dye; first prize at 1975 Scottsdale; very good condition; $9,200–$10,350.

Blankets/Rugs, New Mexico Colcha; hand-spun wool; brown, eggshell, rust, pink, green, blue, yellow, violet, mocha, plum, gray, white; red and orange are synthetic, all other colors are natural, white is no dye; 13 x 13 inches; $200–$300. Courtesy of Dewey Galleries, Ltd., Andrew Nagen. Photo by Robert Reno.

NEW MEXICO COLCHA

New Mexico Colcha: hand-spun wool; brown, eggshell, rust, pink, green, blue, yellow, violet, mocha, plum, gray, white; red and orange are synthetic, all other colors are natural, white is no dye; 13 x 13 inches; $200–$300.

NEZ PERCE

Nez Perce rump throw: native tanned hide beaded in a floral pattern in dark blue, light blue, green, rose, and red on a light blue background with old trade cloth edging with light blue beads and brass bells; 6 feet 6 inches long; very good condition; $1,000–$1,300.

Nez Perce horse blanket: floral beaded, black with red trim; 33 x 54 inches; fair/good condition; $400–$460.

NORTHERN PLAINS

Northern Plains (possibly Cree) rump throw: tanned hide with red trade cloth beaded in floral design in green, blue, and yellow; 50½ inches long; good condition; $400–$600.

NORTHWEST COAST

Northwest Coast button blanket: eagle design blue trade cloth with red trim; 36 x 51 inches; very good condition; $70–$90.

Northwest Coast button blanket: ceremonial blanket; wonderful graphic owl figure in red trade cloth outlined in mother-of-pearl buttons on purple; ca. late 19th century or early 20th;

53 x 58 inches; good condition (two nailhead-size moth holes); $1,000–$1,150.

Northwest Coast button blanket: frog design; blue trade cloth with red trim; contemporary; 60 x 77 inches; very good condition; $230–$300.

Northwest Coast, Haida/Tlingit button blanket: on blue and red trade cloth with mother-of-pearl buttons forming the bear clan depiction; ca. 1918; 72½ x 52½ inches; good condition; $6,000–$8,000.

Pendleton Indian blanket: 100 percent wool in attractive design; very good condition; $50–$100.

Pendleton Indian: striped, "Beaver State"; ca. 1935; 19 inches x 2 feet; very good condition; $60–$85.

Pendleton Indian: wool; ca. 1920; 58 x 36 inches; very good condition; $115–$175.

Pendleton Indian: striped, "Beaver State"; ca. 1950; 76 x 64 inches; very good condition; $85–$115.

Pendleton Indian: blue background wool Indian blanket with geometric designs; ca. 1940; very good condition; $75–$115.

Pendleton trade: double-faced geometric design; ca. 1920; 70 x 63 inches; very good condition; $70–$115.

Pendleton: wool double weave in golds shading to red and green on brown background; reverse diamond design in same colors; original felted binding worn off and label gone; 60 x 80 inches; good/very good condition (minute wear to blanket); $85–$175.

Pendleton: yarn fringe on all four sides; brown; 61 x 58 inches; very good condition; $60–$85.

Pendleton: yarn fringe on all four sides; green; 62 x 54 inches; very good condition; $60–$85.

Pendleton: line design in black, green, red, blue, and white with green fringe; 71 x 60 inches; very good condition; $35–$60.

Pendleton: striped wool trade blanket; ca. 1940; 88 x 56 inches; very good condition; $70–$90.

Pendleton: large, 100 percent wool; ca. 1940; very good condition; $100–$115.

Pendleton: large, classic striped wool blanket; ca. 1930; very good condition; $40–$60.

Pendleton: fine old striped blanket; ca. 1920; 60 x 55 inches; very good condition; $40–$60.

Pictorial: won award in 1980 at the New Mexico State Fair; very good condition; $1,300–$1,600.

Prairie, tribe cloth: decorated shawl, Oto, Osage, Winnebago, Illinois, Omaha; dark blue with sky blue and fuchsia satinlike decoration; 43 x 65 inches; very good condition; $80–$125.

RIO GRANDE

Rio Grande blanket: hand-spun wool, woven in two sections; red, blue, light blue, pink, gray, white, orange; ca. 1900; 78½ x 51½ inches; excellent condition; $1,400–$2,000.

Rio Grande lap blanket: colorful figure blanket; ca. 1935; 44 x 22 inches; very good condition; $35–$60.

Rio Grande serape: Chimayo joined in center; blue on white background; black and red design elements; ca. 1800s; very good condition; $1,725–$2,300.

Rio Grande wearing blanket: Germantown; "Vallero"; woven with two panels joined at the center in an eye-dazzling pattern of diamond forms, repeated chevrons, and two "Vallero Stars" of eight points placed at the tips of the central figures; side borders of serrated, indented lines and eight pointed geometrics in deep red, crimson, teal green, dark blue, ocher, and white, warps are two-ply hand-spun wool, all colored areas in four-ply

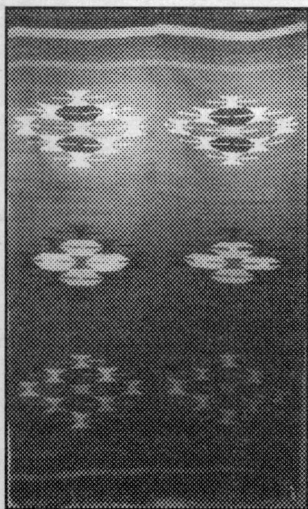

Blankets/Rugs, Rio Grande blanket, ca. 1900, hand-spun wool, woven in two sections; red, blue, light blue, pink, gray, white, orange; 78½ x 51½ inches; excellent condition; $1,400–$2,000. Courtesy of Dewey Galleries, Ltd., Andrew Nagen. Photo by Robert Reno.

Germantown wool yarns, the white elements are single-ply home-spun wool; this wearing blanket is a classic example of Vallero weavers active from 1860 to 1890s, a subgroup of the Rio Grande people; Vallero stars are always eight-pointed; ca. 1880; 50 x 89 inches; one side with slight faded area, but in overall excellent condition with vibrant colors; $4,000–$4,600.

Rio Grande wedding or utility blanket: tightly woven in single-ply hand-spun Rambouillet-merino fleece wool on a four-ply cotton warp in two widths seamed at the center, forming a traditional pattern of broad and narrow stripes in deep indigo blue, natural undyed white, and a yellow ocher (gold) from rabbitbrush dyes; the striped pattern has been overembroidered with wool yarn geometrics, giving an overall design disguising the stripes; ca. 1885; 86 inches long x 45⅛ inches wide; condition very good with embroidery overlay worn in spots, the fringe worn but knotted and intact, the basic woven body without impairments; $700–$800.

SALISH

Salish: Frazer River; rare hand-woven wool blanket; ca. 1965; 40 x 21 inches; very good condition; $65–$85.

SIOUX

Sioux blanket strip: beaded in white with four circular medallions, deaccessioned from a Maine museum; 56½ inches; very good condition; $700–$900.

Sioux blanket strip: beaded hide blanket strip; stitched in lime green, greasy yellow, blue, and white-heart reds on a white beaded ground; sinew-sewn; 64 inches long; good condition (minor bead loss); $800–$1,000.

Sioux saddle blanket: canvas backer beaded in H shape, beaded strips in geometric designs in red, green, cobalt, and yellow on white beaded background; twisted rawhide fringe and attached brass bells; sinew-sewn; 65 x 27 inches overall; very good condition; $800–$1,000.

Sioux saddle: classic hide saddle blanket with sinew geometric beadwork and fringe; ca. 1940; 75 x 28 inches; very good condition; $1,450–$2,100.

Chapter Five

Clothing

❧

When people from other backgrounds picture an American Indian in his or her clothing, what they call to mind is an image of the Plains Indian, but there are scores of other tribes, and their ways of dress are as varied as the rest of their lifestyles.

Most of the tribes wore breechcloths as a primary garment, as well as moccasins. Breechcloths, worn only by men, provided an equally long apron in both front and back.

Leggings, also worn by a variety of tribes, often sported quillwork or beaded trimming down the flap, which ran down the side of the leg. The flap was frequently fringed. The hip portion of the leggings was cut higher for men than for women, and the outer part of the legging was tied to a belt to keep them up.

Shirts and/or capes were also common to many tribes. Hats or bonnets, though an accepted piece of clothing, vary greatly, even among those Indians who belong to the same tribe.

Footwear was adapted to the climate that particular tribes endured, though most Native Americans went barefoot for at least part of the year.

CLOTHING DECORATION

QUILLWORK   The Plains Indians used quills in decoration, and their artistry with this technique reached its peak after horses became a part of their lifestyle. Before they acquired horses, the Plains tribes stayed in one place for long periods of time, giving the women a chance to take their time with the artwork they produced weaving quills into fabric and leather.

Their skill at the craft was a subject of pride, and there were very established levels of expertise among the women in the tribes. The most creative of the quillwork artists perfected dyes, designs, and stitches that the other women willingly copied. It was an honor for a woman of great skill to pass her secrets along to another. The patterns used were mostly geometric designs before 1880. After that, some tribes began using floral designs.

With the use of trade beads becoming more widespread in the early 1880s, the decorative art of quillwork was threatened. It did not begin to disappear, however, until seed beads were readily available (after 1840). Today the Sioux tribe produces most of the available quillwork.

Sewing the quills of a porcupine onto a soft hide was an ancient Blackfoot method of decorating clothing, a method shared by other tribes as well. Before the quill was sewn down onto the fabric, the quill maker soaked them in her mouth to soften them. She then sewed the quills in such a way that they would form patterns and designs.

Quills could be used in their natural colors or dyed; most Native American quill artists used red, yellow, and green dyes. The dyes were derived from plants, which were moistened, covered by the quills, and then wrapped until dry. When dry, the plant color had permanently soaked into the quills. Other times the quill maker would boil the quills with an appropriate dye material and a mordant. Of course, the quill maker's palette of colors expanded greatly when aniline dyes became available.

Tools used in quill decorating include a piece of hide upon which to work, an awl, a smooth object used to flatten the quills once they are sewn down, and strands of rolled sinew.

Quill makers kept their quills in special bags fashioned out of buffalo bladders. A slit was made in the bag, through which the quills were inserted, and the bag was usually stiff enough so that the quills inside would be kept straight. Quillworkers preferred to work with thin quills because they didn't split as easily as the larger, older ones.

Blackfoot quill makers go through a traditional initiation and have to follow rules as they practice their art. They cannot eat porcupine meat or allow anyone to pass in front of them while they quill. An older woman will initiate a younger woman into the art. Unfortunately, because of the advent of beadwork and the lack of knowledge of the art of quillwork among the older women, there are few quillworkers left among the Blackfoot women today.

BEADWORK DECORATION

TRADE BEADS   Glassmaking's secrets were closely guarded in the early history of the art. Egyptians were among the earliest producers of glass beads, although much of the early glassmaking as we know it came from areas in what is now Eastern Europe. Though factories were built in Lebanon thousands of years ago, and still produce glass today, Venice, Italy, is known as the "Mother of Modern Beads."

We can credit Christopher Columbus with being the person to introduce beads to the Indians when he gave a string of red beads to the natives of San Salvador. As other early explorers arrived in America, they, too, brought beads. We can determine the age of trade beads by identifying where the beads were made, then researching when colonists from that country arrived in America. Though that will not always give you an accurate age of the beads, it at least will give you a starting point from which to proceed.

The first beads used freely in trading were Spanish. Close on the Spaniards' heels came Dutch, French, English, and Russian settlers. In 1622 Jamestown, Virginia, became home to the country's first glass factory. Explorers spread glass trade beads until they reached Alaska. The "Russian Blue" bead became the most popular bead in that part of the country and was soon dubbed the "Chief" bead.

Other popular beads include the "Hudson Bay" bead, a red bead with a translucent center, used in Canadian trade; the "Vaseline" or "Cave Agate" bead, a faceted and transparent bead with a hole through its center, made in a variety of colors; and the "Hubbell" bead, made in Czechoslovakia between 1915 and 1920, and sold by the Hubbell Trading Post in Ganado, Arizona, located on the Navajo Reservation.

Different patterns are used in beading techniques, such as weft and warp combinations; the bias-diagonal stitches which are very difficult to perfect and most often used throughout the Great Lakes region; oblique weaving; concentric circling; bead wrapping; spot or overlay stitching; spiral stitching found in Native American coiled basketry, a stitch that was used by the midwestern Musquakiis; the spoked pattern, used by the Indians of Oklahoma; scalloped bead winding, used by the Utes and Comanches; and the lazy stitch, used by most Indians west of the Mississippi, the most commonly used stitch.

Plains Indian beadwork was born shortly after Europeans introduced the beads as trading material. The Plains women immediately put them to use as decorative accents on most of their leather garments. The beads were fashioned into geometric patterns, animals, or human figures, which were only a part of the intricate designs created by this artistic group of people. Their garments reflected light and movement, as well as their feeling of being one with the earth.

After 1910, the beadwork made by the Plains tribes declined in quality. Many believe the decline stems from the transition to a culture that no longer hunted. The work they created was almost strictly for the tourist trade instead of for themselves. They did not have cause to use animal skins, which had been readily available, as clothing. Another theory is that being confined to the reservations left the Indian with a lack of interest in the old crafts that had once reflected their pride. However, other experts say that beadwork and quillwork were at their peak between 1880 and World War I because the tribes now confined to reservations had more time to create work for the tourist trade. They beaded everything they could find, including shoes, doctor's bags, bottles, and violin cases, as well as traditional items. They began to use beadwork on woolen cloth and canvas since buffalo hides and deerskin were not so readily available. Some consider this period a time of quillwork and beadwork renaissance, especially among the Western Sioux.

Because of the interaction between the tribes occupying the plains area, certain crafts of one tribe bear close resemblance to those of another. Cheyenne and Arapaho artwork is quite similar, for instance. Kiowa, Comanche, and Plains Apache beadwork is sparse on their clothing—their beadwork talents were displayed on borders or in isolated figures instead. The Sioux used the lazy stitch when sewing their beads, which leaves the beads in loose rows. They do not lie flat, but have a bumpy appearance. Blackfoot beading was done with the appliqué stitch, requiring the simultaneous use of two threads—one thread strings the beads, the other stitches them down.

Bead colors that were popular with the Blackfoot tribe include blue, "greasy" yellow, "Cheyenne" pink, green, and rose. Italian seed beads are common and are a good-quality glass with soft, subtle colors. New beads, however, arrived with each ship to the New World, and Indian beadwork incorporated Russian cobalt and Czechoslovakian glass beads as well.

The geometric beadwork of the Blackfoot consists of large figures made up of other smaller ones (i.e., squares, triangles, rectangles). The "feather design" and "mountain design" are commonly used, but there are no tribal meanings to a bead maker's designs.

Some trade beads may have reached the Blackfoot as early as the beginning of the 1700s, through trade with other tribes who had direct contact with merchants. Pony beads were widely used on Blackfoot garments beginning around 1830. The most common color combination was white and sky blue. Beads were used to trade for a good buffalo robe or horse—eight shanks being the equivalent of a buffalo robe in 1870.

During the 1870s, when seed beads were introduced, Blackfoot beadworkers turned to the style of beadwork most common today. Once the smaller beads were available, whole articles of clothing were beaded, instead of just the edges, and flower and leaf designs became popular.

Though beading is considered a Native American art, it has its roots in Indian trade with the white man.

WAMPUM Along the East Coast of the continent, North American Indians called their beads "wampum" and made them from quahog (thick-shelled clam) shells. Their arrangement, by color, on a string was used to send messages between tribes. When woven into belts, wampum were used in ratifying treaties.

Wampum was used as a form of money until 1792 when the United States government brought silver dollars, coins, and ten-dollar gold pieces into use.

CLOTHING OF THE VARIOUS TRIBES

Some of the tribes noted are grouped into areas (such as Northwest, Plains, Plateau), while others are listed individually. If individual characteristics are recognized, the tribe is separately noted. If the clothing was consistent throughout the region, then identifying information is given under the area. First check to see whether the tribe you're interested in has its own listing, then check under the area for additional, more general, information.

ALGONQUIAN

This northeast tribe cut and used rabbit skins for capes, mantles, and other garments, and used beaver pelts for robes and fur hats.

Shirts were made by taking two skins of approximately the same size and shape and piecing them together. Leggings were made from single folded and trimmed skins.

APACHE

A young Apache girl wore a two-piece white buckskin bead-work-decorated dress during her "coming out" ceremony (when she reached puberty). The dresses were elaborately painted and beaded, fringed with dangling tin cones, so that the women made music as they danced. (For further information see "Plains Tribes".)

ATHABASKANS

This tribe habitually used beaver pelts for hats and robes. They also made a unique kind of trouser which was attached, in one piece, to their moccasins.

During the winter, these warm pants/moccasins worked well with snowshoes, which the Athabaskans found useful when tracking their prey through deep snowdrifts.

BLACKFOOT

The Blackfoot women of the 1910s and 1920s wore long trade cloth dresses with bands of different colors (perhaps ribbons) around the bottom. Often the upper half was decorated with quill-work and/or beading.

Children generally dressed in miniature versions of adult styles, including the fancier headdresses and buckskin outfits.

Women's buckskin dresses decorated with shells and fanciful beadwork were used for special occasions and ceremonies only, and often lasted a lifetime. Usually women were buried in this clothing.

Wrinkled clothing was worn by the women as a sign of grief when someone close to them died. They would also cut off their hair or leave it unbraided, gash their arms and legs, or, if the one who died had been deeply loved, cut off one of their fingers.

Blackfoot clothing was generally made of white hides, and the designs followed basic patterns, which were easily recognizable by members of other tribes.

Robes were the Indians' outer clothing. These garments were indispensable for most men, as they often wore only a breechcloth and moccasins underneath. Buffalo or elk robes were decorated with stripes, which were either painted, quilled, or beaded. These robes were reserved for special occasions.

Men decorated their clothing with symbols of their war triumphs or religious strengths. Their distinctive war bonnets stood upright.

Though blankets were given to the Indians (Pendleton and Hudson's Bay) by the government or were traded to the Indians in exchange for beadwork, quillwork, basketry, or jewelry after the 1920s, the elk-hide robes were also used during that period. They are still worn by holy women during the Sun Dance ceremony. However, the Hudson's Bay blankets themselves were used for clothing as early as the 1850s.

Summer and winter clothes were basically the same styles, either elongated to cover more of the body or worn in layers for extra warmth during the winter. Hides, heavy and often not conducive to easy washing, were readily exchanged for the wool trade cloth of the early settlers and traders. Though the wool was just as heavy and warm as the hides, it was easier to wash.

Indian women began to wear a calico print blouse under their cotton dresses once trade cloth dresses became popular. They also wore head coverings and became quite fond of peasant-style scarves.

The Blackfoot made two different styles of moccasins. The oldest style (called "real moccasins" in the Blackfoot language), was soft, but wore out quickly and was hard to repair. It was constructed from a single soft hide which was folded in half, then sewn. "Extras" like tongues and ankle flaps would be added separately. The two-piece moccasin construction began in the early 1900s. The bottom of this moccasin was made separately, then sewn to the sides. Thus, the bottom can be easily replaced or patched when worn. For winter wear, moccasins were made of shearling sheep hide instead of the usual buckskin.

If a woman was adept at making moccasins, she was wise to keep a set of foot patterns for all of the people for whom she had made moccasins. Traditionally women used sinew to sew up moccasins, but some of the modern makers use thread or "imitation sinew."

A notable characteristic of a Blackfoot moccasin is the small fringed trailer that sticks out from the moccasin's heel. This characteristic has also intermittently appeared on other tribes' moccasins. Red wool was usually sewn into the seam between moccasins and high ankle flaps.

The majority of Blackfoot moccasins are decorated with small designs between the toe and instep. Some have been found fully covered with quillwork and beadwork; however, those forms of decoration are more commonly found on moccasins made by other tribes.

Some Blackfoot moccasin designs are sketched below:

Crooked Nose

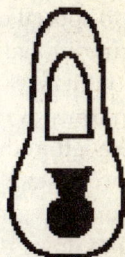
Round

Striped

Three Finger Beadwork
(most definitely Blackfoot design)

Basic Floral Design

BASIC FLORAL DESIGN

The common, traditional style of Blackfoot women's dresses was first noted around 1800; the same style was also worn by neighboring tribes. The style of today's Indian women (who may wear such a dress to special occasions) has a cape sewn to the main body, whereas the traditional style resembled a slip and did not cover the arms and shoulders.

The bottoms of dresses made out of hides are wavy because the hides were left in their natural shape. The skins that were made into dresses were sewn with the flesh side out, making it easier to apply beadwork designs. If deerskin was used, the tail of the deer was often hung down the center of the chest as decoration.

Characteristics of Blackfoot dresses include: (1) a curve in the beaded breastband which mimics the shape of a deer hide's back end; (2) a triangular symbol on the lower front of the dress, symbolizing womanhood; and (3) two more symbols on the lower part of the dress which are said to represent kidneys.

Pony beads were used in early beadwork. These beads are what some call "real beads." Typically, two bead colors were used for the breastband; dark and light colors were combined for contrast. Though geometric sections were used to break up the colored stripes, as a rule, no other designs were used. Shoulder bands, however, were decorated with smaller beads, and new colors and designs.

Red, black, or blue trade cloth was used for patches on the bottom of most dresses, with one color backing the other. These pieces of trade cloth were trimmed with beads.

Before the introduction of trade beads to the Indian culture, quillwork was used for decoration (see Chapter Nine for further information).

Dresses made of red or blue trade wool were known to ravel, so a beaded white edge of the cloth was often used for the bottom hem.

Another style of beadwork involved alternating the rows of beads with cowrie shells or elk's teeth. This particular style was popular during the Victorian age and through the 1920s. "Basket beads" (large, tubular beads) were used with this kind of beadwork. Full, colorful skirts, trimmed with rows of bright ribbons, completed the dress.

The induction of trade cloth and cotton changed a lot about the Blackfoot way of life, including the style of women's clothing.

Capes became popular and were worn over calico dresses. Some dresses were even made from velvet.

CHEYENNE AND ARAPAHO

Clothing made by these two tribes was characterized by the long fringe of buckskin trimming the majority of their garments.

In the 1950s a company called the Plume Trading and Sales Co. began selling kits to Boy Scout groups and Indian hobbyists to make "Cheyenne clothing." We've discovered that some people dealing in Native American collectibles have been fooled into believing that clothing made with the kits is antique. According to some of my sources, these kits are still available through companies working from Japan or Hong Kong. One way of differentiating, for example, period leggings from these kit-made examples is to look for scoop crotches, belt channels, or hair locks applied to the flap edges, none of which are found on authentic pieces. Period leggings would have been made from a rough woolen cloth with an undyed selvage called a stroud. The selvage was usually noticeable on the front legging flap and would not be bound on that edge. Sometimes period leggings were also made from Mackinaw or Hudson's Bay blankets (also check under "Plains Tribes").

Cheyenne moccasins are designed so that the upper part of the moccasin is made primarily of one piece with an added tongue. They seldom decorated the tongues of their moccasins, though beadwork decorates other parts of the shoe. The Cheyenne made moccasins with narrow soles and a straight inner edge. They protected the sole seam of their moccasins with a welt. The upper part of the moccasin was cut to provide short extensions or tabs in the rear of the shoe.

CROW

The women's dresses made by the Crow tribe were made of red wool trade cloth (red was of the highest value) and often decorated with many elk teeth. Some Indians referred to the teeth as "the diamonds of our ancestors" (also check under "Plains Tribes").

EASTERN TRIBES

The tribes in the eastern part of the United States wore robes of animal skins which were sewn together and fringed. If the hair was left on, they were considered to be of the finest quality. These pieces were decorated according to the maker's individual taste.

Summer clothing was often woven from natural grasses and light barks. The robes and mats woven were not rough, as you might imagine, but sweet-smelling and light enough to be worn on hot summer nights. Unfortunately, few have survived the test of time. They are not truly collectible because of their scarcity.

EASTERN WOODLANDS
Moccasins worn by Eastern Woodlands tribes were usually decorated single pieces of leather, the cuff of which was often added later.

ERIE AND SUSQUEHANNA
Notable among the clothing of these two tribes was their practice of wearing animal heads, such as panthers and bears, as hats.

FOREST TRIBES
Skirts made by some of the forest tribes were of a single skin, wrapped around the waist and secured with a belt. Though simple, these beautiful garments were carefully tailored, decorated, and fringed.

Shirts worn by the women of these tribes were shorter than the ones men wore, and were poncho-shaped. The women's short leggings came just above the knee, and their moccasins were cut differently from the men's. Belts and sashes were both decorative and worn to support or tailor their clothing.

HAVASUPAI
This tribe dressed somewhat like the Paiutes. The women wore aprons and basketry hats decorated with beads. The men wore breechcloths, and winter wear for the tribe was made of rabbit skins.

HIDATSA
The quillworkers of the Hidatsa tribe favored many brilliant shades, and their work can be identified by distinctive plaited quillwork. Examples of this type of quillwork can be seen at the American Museum of Natural History's Department of Anthropology.

A beautiful bonnet was not necessarily the mark of an honorable man; however, the man who wore such a bonnet in battle had to be brave because his enemy would likely want to kill him to win the bonnet as spoils! One example of a Hidatsa headdress (in the collection of Gilbert Wilson) was 67½ inches long and 18¾ inches wide across the horns. It was made from a gray felt cap and "decorated with loom-woven glass beads, silk ribbons, ermine fur strips, dyed feathers, bison horn, horsehair, and a red wool trail with eagle feathers" (*American Indian Art* magazine, Spring 1988).

After 1885, the Hidatsa tribe underwent some changes and became, in many respects, modernized. They began to make clothes of calico and wool. Quilts made from cotton replaced painted buffalo robes. Their beadwork was produced for the tourist trade, and in the style of other Plains and Woodland tribes.

Though the Hidatsa were being pressured by European life, they clung tightly to their identity (also see "Plains Tribes").

HUPA
Hupa women wore basketry skullcaps. (See Chapter Three for further information.)

IROQUOIS
The Iroquois, who lived in the Northeast, endured harsh winters and wore peaked fur caps to keep their heads warm.

Iroquois women combined their beadwork with ribbon appliqué, while other tribes, like the Apache, used trade cloth to make appliqué designs (also see "Northeast").

IROQUOIS AND PUEBLO
The men of these two tribes, though not geographically close, wore kilts. Iroquois kilts were made of doeskin, while Pueblo kilts were of woven fabric. (Also see "Northeast" for more Iroquois information, and "Pueblo").

KUTCHIN
The Kutchin Indians of western Alaska made finely tanned caribou outfits. A typical skirt hangs below the knees and is V-shaped, decorated with beadwork, and fringed. The trousers are attached to moccasins, even on summer outfits (also see "Northwest Coast").

LAKES AND PRAIRIE AREA

Appliqué decorations were used on clothing of the Lakes and Prairie area tribes, as well as some southern tribes.

LENAPE OR DELAWARE

These tribes wore robes made of bark or hemp fibers. Feathers were twisted into the robe to completely cover the outside, and the weaving was done in such a way that the feathers lay flat (also see "Northeast").

MANDAN

In the Mandan society, only the men who had won honor marks were permitted to paint those marks on their clothing and other objects. Leggings were often decorated. If the man hadn't won the marks he wanted painted on his clothing, he hired someone else to paint them for him. Often this inconsistency caused arguments among members of the tribe, as to whether a man had the right to the honor marked on his clothing (also see "Plains Tribes").

MENOMINI AND OMAHA

These two tribes were known to wear turbans as headgear.

MICCOSUKEE

As they are located in the same region of the country, it's not surprising that this tribe's clothing closely resembles the Seminole. The Miccosukee live in the Everglades today, but they were originally native to Georgia and Mississippi. Their colorful clothing is made from pure cotton and created by sewing bands of the cloth in intricately folded patchwork strips. Row after row of multicolored rickrack trim makes the clothing bold and dramatic.

The men wear wide-sleeved, waist-length jackets that have small, pointed collars and extra-wide cuffs. They also wear vests and shirts with patchwork details. In the past, the men wore knee-length dresses; however, today such clothing is only worn for special occasions, such as the sacred Green Corn Dance celebrated each spring.

Miccosukee women wear ankle-length full skirts with elastic waistbands. They also wear net capes that fall to the waist and are trimmed with lace or rickrack. Originally the capes were practical, meant to protect the wearer from the mosquitoes and sharp grasses common in the Everglades.

The art of making this type of patchwork clothing is passed down from generation to generation. Mothers teach their daughters in chikees, traditional open-air huts where tribe members live and work.

MOHAVE

By the 1880s, Mohave women had demonstrated their talents with beadwork by developing a fully beaded collar that extended over their shoulders like a capelet. The technique used is usually referred to as *netting*. The Mohave called it "vethamam" or "hulap." There are few available to today's collectors because the Mohave people usually destroyed the property of their deceased friends and relatives. Thus the deceased's clothing and beadwork ornaments were burnt with the body.

Today's Mohave women still wear the beaded collar. The value of a beaded collar is determined by its length, bead size, and design. Longer collars are considered more collectible than the smaller because of the additional time and effort required to make the longer version. Work decorated with small beads is more valuable than work decorated with larger beads, and designs that require the maker to count beads and measure their work are more popular than simpler designs.

A Mohave collar that properly fits should reach the end of the shoulder, but should not hang below the wearer's upper arm. Other tribes, such as Apache, Paiute, Yavapai, Cahuilla, and Cocopa, have also produced collars, but all have a much larger mesh than the Mohave; thus the Mohave collars are more highly prized by collectors. Identifying Mohave collars requires that one examine the direction of the netting (always vertical), beads (Mohave used diamond, hexagon, and hourglass shapes—more than two designs in one pattern is rare), and color (Mohave collar makers favored navy blue on a white background and still use white as the preferred background).

NASKAPI

The Naskapi Indians removed the hair from their caribou skins, then painted complex designs on them (also see "Northwest Coast").

Navajo

The men's moccasins made by these tribes are ankle-length and can be tied or strapped. Women's moccasins are white and have a wide strip that is wound around the leg until it reaches the knee.

Contemporary Navajo women's clothing usually consists of midcalf velvet skirts in a deep burgundy color. The women wear loose, peasant-type blouses with them.

The Navajo people made dresses similar to the Pueblo Indians' (black with red borders); however, instead of using one wraparound blanket, the Navajo put two rectangles together and fashioned them to make a tube. They wore silver concho belts around their waists and bootlike moccasins (already mentioned) with silver buttons.

The southwestern Indian's dress is always accented by their wonderful turquoise and silver jewelry. Squash-blossom necklaces are worn by both sexes, as are concha belts and bracelets. (For more information, see Chapter Eight.)

Northeast

In the Northeast, the northern Plains and Lakes areas, women's dresses resembled jumpers and were made with separate sleeves. This style was eventually replaced by skirts and blouses.

Northwest Coast

Hats worn by Indians of the Northwest Coast tribes are often made of finely woven basketry materials. Their conical forms are similar to those hats worn by immigrant Chinese workers in the late 1700s.

These hats are often painted with decorations, but decoration could also be woven into the hat during the making. Sometimes the hats are used to display lineage emblems. Cedar bark, spruce root, and grass were used to make these basketry hats.

The warriors in tribes that lived near the ocean (Nootka, Haida, Tlingit, and Tsimshian) often wore wooden armor and large carved helmets. Some helmets were designed to resemble grotesque faces, which were intended to scare their enemies.

Masks designed by these people were stylized and meant to resemble the animals they knew—beavers, whales, seals, bears.

The tribes of the Northwest Coast made their own cloth, often out of mountain goat wool, for their garments. These garments were decorated in much the same way as their blankets, with stylized figures of humans, birds, and animals, and were extremely complicated in design, as well as warm and soft to the touch.

Animal skins were used as clothing during the long, extremely cold winters, and often the boots or footgear would be tempered with oil from seals or whales to make them warmer and waterproof.

The women made capes and wraparound skirts from shredded cedar bark and also made conical basket hats, which easily shed the rain so common to the area. The shredded red cedar bark capes were slipped over the wearer's head, and the flared edge came just below the elbows. The length enabled a person wearing the cape to paddle a canoe or work. Often the neckband was trimmed with fur to prevent chafing. Other shredded bark garments were decorated with strands of mountain goat wool.

OMAHA AND OSAGE

The Omaha and Osage tribes wore brimless otter-fur hats. These hats were decorated with quill and beadwork, shells, large beads, and jinglers. Sometimes the back of the hat had streamers or feathers.

Osage wedding hats looked like bowlers gaily decorated in feathers. They often used red, white, and blue, not coincidentally the colors of the American flag.

Everything—the lodge, clothing, utensils, gardens, children—belonged to the wife in the Osage tribe. The man was simply expected to be a good provider for his wife, their children, and his wife's family. The men were noted hunters, hunting buffalo in the fall with their swift horses, and were also exceptionally successful warriors, though most of their battles appear to be retaliatory (e.g., revenge for a slain family member). Animal skins acquired in the hunt were used for clothing. Traditionally the Osage men left their chests bare and wore leggings and moccasins. Their heads normally remained uncovered, except when celebrating a special occasion—in which case they wore feathered warbonnets or other elaborate headgear. The women wore long dresses, leggings to the knee, and moccasins. Their clothing was decorated with porcupine quill embroidery, and, later, with beadwork (also see "Plains Tribes").

PAIUTE

This tribe wore little clothing due to the harsh, primitive, and hot climate in which they lived. Men wore a breechcloth, while women wore aprons made of cedar bark that covered both front and back. Women wore basket hats, and both sexes wore sandals. In the winter, the tribespeople wore rabbit-skin robes.

PLAINS TRIBES

The Plains Tribes created the style of clothing worn during the Ghost Dance period of the 1890s, at the peak of their frustration with the white man. Created by Wovoka or "the Cutter," son of Tavibo, the Prophet, the Ghost Dance religion promised the Indians their messiah. Though painted clothing was fairly common among the Plains Indians, clothing made during the Ghost Dance period is distinctive, as it was decorated with supernatural designs of unusual colors.

This type of clothing is highly collectible and usually very expensive. Once you see and feel Ghost Dance clothing, you will automatically recognize it the next time you have the opportunity to study an example. The designs uniquely convey the significance of what was happening at that time in Indian history. Collectors should be cautious when purchasing an item presented as an example of this work, as a good portion of them are spurious.

Clothing of the Ghost Dance period is not representative of Plains clothing in general. Skirts worn by Plains women were shaped like a short-sleeved nightgown and combined a waist with the skirt. Plains, Prairie, Eastern Apache, and some Basin and Plateau tribeswomen wore skin dresses of a very simple design. Two elk hides were required to make a woman's dress, and they were attached at the shoulders by a yoke. The natural curve of the hide would form the uneven, graceful hem of the dress, and more often than not, the animal's tail remained on the hide and acted as natural decoration. Sioux women's dresses for special occasions were often made of elkskin and paired with a solid beaded yoke and bone breastplate.

During the colder months, Sioux women often wore painted robes. The designs drawn on the robes sometimes symbolized the buffalo or other animals familiar to the tribe. Sioux women often bartered for shells, considered to be quite valuable, from the California tribes. They used shells to decorate the yokes of their dresses, announcing their wealth to the rest of the tribe.

Most Plains warriors went naked to the waist or wore robes; shirts were worn only for ceremonies or special occasions. Older shirts are like ponchos with open sides. Decorations on warriors' shirts included beading, quillwork, tassels, fringe, painting, and hair or ermine.

Both male and female Indians of the Plains wore leggings; the female version only came to the knee, while the male version extended to his hip. The leggings, plain or decorated, were basic tubes made out of buckskin, slid over the legs like pants, but without the waist and crotch. They were attached to the owner's belt.

Plains moccasins were one piece, soft-soled, and secured by a drawstring. Decoration included quillwork, beading on the toe, and painting—sometimes even a combination of the last two.

Sioux men earned the feathers they wore on their heads. After a first coup, a man was entitled to wear a golden eagle feather standing straight up at the back of his head. Additional coups were signified by the way the feathers were angled on the man's head. Obviously a warrior who wore many feathers was considered quite brave and was well respected.

POWHATAN

The Powhatans, a Woodland area tribe, were first encountered by the white European settlers in the Virginias. The tribe's clothing was made by the women and consisted of a string of shell beads, a skin apron, and little else. Both men and women dressed alike. In the winter the tribespeople used tanned deerskin robes and turkey-feathered mantles to keep warm.

PUEBLO

In the early days of the Pueblo dwellers—Acoma, Zuni, and Hopi are all descendants of the Anasazi and Cliff Dwellers—the men farmed during the summer and wove cotton dresses with diamond and diagonal twill patterns on an upright loom during the winter. Men made themselves white kilts and embroidered the edges with black and red geometric designs.

Dresses, traditionally black with a black or brown woven diagonal twill center, were embroidered in blue by the Zuni and in red by the Acomas and other Pueblos.

Later an apron, gingham underdress, and shawl were combined with the plain, one-shouldered black dress. For celebrations, a manta was hung from the shoulders by ornate silver pins.

Maiden's shawls and buckskin leggings are worn by unmarried Pueblo women, and their hair is done in the "butterfly" style.

The Hopi wedding robe is a plain white cotton weave whitened with chalk and is the largest cotton fabric woven by the tribe. It is woven by the groom's male relatives and worn by the bride. A reed case is made to carry her wedding sash and other garments. The case has long tassels (symbols of fertility), which hang from the corners. After the wedding, the robe is embroidered with colorful yarn and is worn during major Hopi ceremonies. The needlework, like the fabric, is the work of men and usually incorporates traditional symbols such as rain clouds, butterflies, and birds.

SALISH

The Salish tribe wear tall, fancy, sombrero-type hats. At each potlatch (a feast in which the host gives away most of his or her property) the wearer of these hats receives a ringed constriction on its peak. The number of rings on a hat indicates the wearer's generosity (also see "Northwest Coast").

SEMINOLE

Seminole men's clothing consisted of turban, breechcloth, calico shirt, and neckerchief. When visiting town, a Seminole would add some brooches, pantaloons or leggings, watch chains, and safety pins to their everyday attire (though few Seminoles actually owned watches).

The man's shirt was simple and full-cut with a decorative area usually adorning the front placket. His turban was made from plaid wool shawls, and his belt was made of leather, woven yarn, or decorated with beads.

Women went barefoot in cotton or calico skirts and long shirts. The skirts reached the ground and had a ruffle and adorned area at the knee, but left a portion of the waist bare. Calico patches of different colors were sewn on as ornamentation. Their long-sleeved midriff-style blouses had an attached cape, also trimmed with a ruffle at the shoulders.

The women wore a great many necklaces made of beads and silver around their necks—as many as they could afford. According to some Seminole historians, the Seminole baby gets the first strand of beads at birth, and an additional one is added every year until middle age. At that point, they start giving them away, one a year, until the final string of beads goes with them to the grave. Other historians report that the women wore fewer beads as they aged because wearing the heavy necklaces simply made the older women uncomfortable.

During colder weather, an additional piece of clothing called a "long shirt," embellished with ruffles, was added for warmth.

Seminoles do not use beadwork on their clothing as other tribes do, but instead weave the beads into belts, fobs, and garters.

While they most commonly used calico, stripes, solids, and plaid material was also used to make their clothing. The Seminole Indians decorate their cotton clothing with appliqué and have made use of the sewing machine in doing their work since 1880.

When they began making their clothes by machine, some changes came about. For instance, the men's shirt began to include a built-in waistband or belt; then the shirt was tucked into trousers and dubbed the "Seminole jacket." The ruffle on the women's cape increased in length, until by 1920 it covered the whole blouse and extended to the wrists. Today such a cape may be made of tulle or another diaphanous material.

Before 1920, the Seminole seamstresses began to sew contrasting color stripes into their garments, and by the turn of the decade, both sexes' clothing was made of horizontal stripes of material. The now famous Seminole patchwork was developed around this time, and early designs featured blocks or bars of different colors. Sometimes a sawtooth design was sewn directly into the body of the garment. Seamstresses became more and more adroit at adapting this design, and contemporary Seminole clothing is often extremely complicated.

SIOUX

Sioux moccasins are similar to Cheyenne; however, there are several differences. The Sioux decorated the tongues of their moccasins with beadwork, while the Cheyenne rarely did. The Sioux moccasin sole is moderately wide and its inner edge curves out. Unlike the Cheyenne, the Sioux did not protect the sole seam with a welt, but they did bind the top edge with cloth.

APACHE

Apache, woman's cape: hide cape, fringed and scalloped around the bottom with a row of coiled red, white, and blue beads around the edges; the neck opening is surrounded by a large circle of tin cones in a double row; also, a smaller circle of brass medallions and of blue and white seed beads in rope pattern; across the bottom is a row of tin cones and a row of large metal medallions; very good conditon; $850–$1,150.

Apache, woman's dress: two-piece, with ribbon work and bells; ca. 1930; very good condition; $85–$115.

Apache, hat band: braided leather band with bead and horsehair decoration; ca. 1985; 32 inches; $40–$80.

Apache, high-top moccasins: high tops with beaded geometric designs in black, white, light blue, green, red, and cobalt; 15 inches long; very good condition; $450–$650.

Apache, moccasins: hide soles and toe guard, tall yellow muslin tops; ca. 1890; 32 x 6½ inches; very good condition; $70–$115.

Apache, shirt and leggings: fringed hide and trade cloth; a red fringed cotton shirt with ribbon trim and pair of trade cloth appliqué-decorated leggings; very good condition; $60–$115.

ARAPAHO

Arapaho, moccasins: classic full-beaded moccasins with buffalo-hide soles and sinew-sewn; ca. 1880; 11 x 4 inches; very good condition; $700–$920.

Clothing, Arapaho, moccasins; ca. late 1800s; sinew-sewn; beadwork in violet, purple, yellow, wine, and light blue; provenance: collection of Burton Thayer. $2,600. Courtesy of Canfield Gallery. Photo by Robert Reno.

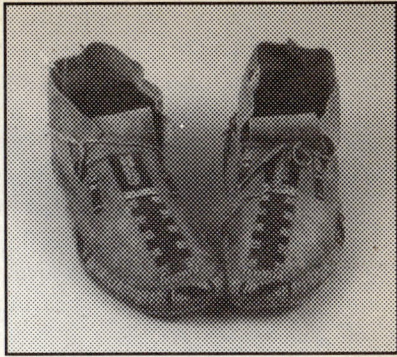

Clothing, Arapaho, moccasins; late 1800s; red, white, and blue beadwork; $2,000. Courtesy of Canfield Gallery. Photo by Robert Reno.

Arapaho, moccasins: sinew-sewn; beadwork in violet, purple, yellow, wine, and light blue; provenance: collection of Burton Thayer; ca. late 1800s; $2,600.

Arapaho, moccasins: red, white, and blue beadwork; late 1800s; $2,000.

Arapaho, moccasins: three pair, each with bead-stitched uppers, all sinew-sewn, all with hard soles; inside one pair: "Made by Arapaho Indians at Ethete, Wyoming—1935"; provenances; 10 inches, 10¼ inches, and 10¼ inches; very good condition; $200–$325.

ASSINIBOIN

Assiniboin, dress: large trade cloth dress with full basket-beaded top; ca. 1900; 50 x 48 inches; very good condition; $750–$975.

Assiniboin, dress: unusual green velvet dress with brass snap and bead decoration; ca. 1900; 52 x 49 inches; very good condition; $575–$800.

ATHABASCAN

Athabascan, boots: high-top moose-hide moccasins with beaded toe and fur and red cloth trim; ca. 1975; 16 x 9 inches; very good condition; $80–$115.

Athabascan, chief's coat: soft tanned buckskin jacket with fringe and floral beadwork on shoulders and front; ca. 1900; 26 x 22 inches; very good condition; $300–$575.

Athabascan, coat: rare hide "chief's" coat with beaded floral designs and fringe; ca. 1890; 29 x 19 inches; very good condition; $275–$315.

Athabascan, moccasins: rare large plaited birch-bark moccasins; ca. 1910; 10½ x 4 inches; very good condition; $55–$80.

Athabascan, moccasins: large moose-hide puckered-toe moccasins with floral beadwork on toes; ca. 1910; 10½ x 3 inches; very good condition; $45–$60.

Athabascan, moccasins: large moose-hide moccasins with fur trim and with flag and eagle beaded on felt toe; ca. 1935; 11 x 4 inches; very good condition; $50–$90.

Athabascan, moccasins; buckskin moccasins with floral beaded toes and fur trim; ca. 1920; 9 x 5 inches; very good condition; $50–$85.

Athabascan, mukluks: moose-hide moccasins with seal fur and wolf trim; ca. 1920; 9 x 3½ inches; very good condition; $50–$90.

BLACKFOOT

Blackfoot, leggings: trade cloth leggings with colorful beaded strip; ca. 1940; 36 x 18 inches; very good condition; $150–$200.

Blackfoot, moccasin: single, beaded on toe, with soft sole; very good condition; $50–$100.

Blackfoot, moccasins: beaded hide; with beaded tops and heels, red and blue trade stroud cloth around on the cutwork cuffs; bead colors: greasy yellow, turquoise, sky blue, pink, black, and white; 10¼ inches long; very good condition; $920–$1,035.

Blackfoot, beaded and fringed hide shirt: with ermine attachments; ca. 1900; $30,000.

Clothing, Blackfoot, beaded and fringed hide shirt with ermine attachments; ca. 1900; $30,000. Courtesy of Canfield Gallery. Photo by Robert Reno.

CHEYENNE

Cheyenne, leggings: blue trade cloth leggings, edged with red silk; a beaded panel featuring crosses and diamonds extends from top to bottom; the outside edges with tin cones with locks of human hair; ca. 1890; very good condition; $700–$900.

Cheyenne, moccasins, child's: geometric beadwork; ca. 1880; 7 x 3 inches; very good condition; $115–$150.

Cheyenne, moccasins: beaded design on green ochered buckskin; old; very good condition; $650–$850.

Cheyenne, moccasins: fully beaded, very narrow, good colors and designs; old; mint condition; $700–$1,100.

Cheyenne, moccasins: fully beaded with rawhide soles; very good condition; $500–$700.

Cheyenne, moccasins: hide with rawhide soles and full-beaded uppers in geometric designs; ca. 1900; 10 x 4 inches; very good condition; $185–$230.

Cheyenne, moccasins: full-beaded hard-soled moccasins with geometric designs; ca. 1940; 10 x 4 inches; very good condition; $160–$185.

Cheyenne, moccasins: full-beaded, sinew-sewn, hard-sole moccasins with geometric designs; ca. 1920; 10 x 4 inches; very good condition; $150–$175.

Cheyenne, moccasins: beaded; ca. late 1970s; very good condition; $400–$520.

Cheyenne, moccasins: pictorial beaded moccasins; eagle effigy denotes warrior society affiliation; beaded in red, white, and blue; $3,000.

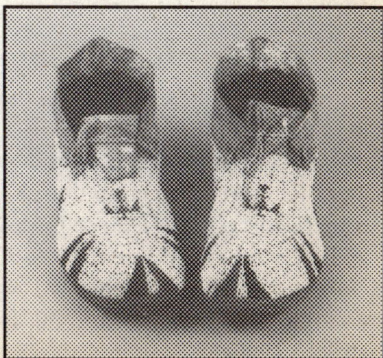

Clothing, Cheyenne, moccasins; pictorial beaded moccasins; eagle effigy denotes warrior society affiliation; beaded in red, white, and blue; $3,000. Courtesy of Canfield Gallery. Photo by Robert Reno.

CHIMAYO

Chimayo, jacket, woman's: wool; red, gray, black, white, and aqua; double pockets and three buttons; 28½ inches long; very good condition; $30–$60.

CHIPPEWA

Chippewa, bandolier bag: beaded; green, blue, and red flower designs on white beadwork field; trimmed with black satin; sewn on old feed sack material; much of beadwork fringe missing; fair condition; $60–$85.

Chippewa, moccasins: pair, one-piece buckskin with beaded designs on cuff and toe; old; very good condition; $100–$200.

CHOCTAW

Choctaw, sash: beaded, of typical white beaded scroll design on brick-colored stroud cloth, with blue-black braided wool accents; good condition; $1,275–$1,725.

COMANCHE

Comanche, boots: yellow-pigmented hide with attached beaded strips in black, white, orange, and blue; fringed and signed "Cynthia Horse," Oklahoma City; 20th century; 20 inches long; very good condition; $100–$140.

Comanche, leggings, man's: beaded and fringed hide, edged with rows of metal studs and beads; ca. 1890; very good condition; $1,380–$1,725.

Comanche, moccasins: rare old hide moccasins with star and cross design; ca. 1890; 9½ x 4 inches; very good condition; $55–$100.

Comanche, sash, woman's: colorful, hand-woven; ca. 1980; 94 x 8 inches; very good condition; $15–$20.

CREE

Cree, moccasins, child's: beaded moose hide; ca. 1920; 8 x 3 inches; very good condition; $55–$85.

Cree, moccasins: beaded moose hide with rabbit-fur cuff; not old, but nice; very good condition; $75–$125.

Cree, moccasins; pair, one-piece buckskin with moose-hair designs; old; very good condition; $100–$200.

Cree, moccasins: choice hard-soled white buckskin with multicolored floral beadwork; ca. 1890; 10½ x 4 inches; very good condition; $200–$260.

CREEK

Creek, ribbon shirt: black crepe fabric with red ribbons; worn for guidance; very good condition; $40–$60.

CROW

Crow, breastplate: choice real hair-pipe bone breastplate with fringe and with Crow bead separators; ca. 1880; 15 x 13 inches; very good condition; $635–$800.

Crow, scout-style child's ¾-length coat/jacket: tailored with fringe at seams, with yellow paint and geometric floral beadwork of salmon, blue, green, red, light brown, greasy yellow, and cobalt, outlined in white; 25 inches overall; very good condition; $4,000–$4,500.

Crow, cuffs; classic full floral beaded dance cuffs with fringe; ca. 1930; 8 x 6½ inches; very good condition; $160–$230.

Crow, dress, maiden's: fine beaded and fringed doeskin, sinew-sewn with red, blue, and green Plains designs on white field; bright, clean; two rows of tin cone hawkbells around fringe; excellent condition; $620–$850.

Crow, gauntlet glove: one only, with beaded design; ca. 1920s; very good condition; $90–$150.

Crow, leggings, woman's: beaded hide and trade stroud cloth; light and dark blue bands; white trim against red cloth; ca. late 1800s; very good condition; $1,725–$2,300.

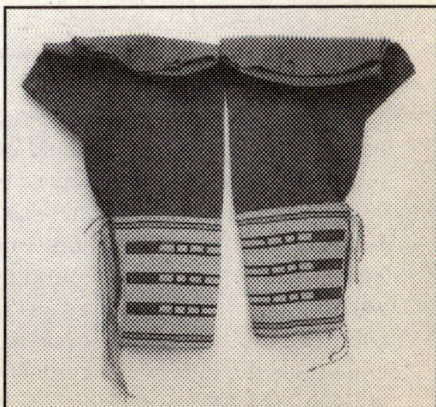

Clothing, Crow, leggings; women's leggings; late 1800s; beaded hide and trade cloth (stroud cloth); light and dark blue bands; white trim against red cloth; $2,000–$2,500. Courtesy of Canfield Gallery, Santa Fe. Photo by Donald Vogt.

Clothing, Crow or Nez Perce, woman's leggings; ca. 1900; made of red trade cloth with beadwork panels at the ankles; $2,000. Courtesy of Canfield Gallery. Photo by Robert Reno.

Crow/Nez Perce, girl's leggings: early seed beads in light blue with red, green, yellow, and blue stripes; old; very good condition; $300–$475.

Crow/Nez Perce, woman's leggings: made of red trade cloth with beadwork panels at the ankles; ca. 1900; $2,000.

Crow, moccasins: beaded in white, light blue, clear, red, green, and cobalt beads; 9 inches long; very good condition; $125–$175.

Crow, moccasins: fully beaded with geometric designs and painted parfleche soles; old; very good condition; $450–$650.

Crow, moccasins: rare old buffalo-hide moccasins with geometric beaded toe and trim; ca. 1880; 10 x 3½ inches; very good condition; $200–$260.

Crow, pants: fringed and beaded in floral design down leg; very good condition; $375–$500.

Crow, painted buffalo robe: native tanned multicolored depictions on a subtle yellow pigment field of exploits such as hunting bear and buffalo and a variety of battles; details from scenes include dancer wearing otter-skin turban with roach and German silver ornamentation, wounded warrior with scalp locks, split-horn warbonnets, and two riders attacking a Crow warrior on foot; provenance: was reshaped into a sleigh/car robe with a plaid flannel cover; had been stored in a sealed crate since the turn of the century; descended through family; 56 x 79 inches; "as found" condition; $7,200–$8,625.

FLATHEAD

Flathead, vest: beaded cloth and hide, decorated with faceted clear dark red, yellow, clear green, iridescent, chili red, and clear beads in large floral and foliate designs on a white beaded background; ca. 1920s–1930s; 27 inches long (including fringe); very good condition; $400–$575.

GREAT LAKES

Great Lakes, dress: beaded and sequined; possibly Winnebago; aqua trim on dark blue background decorated with red beads and red, copper, and black sequins; ca. 1930s–1940s; very good condition; $230–$375.

HAIDA

Haida, apron: cloth apron decorated with miniature coppers and shells; ca. 1930; 34 x 22 inches; very good condition; $150–$230.

HOPI

Hopi, Armbands; constructed of yarn-wrapped pieces in red, yellow, and green, trimmed in black; ca. 1940; very good condition; $300–$500.

Hopi, manta, woman's: cotton in a classic woven design of red, black, and natural; ca. 1930s; 3 feet 1 inch x 3 feet 11 inches; good condition; $700–$1,000.

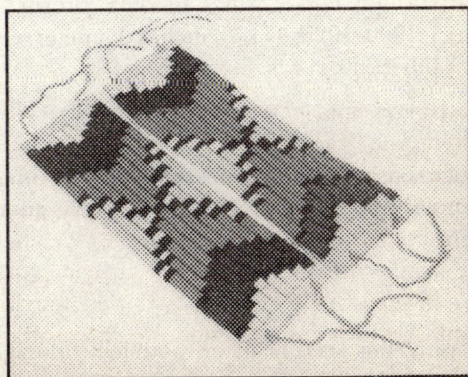

Clothing, Hopi, armbands, ca. 1940; constructed of yarn-wrapped pieces in red, yellow, and green; trimmed in black; $300–$500. Courtesy of Canfield Gallery. Photo by Donald Vogt.

IROQUOIS

Iroquois, cap: beaded floral design and red trade cloth; very good condition; $400–$500.

Iroquois, cap, man's: red wool with beaded band and bill; ca. early 1900s; good condition; $100–$150.

Iroquois, moccasins, child's: choice, with fine pony-beaded designs; ca. 1880; 5½ x 3 inches; very good condition; $100–$140.

Iroquois, moccasins, child's: pony-beaded, white with floral designs in yellow and translucent white beads with metal discs; 7 inches; very good condition; $50–$90.

Iroquois, moccasins and small purse: beaded; ca. 1900; very good condition; $70–$150/set.

Iroquois, Seneca/Oneida, moccasins: black velvet vamps and cuffs beaded in floral design, hide soles; ca. 1890; 10 inches long; excellent condition; $100–$200.

KIOWA

Kiowa, leggings: red trade cloth lining, red, green, and white beading down the side of the leg; ca. 1880–1900; very good condition; $1,150–$1,530.

Kiowa, shirt: fringed buckskin with many painted Ghost Dance symbols; ca. 1890; 42 x 18 inches; very good condition; $775–$920.

KLAMATH

Klamath, hat: twined basketry hat in dark brown and mottled brown; ca. 1900–1925; 4¾ x 7½ inches diameter; very good condition; $155–$260.

KUTENAI

Kutenai, moccasins; high-top buckskin with geometric beaded designs; ca. 1935; 9 x 4 x 9 inches; very good condition; $55–$85.

LAKES

Lakes, moccasins: tiny seed beads in double-head eagle design on red trade cloth backing, soft soles; very old; very good condition; $200–$300.

MICMAC

Micmac, Eastern Woodlands, 14–piece dance costume: beaded dress, leggings, moccasins, coat, ankle bands, bag, beaded strip, shawl, waistband with double curve motif and diamond design on red trade cloth; ca. late 19th century; very good condition; $3,000–$4,500 each.

MODOC

Modoc, cap, woman's: rare twined cap with purple and green diamond designs; ca. 1880; 7½ x 4 inches; very good condition; $135–$155.

NAVAJO

Navajo, blouse: squaw's traditional "plush" in rust color, decorated with 25 fluted, round, and repoussé butterfly ornaments; very good condition; $115–$175.

Navajo, dress, woman's: one panel, finely woven with a dark brownish black center flanked by two rows of stepped terrace and linear designs in indigo blue against red panels, fine narrow stripes in green, cotton warp; 45 x 33 inches; very good condition; $1,265–$1,600.

Navajo, sash, child's: small hand-woven sash belt; ca. 1940; 31 x 1½ inches; very good condition; $15–$20.

Navajo, sash: handmade orange, white, and pink sash, often used in birthing; very good condition; $35–$45.

Navajo, serape: colored stripes with blue band; 46 x 82 inches; very good condition; $50–$90.

Navajo, vest, man's rug: rust, aqua, black, gold, and gray in serrated diamond designs; $85–$155.

NEZ PERCE

Nez Perce, gauntlets: high-top buckskin gloves with bow and arrow beaded decoration; ca. 1935; 11 x 7 inches: very good condition; $55–$90.

Nez Perce, moccasins, infant's: beaded hide, sinew-sewn and decorated with cobalt blue, lavender, red with white centers, and white beads in a narrow T design; ca. 1900; 4¼ inches long; mint condition; $50–$115.

Nez Perce, moccasins: soft-soled and fully beaded with geometric designs; ca. 1900; 10 x 4 inches; very good condition; $175–$230.

Nez Perce, vest: full-beaded "Dreamer Society" contour-beaded vest with floral designs; ca. 1900; very good condition; $920–$1,150.

Nez Perce, vest: large; buckskin with classic multicolored floral beaded designs; ca. 1920; very good condition; $400–$575.

NORTHERN PLAINS

Northern Plains, leggings, woman's: fully beaded in geometric designs of red, light blue, green, light brown, white, and dark blue, with fringe; 15 inches long; very good condition; $650–$850.

Northern Plains, moccasins, child's: beaded hide fully decorated across the vamp, toe, sides, and around back with cobalt blue, chili red, clear red, yellow, and white beads; 4¾ inches; mint condition; $80–$115.

Northern Plains, moccasins: fully beaded hide, decorated with clear red, lime, cobalt blue, orange, sky blue, chili red, metallic, and white beads; 9 inches long; excellent condition; $350–$450.

Northern Plains, vest, man's: possibly Northern Arapaho; sinew-sewn beadwork on buffalo hide; ca. 1870; excellent condition; $3,000–$4,000.

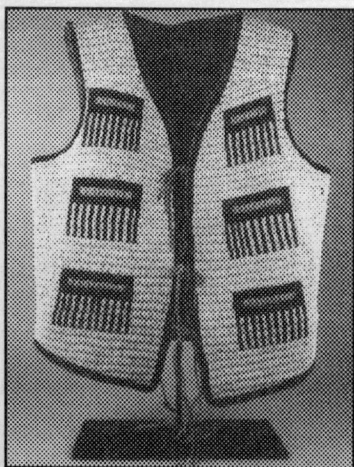

Clothing, Northern Plains, man's vest; ca. 1870s; sinew-sewn, beaded on bison hide, geometric motifs on white background; $8,500–$9,500. Courtesy of Canfield Gallery. Photo by Robert Reno.

Clothing, Northern Plains, moccasins; fully beaded hide moccasins; 9 inches long, decorated with clear red, lime, cobalt blue, orange, sky blue, chili red, metallic, and white beads; excellent condition; $350–$450. Courtesy Jack Sellner, CAI.

Northern Plains, vest, man's: sinew-sewn, beaded on bison hide, geometric motifs on white background; ca. 1870s; excellent condition; $8,500–$9,500.

Northeastern, snowshoes, child/youth: high-strung webbing, leather foot straps, and tufts of red bayeta/Germantown yarn along the sides; the name Irene Farnham is carved into the tail of each; 36½ inches long x 11 inches wide; very good condition; $75–$120.

Northern Plains, vest: beaded cloth vest; decorated with cobalt blue, sky blue, red, clear green, and faceted brass beads; ca. 1900–1930; very good condition; $400–$600.

NORTHWEST COAST

Northwest Coast, headdress: polychrome, in the form of an elongated wolf's head, with hinged lower jaw, flaring nostrils, abalone inlaid eyes and snout, horsehair tufting on ears, applied bone teeth, tacked copper strips forming eyebrows; paint colors: black, red, and turquoise; ca. 20th century; very good condition; $1,035–$1,380.

Northwest Coast, mukluks: sealskin and white and brown leather; 9 inches high; very good condition; $40–$60.

Northwest Coast, Nootka, hat: made of twisted spruce root with totemic designs, painted in red and black; good condition; $1,800–$2,000.

OJIBWAY

Ojibway, moccasins: soft buckskin moccasins with rows of beaded decoration; ca. 1940; 8 x 3½ inches; very good condition; $45–$90.

Ojibway, buffalo robe: painted, with polychrome Ojibway figures; dated 1884; 6 feet 6 inches x 5 feet 9 inches; very good condition; $450–$650.

OSAGE

Osage, leggings, woman's: ca. 1900; very good condition; $865–$975.

Osage, shirt; ribbon-work shirt in mint green, pink, and purple panels; made of Chinese silk; construction technique is reverse appliqué; ca. 1860; very good condition; $4,600–$5,750.

Osage, wedding hat and coat, woman's: ca. 1920; very good condition; $1,380–$1,725/set.

Osage, pants, man's: buckskin; fringed and beaded; floral beadwork designs of green, brown, blue, pink, yellow, and white; button fly; good condition; $185–$230.

PLAINS

Plains, belts: five full-beaded leather belts with loom-strung beadwork; very good condition; $60–$85.

Plains, belts (two): loom-strung with red, yellow, and blue designs on white; 1½ x 36 inches; and belt with same colors, 1½ x 32 inches; very good condition; $15–$20.

Plains, blouse, lady's: sleeveless deerskin; fringed, beaded, and embroidered; embroidered silk flowers accented with beadwork scrolls; long fringe at shoulders (10 inches), fringe down sides and at hem; very good condition; $135–$200.

Plains, dress, girl's: hide; beaded and fringed with translucent-blue-beaded yoke containing crosses and triangle motifs in white, dark blue, bright green, translucent red, and faceted silver, and white beaded panels containing rows of crosses in similar colors, tiny beaded rectangles on the skirt, large glass beads on the fringe; 38 inches long; very good condition; $5,175–$5,750.

Plains, dress: large beaded and fringed deerskin dress; beadwork around neck and sleeves; fair condition; $100–$155.

Plains, hatband: wide geometric-design loom-beaded hatband; ca. 1980; 14 x 2 inches; very good condition; $35–$60.

Plains, headband: beaded, red and white on green; very good condition; $40–$50.

Plains, leggings, child's: beaded deerskin with 4-inch-wide band of red, blue, green, and pink geometric designs on white field; sinew-sewn; very good condition; $80–$115.

Plains, leggings, man's: large, full-length beaded buckskin leggings; ca. 1940; very good condition; $60–$90.

Plains, leggings: blue trade cloth decorated with ribbons and a beaded breechclout; the clout is badly damaged by moths, but the beaded areas are intact; $75–$100.

Plains, vest, man's: fully beaded with blue background and floral design in orange, yellow, salmon, green, red, and purple metallic cut beads; 22 inches long; very good condition; $800–$1,000.

Plains, moccasins and beaded bag: green, white, red beads in buffalo-track design; drawstring bag with blue and white hourglass design; very good condition; $200–$350 each.

Plains, moccasins: beaded hide, hard-soled, with triangles in light and dark blue and translucent red against similar grounds, translucent-green-beaded panels on the fronts and ankles; 10 inches long; very good condition; $700–$920.

Plains, moccasins: beaded hide, hard-soled, decorated with thunderbirds in yellow, blue, and translucent red against white-beaded ground; 10 inches long; very good condition; $700–$920.

Plains, moccasins; deerskin: beaded panels on instep; green, orange, blue, red, and white design; 1 x 4 inches; good condition; $55–$85.

Plains, moccasins: large; trimmed with narrow beaded panels in orange, blue, green, black, and white designs; good condition; $35–$60.

Plains, moccasins: roughly tanned, rawhide-looking with red, white, and blue beaded design; very good condition; $25–$50.

Plains, moccasins: sinew-sewn with multicolored beadwork borders and toe designs; good condition; $55–$80.

Plains, moccasins: rare Southern Plains beaded hide moccasins, sinew-sewn, decorated with cobalt blue, lavender, waxy yellow, pony trader blue, green, black, white, and clear red beads; old; 10 inches long; excellent/near mint condition; $460–$700.

Plains, moccasins: beaded; very good condition; $65–$100.

Plains, moccasins: three pairs, one each for child, youth, adult; beaded hide, with geometric devices; provenance: Cephas

Buttes, Dakota Territory, 1885; very good condition; $875–$975/set.

Plains, moccasins: two pairs, beaded in geometric designs in white, red, cobalt, light blue, and orange; 10½ inches long and 9 inches long; very good condition; $125–$175 each.

Plains, pouch: small, beaded, with geometric decoration; very good condition; $55–$115.

Plains, pouch: beaded; very good condition; $50–$115.

Plains, robe: central sunburst design in green and red with four smaller sunbursts in corners; branded "DL"; 7 feet 3 inches high x 7 feet 10 inches; very good condition; $400–$600.

Plains, miscellaneous Indian beadwork: beaded loom-strung belt with red, yellow, and blue geometric designs on white, 1½ x 30 inches; and beaded belt with orange, black, red, blue, and yellow thunderbird design on white, 1½ x 24 inches; very good condition; $15–$20 each.

Plains, miscellaneous, vest and watch fob: beaded pockets and back in floral designs; loom-beaded fob with hearts; ca. 1930–1940; very good condition; $65–$85.

Plains, vest, man's: fully beaded with white background; front: crosses and stars in red, black, and metallic beads; back: clear-cut basket beads; 21½ inches overall; very good condition; $600–$800.

PLATEAU

Plateau, beaded belt, lady's, multicolor floral designs on a white background, with buckle and deerskin ties; ca. 1890–1920; 28 inches long; excellent condition, $100–$200.

Plateau, belt: beaded geometric designs; 4 x 36 inches; very good condition; $190–$240.

Plateau, cuffs, two pairs; one pair with multicolored beads on a white-bead background with a floral and heart design with quills in red and green on the fringe; other with geometric design in dark blue, orange, and yellow on a light-blue-beaded background and translucent gold beads on the fringe; very good condition; $250–$350/set.

Plateau, dress; mountain sheep buckskin dress with red and white pony beads, fine hairlike fringe; rare; ca. 1900; very good condition; $6,500–$7,500.

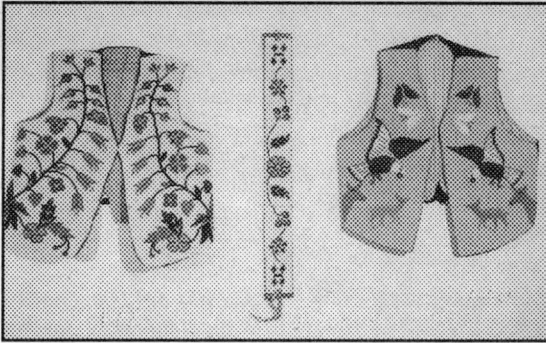

Clothing, Plateau pieces—from left to right: Plateau beaded vest, intricate floral design with trailing blue bells, multi shades of blue and green, reds, yellows, on white background with label "Vest of Big Moose, Salteaux," ca. 1890–1920, 23 inches long, excellent condition, $1,000–$1,250; Plateau beaded belt, lady's, multicolor floral designs on a white background, with buckle and deerskin ties, ca. 1890–1920, 28 inches long, excellent condition, $100–$200; Plateau beaded vest, butterflies, deer, and flying eagles in gold, brown, white, black, blue, and red on a rose background, trimmed in light blue, ca. 1890–1920, 21½ inches long, $850–$1,000. Courtesy of Willis Henry Auctions, Inc.

Plateau, gauntlets: beaded elk/moose hide; decorated with sky blue, lavender, faceted black, brass metallic cut, clear lime, clear gray, and light blue beads in floral and foliate designs; ca. 1920–1930; 13 inches long; very good condition; $125–$175.

Plateau, vest: beaded floral design with blue background, back of yellow-painted hide; 19 inches long; very good condition; $600–$800.

Plateau, beaded vest: butterflies, deer, and flying eagles in gold, brown, white, black, blue, and red on a rose background, trimmed in light blue; ca. 1890–1920; 21½ inches long; $850–$1,000.

Plateau, beaded vest: intricate floral design with trailing blue bells, multi shades of blue and green, reds, yellows; on white background, with label "Vest of Big Moose, Salteaux"; ca. 1890–1920; 23 inches long; excellent condition; $1,000–$1,250.

Plateau, figural vest: fully beaded with spread-wing eagles on a red, white, and blue American shield, and floral beadwork on a light blue background; fringed suspension around collar; 20 inches long; very good condition; $500–$700.

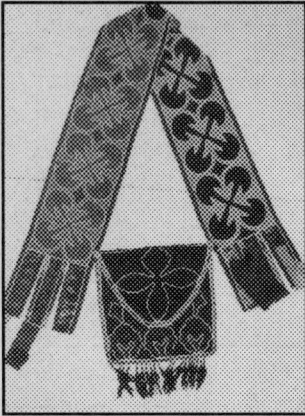

Clothing, Potawatomi, bandolier shoulder bag; appliqué beaded flap and pocket in cobalt, green, and red, outlined in white; decorated with tin cones; red wool; 6-inch straps beaded in cobalt, light blue, outlined in white, with red and green diamonds, blue and beige silk strips; 55 inches long; excellent condition; $20,900–$25,000. Courtesy of Willis Henry Auctions, Inc.

Plateau, vest, man's: fully beaded with light blue cut bead background and floral design in red, green, salmon, light brown, and metallic beads; 25 inches long; very good condition; $800–$1,000.

POTAWATOMI

Potawatomi, bandolier shoulder bag: appliqué beaded flap and pocket in cobalt, green, and red, outlined in white; decorated with tin cones; red wool; 6-inch straps beaded in cobalt, light blue, outlined in white, with red and green diamonds, blue and beige silk strips; 55 inches long; excellent condition; $20,900–$25,000.

PUEBLO

Pueblo, boots, girl's small: beaded doeskin; geometric designs in orange, blue, yellow, and red on white panels; white and orange border design around sole edges; row of brass spots up outside of leg; 15-inch fringed top; old but not worn; very good condition; $200– $240.

Pueblo, moccasins: ocher-dyed coin button "high-top" moccasins with six Washington quarter buttons; 16 inches high; very good condition; $200–$300.

Pueblo, sash: with red, white, and green in geometric designs; 2½ x 51½ inches long (including fringe); very good condition; $25–$45.

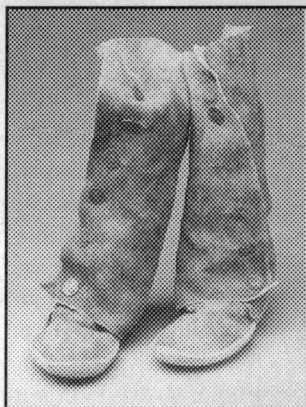

Clothing, Pueblo, moccasins; ocher-dyed coin button "high-top" moccasins; 16 inches high with six Washington quarter buttons; $200–$300. Courtesy Jack Sellner, CAI.

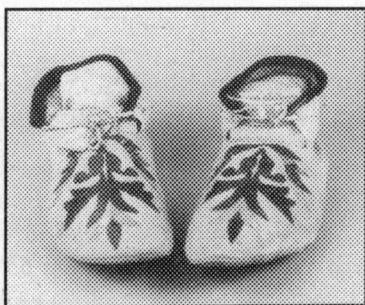

Clothing, Santee Sioux, moccasins; early 1900s; Plains, quillwork on sinew-sewn hide, elaborate curvilinear motifs; $1,900. Courtesy of Canfield Gallery. Photo by Robert Reno.

Pueblo, sash: colorful hand-woven sash belt with fringe; ca. 1950; 50 x 4 inches; very good condition; $30–$60.

Pueblo, shawl: woven wool manta; black with ties and tassels; type used in Pueblo Indian ceremonies by Kachinas, dancers, and women; 39 x 56 inches; very good condition; $115–$225.

SANTEE SIOUX

Santee Sioux, moccasins, lady's: soft buckskin, hard-soled, floral beadwork; ca. 1890; 9 x 3½ inches; very good condition; $150–$200.

Santee Sioux, moccasins: quilled high tops, Santee floral designs, leggings made on; fine, early; very good condition; $800–$1,100.

Santee Sioux, moccasins: quilled in floral design; old; fair to poor condition; $125–$300.

Santee Sioux, moccasins: quilled; ca. 1900; good to better condition; $400–$500.

Santee Sioux, pants: deerskin with beaded floral designs and fringe running the entire length of the outseam, with two large beaded birds at top; 45 inches long; very good condition; $1,300–$1,600.

SEMINOLE

Seminole, dress and jewelry: cape dress with wedding collar and earrings; cape is black, jewelry is black and red; very good condition; $60–$115/set.

Seminole, life jacket and jewelry: contemporary life jacket made of Seminole patchwork with no seams; paired with old Seminole earrings and necklace made of bone, brass, and old cut glass; very good condition; $350–$575 each.

Seminole, woman's blouse and skirt: quilted and banded strips of fabric, multicolored; blouse with blue yoke and green body; mainly blue and red skirt; ca. late 19th century; 50 inches long; very good condition; $100–$200/set.

Seminole, shawl, Pendleton: double-faced and fringed Pendleton Indian shawl; ca. 1965; 64 x 44 inches; very good condition; $50–$80.

SIOUX

Sioux, baby's bonnet: fully beaded; very good condition; $300–$500.

Sioux, baby's bonnet: beaded in striped red, blue, yellow, green, and white with beaded and fringed tab, sinew-sewn; 7 inches overall; very good condition; $800–$1,000.

Sioux, baby's bonnet: indigo trade cloth decorated with dentellium shells, trimmed in printed calico; ca. 1880–1890; very good condition; $350–$450.

Sioux, boots, girl's: decorated with brass spots and fine beadwork designs in red, blue, greasy yellow, and white; sinew-sewn; 14 inches; good condition; $115–$175.

Clothing, Sioux, moccasins; beaded hide; 9 inches long; green back; figured white bands with red, blue, yellow, and black accents; ca. 1890; $750–$1,000. Courtesy of Canfield Gallery. Photo by Donald Vogt.

Sioux, breastplate, woman's: with glass trade beads on store string with old coin dangles; very good condition; $600–$800.

Sioux, breastplate, woman's: necklace of tubular bone beads and brass and glass trade beads with a fringe of Indian-head pennies; such adornment, popular all during the 19th century, reached its zenith in the Roaring Twenties when some Sioux women even wore these necklaces with flapper dresses; ca. 1920s; excellent condition; $3,200–$3,800.

Clothing, Sioux, woman's breastplate; ca. 1920s; necklace of tubular bone beads and brass and glass trade beads with a fringe of Indian-head pennies; such adornment, popular all during the 19th century, reached its zenith in the Roaring Twenties when some Sioux women even wore these necklaces with flapper dresses; $3,200–$3,800. Courtesy of Canfield Gallery. Photo by Robert Reno.

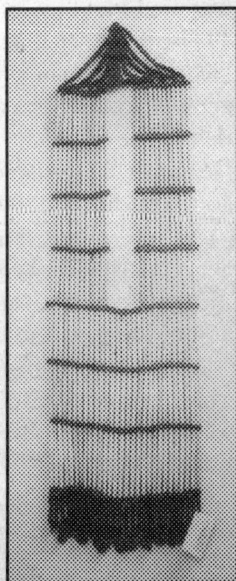

Clothing, Sioux, woman's necklace or breastplate; Dakotas; ca. 1920; elaborate construction of porcupine-quill-wrapped hide strips, medicine wheels, tin cones, and feathers; $9,500–$10,000. Courtesy of Canfield Gallery. Photo by Robert Reno.

Sioux, breastplate, woman's: Dakotas; elaborate necklace constructed of porcupine-quill-wrapped hide strips, medicine wheels, tin cones, and feathers; ca. 1920; excellent condition; $9,500–$10,000.

Sioux, cape, child's: black velvet with beaded eagle and cowrie shell trim; ca. 1910; 18 x 13 inches; very good condition; $40–$80.

Sioux, child carrier: bonnet of bead-trimmed red trade cloth with rosette design in center, with blue and belled bead designs on bonnet front and cross design on back flap; 25 inches long; very good condition; $750–$950.

Sioux, dress: large size; woman's buckskin dress with beaded strips; very good condition; $1,500–$1,900.

Sioux, dress and accessories: full-beaded yoke, geometric design on blue background with later-made matching headband, belt, and moccasins; thousands of early glass beads on fringed buckskin body; ca. 1900; very good condition; $8,000–$10,000/set.

Sioux, gloves: beaded gauntlet gloves with geometric designs on fringed panel; ca. 1880s; very good condition; $800–$1,300.

Sioux, leggings: blue wool with attached beaded strips on hide in H and tepee designs in green, red, cobalt, and greasy yellow on a background of white; sinew-sewn; attached brass beads; trimmed in white beads, cowrie shells, and twisted rawhide; 30½ inches long; good condition; $500–$700.

Sioux, leggings, woman's: beaded buffalo hide with classic beaded geometric designs; ca. 1880; 18 x 7 inches; very good condition; $750–$1,035.

Sioux, leggings: beaded and fringed, on commercial hide; ca. 1920; good condition; $300–$500.

Sioux, leggings, man's: buckskin leggings with geometric design, beaded strips; very good condition; $600–$800.

Sioux, leggings, man's: buckskin leggings with wide-fringed wings and beading on the hide; very good condition; $350–$550.

Sioux, leggings: each beaded with geometric patterns against a white ground; bead colors: apple green, bright blue, and white heart reds; sinew-sewn; 18 inches long; very good condition; $635–$800.

Sioux, moccasins: fully beaded in hourglass and cross designs in cobalt, green, and red on a background of white; 10 inches long; very good condition; $550–$750.

Sioux, moccasins: fully beaded in geometric patterns in cobalt, green, and red on a background of white; sinew-sewn; 11 inches long; very good condition; $750–$950.

Sioux, moccasins: beaded in cross design in red, white, green, and cobalt; 9½ inches long; very good condition; $450–$650.

Sioux, moccasins, child's: beaded leather; late but good-looking; very good condition; $100–$150.

Sioux, moccasins, infant's: hide soles, the entire surface covered with small beads in blue, red, yellow, white, in geometric designs; each moc with three tin cone and feather tassel pendants; 4¼ inches long; very good condition; $175–$380.

Sioux, moccasins, child's: beaded, triple-box design with rawhide soles; very good condition; $100–$150.

Sioux, moccasins: beaded buckskin, sinew-sewn; late but good-looking; very good condition; $100–$200.

Sioux, moccasins: beaded in simple design, buckskin; ca. 1900; very good condition; $190–$290.

Sioux, moccasins: commercial buckskin, fully beaded; very good condition; $100–$200.

Sioux, moccasins: full-beaded with canvas uppers and rawhide soles; early; good condition; $300–$400.

Sioux, moccasins: fully beaded in geometric designs with buckskin uppers and rawhide soles; late; very good condition; $150–$200.

Sioux, moccasins: fully beaded with rawhide soles and geometric designs; very good condition; $350–$550.

Sioux, moccasins: fully quilled; ca. 1900; in rare good condition; $1,000–$1,500.

Sioux, moccasins: quilled bar designed with rawhide soles; pre–1900s; good condition; $750–$950.

Sioux, moccasins: fine old Sioux full-beaded, sinew-sewn, hard-soled; ca. 1890; 11 x 4 inches; very good condition; $220–$250.

Sioux, moccasins: beaded hide, green back; figured white bands with red, blue, yellow, and black accents; ca. 1890; 9 inches long; very good condition; $700–$1,035.

Sioux, moccasins: old buffalo hide with geometric designs on the toes; ca. 1880; 9 x 3½ inches; very good condition; $85–$160.

Sioux, moccasins: pair of fully beaded; green, white, red, and blue on white; sinew-sewn; very good condition; $75–$110.

Sioux, necktie: beaded; old; good condition; $100–$200.

Sioux, robe, child's: painted buckskin; box and border with unusual center design; very good condition; $1,300–$1,700.

Sioux, shirt and leggings: matching set of beaded buckskin war shirt and leggings with geometric beaded strips; ca. 1930s; very good condition; $4,500–$5,500/set.

Sioux, shirt: wide quilled buckskin war shirt with strips and bib; very good condition; $2,000–$3,600.

Sioux, war shirt, boy's: sinew-sewn fringed buckskin beaded with geometric figures against a medium blue background; triangular panels at the neck front and back beaded with stylized flags on blue background; ca. 1900; $9,000.

Sioux, shirt: hide, beaded and fringed, stitched across the shoulders and along the arms with white beaded panels of diamond and arrow-feather motifs alternating with rectangles in yellow, bright green, pale orange, shades of blue, and translucent red; a triangular bib on the front and back, each beaded in similar colors; 31½ inches; very good condition; $4,600–$5,175.

Sioux, shirt: fringed and painted muslin shirt, used for Ghost Dance; decorated on one side with sun and star; a spread-winged eagle with lightning bolts surmounted by a sun, star, and crescent moon on the reverse; feather suspensions; 36½ inches long; very good condition; $1,730–$2,000.

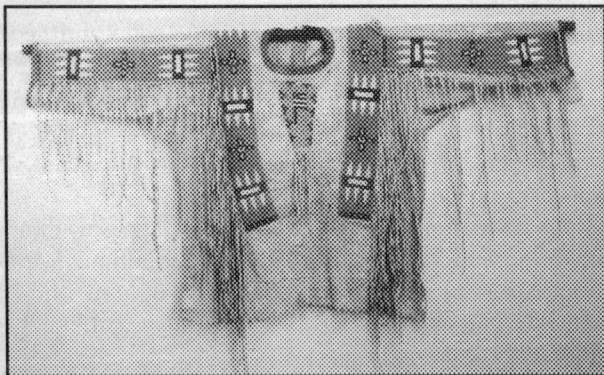

Clothing, Sioux, boy's war shirt; ca. 1900; sinew-sewn fringed buckskin beaded with geometric figures against a medium blue background; triangular panels at the neck front and back beaded with stylized flags on blue background; $9,000.
Courtesy of Canfield Gallery. Photo by Robert Reno.

Sioux, vest: beaded bison and mounted chiefs on front and reverse in blue, red, black, green, and yellow on white beaded background, some attached red trade cloth; 17 inches wide, 22 inches overall length; very good condition; $11,000–$13,000.

Sioux, vest, man's: beaded hide, lined with blue and white cotton cloth and trimmed along the edges in maroon silk; the front stitched in yellow, bright green, dark blue, and translucent red and blue against a white beaded ground, with two stylized dragonflies and angular devices; a tracked line surmounted by similar devices on the back; 18¼ inches long; very good condition; $1,180–$1,725.

Sioux, vest; buckskin, beaded and fringed; very good condition; $375–$475.

Sioux, yoke and dress, girl's: vest-style beaded yoke on velvet dress, geometric designs on buckskin; very good condition; $1,000–$2,000.

SOUTHERN PLAINS

Southern Plains, moccasins: each hard-soled, beaded on the front and sides with a tapering column between rows of parallelograms and diamonds in white, pink, dark blue, and translucent red, yellow, and green against a cobalt blue ground; decorated with rectangular ankle flaps, each with red trade cloth and beaded trim; thick panels of hide fringe on the heels; ocher pigment; 10½ inches; very good condition; $1,380–$1,725.

Southern Plains, boot moccasins: with yellow and red pigment and white beaded panels of blue and translucent red geometric motifs around the ankles and up the calves; provenance: Cephas Buttes, Dakota Territory, 1885; very good condition; $700–$920.

Southern Plains, painted buffalo robe: native tanned hide decorated with the "black bonnet" or "feathered circle" design in black and red; central decoration of four circles encompassed by wavy line; native sinew-sewn repair; 92 inches long x 67 inches wide; very good condition; $920–$1,380.

TLINGIT

Tlingit, moccasins: sealskin low-top moccasins with beaded geometric designs on the toe; ca. 1935; 10 x 4 inches; very good condition; $50–$85.

WARM SPRINGS

Warm Springs, dress, girl's: buckskin with fully beaded black, white, and orange geometric yoke; ca. 1940; 38 x 34 inches; very good condition; $400–$575.

WOODLANDS

Woodlands, Great Lakes, waistband: loom-beaded with leaf designs in cobalt, light blue, green, white, pink, and red; 31¼ inches; very good condition; $100–$300.

Woodlands, moccasins: soft leather with cuffs, instep with floral bead design, cuffs with black and white bead edging; 11 inches long; very good condition; $25–$75.

Woodlands, moccasins: beaded hide, decorated with dark red, lime, blue, faceted clear purple, and white beads; 8½ inches long x 9½ inches high; excellent condition; $1,500–$2,000.

Woodlands, purse: bead-trimmed, blue cloth, 3½ inches; very good condition; $15–$20.

Woodlands, sash: beaded, cross and geometric motif; very good condition; $75–$115.

Woodlands, Great Lakes Menomini, sash: loom-beaded, blue background and multicolored stylized floral design with multicolored wool tassels and braided fringe; 55 inches long; very good condition; $250–$300.

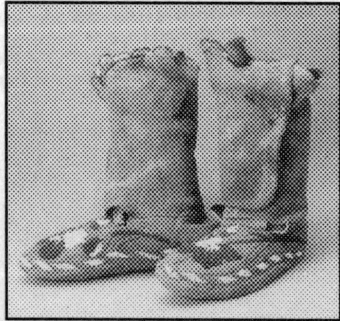

Clothing, Woodlands, moccasins; beaded hide moccasins, 8½ inches long x 9½ inches high; decorated with dark red, lime, blue, faceted clear purple, and white beads; excellent condition; $1,500–$2,000.
Courtesy Jack Sellner, CAI.

YAKIMA

Yakima, leggings, child's: beaded cloth with geometric designs; ca. 1940; 11 x 8 inches; very good condition; $50–$80.

Yakima, moccasins: soft-soled, beaded hide with colorful geometrics; ca. 1930; 9 x 4 inches; very good condition; $110–$155.

Yakima, purse: fully beaded with floral designs and with a metal top and latch; ca. 1925; 10 x 6½ inches; very good condition; $200–$230.

Chapter Six

Dolls, Games, and Sports

～

Every culture has its share of recreational activities, and the Native American cultures are no exception. Before the Europeans ever set foot on this continent, the Indians had developed a battery of games. Often different tribes had slightly different versions of a particular game. Some of the sports that are vital to weekend activities with today's American families—football, for instance, and lacrosse—developed from Native American leisure activities. Even racquetball has its origins in Indian history.

Indian dolls are among the finest and most imaginative in the world. Their creators used the tools available to them, never shirking the opportunity to decorate even the most miniature of toys or dolls.

If you, as a collector, have chosen to collect strictly Indian dolls, toys, and games, you have a wide and interesting field from which to choose.

DOLLS
HOPI

The Hopi artisans have contributed significantly to the field of Indian collectibles, but perhaps their most noted contribution is that of Hopi Kachina dolls.

The Kachina cult is arguably the most important part of the Hopi religion; it has undoubtedly received more attention than the religions of other Pueblo cultures. The Hopis believe it is extremely important to preserve harmony with the world and nature, and the Kachinas provide the Hopi guidance to seek this peaceful way of life. Kachinas are benevolent Hopi spirits said to exist in the San Francisco Peaks. It is said that the spirits rehearse in those peaks and prepare themselves for their main function: the making of snow or rain. The Kachinas represent the spirit essence of everything about the world as we know it: plants, animals, food, insects, birds, power, weather.

The Kachinas are extremely important to Hopi society, thus the San Francisco Peaks are considered sacred. When developers built a ski lift several hundred feet below a sacred site in these peaks, the Hopis objected strenuously, and their Navajo neighbors, to whom the peaks are also sacred, joined them in protesting. This and other developments have seriously endangered the religion the Hopis practice.

The Kachinas traditionally begin to appear in villages after the winter solstice when the kivas—underground ceremonial chambers which the Hopis believe are entrances to the Underworld—are opened. They join with the men there to dance in the kiva and pray for the new year. Until late July, when the path to the kivas is closed, the Kachinas dance in one of the twelve Hopi villages. As August approaches, the villages host *Niman* ceremonies (Home Dance) for the Kachinas to return to their homes in the mountains. This dance is the time when Hopi brides, dressed in white cotton robes traditionally woven by their husbands' uncles, are presented to the Kachinas.

Three main ceremonies are held by the Hopis. The *Soyal* (opening of Kachina season) is in December, when the Kachinas arise sleepily from the now open kivas and dance there, performing rites to strengthen the individual, the clan, and the village during the coming year. The *Powamu* ceremony is held in the villages in February, to celebrate the false advent of spring and to prepare for a new growth season—this is the time when children are initiated into the Kachina cult. The final ceremony is held when the corn the men have planted is ready for harvest—and the Kachinas are sent home to their mountain peaks, through the kivas whence they came.

Because of their holy place in Hopi society, Kachinas may never be photographed. In fact, most Hopi villages maintain their privacy by forbidding the use of cameras, tape recorders, and sketching.

During the planting season, gifts of Kachinas are given, and the distributors of these gifts can select whatever Kachina they care to represent, as well as name their successor for the next year.

The young children are given the dolls that have been made by their male relatives and allowed to play with them in the ensuing days. These figures are called *tihu* by the Hopi and Kachina dolls by everyone else. Most Hopi children have no toys other than those they receive from the Kachinas or make for themselves.

Sprouts are wrapped around the Kachinas that are given as gifts for the new children born that year, and some sprouts are also left as a gift for the Kachina impersonator who will distribute the gifts.

Hopi children have, apparently, learned a valuable lesson from receiving Kachina dolls as gifts. Because the times when a Hopi child receives presents are few and far between, few children have a great love of money or get a thrill from possessing material things. Instead they give to those who give to them—mainly by returning good thoughts and behavior.

Kachina initiation for the Hopi children begins around the age of eight. Before their initiation, the children have close haircuts (the girls are left with a tuft in the front). The initiation takes place every fourth February as part of the *Powamu* ("Bean Dance"). The ceremony introduces the child to his ancestors, the Kachinas, as his birth introduced him to his father, the Sun.

The Kachina cult initiates every Hopi over ten years old as a member. In Third Mesa initiations, the affiliation of the godfather with the Kachinas determines whether or not the child goes through the whipping ordeal (reserved for discipline problems). In this training procedure, the Mother of the Kachinas holds a bunch of yucca switches while the Whipper Kachina applies them to the nude boy or clothed girl, who is supported by his or her godfather and the godfather's sister. The initiation is meant to teach the child the difference between the supernatural and reality and what the child's role is in the scheme of things. After the ritual, boys join one or more of the secret societies, and girls join those of their ceremonial aunts.

During the season when the Kachinas take part in the dances and festivals held in the Hopi villages, the Hopis are reacquainted with the approximately five hundred Kachinas who exist in their religion. There are approximately three hundred currently active Kachinas and another two hundred who make infrequent appearances. The men of the tribe act as the Kachinas, using masks and costumes to resemble the Kachina spirit they represent. When the men are representing their Kachinas, they are said to be invested with that particular Kachina's spirit.

The Chief Kachinas are the most important and have jurisdiction over other Kachinas as well as over village life. They appear at every ceremony, but dolls are not usually made in their likeness.

The warriors or police Kachinas comprise another important group. It is their job to see that the public does not interfere with the dancers or venture into the wrong areas.

The mudhead Kachinas are the cult clowns. They function to lighten the atmosphere and to tease some of the other more serious Kachinas.

Though Hopi men are traditionally the Kachina carvers, Oraibi women have been known to make Kachinas, thus intruding on what has traditionally been a male occupation. Old Kachinas were carved from cottonwood *(ba'ko)* and painted with natural colors. They were usually decorated with real feathers, and pieces of leather were used as skirts or tops. Fabric was used to make other accessories.

The Kachinas made today are extremely beautiful and carved out of a single piece of cottonwood. Instead of being completely painted, as the old ones were, these new Kachinas are only partially painted, and sometimes no other materials are used to decorate them.

Doll dances, once too secret to be discussed, were held by the Hopi. It's unclear whether this practice continues today at Hotevilla. The dolls were worked by strings and represented Corn-Grinding Maidens (Gnumamantu), Shalako Girl (Shalakmana), or Water-Drinking Girl (Palhikmana). They were, apparently, worked much the same as puppets.

Some of the Kachinas a collector might see include:

Bear Kachinas have red *nakwakwosi* ("prayer feathers") placed on their heads. The bear is a warrior, and all warriors have red feathers.

Eototo appears every year on each of the three mesas. He is the equivalent of the village chief and the "father" of the Kachinas.

Aholi appears in the company of Eototo, but only on the Third Mesa during the Powamu ceremony.

Kokosori is one of the oldest recorded Kachinas. This Kachina is always portrayed by a boy.

The angry-looking **Wuyak-kuita** is one of the police or guards who protects the ceremonies. He often is at the rear of the Bean Dance Procession, and his appearance terrifies the clowns.

Tsitoto appears on all mesas and is a well-known ancient Kachina. He is a very colorful figure with a brightly colored birdlike helmet mask. He carries a bunch of yucca leaves and often appears at the Bean Dance.

Talavai Kachinas used to wake the people in the village by singing on the rooftops in pairs.

The only masked Kachina who is truly a woman is **Pachavuin Mana**. She brings bean sprouts into the village during the Pachavu Ceremony.

The **Eagle Kachina** or **Kwahu** dances during one of the March night ceremonies or during the Powamu. The dancer imitates the eagle as closely as possible.

The **Buffalo Kachina** is always masked and dances for the life and population of the buffalo. He usually holds a lightning stick and rattle.

Tawa Kachina or **Sun Kachina** appears with a spruce tree in his left hand and a bell in his right. He is not often impersonated.

Deer Kachina are very popular in the Plaza Kachina dances. He prays for an increase in the deer population and has power over the rain.

One of the best-known Kachinas is the **Hemis Kachina**. He is said to come from the Jemez Pueblo and dances a stately dance in the final dance of the ceremonies.

Kokopele is the humpbacked Kachina who plays a flute.

There are hundreds more, and all collectors have their favorite.

SEMINOLE

Seminole dolls are made in all shapes and sizes, though the look of them is generally the same. They are cloth dolls, dressed as the Seminole women themselves—in brightly striped long cotton shirts with matching full blouses, a number of beaded necklaces around the throat, and a black felt hat.

Dolls are the Seminole's major craft. Some are made for decoration, others to be used as doorstops.

YUMA AND MOHAVE

The Yuma and Mohave tribes of the Colorado River designed and decorated pottery dolls for the tourist trade. These dolls were embellished with beads and cloth.

ZUNI

The Zuni tribe produces Kachinas, as the Hopi do. However, they produce far fewer dolls. Zuni Kachinas are identified by movable body parts and miniature clothing. They are also taller and thinner than their Hopi counterparts.

HOW TO COLLECT
NATIVE AMERICAN DOLLS

First and foremost, choose which type of dolls you like best so that you focus your energy on extensive study of one kind of doll.

Second, when collecting carved dolls (such as Kachinas), check the quality of the carving by making sure that the body parts are in proportion and properly placed. Also check to see that the wood is not cracked. If collecting cloth dolls, make sure there are no tears in the body seams and that the original clothing appears to be intact.

Third, determine the material from which your doll was made. Cottonwood is lightweight; balsa wood is extremely light and can be damaged with the edge of a fingernail (indicating it is not a good doll); red trade cloth on a cloth doll or bits of animal skins indicates a doll predates machine-made fabrics.

Fourth, check the painting on Kachinas to see that the artist paid close attention to detail. If the face of your cloth doll is painted, make sure that the features are recognizable; if it is sewn, check to see if there are loose stitches.

Fifth, be sure that the doll's parts are all intact. For instance, if you have a Kachina with a hole in his hand, it was probably meant to hold something. You should note that very few dolls—Kachinas or other types—are without ornamentation.

Sixth, the collector should note that many Native American dolls are being reproduced by Asian manufacturers. Most dealers worth their salt will be able to tell a real doll from a fake. It is also a law that imported dolls must be marked as such, so check the bottom stand or the tag to see where the doll was made. If it is signed with what appears to be a Native American name, you can be relatively sure that it is authentic.

Seventh, identifying Kachina dolls may be quite difficult as few publications have photographed every single Kachina that exists. However, Barton Wright's *Hopi Kachinas: The Complete Guide to Collecting Kachina Dolls* is one of the best resources. His book lists numerous other sources to investigate. Other dolls may be identified through sources on the Native American tribe to which you believe your doll belongs (see the Bibliography).

BIOGRAPHIES OF SOME KNOWN DOLL MAKERS

JOHNSON ANTONIO (1932–)

Antonio is a Navajo who carves dolls that are folk art in design. His works are now becoming collector's items. He first tried his hand at carving dolls in an effort to earn the money he needed to send his children to school. Antonio's carvings capture the Navajo spirit and culture and are authentic in their clothing and costumes.

His work has been shown at the Wheelwright Museum of the American Indian in a one-man show; other museums and galleries have also begun to show his work.

CECIL CALNIMPTEWA (1950–)

A Kachina carver held in high regard, Calnimptewa is well known for his true one-piece carved Kachinas, as well as for his understanding of draping materials. To make sure his carving truly represents the way material falls, he often practices draping the material on himself or his wife.

Born in the village of Moenkopi, Arizona, Calnimptewa learned about carving Kachinas from his father, who would let his son sand the dolls and paint them. He has passed on that knowledge to his own students, including Dennis Tewa, winner of the 1983 Gallup Inter-Tribal Ceremonial.

The artist's innovations have given new nuances of artistic rendering to his Kachina carvings. He has won many awards for his carvings.

NEIL DAVID, SR.

David is a Hopi from the First Mesa who is an excellent artist versed in several media. He belongs to the Artist Hopid, a group of Hopi artists, and may have been the first to convert the painted Kachina into a three-dimensional being.

David is prolific and versatile and brings to his figures a spirit that makes them truly appear alive.

JAMES (JIM) FRED (1945–)

Jim was born in the village of Bacavi, Arizona, on April 25, 1945. He creates realistic all-wood Kachinas, even carving the feathers that adorn his creations.

He began carving full-time after working for the Hopi Center for Human Services, teaching the mentally handicapped.

He tries to carve the dolls the way he sees the Kachinas move during the traditional dances, capturing the movement of certain motions. He does not attempt to carve unless he's "in the mood to carve a particular type of doll."

WALTER HOWATO

One of the first Kachina carvers to partially paint his figures, Howato entered his Kachina in the Santa Fe Indian Market in the early 1970s.

BRIAN HONYOUTI

Honyouti carved a Crow Mother emerging from the kiva, which is said to be one of the first wood Kachinas that was only partially painted. (Howato did the other.)

RONALD HONYOUTI

Brian's brother Ronald began carving later than Brian, and Ronald's Butterfly Girl won Best of Class at the Gallup Inter-Tribal Ceremonial in 1983.

ALVIN JAMES MAKYA

This Kachina artist was born in Old Oraibi and attended high school in Carson City, Nevada, where he learned carpentry. He was in the Marine Corps from 1957 to 1960 and lived as a carpenter after returning home.

Makya studied Peter Shelton's Kachinas and vowed to make Kachinas as good, or better, than those he studied.

Makya considered his Kachinas something that "makes my living worthwhile."

During the early 1970s Makya Kachinas were not on the market, but those that had been sold earlier brought four-figure prices.

MARLIN PINTO (1957–   )

Born in Zuni, New Mexico, to a Zuni father and Tewa mother, this Kachina carver began creating dolls when he was eleven and began selling them by the time he turned fifteen. He specializes in miniature Zuni, Hopi, and Tewa dolls, since those tribes interchange Kachinas. Every time he carves a Kachina, he purposely makes a mistake to let the spirit out.

A pocket knife is his primary tool. He uses acrylic paint to make his dolls more realistic.

His family is well known since his grandmother, Daisy Nampeyo, was a famous Tewa potter; his uncle, Ray Naha, a Tewa painter; and his mother, Shirley Ben, a Tewa jewelry maker.

HENRY SHELTON

Shelton was first persuaded to carve a raw wood Ho-ote about forty years ago and found it "very difficult." During the mid-1960s he went on to carve two Snake Dancers and an Eagle Dancer, both of which were eventually cast in bronze.

His Kachina figures have been more influential in producing change in the carving of these beloved dolls than any other artist's work.

LOWELL TALASHOMA

A well-known carver, Talashoma creates small traditional dolls in a contemporary style.

His carved wooden Kachinas are now being cast in bronze. Talashoma's agent markets and sells copies to galleries and collectors.

WILFRED TEWAWINA

Tewawina carved several plain wood Hopi figures during the period from 1965 to 1970.

NATIVE AMERICAN TOYS

APACHE PLAYING CARDS   No one really knows when the Apache began making playing cards, and it is argued whether the game was introduced to them by white men or by Spanish-Mexican traders.

The cards acknowledged as Apache designs were often named with words of Spanish derivations, and Apache suit terms were identical to the Spanish. The Apache version of playing cards was usually larger than Anglo ones, and included picture cards. A full deck consisted of anywhere from thirty-two to fifty-two cards and did not reflect the mathematical parallel that served as the foundation of the playing cards of the white men.

The cards averaged 9 by 6.5 centimeters. Only the faces of the cards were painted and decorated. They were usually made of rawhide, and all decoration was hand-painted by the best of their artisans. Produced in limited quantity, the cards have increased in value because of their scarcity.

The red color used on the cards was produced by mixing a combination of barks, roots, and ashes, while rabbitbrush blossoms made yellow pigment, and purple amaranth was used to make purple. Green pigment came from turquoise stones, and black from a mix of yucca juice and charcoal. Brown was derived from walnuts, and cactus juice served as a fixative.

Natural phenomena, special events, places, and people, as well as items associated with soldiers and pioneers, were depicted on playing cards. The early round version of the cards featured suits represented by fish and shells, while others had flowers or coins as symbols.

In the latter part of the 1800s, cards made by Apaches evolved into cards painted with designs such as rifles, swords, and soldiers. The Indian painted what most influenced his life, and at that point, the American soldier was upsetting his cycle of life.

Men, women, and children all played games of chance, and all risked losing everything they possessed in a card game. Everything that was "bettable" was anted up (e.g., money, horses, blankets). The Apaches were professional card players and would take on anyone—including soldiers—at the game.

Though the details of actual games played with these cards are vague and largely unknown, it *is* certain that the Yavapai and Mohave tribes often used the cards as misleading clues, leaving them scattered on the ground after a holdup or wagon attack when they wanted settlers to believe that the Apache, their enemy, were to blame.

Though card playing was known to exist as a social custom in other North American tribes, no other tribes are known to have made playing cards.

BOYS' TOYS Boys' toys included child-sized bows and arrows, tops, drums, whips, and horse gear. Also common were boy or warrior dolls.

CUTOUT FIGURES Cutout figures made from birch bark were designed by Indian women of the North, Northeast, Subarctic, and Lakes areas. Some forms were human, while others were of animals and birds.

The Athabascans sewed such ornaments on their birch-bark containers; others were used as toys.

GIRLS' TOYS Young girls often had miniature tepees and scaled-down furnishings with which to play. Older members of the tribe made child-sized tepees for the girls to play in.

Girls would fashion their own dolls out of available materials and dress them, Indian style, with leftover skins discarded by their mothers or other members of the tribe. If the girl was extremely ambitious, she might talk one of the boys into hunting a squirrel or some other small animal to use as material for doll clothing. Small tepees and furnishings were often just as elaborately decorated as adult versions.

The girls with the longest hair donated hair for the dolls, and sometimes fathers from well-to-do families would make special toys for their favorite daughters. Miniature pipe bundles, small play horses, or small travois packs in which the girls could put their dolls are examples of these "special" toys.

WOODEN ANIMALS Plains Indians fashioned wooden animal toys for their children. Bears, buffalo, and horses were the most common forms carved.

Northern Plains Indians used willow branches to make toy horses. One piece could be split to form the neck and ears; the other half of the same piece could be split to make the forelegs. The tail and back legs were made the same way. Examples of these toy horses are held by the Montana Historical Society.

Dice, used by the Plains Indians as gaming pieces, were often carved in the shape of small animals. Some examples of these pieces, carved of wood or bone, can be found in the American Museum of Natural History in New York City.

DANCE COSTUMES AND REPRESENTATIONS

DANCES Dances play a major role in Native American life, and though it's impossible to collect the dances themselves, one might collect the costumes used in their dances or photos and drawings of the dances performed by different tribal members.

The American Indian Dance Theatre has recently come to prominence, touring throughout the United States and fascinating audiences with their talents. The Theatre performs Native American social dances, the same type of dances performed at competitions staged at powwows and tribal ceremonials.

One group of dances is known as "Traditional Dances." An example is a warrior dance with both men in full regalia, including double bustles of eagle feathers and brightly painted shields and spears. The Traditional Dances represent different facets of Indian life—such as hunting and spotting a bird or prey—and often imitate birds or animals.

The Zuni tribe's women perform a "Butterfly Dance," which teaches children an appreciation for the jobs a butterfly performs. For this dance the women wear knee-high white leather boots that close on the side with conchas, a sleeveless white dress, and a colorful butterfly headdress.

The "Eagle Dance," another Zuni dance, celebrates the bird's power and wisdom and is dedicated to all tribes. The men who dance as eagles are decorated with feathers along their arms. Other tribes also perform eagle dances, which are distinguished from the Zuni version by more active, swooping motions.

The Kwakiutl do a dance called the "Hamatsa Dance" where the dancers are dressed in Raven and Crooked Beak of Heaven wooden, painted, and carved masks.

"Fancy Dances" feature tribe members trying to outdo each other, putting a great amount of high energy into their spins, leaps, and kicks. Their outfits are highly colorful, including full headdresses, spears, shields, decorated breastplates, leggings, and moccasins.

GAMES/SPORTS

ARCHERY   This category includes any games in which an arrow or dart was used to shoot at a mark or object. Grass or bark targets were used by tribes including the Crow, Zuni, and Potawatomi, while the Navajo shot at a yucca ball, and the Makah used kelp. The Omaha tribe shot at arrows lodged in a tree or cacti.

BULL-ROARER   A bull-roarer was a thin piece of wood to which a thong with a piece of wood on the end was attached. Youngsters of the Oglala, Teton, or Omaha tribes grasped the end of the stick and whirled the thong overhead. The piece of wood on the end of the thong would whip through the air, making a whizzing noise.

BUZZ   Another whirling toy common to Indian children was the "buzz." It was made of a flat piece of shell, bone, pottery, or gourd threaded through the center hole with a cord.

By pulling the twisted ends of the cord, the piece in the middle was forced to spin, producing a buzzing noise.

CAT'S CRADLE   Common to quite a few Indian tribes, the cat's cradle game has its roots in mythology. The Zuni say the game was taught to them by their grandmother, the Spider; the Navajo also say they were taught this game by the Spider people.

The game is played with a simple piece of string which is wound through the fingers, making various designs.

Such tribes as the Sauk and Fox, Apache, Hupa, and Navajo have histories of playing this game.

CHUNKEE   Chunkee is the southeastern Indian version of the hoop-and-stick game. It was played with a stone disc, and the object of the game was to come as close as possible to where a player's rolling disc would stop through a pole.

The artist George Catlin, well-known for his intense studies of the American Indian, painted members of the Mandan tribe playing this game, which was also enjoyed by Creek men.

DICE   Games played with dice were common to approximately 130 Indian tribes. It's safe to say that all North American tribes had some knowledge of dice. To play the game, one needed only dice and counting tools. These counting tools could be as simple as sticks or as sophisticated as an abacus.

Some museums attribute beaver-teeth dice to the Karok Indians. The game, originally known to have come from Oregon, may have only come to the Karoks through occupation of their land by the white men.

Arapahos and other tribes made a basket that was used in dice games. The basket, flat with slanted sides, is usually not fancy. The dice can be made from a variety of materials, though Arapaho are known to use bone or plum stones. The dice are tossed in the air, landing in the basket. Points are scored based on the way the dice land.

The game of dice was very detailed, and more often than not, serious gambling was employed on the part of the players. Though both men and women played dice games, ceremonial games were played strictly by men. The game of dice was considered sacred to the Zuni war god, and cane dice were sacrificed to him.

Dice made of bone have even been found in archaeological diggings done in the Southwest.

FOOTBALL   The National Football League did not invent football, as many fans have been led to believe. The game was first played by Indians in the Algonquian tribes, specifically the Massachusetts, Micmac, Narragansett, and Powhatan; the Micmacs are best known for their love of the game. That might explain why the great Indian football player Jim Thorpe had no trouble comprehending, as well as mastering, the game. Other tribes have also been known to play some form of the game.

The balls were made of buckskin or stone, and the goals were two erect sticks, or lines, at the ends of the playing field.

The Indians would play "county against county," and the goals were often a mile apart. Before playing, they would put on war-type paint, and weapons were set aside in the spirit of good sportsmanship.

FOUR-STICK GAME   Played by the Klamath, Modoc, Achomawi, Paiute, Washo, and possibly Chinook tribes, this game includes four sticks that are also referred to as the war gods and their bows.

Players sit opposite each other, with one player in possession of the four sticks. That player's hands are covered with a mat as he rearranges the sticks under the mat, out of sight. The other players are then required to guess how the sticks are arranged, and if someone guesses correctly, he wins a point and the game is handed to him.

The game is accompanied, as are many others, by the harmonious singing of the players.

HOOP AND POLE   Hoop and pole games were popular year-round with the Indian tribes who lived along the American-Canadian border.

The Plains tribes played this game by throwing spears at webbed hoops that were rolled along the ground.

LACROSSE   The game of lacrosse was an Indian invention. It was borrowed by the whites, who now play the game with equal fervor.

Lacrosse was played by most eastern tribes. The Iroquois tribe used a racket that closely resembles the ones modern lacrosse players use. Southeastern tribes used smaller sticks with round nets on the end, while Lakes area tribes used single sticks.

The game was also played by the Chippewa, Huron, Miami, Penobscot, Sauk and Fox, Shawnee, Skokomish, and Winnebago tribes.

RACQUETBALL Racquetball was almost exclusively a game for Indian males. Many tribes played, but only one that we know of, the Santee, allowed men and women to play the game together.

Though it is played by a number of different eastern, northern, and Great Lakes tribes, the game was apparently unknown in the Southwest.

The ball employed in the game was made of wood or buckskin that was stuffed with hair. The racquet was a stick with a round net on its end. The field used was much the same as the field used for football.

RING AND PIN Quite a few Indian tribes played the game known as ring and pin. Its popularity was in part due to the fact that one did not need another player to enjoy the game.

The ring is attached to a thong and swung into the air. The object of the game is to catch the ring on a pin or dart that is fastened to the other end of the thong.

The game was played by Indians all over North America, and to this day, there are games made that resemble this ancient favorite.

SHINNY Most tribes from the Plains area to the Pacific Coast played a game called shinny, which resembled baseball in that a stick and ball were used. Unlike a baseball bat, the stick had a curved end, more like a hockey stick.

SNOWSHOES Snowshoes were used by eastern and western Indians. The frames for snowshoes made by the eastern tribes were usually oval, while the western snowshoes were notably narrower.

The northern tribes such as Algonquians and Athabascans used rawhide strips to make the netting for their snowshoes.

Maidu snowshoes are similar to those worn by other California Indians. One or two thongs cross over the width of the shoe, and two to four thongs crisscross those. The hoop is a small oval with no netting, no tailpiece, and no provision for heel play.

SNOW SNAKE Western tribes, as well as the Iroquois, played this game in which a stick called a snow snake was flung, and the distance measured. It appears to have been the predecessor of the javelin toss now a highlight of the modern Olympic games.

TOBOGGANS   Northern Indian tribes used wooden toboggans for many different purposes—to carry belongings from one place to another, to transport people unable to walk, and sometimes just for the sport of riding the flat piece of wood with one curved end down a hill.

Musical Instruments

Simple rhythm instruments or musical rasps were made from the shoulder blade of a deer. A stick was rattled along the notches of the bone to create rhythmic sounds.

A variety of instruments, such as the flutes made by the Hupas and the dance whistles of the Plains Indians, were made from tubular bones. Some were decorated or engraved.

The Yurok flute was an open tube of elder wood with three or four evenly spaced holes. To produce noise, one would blow diagonally across an end. Though the flute was usually played by a young man during courtship, older people would often play the flute for meditation.

The Pomo whistle may be made of bone or reed, single or double, and may be tied, pierced, or cut off. Cahuilla whistles are made of huikish, elymus cane, and were played by men who sang and danced about the young men who underwent the ordeal of the ants.

PRICES

Note the price listings for this chapter are divided into four sections: Dolls, Games, Sports, and Toys.

Dolls

CHEROKEE

Doll: Cherokee, Spirit; by Hank Orr (Cherokee); hand-carved and masked fox dancer; ca. 1984; 14½ inches; very good condition; $1,250–$1,500.

CREE

Doll: Cree, squaw with papoose; fine buckskin costume with beading around yoke and fur trim; felt face; papoose on back; 11½ inches high; very good condition; $175–$200.

Dolls/Toys, doll, Cherokee, Spirit, Hank Orr (Cherokee); hand-carved and masked fox dancer; 14½ inches; 1984; $1,250–$1,500. Courtesy of Naranjo's, Houston, Texas. Photo by Donald Vogt.

Dolls/Toys, Cheyenne, doll cradle; ca. 1890; beaded hide on wood frame with brass tack decoration; overall length 14½ inches; $500–$600. Courtesy of Canfield Gallery. Photo by Donald Vogt.

Doll: Cree, Stone Face; ca. 1950; 12 inches high; very good condition; $300–$350.

Dolls (two): Euchee; large one made by Milo Yellowhead of Euchee tribe of Oklahoma; small one made by Hattie Harris; both very good condition; $50–$90 each.

Doll: dresses; bead-decorated blue trade cloth and black cloth dresses, beaded with lace sleeves; very good condition; $60–$85.

GREAT LAKES

Doll: Great Lakes style; carved wood and birch-bark-wrapped; 6 x 2½ inches; very good condition; $20–$35.

HOPI

Doll: Hopi, Kachina; polychrome painted dancer "Kitten" signed "Stacy Talahytewa"; 10 inches high; very good condition; $100–$200.

Doll: Hopi, Kachina; well-detailed, "Motsin" dancer signed "Virgil Namoki"; 12½ inches high; very good condition; $65–$90.

Doll: Hopi, Kachina; cottonwood, with wool and remnants of feather decoration painted in white, green, blue, black, pink, cranberry, and yellow; one foot missing; 13 inches high; fair condition; $175–$300.

Doll: Hopi, Kachina; Eagle by Nate Ahownewa; 1991; 11 x 5 inches; mint condition; $2,500–$2,800.

Doll: Hopi, Kachina; Koroasta by Ariel Navasie (Muriel Navasie's niece or cousin—Ariel learned from Cecil Calnimptewa, Muriel's husband); 3½ inches tall; near mint condition; $445–$500.

Dolls/Toys, Euchee; large doll made by Milo Yellowhead of Euchee tribe of Oklahoma; small one made by Hattie Harris; large doll currently in author's collection; small doll; $50–$90 each. Collection of Joyce Williams. Photo by Donald Vogt.

Dolls/Toys, basket, Hopi; Shalako doll in basketry; done by Bertha Wardsworth for the 1987 SWAIA Indian Market; won first place and best in division. Courtesy of Miniatures at the Kiva/Steve Cowgill. Photo by Donald Vogt.

Dolls/Toys, Hopi, Kachina; 12½ inches; older Kachina "H. Hano Clown," made by Tino Youvella; has a "surprise" under his breechcloth; $350–$450.
Courtesy Jack Sellner, CAI.

Dolls/Toys, Hopi, Kachinas (two); left— 15 inches high, Hemis (Jemez Ripened Corn), signed Mocktima; right—12 inches high, Talavai (Morning Singer), signed W. Maktima; $200– $350 each.
Courtesy Jack Sellner, CAI.

Doll: Hopi, Kachina; Koshare (or Hano Clown) by Marlin Pinto; 1993; in squatting position it is 5¾ inches; mint condition; $2,500–$3,000.

Doll: Hopi, Kachina miniature; by Dwayne Dwahough; ca. 1984; excellent condition; $1,380–$1,725.

Doll: Hopi, Kachina miniature; mudhead; carved and painted; ca. 1970; 3½ x 3 inches; very good condition; $45–$60.

Doll: Hopi, Kachina; Pahlik Mana by Brian Honyouti; 1992; 8¾ inches; mint condition; $2,800–$3,200.

Doll: Hopi, Kachina; Piggyback Mudhead by Jim Fred; 1984; 14½ x 10 inches; near mint condition; $2,500–$2,800.

Doll: Hopi, Kachina; Sun or Tawa, by Cecil Calnimptewa; 1993; 18¼ by 9 inches (width of pedestal); mint condition; $9,500–$10,000.

Doll: Hopi, Kachina; Warrior Maiden (H.e.e.e) by Adrian Poleahla; 1992; 15¼ inches to top of scabbard x 7½ inches deep on pedestal; mint condition; $4,500–$4,800.

Night Hawk, *cast bronze, 280 pounds, life-size figure of warrior with hawk on shoulder, 6 feet x 26 inches x 21 inches; stones in center of robe are yellow lip shell, and red is man-made stone; 1993; $28,000.*

Courtesy of Charlie Pratt.
Photo by Robert Reno.

Blue Sky, *turquoise nugget out of Senora mine in Mexico; feathers are fabricated brass, and medallion is turquoise, coral, and Pacific clam; 17 x 10 inches; 1993; $2,600.*

Courtesy of Charlie Pratt.
Photos by Robert Reno.

Hopi Kachina, Sun or Tawa, by Cecil Calnimptewa; 1993; 18¼ x 9 inches (width of pedestal); $9,500.
Courtesy of Alexander Anthony/Adobe Gallery. Photo by Robert Reno.

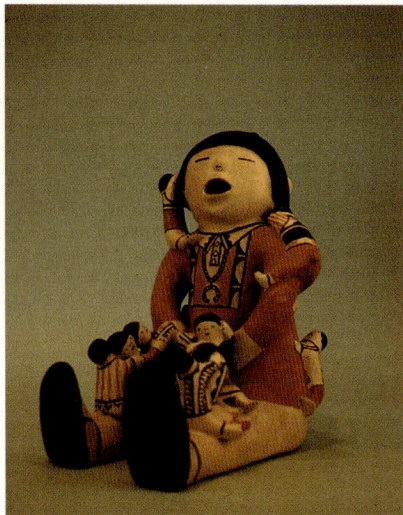

Storyteller, made by Helen Cordero in 1985; 11 inches; has 14 children; male storyteller; $8,500.
Courtesy of Alexander Anthony/Adobe Gallery. Photo by Robert Reno.

Storytellers, two made by Tony Dallas, a Hopi who lived with a Cochiti family and learned how to make storytellers there (Cochiti potters are not allowed to make mudheads or Koshares, but since Tony is a Hopi, he can); the Koshare (right) is 9 x 3½ inches, $1,050; the mudhead is 6 x 3 inches, $795.
Courtesy of Alexander Anthony/Adobe Gallery. Photo by Robert Reno.

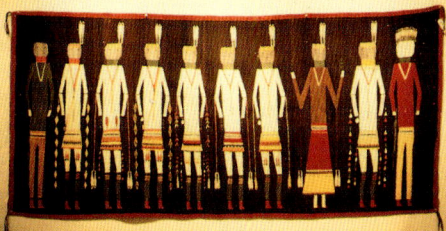

Navajo Yeibichai rug, ca. 1920s, hand-spun wool and commercial yarn; red, black, yellow, tangerine, orange, green, gold, carrot, brown, tan, purple, white, gray; all colors synthetic dyes; 39 x 86 inches; excellent condition; $6,500–$8,500.

Courtesy of Dewey Galleries, Ltd.,
Andrew Nagen.
Photo by Robert Reno.

Navajo Germantown blanket, ca. 1885–1895, cotton warp, excellent condition; red, green, yellow, orange, purple, black, white, burgundy; 83 x 69 inches; $18,000–$24,000.

Courtesy of Dewey Galleries, Ltd.,
Andrew Nagen.
Photo by Robert Reno.

Navajo Crystal area pictorial rug, ca. 1915–1925, hand-spun wool; brown, gray, white, red, burgundy, gold, salmon; 41 x 64 inches; excellent condition; $7,500–$9,000.

Courtesy of Dewey Galleries, Ltd.,
Andrew Nagen.
Photo by Robert Reno.

Nas Bah, *bronze bust of girl with necklace, turquoise inset, wears different pairs of earrings; combination of the faces of his sister-in-law and wife; 17½ inches tall x 10 inches wide; 1987; $3,200.*

Courtesy of Jake Livingston.
Photo by Robert Reno.

Necklace, silver hand-stamped beads; won Best in Division for Traditional Jewelry in Santa Fe Indian Market in 1992; pendant part has Nevada Blue Spiderweb turquoise stone in center; 18 inches; $2,500. Courtesy of Jake Livingston.
Photo by Robert Reno.

Necklace, coral strands supporting 14 carat hand-tooled gold pendant with coral center; 18 inches long; 1992; $7,800.

Courtesy Jake Livingston.
Photo by Robert Reno.

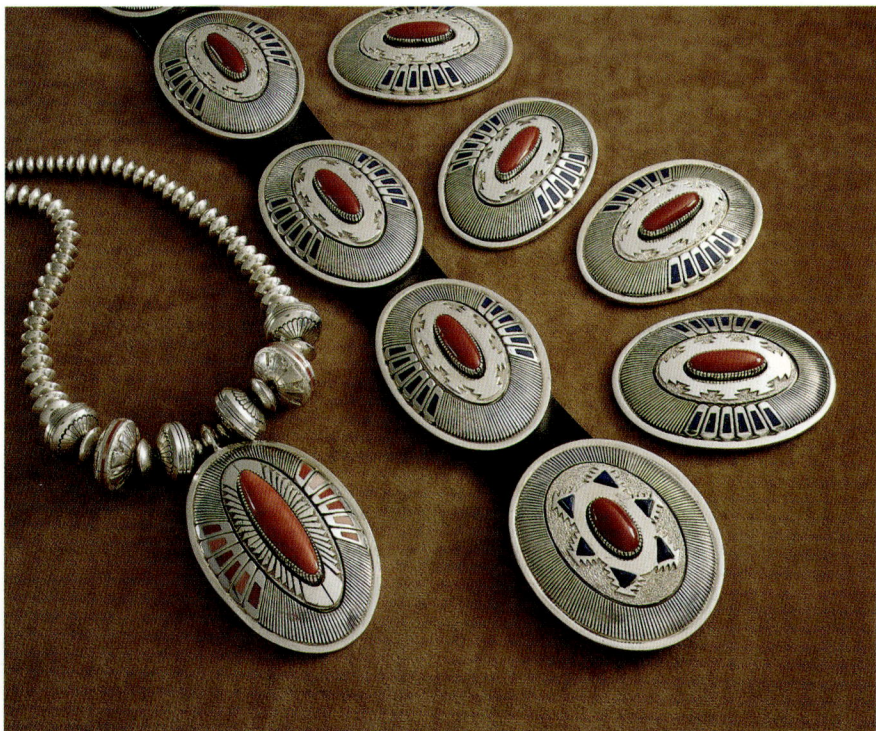

Concha belt and pendant, Mediterranean coral, overlay hammered, stamped with inlaid lapis; pendant inlay is pink and red coral, beads are inlaid as well; 1992; $10,000 for belt; $2,200 for pendant. Courtesy of Gibson Nez.

Photo by Jerry Jacka.

Cheyenne knife and sheath; ca. 1860s; beaded hide with traditional Cheyenne design; chain suspensions; trade knife with hilt wrapped in copper wire; $5,000.

Courtesy of Canfield Gallery.
Photo by Robert Reno.

Northwest Coast/Tsimshian doll; 11½ inches high; carved and painted wood doll; hair wig; applied eyes; animal skin costume with painted symbols; trimmed with caribou fur.

Collection of, and photo by, Evelyn Ackerman.
© Evelyn Ackerman, 1990.

Sioux, Warrior Society, dance harness; ca. 1900; a cape or bandolier worn over the shoulders and draping front and back; constructed of panels of quill-wrapped rawhide strips edged with tin cone and dyed feather tassels, a whitetail deer tail attached at the center; $9,500.

Courtesy of Canfield Gallery.
Photo by Robert Reno.

Koshare and mudheads, chess set, cast bronze with paint, each figure is 4¼ inches tall, unlimited edition, cast in 1992, chessboard is walnut and birch; $4,500.   Courtesy of Charlie Pratt.
Photo by Robert Reno.

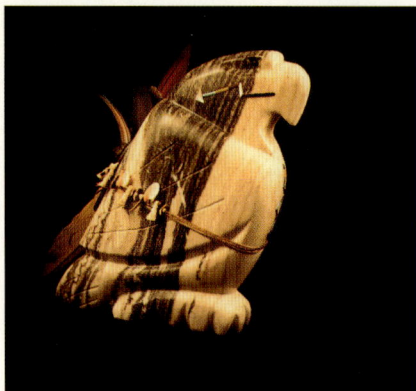

Pueblo, zebra alabaster heart-line fetish eagle with medicine bundle, 14 x 13 inches; $1,350.   Courtesy of Andy Abeita and Silver Sun Gallery, Santa Fe. Photo by Robert Reno.

Pueblo, taupe alabaster fetish bear with medicine bundle, 1993, 8 x 5 inches; $690.   Courtesy of Andy Abeita and Silver Sun Gallery, Santa Fe. Photo by Robert Reno.

Pueblo, steatite (black soapstone) heart-line deer with medicine bundle, 11 x 8 inches; $525.   Courtesy of Andy Abeita and Silver Sun Gallery, Santa Fe. Photo by Robert Reno.

Spirit Stone, white alabaster with brass Rainbow Kachina in paw, weighs over 300 pounds, 2 feet x 20 inches; will be cast bronze in an edition of ten; $6,800.   Courtesy of Andy Abeita and Silver Sun Gallery, Santa Fe. Photo by Robert Reno.

Doll: Hopi, Kachina; Yellow Ahote (front and back shots) carved by Bryce Quamahongnewa, Hotevilla, Arizona; cottonwood (one piece except for feathers, bow, and rattle); 1993; 10½ inches (including pedestal); mint condition; $2,500–$2,800.

Doll: Hopi, Kachina; "Yapa," with white head and large red ears; signed Leo Barber; very good condition; $80–$175.

Doll: Hopi, Kachina; "Hon Bear"; action figure on wood stand; 10½ inches high; very good condition; $90–$160.

Doll: Hopi, Kachina; "Chakwaina"; signed John Martin; 10¼ inches high; very good condition; $130–$160.

Doll: Hopi, Kachina; "Squash"; wood base; 10¾ inches high; very good condition; $150–$200.

Doll: Hopi, Kachina; "Squash," carved by Malcolm Fred; Hopi Third Mesa; contemporary; 10 inches high; mint condition; $920–$1,150.

Doll: Hopi, Kachina; "Kau-a"; 10-inch figure on base; very good condition; $150–$175.

Doll: Hopi, Kachina; "Snake Dancer"; standing figure on wood base; 10 inches high; very good condition; $115–$175.

Doll: Hopi, Kachina; "Sipikne"; action figure on wood base; 11¾ inches high; very good condition; $80–$175.

Dolls/Toys, Hopi, Kachinas—from left to right: 9-inch-high Kachinalike Hopi female figure with bowl atop head, carved in one piece; 8-inch-high Hopi Kachina Mudhead, unusual because it is painted putty color instead of rust (also, not beaklike mouth); 8½-inch Hopi Kachina (Hummingbird Kachina?). Collection of, and photography by, Evelyn Ackerman.

Dolls/Toys, Hopi, Kachinas; set of three Hano Clown Kachinas (Hear no Evil, Speak no Evil, See no Evil); sitting on a piece of driftwood; ca. 1968. Collection of, and photography by, Evelyn Ackerman.

Doll: Hopi, Kachina; mudhead; 11½ inches high; very good condition; $75–$120.

Doll: Hopi, Kachina; painted cottonwood root; polychrome; ca. 1900; 11 inches high; very good condition; $2,900–$3,450.

Doll: Hopi, Kachina; "Left Hander"; action figure on wood base; 11 inches high; very good condition; $125–$200.

Doll: Hopi, Kachina; "Mastof"; standing on wood base; 11 inches high; very good condition; $110–$175.

Doll: Hopi, Kachina; older Kachina "H. Hano Clown," made by Tino Youvella; has a "surprise" under his breechcloth; 12½ inches high; excellent condition; $300–$400.

Doll: Hopi, Kachina; older "Polik Mana" (Butterfly Maiden); 12¾ inches high; very good condition; $125–$210.

Doll: Hopi, Kachina; "Sio Hemis" Kachina by Lauren Honyoti from Hopi Third Mesa; wood, stained, all one piece; contemporary; 12 inches high; very good condition; $2,075–$2,300.

Doll: Hopi, Kachina; "Chop/sowi-ing" (Antelope); signed Pat Sauphe; 12 inches high; very good condition; $125–$180.

Doll: Hopi, Kachina; probably representing "Tawa," the Sun Kachina, with deep red painted body and yellow legs, forearms, and shoulders, the helmet mask with pale blue face, rainbow decoration along the chin, triangular mouth, rectangular eyes, warrior marks on the cheeks, and a concentric wedge of spotted rainbow decoration on each temple, wearing a tall crown of feathers; an old label remaining on the underside reading "Kachina doll, Grand Canyon, Arizona, 1939"; 13⅜ inches high; very good condition; $1,380–$1,725.

Doll: Hopi, Kachina; "Pong" (Mountain Sheep); 13½ inches high; very good condition; $150–$230.

Doll: Hopi, Kachina; dancing figure with mask and fur cape, wearing kilt; 13 inches high; very good condition; $175–$230.

Doll: Hopi, Kachina; "Sun Kachina"; figure standing on wood base; 14½ inches high; very good condition; $110–$185.

Doll: Hopi, Kachina; dancing figure with tableta headdress and fur cape; 14 inches high; very good condition; $200–$220.

Doll: Hopi, Kachina; "Hemis," wearing a terraced tableta with rain cloud and phallic symbols, his body painted black; Jemez or Ripened Corn; 15¾ inches high; very good condition; $575–$875.

Doll: Hopi, Kachina; Wolf Kachina in action position; 15 inches high; good condition; $140–$175.

Doll: Hopi, Kachina; "Avachoya-QA-O"; ca. 1940s; 15 inches high; very good condition; $270–$400.

Doll: Hopi, Kachina; "Poli Sio Hemis" (Butterfly Kachina); wood, painted overall in white, with tubular snout, concentric rectangular eyes, and tall tableta with terracing across the top painted with corn and butterflies; 16½ inches high; very good condition; $575–$850.

Doll: Hopi, Kachina; mudhead with drum; bun missing at back of head, and feathers on head worn off; crack at joint of right arm; 16 inches high; fair condition; $175–$230.

Doll: Hopi, Kachina; Snake Kachina dancer; painted leather, horsehair fringe on mask; one of finest of contemporary work; 18 inches high; excellent condition; $660–$800.

Doll: Hopi, Kachina; carved and painted wooden "warrior"; ca. 1986; 20 x 9 inches; very good condition; $150–$285.

Doll: Hopi, Kachina; "Palhik Mana" (Butterfly Girl) by Walter Hawato; 24¾ inches high; very good condition; $375–$500.

Doll: Hopi, Kachina; signed Silas Roy; 3⅝ inches high; very good condition; $125–$200.

Doll: Hopi, Kachina; "Kwikwilyaka" (Mocking); signed Silas Roy; 3½ inches high; very good condition; $200–$260.

Doll: Hopi, Kachina; "Kokopelli" (Assassin Fly); signed Silas Roy; 3½ inches high; very good condition; $135–$200.

Doll: Hopi, Kachina; wooden Coyote Kachina; yellow body with black spotting and white kilt; accompanying mount inscribed "Kachina Doll from Hopi Indian, Oraibi Mesa, Painted Desert, Arizona, August 1, 1932"; missing one ear; 6¾ inches high; fair/good condition; $260–$460.

Doll: Hopi, Kachina; "Mongwu" (Great Horned Owl); signed Taiz; 7½ inches high; very good condition; $55–$85.

Doll: Hopi, Kachina; "Sipikne" (Zuni Warrior God); ca. 1930s–1940s; 7½ inches high; very good condition; $100–$175.

Doll: Hopi, Kachina; "Kocha Mosairu" (White Buffalo), signed Taiz; 7¼ inches high; very good condition; $75–$100.

Doll: Hopi, Kachina; "I'She" (Mustard Green); signed Wiefred Huma; 7 inches high; very good condition; $40–$85.

Doll: Hopi, Kachina; "Tema" (Left Hand Hunter); 8½ inches high; very good condition; $110–$175.

Doll: Hopi, Kachina; "Ota/Kwasa-itaqa" (Skirt Man—Third Mesa type); older type; 8¾ inches high; very good condition; $85–$135.

Doll: Hopi, Kachina; finely carved and painted Crow Mother Kachina with basket; 8½ x 4½ inches; very good condition; $70–$100.

Doll: Hopi, Kachina; carved wooden, decorated with hand-ground pigments; 9¼ inches high; very good condition; $110–$150.

Doll: Hopi, Kachina; "Crow Mother"; standing figure on wood base; 9¾ inches high; very good condition; $100–$175.

Doll: Hopi, Kachina; dancing figure with paralyzed Kachina mask and fur cape; 9 inches high; very good condition; $65–$100.

Doll: Hopi, Kachina; Black Buffalo Dancer; very good condition; $150–$185.

Doll: Hopi, Kachina; carved and painted Corn Kachina with hoop and dance rattle; very good condition; $70–$100.

Doll: Hopi, Kachina; "The Cumulus Cloud"; done by Henry and Mary Sheldon (husband and wife carvers); Mary does miniatures and Henry does large Kachinas (Mary's work averages $460–$700); excellent condition; $2,300–$2,875.

Doll: Hopi, Kachina; Prickly Pear Kachina by Warren Phillips; very good condition; $6,300–$6,900.

Doll: Hopi, Kachina; Mudhead with fur ruff and drum and stick in hand; signed Edison Brown; very good condition; $115–$175.

Doll: Hopi, Kachina; Mudhead with shaker and feather in hands; signed Sanfard Honyamtowa; very good condition; $140–$185.

Doll: Hopi, Kachina; traditional-style "Corn Maiden"; made by contemporary artist J. Michael Bear (Acoma/Sioux); near mint condition; $920–$1,150.

Doll: Hopi, Kachina; two-piece Kachina "Koshare"; made by Dawa, Hopi Kachina carver; certificate of authenticity included; very good condition; $1,150–$1,430.

Doll: Hopi; "Rainbow Dancer"; not Kachina, but social figure; 14¾ inches with feathers; very good condition; $70–$115.

Dolls: Hopi, Kachina; Snake Dance set done by Cecil Calnimptewa; one of the most famous single sets of Kachinas carved to date; the Snake Dance is rare. Many carvers won't even attempt something as intricate as this; mint condition; $17,250–$20,700.

Dolls: Hopi, Kachinas (two); 12-inch Eototo (White Mask) and 13½ inch Aholi (turquoise mask); two of the Chief Kachinas; always travel in a pair; done by Manuel Kooyahoema of the Hopi Third Mesa; contemporary; near mint condition; $920–$1,150 each.

Dolls: Hopi, Kachinas (two); "Hemis" (Jemez Ripened Corn), signed Mocktima, 15 inches high, very good condition; $175–$315; "Talavai" (Morning Singer), signed W. Maktima, 12 inches high, very good condition, $200–$315.

Dolls: Hopi, Kachinas (three); by Cecil Calnimptewa and Muriel Navasie, husband and wife award-winning carvers (wife taught husband to carve); "Muriel's Crow Mother," near mint condition, $4,600–$5,750; "Cecil's Ram," near mint condition, $4,830–$5,175; "White Buffalo," near mint condition; $6,900–$7,360.

Dolls: Hopi, Kachinas (four); "Female Ogre" by Neal Kayourptowa, very good condition, $170–$230. "Whipper's Uncle" by Finkle Sahmu, Hopi Tewa, Pulacca, Arizona, very good condition; $175–$230; "Telauai Kachina" (Morning Kachina) by Bear Dance, very good condition, $225–$300; "Wolf Kachina," very good condition; $50–$85.

Dolls: Hopi, Kachinas (five); made by Lucy Dougi, Chinle, Arizona; "Sundancer," "White Wolf," "Eagle Dancer," "Black Buffalo," "Angry Kachina"; contemporary; very good condition; $35–$60 each.

Dolls: Hopi, Kachinas; six cottonwood Kachinas representing Salako Mana, Owl, Mudhead, and others; 4 and 5 inches high; good condition; $300–$500 each.

Dolls: Hopi, Kachinas; by award-winning carver Cecil Calimptewa; contemporary; near mint condition; $8,050–$10,350 each.

NAVAJO

Doll: Indian woman with child and wool blanket; very good condition; $60–$85.

Doll: Navajo; wood carved healing doll with traces of paint; 5½ x 1¾ inches; very good condition; $115–$175.

Doll: Navajo; "Yeibichai"; carved and painted, signed Tom W. Yazzie; 12½ inches; excellent condition; $115–$150.

Doll: Navajo; woman working at a loom; 17 x 15 inches; very good condition; $35–$60.

Doll: Navajo; traditionally dressed squaw with plush blouse, real hair tied in native "bun" style, full-length pleated skirt, authentic sash around waist, and miniature jewelry; 19½ inches high; very good condition; $230–$285.

Doll: Navajo; female figure with sewn dress, velour shirt, bead necklace, painted rag face, body, tin metal concho belt; lacking bandana; ca. 1900; 8 inches high; very good condition; $40–$60.

Doll: Navajo; female; ca. 1975; very good condition; $15–$25.

Doll: Navajo; signed on leg "Naz Bah" and dressed in traditional wine-colored dress; very good condition; $115–$150.

Dolls: Navajo (three); each wrapped in colorful blankets, real black hair, leather headband, fabric shirts, pants, two with necklaces of beads, two with leather moccasins, one with wood feet and leather fringe pants, painted faces, eyes and lips on some sort of composition head; old; 6 inches tall; very good condition; $75–$250 each.

Dolls: Navajo (two); apparent wooden bodies, composition heads with painted eyes, lips, black real hair, headbands, fabric clothing and blanket wraps; early; approximately 7½ inches tall; very good condition; $150–$200 each.

Dolls: Navajo; handmade man and woman, traditional dress; Rose Hadley; 18 inches high; very good condition; $85–$130.

Dolls: Navajo; pair of china dolls dressed in Navajo costumes; woman's costume is red velvet with brocade sash and turquoise

Dolls/Toys, North Cheyenne, pair of dolls; 14-inch-high male; 13-inch-high female; buckskin; both have identically fashioned bead eyes and mouth and black hair wigs. Collection of, and photography by, Evelyn Ackerman. Copyright Evelyn Ackerman 1990.

Dolls/Toys, doll, Northern Plains; beaded clothing, 12 inches tall; $460–$700. From the Collection of David L. Atteberry. Photo by Donald Vogt.

bead buttons; man wearing white velvet trousers and red velvet shirt with silver and turqoise buttons; 19 inches; very good condition; $160–$215.

Dolls: Navajo miniature (five); handmade costumes of velour and other fabrics, with metal concho belts, beaded necklaces on the females, painted rag faces; ca. 1900; each approximately 3 inches; very good condition; $60–$100/set.

NORTHERN PLAINS
Doll: Northern Plains; buckskin, beaded; 12 inches tall; very good condition; $460–$700.

NORTHWEST COAST
Doll: Northwest Coast; Dancer, in full costume, by Erla Graham; ca. 1975; 30 x 6 inches; very good condition; $430–$575.

Dolls/Toys, Plains/Plateau doll and miniature saddle; doll is 6 inches high and made of buckskin; costume and saddle are decorated with seed beads in floral design; features are delicately painted black, and his nose is needle-molded. Collection of, and photography by, Evelyn Ackerman. Copyright Evelyn Ackerman 1990.

PLAINS

Doll: Plains; buckskin doll with beaded belt; ca. 1930s; 12 inches high; very good condition; $175–$230.

Doll: Plains; doll form on wooden cradleboard; 13½ x 5 inches; very good condition; $30–$60.

Doll: Plains; polychrome hide doll/charm, small stuffed figure, with red linear and circle designs over yellow pigment ground with blue pigments along seams, human hair coiffure, rawhide suspension at back of featureless head; 4¼ inches tall; very good condition; $750–$920.

Doll: Plains; made of leather and horsehair; very good condition; $235–$350.

Doll: Plains; warrior doll; constructed of cloth and buckskin with beadwork detail; ca. late 1800s; very good condition; $1,500–$1,800.

Dolls: Plains; pair of dolls, buckskin with clothing of beads in white, red, and shades of blue; one doll has human hair and red paint on the face; 10 inches high; very good condition; $900–$1,300.

PUEBLO

Doll: Pueblo; Kachina; "Katoch Ang-ak-china" (barefoot, long-haired Kachina); 8 inches high; very good condition; $115–$155.

Dolls: Pueblo (two); handmade pottery dolls; ca. 1935; very good condition; $70–$90.

Doll: Santa Clara, Kachina miniature; clown; signed by Margaret and Luther; ca. 1965; 1½ x 1½ inches; very good condition; $50–$70.

SEMINOLE

Doll: Seminole; palm fiber with banded cloth costume; 4 inches high; good condition (small tear in cloth); $20–$30.

Dolls: Seminole (three); palm fiber bodies, hand-stitched dresses of various-colored fabrics and rickrack, each wearing black hats or with black hair, yarn features, the larger figure with three rows of bead necklace, the smallest with deep purple bead necklaces; probably early 1900s; 11 inches, 8 inches, and 7 inches tall; very good condition; $75–$210.

Dolls: Seminole, doll collection; dressed in traditional Seminole clothing; a couple (man and woman) are unusual in that they have molded noses; all approximately 6 inches high; very good condition; $200–$230 for collection.

SIOUX

Doll: Sioux; beaded yoke, belt, moccasins, and dress in green, yellow, red, blue, and white, sinew-sewn, fringed; 15 inches long; very good condition; $2,000–$3,000.

Doll: Sioux; beaded hide doll wearing a fringed hide dress with a fully beaded yoke, body of dress with dyed red plaited quillwork and beaded ornamentation, fully beaded high boots,

Dolls/Toys, Sioux, doll; 14 inches high; buckskin; female doll with traditional wide beaded band stretching across her chest; beaded facial features and red blushed cheeks. Collection of, and photography by, Evelyn Ackerman. Copyright Evelyn Ackerman 1990.

long horsehair coiffure, beaded earrings on edge of face, bead colors: white heart reds, light blue, clear and greasy yellow, white and royal blue; 17¼ inches tall; very good condition; $1,600–$2,075.

Doll: dress, Sioux, miniature; woman's dress; yoke beaded in blues and red on a white ground on buffalo-hide backing; rest of dress is hand-spun from cloth stenciled (inside dress) "U.S. Indian Agency"; beaded and fringed decoration on dress skirt; all beading sinew-sewn; 12 inches wide x 13½ inches long; very good condition; $850–$1,150.

SKOOKUM

Doll: Skookum; early; 14 x 5 inches; very good condition; $115–$175.

Doll: Skookum; 16 inches high; very good condition; $30–$55.

Doll: Skookum, male; right-facing eyes; original headdress; ca. 1920–1940; 18 inches; mint condition; $250–$300.

Doll: Skookum; blanket and paper label on bottom (Pat. Feb. 17, 1914); very good condition; $70–$90.

Doll: Skookum; male; souvenir of 1933 World's Fair; also, dolls with hats are very desirable; 9 inches; mint condition; $150–$250.

Dolls: Skookum (and other types); ca. 1930s; very good condition; $25–$75 each.

Dolls/Toys, Skookum doll, 18-inch male; right-facing eyes; original headdress; ca. 1920–1940; mint condition; $250–$300. From the collection of Bette Nussbaum. Photo by Joel Nussbaum.

Dolls/Toys, Skookum male; 9 inches; souvenir of 1933 World's Fair; also dolls with hats are very desirable; mint condition; $150–$250. From the collection of Bette Nussbaum. Photo by Joel Nussbaum.

Dolls/Toys, Skookum family; "apple-faced" skookums; made 1895–1915; sizes: 15-inch chief, 14-inch squaw, 10–inch child, 9-inch child; extremely rare to find in good condition; glass eyes looking straight ahead; bodies are blocks of original wood; very good condition; $1,000–$1,250/set. From the collection of Bette Nussbaum. Photo by Joel Nussbaum.

Dolls: Skookum family; "apple-faced" Skookums; 15-inch chief, 14-inch squaw, 10-inch child, 9-inch child; extremely rare to find in good condition; glass eyes looking straight ahead; bodies are blocks of original wood; made 1895–1915; very good condition; $1,000–$1,250/set.

Dolls: Skookum family; 15-inch chief, 14-inch squaw with papoose, two children (6½ inches); ca. 1920–1940 (note: plastic shoes on one child indicates late manufacture—1940s); mint condition; $400–$500/set.

Dolls: Skookum pair; 22-inch pair and papoose with doll of her own; extremely rare; ca. 1920–1940; mint condition; $800–$1,000/ pair.

Dolls/Toys, Skookum family; 15-inch chief, 14-inch squaw with papoose, two children (6½ inches); ca. 1920–1940 (note: plastic shoes on one child indicates late manufacture—1940s); mint condition; $400–$500/set. From the collection of Bette Nussbaum. Photo by Joel Nussbaum.

Dolls/Toys, Skookum pair; 22-inch pair and papoose with doll of her own; extremely rare; ca. 1920–1940; mint condition; $800–$1,000/pair. From the collection of Bette Nussbaum. Photo by Joel Nussbaum.

Dolls/Toys, Skookum pair; unusual left-facing pair—some consider left-facing Skookums to be bad luck; 16-inch male; 14-inch squaw with papoose; ca. 1925–1940; mint condition; $300–$500. From the collection of Bette Nussbaum. Photo by Joel Nussbaum.

Dolls: Skookum pair; male 16¾ inches tall, female 16 inches tall; in finely detailed blanket costume; pristine condition; $150–$185.

Dolls: Skookum pair; one 11 inches high and the other 12½ inches high; very good condition; $50–$75.

Dolls: Skookum pair; unusual left-facing pair—some consider left-facing Skookums to be bad luck; 16-inch male; 14-inch squaw with papoose; ca. 1925–1940; mint condition; $300–$500.

SOUTHWEST

Doll: Southwest; doll in case; mother and papoose in leather and cloth, seated in front of a loom, in glass case measuring 19 x 14 x 11 inches; very good condition; $65–$150.

VARIOUS TRIBES

Dolls: collection; glassed case containing 32 Indian and Eskimo dolls, including three with ivory faces; ca. 1920; very good condition; $800–$1,500 for collection.

Dolls: Indian doll collection; glass case (37 x 22 inches) containing 37 assorted Indian dolls; ca. 1920; very good condition; $1,575–$1,800 for collection.

Dolls: four Indian dolls, all stuffed cloth with various costumes; 8 to 10 inches in height; good condition; $90–$115/set.

Dolls/Toys, Ute doll; 7 inches high; labeled "Ute male buckskin doll"; colorful and fully beaded head and hair. Collection of, and photography by, Evelyn Ackerman. Copyright Evelyn Ackerman 1990.

Dolls: hand-carved man and woman dressed in blankets and hand-made clothing; wooden faces, straw-filled bodies; good condition; $145–$185.

Dolls: (11); including polychromed carved wood ceremonial figures, fabric dolls, rope doll, and carved bone doll; largest 17½ inches; very good condition; $440–$575/set.

GAMES

APACHE

Game: cards; ten birch-bark cards; very good condition; $35–$70.

SIOUX

Game: Sioux, finger bone game played by women; five carved bones with lance; very good condition; $70–$100.

Game: Sioux, pin and bone child's game; traces of paint; ca. 1870; 5 x ¾ inch; very good condition; $80–$115.

Game: Sioux, whip and top game; very good condition; $90–$175.

VARIOUS TRIBS

Game: chess set; metal sculptured chess set of cowboys and Indians with a wood and metal board by Charlie Pratt; very good condition; $630–$850.

SPORTS

ATHABASCAN

Sports: Athabascan, snowshoes; fine and fancy painted; ca. 1880; 80 x 46 inches; very good condition; $550–$575.

CREE

Sports: Cree, snowshoes, large; intricate lacing; very old; very good condition; $350–$550.

MICMAC

Sports: Micmac, snowshoes; 42½ inches long; good condition; $75–$100.

VARIOUS TRIBES

Sports: snowshoes; handmade "True Temper" snowshoes, ca. 1930; 61 x 10 inches; very good condition; $65–$85.

Sports: snowshoes; pair of toy snowshoes, handmade; 13 x 13½ inches; very good condition; $50–$75.

Sports: snowshoes; rawhide and bentwood snowshoes; good condition; $40–$70.

TOYS

APACHE

Toy: Apache, cradleboard; woven willow; old; very good condition; $90–$160.

Toy: Apache, doll cradleboard; carved and beaded stripped willow with attached strips in cobalt and white; 19th century; 12 inches long; very good condition; $100–$200.

Toy: Apache, cradleboards (four), miniature; made of silver and wood; very good condition; $15–$20 each.

CHEYENNE

Toy: Cheyenne, cradle; beaded hide on wood frame with brass tack decoration; ca. 1890; 14½ inches overall length; very good condition; $2,875–$4,000.

Toy: Cheyenne, moccasins, miniature; full-beaded hide toy moccasins, ca. 1920; 2 x 1 inch; $75–$100.

NAVAJO

Toy: Navajo, diorama; Navajo woman weaving rug in diorama; she's wearing maroon dress, and child is dressed in same fabric and color; very good condition; $60–$85.

Toy: Navajo, doll pin cushion; handmade; ca. 1935; 6 x 4 inches; very good condition; $20–$30.

NORTHEASTERN

Toy: canoe; birch-bark toy canoe; 25 x 8 inches; very good condition; $35–$55.

PAIUTE

Toy: Paiute, toy cradle; geometric beaded design on hide with basketry sun visor; ca. 1950; 22 x 7 inches; very good condition; $150–$300.

PLAINS

Toy: cradle, miniature; hide-covered cradle with round top, some beadwork; 9 x 5 inches; very good condition; $50–$70.

SIOUX

Toy: Sioux, doll cradleboard; 4½ inches; very good condition; $100–$150.

Toy: Sioux, flute; duck-head flute, carved and painted with old museum tag indicating it was used for the Grass Dance; old; 16 inches; very good condition; $200–$400.

Toy: Sioux, painted buckskin toy tepee; with poles and accessories; very good condition; $250–$450.

Chapter Seven

Ephemera and Advertising/
Photography/Books

～

This section offers general information on a smattering of tribes of special interest to the collector. It is by no means complete or even representative of the hundreds of tribes who lived in North America; nor is this chapter meant to deliver all the information necessary for you to fully understand the arts and crafts the Native American produced. For more specific information about the arts and crafts of particular tribes or about their culture, consult the index or the chapter regarding the subject of interest.

EPHEMERA

White European settlers and their descendants have been fascinated with the Native American way of life—and recorded information about it—since the first encounter between these two cultures. Such information, whether factual, apocryphal, or downright misleading and untrue, has been the basis for representations of Native American peoples and culture used to advertise various products. It is a category of American Indian collecting that purist collectors of Indian arts and crafts may consider entirely unworthy of their attention—or anyone else's.

However, the newspapers, magazines, and books that have focused on the Amerind—some of which were written by American Indians—are, indeed, collectible and constitute a rich well of knowledge for those more interested in the written word than in painted images, jewelry, and other items that bespeak the Indian heritage. Writers are as much a part of the arts community as are the potters, jewelers, and painters mentioned in other chapters of this book.

Because of the vast number of periodicals published that in various ways describe and detail Native American life, I have not attempted to list all of those that have taken a special interest in the subject. I will say, however, that magazines and newspapers such as *Harper's* and *Leslie's*, in the early days of U.S. publishing history, chronicled Indian events with much relish, and articles published in their pages were often embellished with engravings or sketches of the various tribes. Interest in the "red man" was extremely high during that period in our history, and the mixture of curiosity and fear that journalists felt for the subject often made them color their articles unfavorably.

In later decades, various tribes began publishing their own periodicals, and though scarce, they are collectible, as are current magazines and newspapers such as *The Indian Trader* newspaper, *American Indian Art* magazine, and the beautiful, glossy magazine put out by the Heard Museum entitled *Native Peoples.*

Books written about the various tribes are also plentiful, some of which date back to the beginning of U.S. history. Being a lover of the written word, this is where my own interests lie, and I have found many fascinating and well-illustrated books on the American Indian from the late eighteenth century and early nineteenth century. Though much of the information related in these early tomes has been proven incorrect, there are some (such as Catlin's *Letters and Notes on the Manners, Customs and Conditions of the North American Indians*) that have survived the test of time and tell a very accurate tale of the habits and lifestyle of the original caretakers of this country.

American Indians have told their own story for hundreds of years. They are the original storytellers, the people who acted out myths and legends around campfires. History was passed on orally, from generation to generation, and to this day, when Native American tribes get together, a storyteller is usually present to pass on time-honored tales about why the sun hangs in the sky, or why a turtle has thirteen moons on its back.

It was not until recent times (the last hundred years or so) that the tribal stories were written down and subsequently published. Indian writers have not yet received their due. When pressed to name a famous Amerind author, most people cannot, but I'm sure that, with time, this will also change.

With the following general information in this chapter about various tribes and specific information about authors, photographers, and uses of advertising, I hope to give you an overview of the written word and the documentation of (and by) the American Indian.

ADVERTISING

The Native American has long been a favored figure in the advertising world. Perhaps the earliest use of the image is the cigar store Indian, but logos picturing an Indian in a headdress or sitting regally on top of a horse are still used by today's advertising firms.

Various companies used the figure of a Native American to promote their products, such as Calumet Baking Powder, Prince Albert Smoking Tobacco, H. B. Gardner Cigars, Sitting Bull Durham Tobacco, and Pontiac automobiles, as well as many others. For more specific information on advertising collectibles that feature Native Americans, see my book *The Confident Collector Advertising Collectibles Identification and Price Guide.*

Because of the many years of propaganda, both from the government as well as missionaries, the Indian people have been forced away from their traditional ways. Though there is a resurgence of interest in Indian tradition, and the reservation schools are encouraging children to learn the old ways, it is still difficult for native people to freely choose a lifestyle. Every time one of the elders in the tribe dies, some portion of that tribe's knowledge goes with him or her.

The size of Indian reservations has diminished between 1880 and 1980, and many have been relocated. Today the largest reservation in the United States is the Navajo reservation, which includes parts of northwestern Arizona, northeastern Nevada, and southern Colorado and Utah. However, you can find reservations all over the United States—from the humid regions of the Everglades to the ice-covered mountains in Alaska.

It is hard for us, so used to modern living, to slow down, learn, and appreciate the ancient ways of the Indian culture. Yet if the younger Indians are not allowed to feel proud of their heritage and to learn all they can from the elders of their tribes, the knowledge built from thousands of years of living with the land could disappear.

The Native American has valuable information to pass on, about their religion, medicine, arts and crafts—information we should *all* be careful to preserve . . . not only in museums but also in the hearts, minds, and hands of all living Americans who can later pass on the traditions to their children.

ABENAKI

The Abenaki Indians call the white ash the "snowshoe tree" because they use its branches to make snowshoes. This tribe has received media attention over the past couple of years in New England because of land disputes due to their concern with the ecology—something that their white brothers have to be reminded is extremely important.

Having lived near the Abenaki tribe, I am aware that they are trying to indoctrinate some of the lost traditions back into their ways of learning, such as making totems, doing beadwork, and painting. Because they were one of the first tribes to lose their lands to the white man, their ways have been lost for a long time. They still endure discrimination, but fight to breathe new life into their traditions.

This tribe is located in Northern New England (Maine, Vermont, New Hampshire) and into Quebec; its origins were Algonquian. Their tribal leader, as of this writing, is Chief Homer St. Francis.

ACOMA

The Sky City of Acoma was located on a mesa in an effort to protect it from attacks by Spaniards. The Europeans did not succeed in driving Indians from their pueblo. The Acomas still live there, and it is one of the oldest continuously occupied villages in the United States.

The people of this tribe are well known for their pottery-making skills, which are covered more completely in other chapters.

ALASKAN TRIBES

The Athabascan, Haida, Tlingit, and Tsimshian tribes have a rich and dazzling heritage of superb craftsmanship. Though we think of the intricately carved totems and dance poles as the focus of their efforts, they are also responsible for wonderful baskets, carved wooden pieces (such as masks), decorated clothing, and unique utensils (covered in other chapters).

Since they made their home by the cold northwestern Pacific, and spent a good deal of their time fishing, they have an extensive knowledge of whales, seals, walruses, sea lions, and other cold-water mammals. Their legends, folk tales, carvings, and art reflect that oceanic erudition.

BLACKFOOT

During the 1800s, the Blackfeet had a cure for cancer, which they called "big boil" or "big pimple." Through the years, the cure has been lost, but the old women of the tribe have told younger members that the cure came from a root of some kind. It has often been noted that the Native American tribes did not experience a great deal of sickness in the early days, except for the diseases passed on to them by traders. Once schools were set up and reservations established, the Indians' natural immunity system broke down and diseases ran rampant.

The Blackfoot men often had more than one wife. Sometimes a man sought a second wife when the first wife became pregnant and needed help. If the man did not choose to have another wife, he would bring a younger sister or his mother into his home. The wife's mother, however, was not allowed to be in his company. There were many superstitions about what the pregnant woman should or should not do. For example they believed a woman with child should not linger in the doorway of her home—she should be either in or out. The Blackfoot believed if she didn't go all the way out of her home, or all the way in, she would have hard labor. The pregnant woman stayed out of her own home while someone took care of her. (In fact, no one remained home while ill.) During this time, the woman's mother, if she was alive and able, cared for her.

After birth, the baby and its mother would be dressed in rags for thirty days. The mother wore her pregnancy clothes. Every four days the young mother would be given a cleansing ceremony, and in addition to daily massages, the woman was given a girdle in order to get her body back into shape. This first thirty days was a period of trial and concern over whether mother and child would survive the birth.

At the end of the thirty-day trial, they would move camp, and the mother would go through one more cleansing ceremony. Both baby and mother would get dressed in new clothes, and the baby would finally get a name. The naming ceremony was held by the father, if he was an important or holy man, or by one of the elders. It was important for the child to have a good name in order to give it an auspicious start in life. The ceremony consisted of blessings and prayers, after which the father or elder would announce the name he was giving to the child. Though the mother was not active in the naming ceremony, she would often give her children nicknames. Men often carry an inherited name, while, surprisingly, women were named for famous war deeds.

It is common for Blackfoot grandparents to raise one of their grandchildren. The closeness between generations has always been fostered, and as a result, traditions were passed on.

Widows who lived alone were often given an orphaned child to care for. That act solved *two* problems—the loneliness of both parties and the problem of who would take care of each of them if they had remained by themselves.

HOPI

The Hopis call themselves *Hopitu Skinumu*—the "peaceful people." They live on three mesas in central Arizona and occupy a dozen small towns there. Their reservation occupies a portion of the much larger Navajo nation.

The Hopi people live much as their ancestors did. In fact, Oraibi is one of the oldest continuously occupied towns in North America. Their buildings are ancient analogies of today's apartment houses, where people shared open fires and prayed to their gods (Kachinas) to give them the rain necessary to bring their crops to fruition.

The tribe has survived such catastrophes as the 1775 smallpox epidemic, which took most of the population, the arrival of white men into their otherwise isolated existence in 1826, and the continuing pressure of those interested in modernizing their culture from the 1850s onward. During this continuous onslaught, the Hopi people have fought to retain their independence and their isolated mesas in the arid eastern region of Arizona.

Today, state highways cut through the villages and mesas of Hopiland, and the Hopis still fight an uphill battle for privacy. The roads leading to the mesas on which the Hopi people have built the majority of their communities have signs that advise visitors to check in, forbid the use of cameras, and caution visitors to have respect for the Hopi way of life.

The Hopi arts and crafts are highly regarded in the Indian collectibles field. Hopi Kachinas, baskets, jewelry, and pottery help to ease some of the economic hardships of the Hopi nation.

Ceremonial life, which the Hopi have kept as close to the original as possible, is as different from the Anglo-ceremonial rituals as a cow is from an eagle. The Hopi Kachinas (gods) are fascinating, and many are models for the Kachina dolls discussed in Chapter Six.

These peaceful people farm the arid fields of their region, using the corn they grow in many of their dishes and utilizing the area's clay in their pottery.

In 1989 the Hopi tribe retrieved a sacred tribal mask that had been on display at New York Fall Antiques Show at the Pier. The tribe's eighty-two-year-old spiritual leader, Herman Lewis, identified the Kachina mask as one that had been stolen eight months before the show from one of the Hopi villages, and the Association of American Indian Affairs helped him confiscate the stolen artifact. The mask had been used for over 150 years in the ceremony that initiates children into adulthood.

IROQUOIS

The Iroquois nation, now known as the Six Nations, is considered the most completely evolved of all North American tribes. The Iroquois Constitution grants not only the majority of freedoms included in the U.S. Constitution, but one-ups the U.S. government by giving women and children rights, and by pledging a certain responsibility to the environment. The Iroquois have believed, since they founded their league, that they would be responsible for bringing peace to all nations.

Tadodaho is the title that means "speaker of the house" for the Grand Council of Six Nations Iroquois Confederacy. The ceremonial staff of office is an eagle-headed cane with a pictograph of each of the original peace chiefs etched onto it. The Iroquois Six Nations consists of the Mohawk, Oneida, Onondaga, Cayuga, Seneca, and Tuscarora. They consider themselves a nation separate from the United States and even issue their own passports. They call themselves *Haudenosaunee* or "the People of the Longhouse."

The Nation is located in central and western New York State (Onondaga Indian Reservation). Inside the reservation, federal and state officials have no jurisdiction. The Iroquois world consists of seventeen separate and distinct communities, ranging from Quebec and Ontario in Canada, to New York, Wisconsin, and Oklahoma settlements.

The Iroquois women play a strong role in the leadership of their society. Clan mothers select and depose chiefs, and the line of inheritance is carried by the women of the tribe.

MANDAN AND HIDATSA

The Mandan and Hidatsa tribes of North Dakota were often studied in the early days of the westward exploration by people such as George Catlin, Prince Maximilian, and Karl Bodmer. The tribes fell prey to smallpox in 1837–1838 and the disease brought by white men killed almost the whole combined population of both tribes. Those who survived pulled together and the two tribes moved to a spot in McLean County, on the Missouri River, that they named "Like-a-Fishhook."

There they started a new village, and once again began to grow traditional crops—corn, squash, beans, and sunflowers—and practice the domestic crafts of pottery, basket weaving, quillwork, and hide painting. After the Arikara tribe joined them in 1862, they came to be known as the Three Tribes.

NATCHEZ, CHOCTAWS, AND CHICKASAWS

Natchez, Choctaws, and Chickasaws originally lived along the Natchez Trail and welcomed travelers at Indian stands from the early 1800s, until the Treaty of Dancing Rabbit Creek forced the Choctaws to Oklahoma. Some Choctaws still remained in the area, and there is talk of building an Indian village and museum.

The Natchez were an elegant tribe with a monarchical ruler called the "Sun." This ruler had absolute power over nine or more villages, which numbered more than four thousand when the French first discovered them in the seventeenth century. The "Sun" was carried on a litter when he traveled, and lived in the plaza in a house specially built atop a ten-foot-high mound. He was considered chief priest as well as ruler, thus tended the fire and guarded bones considered sacred in the tribe's temple. He appointed war chiefs, though these appointments could not be his direct descendants. His word was law and he dictated every aspect of Natchez life. Females also held positions of power within the society. The matriarch picked the Great Sun from her brothers or sons.

The highly evolved Natchez social structure was divided into classes, with the Sun at the top and the "Stinkards" on the lowest rung.

The Choctaws, known as skillful farmers, were one of the tribes removed from their homeland and escorted to the government's Indian territory along the "Trail of Tears." They also managed to cause some trouble for their neighbors, the Natchez, by siding with the French in the mid-1700s. They later signed a treaty with the United States during the mid-1800s that allowed the railroad to come through their lands. In 1811 the Choctaws joined Andrew Jackson to fight against the Creeks. Chief Pushmataha and his warriors were much admired by Jackson, not known as an Indian lover. In fact, Jackson was largely responsible for sending the Chocktaw on the Trail of Tears to Oklahoma.

During the Civil War they joined the Confederacy along with some other tribes, and it should be noted that some Choctaws actually held slaves.

One of the best-known Choctaws was Private Joseph Oklahombi, an Indian volunteer in the 141st Infantry during World War I. He captured 171 German soldiers and received the croix de guerre from Marshal Philippe Pétain.

During World War II, Choctaws joined with other tribes to create an unbreakable code using their own language. Two Choctaw officers were able to transmit telephone messages regarding such sensitive subjects as troop movements.

The Chickasaws, considered warlike troublemakers, were one of the Five Civilized Tribes. They, too, were part of the group that traveled the Trail of Tears. While the Choctaw allied with the French, the Chickasaws sided with the English during the Revolutionary War.

Chicasaws were a slave-owning tribe and utilized the cotton gin before the Civil War. They, along with the Choctaw, signed an agreement with the United States to let the railroad pass through their territory. During the Civil War, they joined the Confederate side.

NAVAJOS

Navajos call themselves the *Dineh*, the "People"; their land is called *Dinetah*, the "People's Country." They arrived from the North, anthropologists say, and settled around Gobernador Canyon. Both Navajos and Apaches speak Athabascan languages, closely related to the Indian languages of the Pacific Northwest, Alaska, and Canada. They are the largest tribe in the United States and own about 14 million acres in Arizona, New Mexico, and Utah.

Navajo legend tells a different story explaining their appearance in New Mexico—they say the People emerged from underworld regions about seventy-five miles north of the Gobernador Canyon, through a hole near Silverton, Colorado.

The Hopis and Navajos are constantly squabbling, and frequently they settle their differences in court; Hopis claim Navajos are "borrowers" of Hopi and white culture.

In 1972 the United States offered the Navajo nation the opportunity to run their own reservation. It was the first time in more than a century that the tribe would control its own future, as well as the $110 million operation that had been run by the Department of Interior's Bureau of Indian Affairs. The Tribe now has its own legislature, police, and courts, and only answers to the federal government on traffic regulations and major crimes, such as murder, rape, and robbery.

The People are comprised of seventy-five clans. Marriage within the clan is considered incestuous. Property is traditionally passed through a wife's clan. The husband lives with her people and does not own anything except his clothes, jewelry, and saddle. In the old days, a man considered himself divorced if his wife put his saddle outside the door.

In 1989 the U.S. Supreme Court agreed to consider the Navajos' right to use peyote in religious practices. Since the First Amendment was written to protect religious freedom, the Navajo people believe that they should be allowed to use peyote, as they have been, in a closely supervised manner. The case came to court after Al Smith, a Klamath Indian and practicing member of the Native American Church, was fired from a job because of his use of peyote and died subsequently without unemployment benefits.

In 1991 the 219,000 members of the Navajo tribe reshaped their government into a more democratic structure. They elected their first tribal president, Peterson Zah, who said, "In unity, we will demonstrate that we have regained our stability."

SEMINOLES

The name Seminole is a derivative of a Muskogee word *cimarro'n*, which in its Spanish form means "something once domestic and now wild." The Muskogee considered the meaning to be closer to "emigrant" or "frontiersman."

The Seminoles were affiliates of the Creek peoples, and when the tribes were banished along the Trail of Tears, the Seminoles escaped to Florida. The U.S. Army gave up trying to follow the tribe after five years of searching and the loss of over fifteen hundred men. U.S. troops fought the Seminoles in three conflicts between 1817 and 1858. The Seminoles, using effective guerrilla tactics, won on the battleground, but lost at the negotiating table. Osceola, their leader, was seized when the tribe violated a truce and he died in prison in 1837.

Some slaves previously held by southern tribes found refuge with the Seminoles and married into the tribe. The Seminole homeland became known as a safe haven for runaway slaves.

Wewoka, the Seminole nation's capital, was put up for sale around 1900. At that time, the people of Wewoka received $15 a year for every citizen—man, woman, or child—of the Seminole nation. The countryside surrounding Wewoka was used for growing wheat, corn, and other cereals, as well as a sizable crop of cotton— sizable enough that the Wewoka Trading Company owned a large cotton gin. Wewoka, halfway between Oklahoma City and South McAlester, was an enviable piece of property.

The Seminoles brought legalized gambling in the form of high-stakes bingo games into their reservation in 1979. Since that time, several other tribes have also engaged in legalized gambling.

TAOS PUEBLO
The land the Taos people live on is divided by a mountain stream. The resulting parts are called North and South Pueblo. Originally these Native Americans farmed on the plateau and hunted in the mountains. They spoke Tanoan and were influenced by the Chacoans. Certain archaeologists believe this tribe originated in the Plains and later moved to the Southwest. They traded their leatherwork and pottery with some of the Plains Indians by traveling through a narrow mountain pass to the east.

The tribe is ruled by a council of elders, half from the North Pueblo and half from the South. Each has equal say in tribal matters. As with other tribes, the Taos Pueblo people would like to keep out the signs of modern civilization. However, it is nearly impossible to do so, given their proximity to the resort area of Taos.

These Indians built their pueblos as high as five stories with no ground-level openings—a protection against enemies. Now pueblos in Taos have ground-floor openings for windows and doors, but little else has changed—the villages have no electricity or running water and count approximately one thousand Indians as residents.

Timucuan

One of the earliest tribes to settle the peninsula of Florida, the Timucuans lived in the northeastern part of the state and along the Saint Johns River. They were considered one of the most civilized tribes in Florida, living in villages of as many as two hundred round wood huts. They were led by a "cacique" or chief. The tribe numbered approximately fourteen thousand people when Europeans first discovered them.

Their clothing was scant—women wore skirts made of moss and adornments of shell or pearl bracelets with brass bells that tinkled when they moved. The chief and his family were tattooed; the decoration was made with thorns.

The tribe believed in sorcery, and a witch doctor often claimed to foretell when and where an enemy would attack. Brave warriors, the people fought their battles during the day; they scalped their enemies, then cut off their arms and legs. These "trophies" were exhibited on tall poles back at the village. If their own warriors were killed, the wives would cut off their waist-length black hair and could not remarry until the hair had grown back to its original length.

Timucuans farmed, and the harvested food was kept in the chief's hut, to be divided evenly among the villagers. They also ate local snakes and alligators, a source of meat in their diets. According to Europeans who discovered the tribe, its members grew to be quite old.

The people traveled in dugout canoes made from indigenous trees. The canoes, flat on the bottom and with higher sterns than bows, were pushed by poles through the shallow waters.

The tribe died as a result of diseases introduced to their culture by Europeans, in battles, and when they were forced to work for the Spanish. By the early 1700s, the tribe was pretty much extinct.

ZUNI

Zuni tribal history states that the first European to visit the Zunis was a black Moroccan slave named Estevanico. When Estevanico demanded tribute, including gifts of turquoise and women, the Zuni men had a conference and decided to kill him with their arrows. Needless to say, more Europeans came, some of whom rode in on an animal the tribe had never seen before: the horse. Though the Zunis refused to surrender their land, the Europeans continued to come, bringing with them other animals (sheep, cattle, pigs, and goats), as well as families to settle the land. Eventually the "conquerors" enslaved the Indians and forced European Christian beliefs on them.

Like the Hopi, Zunis have Kachina gods who dance for them on special occasions. One such god, the Shalakos, are giant Zuni Kachinas whose dance blesses new houses.

The Zunis own many horses and consider them a sign of wealth. They are among the most prosperous of the Indian tribes. The first jewelry makers of the tribe learned to work silver from the Spanish, and today's Zuni silverworkers are considered some of the finest in the world (see Chapter Eight).

The Zuni now have complete control over their tribal affairs.

SPECIFIC EPHEMERA AND ADVERTISING ITEMS

APACHE CORN—MEDAL AND BOOK

Apache Corn—medal and book was issued in 1971 to mark the hundredth anniversary of the White Mountain Indian Reservation. The book and medal were placed in a time capsule on the reservation, to be reopened in another one hundred years. One side shows a "Gan" Dancer (the official symbol of the tribe), while the other depicts an Apache scout astride his horse.

Thirty-eight coin medals and accompanying books were issued, depicting the thirty-eight representative American Indian tribes.

CALUMET BAKING POWER

Calumet Baking Power has used an Indian as their advertising symbol since the 1920s. The company, located in Chicago, made three or four different sizes (one pound, eight ounces, etc.), and the original red, black, and yellow label has changed little from the original design. Large cans are valued at $20–$25, and small cans are valued at $15–$20.

CIGAR STORE INDIANS

Cigar store Indians originated with Sir Walter Raleigh, the Englishman who introduced tobacco to America. Though these figures are called "Indians," they are actually composite figures, comprised of: the Indians, who smoked the "weed" (as Raleigh termed the tobacco plant); the plantation owner, who grew it; and the Negro slave, who worked the fields.

These carved Indians, placed at the front door of tobacco shops, were an early form of advertising.

The people who made their living carving these figures were often craftsmen who had turned away from carving figureheads for ships when that industry fell into decline. Master carvers such as Charles Robb, Gustav Hentzel (also known for his carousel figures), Wilhelm Schimmel, John Bellamy, and Louis Jobin (a Canadian carver who created ship figureheads and religious figureheads before attempting to carve cigar store Indians) are represented in collections such as the superb representation of carvers held by the Shelburne Museum in Shelburne, Vermont.

The carvers depicted their wooden Indians with full headdresses whether the figures were male or female. Female figures often wore skirts much shorter than the acceptable style of the day, or had breasts that were exposed—a shocking sight in the mid-1800s.

A likeness of "Seneca John," a well-known Indian personality, was carved for the purpose of selling tobacco and was completely recognizable, right down to his headdress, rifle, and deerskin leggings. Other cigar store figures included an Indian trapper, Indian princesses, and a large variety of chieftains.

In 1987 the National Museum of American Art in Washington, D.C, acquired a pair of cigar store Indians entitled "Indian Squaw" and "Indian Brave." Carved of wood, painted, and stained, with metal accessories, this pair is thought to have been made around 1870 in New Jersey because they are similar to a figure that has been owned by a New Jersey family since the late nineteenth century. (Also see my book *The Confident Collector's Guide to Advertising*.)

OJIBWAY

Ojibway fine-cut tobacco was packaged in a yellow tin with red and black lettering. Made by the Scotten Dillion Company of Detroit, Michigan, the flat, round tin featured an Indian with one hand outstretched and the other holding tobacco leaves.

These round tins are valued at $85–$115.

ROUND OAK

Round Oak made stoves, ranges, and furnaces, and used an Indian chief, wearing three red feathers in his hair and a bear claw necklace around his throat, as an advertising symbol on its round cardboard sign. The sign was trimmed with a pattern of oak leaves. The Indian's face was centered with the words "Round Oak" in a semicircle around his head. Below the Indian's face are the words "Doe-wah-Jack" and "Stoves, Ranges and Furnaces." The signs are valued from $275 to $300, and the trade cards from $30 to $35.

SLEEPY EYE FLOUR

Sleepy Eye Flour's trademark was a profile of an older Indian whose name was (appropriately) "Old Sleepy Eye." The Sleepy Eye Milling Company made flour and cereal products in Sleepy Eye, Minnesota, and the Massachusetts-based company offered their customers a large assortment of premiums, all adorned with their Indian trademark. The company's metal signs, stoneware pitchers, and paper or canvas banners are becoming increasingly difficult to find. Signs are valued at $800–$1,000.

SURE SHOT

Sure Shot chewing tobacco was displayed on country store counters in its own metal display case, which depicted an Indian with an arrow on his bow and at the ready. Their slogan was "Sure Shot Chewing Tobacco—It Touches the Spot." The metal case held individual paper packages of tobacco. The metal case is valued at $250–$300, and the packages at $15–$18.

INDIAN WOMEN IN ADVERTISING

From 1915 to the 1940s, Indian maidens were used for various types of advertising. They graced calendar covers, playing cards, postcards, and almanacs.

Companies such as Brown and Bigelow of Saint Paul, Minnesota, hired Caucasian women to pose as Indian maidens, posing them seductively against the backdrop of a blue mountain or a clear moonlit lake. American Art Works of Coshocton, Ohio; Hayes Litho of Buffalo, New York; Arthur B. Cotas; the Fairman Company; and Knapp Company joined Brown and Bigelow in zealously producing the calendars that were in vogue.

The Flemish Art Company captured the female Indian image, Gibson girl style, on wooden boxes, mirrors, and trinkets, burning the image on the cover of their boxes.

Illustrators known for their images of Indian maidens included Walker, Burrich, McKenzue, Arthur, F. J. Harper, J. Knowles Hare (who also did covers for the *Saturday Evening Post*), Henry H. Intermeister (who worked for the Knapp Company), and Zula Kenyon, the only female artist to illustrate Indian women.

PHOTOGRAPHY

Photographers who worked during that early groundbreaking period to capture the elusive societies of various Indian tribes (1850–1900) often reflected the attitude of the white race toward the native peoples of America. Because these photographers were the first to record that presence, they dealt with Indian reluctance to use the sacred sun to make images that neither moved nor spoke. They took photographs that preserved the knowledge they had uncovered, and created a historical legacy. Early photographers such as Jean-Jaques Rousseau, John Mix Stanley, John Wesley Jones, and Robert Vance produced images that served to form valuable archives of visual information.

These early contacts were, for the most part, healthy and gratifying for both parties. White people were learning about the other occupants of the continent, and if they had tried harder to understand, may have even learned why the tribes grew threatened when the lands of their ancestors were invaded with wagon trains full of new settlers. The "noble savage" the early photographers encountered was now feared and fought against.

A different group of photographers began taking photos of those tribes not yet in conflict with American military. Government photographers, whose work was part of a survey of the land, included William Henry Jackson, Jack Hillers, and Timothy O'Sullivan. Army photographers like Will Soule and Ben Wittick produced worthy collections of images for the military. In Washington, Alexander Gardner and Zeno Schindler used their talents to capture on film Indian delegates to the capital in formal and dignified poses.

During the first two decades after the Civil War, tensions between the U.S. government and the Indians were so volatile that few photographers were able to create images of them in natural settings. The anti-Indian feeling that "any good Indian is a dead Indian," promoted by President Andrew Jackson, colored photographers' abilities to portray the Amerind with any measure of humanity. The photos of this period were "safe," romanticized views of Native Americans, not portraits of successful tribal leaders.

During the age of Queen Victoria, the dime-store novel was popular, and Indians starred in Wild West shows, such as the one put together by the legendary Buffalo Bill Cody. The Indian grew into something of a circus figure, someone who could be watched from a distance and degraded to the point that Americans of European heritage knew little, and did not care to know more, about Indian civilizations.

BIOGRAPHIES OF PHOTOGRAPHERS OF NATIVE AMERICAN CULTURE

EDWARD S. CURTIS (1868–1952)

Edward S. Curtis invested many years of his life to create more than twenty volumes of photographs of Native Americans. (A complete set of his photos brought $79,200 at a 1991 Sotheby's auction.) He believed the life they led, before the invasion of the white man, to be an idyllic one, and he approached them with that attitude. That philosophy is reflected in the many images he captured of the people other photographers turned away from.

Curtis spent many years learning the Indians' ways, traveling with them, and sharing his respect for their culture. He posed his subjects so that he could photograph them in powerful, deeply moving compositions. Historians often wonder how many of Curtis's photos were planned, how many of his subjects wore props Curtis decided they should wear, and even whether his subjects wore their own hair.

JOHN H. FITZGIBBON

A daguerreotype taken by this photographer in 1853 of "Kno-Shr," a Kansas chief, became part of an exhibit called "The Waking

Dream" shown at the Metropolitan Museum of Art in New York City through July 4, 1993.

SHAN GOSHORN

Shan Goshorn was a Cherokee woman born in Baltimore, Maryland. Her Cherokee name is *Noon da Da Lon a ga el* ("Yellow Moon"). Goshorn majored in silversmithing at the Cleveland Institute of Art, but changed her major to photography in her third year and then transferred to Atlanta College of Art. Her work has been shown at the Southern Plains Indian Museum.

TIMOTHY O'SULLIVAN AND WILLIAM BELL

Timothy O'Sullivan and William Bell were responsible for numerous documentary photographs of the American West. The photos were taken from 1871 to 1873, and assembled in 1875 by First Lt. George Montague Wheeler of the Army Corps of Engineers.

The photos were taken during expeditions through regions of the West that are now the states of Utah, California, Arizona, and New Mexico.

During the 1871 expedition, O'Sullivan photographed areas of the Southwest that included part of the Grand Canyon, Death Valley, and the Apache territory.

In 1872 Bell swung north to photograph more of the areas in and around the Grand Canyon, parts of Utah and Nevada, and the Colorado River. In 1873 O'Sullivan chronicled sights in Arizona and New Mexico. He traveled in a crescent shape through what is now the Navajo reservation in the northern parts of those states, and south through the states' central regions.

Born in 1842, Wheeler, the leader of the survey, was a Hopkinton, Massachusetts, native and a topographical engineer. The photos were used, as Wheeler proposed, to chart "astronomical, geographical, and topographical observations, artificial and economic features, the geologic and natural history branches being treated as incidental to the main purpose." The photos were not simply used for topographical reference; they were also used to help the U.S. Army gather and exterminate tribes of Indians who lived throughout the Southwest. Paiute, Apache, Zuni, and Navajo lifestyles and people were photographed during the expedition.

Wheeler chose O'Sullivan on the recommendation of William Henry Jackson, a famous frontier photographer, who called

Timothy O'Sullivan, an Irishman born in 1840, "one of the best of the government photographers." O'Sullivan was apprenticed to Matthew Brady during the early part of his career and later joined Brady's semiofficial corps of photographers during the Civil War. Many of O'Sullivan's pictures are included in *Photographic Sketchbook of the Civil War*, by Alexander Gardner, though Brady and Gardner took credit for many of them. He was later hired as the official photographer for the expedition through the Isthmus of Darien, which later resulted in the construction of the Panama Canal.

In the course of O'Sullivan's at times perilous treks, he nearly drowned, one of his men died in the desert, and two civilian guides disappeared. The photographs, however, survived the perilous journey down the white-water rapids of the Colorado River. The expedition drew to a close with the onslaught of winter, and Wheeler, as director of the dangerous journey, sent a group back to Congress with the photos. Unfortunately, some of the photos, which had survived the rough ride down the Colorado, were lost when the stagecoach was ambushed en route to Washington, D.C., and one of the party was killed.

William Bell replaced O'Sullivan in 1872 for the Wheeler survey. Bell was a Philadelphian who used a dry photographic process, unusual for photographers who worked with this particular subject matter. In 1873 O'Sullivan returned to complete the survey and produced some of his more memorable work. His work showing the Zuni Indians and their ancient pueblo were some of the first photos to document that tribe's lifestyle. The expedition produced a variety of documents, as well as photographic data, that remain a powerful testament to the rich heritage of southwestern tribes.

JULIUS VANNERSON

Julius Vannerson, the manager of a studio in Washington, D.C., in 1858, photographed Indian delegations and treated them as he would any other type of delegation. He was not concerned whether one Indian was more important than another, he just did the best work he could for his rather disinterested client—the American government.

ADAM CLARK VROMAN

Adam Clark Vroman had a clear, realistic vision of the Indian way of life and chronicled the Hopi with empathy few have ever accomplished before or after. His work, during the late 1890s, chronicled his anger at the conditions under which the Indians were forced to live, as well as his determination to take action. His photos strived to raise the consciousness of others.

He photographed the Hopi, Taos, Navajo, and Zuni tribes, not with full warbonnets and memorabilia as Curtis did, nor in a room that was foreign to them as Vannerson did, but instead as human beings who were struggling to eke out an existence on the arid plains and mesas of the Southwest. His photos clearly showed their subjects' strong religious character and the depth of their belief, and exposed the truth of the Indians' lives as no white man ever had before.

The Native American in Fiction and in the Cinema

Many popular magazines, with wide distributions at the turn of the century, published short stories about the American Indian. Though some were predictably stereotypical, an amazing portion of fictionalized Native Americans were realistically depicted. Later, when movies and television drew visual portraits of Indian characters, they were, more often than not, stereotyped more than their earlier literary counterparts.

In reading what has been written by, as well as about, the American Indian, you can decide for yourself which stereotypes have been carried through the years. Writers, like other people chronicling Indian life, drew generalizations about tribes, their habits, customs, and speech patterns. Remember, though, that we are speaking of *fiction* and that writers of fiction are bound to treat Indian subjects far differently from nonfiction writers who attempt to accurately portray the Native American and his or her place in society.

Collections of Indian stories include *Indians, Indians, Indians,* edited by Phyllis R. Fenner and published by Franklin Watts in 1950. This anthology features a story called "The Second Race," by Merritt P. Allen.

In 1990 an article in the *New York Times* declared "Hollywood's War on Indians Draws to Close." It went on to say that the movie *Dances with Wolves* proved their claim since Native Americans rather than white actors represented the film's Native American characters. The film was shot on location in South Dakota (Sioux country), and Kevin Costner, the lead actor, learned how to speak the Sioux language, Lakota, for his role as Lieutenant John J. Dunbar. Other details such as set design and authentic clothing were attended to by Sioux experts.

The American Indian Registry for the Performing Arts in Hollywood has been instrumental in influencing the industry to hire Indian actors to portray Indians on stage and in film.

NATIVE AMERICAN WRITERS AND OTHERS WHO WROTE ABOUT INDIANS

PAULA GUNN ALLEN

Allen has been largely responsible for introducing women to the powers the American Indian women have through her books *The Sacred Hoop: Recovering the Feminine in American Indian Traditions* and *Grandmothers of the Light.* Her books deal with all the Native American tribes, rather than just one or two, and have been accepted as feminist treatises on the goddess theory and the American Indian way of life.

FRANK APPLEGATE

Native Tales of New Mexico (Lippincott, 1932) featured Frank Applegate's stories "The Apache Kid," "The Buried Treasure of Cochiti," "The Founding of Hano," and "Hopi Susanna Corn Blossom." His stories were also featured in *Indian Stories from the Pueblos* (Rio Grande Press, 1929).

MARY AUSTIN

Another Indian story anthology, *One Smoke Stories* (Houghton, Mifflin, 1934), featured stories about many different tribes with realistic overtones about the culture of the various tribes they depict. Mary Austin was a prolific writer of the time.

GEORGE A. BOYCE

In the anthology *Some People Are Indians,* it appears the editors were trying to convince white people that the Native American was a human being. George A. Boyce was an author published by this anthology on a regular basis.

DEE BROWN

Brown was born in a Louisiana lumber camp; his father was a timberman who died when Dee was five. While living with his two sisters and mother in the Southwest, he became friends with an Indian boy and came to realize that the Indians portrayed in the movies he and his friend went to see were not at all like the people themselves.

Brown attended Arkansas State Teachers College and George Washington University in Washington, D.C.

Because of his strong belief that the Native Americans deserved fair treatment and representation, Dee Brown spent over two years researching and writing the fabulously successful book *Bury My Heart at Wounded Knee* (1971).

JOSEPH BRUCHAC

An Abenaki storyteller, poet, and publisher, Bruchac has authored several books, including *Keepers of the Earth: Native American Stories and Environmental Activities for Children* and *Thirteen Moons on Turtle's Back: A Native American Year of Moons* (1992).

His stories and poetry have been published by more than four hundred anthologies and magazines.

He lives in Greenfield, New York, with his wife, Carol, and two sons, Jesse and Jim.

ROBERT J. CONLEY

Robert J. Conley was a Cherokee Indian who wrote for *Indian Voice*. He wrote short stories about Indians who struggled to make their way in the white man's world.

ADELINA DEFENDER

Adelina Defender, a Pueblo Indian, is best known for her short story "No Time for Tears," included in *An American Indian Anthology* (Blue Cloud Abbey, 1971). It is a story of the way a woman was treated in a mission school, forcing her to turn her back on her Indian ways.

CHARLES A. EASTMAN

Charles A. Eastman, a popular Santee Sioux short story writer, was published in *Old Indian Days, Harper's, Sunset, Craftsman,* and *Ladies' Home Journal.*

His stories, written in the early 1900s, are a combination of realistic Indian stories and tales of how various Indians coped with the ways of the white men.

ALEXANDER EWEN (1959–   )

The editor of *Native Nations*, a magazine begun in 1990, Ewen attended the University of Virginia and decided to start the magazine in response to the anniversary of Columbus's "discovery" of the Americas. Its first issue was decorated with a cover painted by Leonard Peltier, the imprisoned Indian leader.

WILLIAM FAULKNER (1897–1962)

Faulkner was a well-known writer who wrote many short stories about the American Indian, which appeared in such publications as *Go Down, Moses,* and *The Saturday Evening Post.*

HAMLIN GARLAND (1860–1940)

Hamlin Garland, a prolific short story writer, published a good number of stories in which the plot focused on the American Indian and his or her conflicts with white men.

The Book of the American Indian, published in 1927, made use of quite a few of his stories, as did *Prairie Son* and *Western Story.*

RICHARD G. GREEN

An Oneida Indian, Green actively wrote in the early 1970s and was featured in such publications as *Indian Voice.* Green's stories are realistic depictions of everyday matters in Indian life and are clearly written from the Indian's viewpoint.

GEORGE BIRD GRINNELL

George Bird Grinnell wrote stories about Indian and animal mythology during the early 1900s for *Harper's.*

ERNEST HEMINGWAY (1899–1961)

Even literary luminary Ernest Hemingway used his pen to create tales of Indian lore. Such short stories as "Indian Camp," "Ten Indians," and "Fathers and Sons" were a part of the collection *The Short Stories of Ernest Hemingway,* published by Scribner's in 1935.

The stories, featuring Hemingway's protagonist Nick Adams, characteristically expose the underside of people's personalities—a side decidedly not understanding of the ways of the Indians.

DOROTHY M. JOHNSON

"A Man Called Horse," a short story that was the basis for the film epic starring Richard Harris, was written by Dorothy M. Johnson and published in 1953 in *Indian Country* (Ballantine Books). The story was first published by *Collier's* magazine.

"A Man Called Horse" was one of many stories Johnson wrote about Native Americans.

MARTHA KOSANKE

Romances about Indians were the focus of Exposition Press's 1954 publication called *Indian Romances of the Western Frontier.*

It appears that most, if not all, of the stories published in this book were written by Martha Kosanke.

JACK LONDON (1876–1916)

Jack London, well known for his tales of the Northwest Territory, devoted a good deal of time to writing stories about Indians, which are included in the collections *The God of His Fathers and Other Stories* and *The Best Short Stories of Jack London.*

N. SCOTT MOMADAY (1934–   )

N. Scott Momaday, a contemporary Indian author, won a Pulitzer Prize for *House Made of Dawn* (1968), a story about a Tanoan Indian World War II veteran reentering society.

Momaday's father was Kiowa and his mother was part Cherokee. He was raised on Navajo, Pueblo, and Apache reservations in Oklahoma.

He also wrote *The Way to Rainy Mountain* (1969), which was illustrated by his father and is about Kiowas visiting his grandmother's house.

Momaday received his Ph.D. in literature from Stanford University and taught at the University of California at Berkeley, Stanford, and elsewhere.

He lives in Tucson, where he teaches at the University of Arizona. He has written two volumes of poetry, a memoir, and a coffee table book called *Colorado: Summer, Fall, Winter, Spring* (1973).

SIMON J. ORTZ

From the Acoma Pueblo, famous for its pottery makers, came the writer Simon J. Ortz, whose work was published in *Howbah*

Indians and *The Man to Send Rain Clouds: Contemporary Stories by American Indians* in the late 1970s. He wrote short stories about modern problems, with Indians as the main characters. The stories are realistic and their characters face problems that could face any average American—some deal with war, others with a character's reaction to life's turmoils.

MARY SUMMER RAIN

Rain is of Shoshone descent and was the last apprentice to No-Eyes, the renowned Chippewa visionary who was the daughter of a tribal shaman. Mary Summer Rain's books *Earthway: A Native American Visionary's Path to Total Mind, Body, and Spirit Health, Spirit Song, Phoenix Rising, Dreamwalker, Phantoms Afoot, Daybreak, Soul Sounds*, and her children's book *Mountains, Meadows and Moonbeams* share the secrets taught to her during her apprenticeship.

Rain lives in Colorado with her husband and three daughters.

VERNER Z. REED

At the turn of the century, Verner Z. Reed produced fiction about the American Indian for anthologies such as *Tales of the Sunland* (Continental, 1897) and *Adobeland Stories* (Badger, 1898) and for periodicals such as *Overland Monthly*.

Using true Indian names, Reed's characters were often Pueblo Indians who dealt with religious problems or related legends of their culture.

FREDERIC REMINGTON (1861–1909)

Frederic Remington, the artist/sculptor, exercised his literary talents writing short stories about the Amerind for *Harper's* during the turn of the century.

His main characters were usually whites or half-breeds, who related the Indians' tale through their eyes.

LESLIE SIKO

Leslie Siko (Laguna Pueblo) published a number of stories in the 1974 Viking book *The Man to Send Rain Clouds: Contemporary Stories by American Indians*, including the title story.

Her work is diversified and includes tales that give a fictional recounting of historical facts, as well as contemporary stories of families and their everyday conflicts.

WILLIAM JOSEPH SNELLING

In the early 1800s, William Joseph Snelling wrote of the Northwest Indian. He must have been intimidated by the public's view of the "noble savage" because much of his work was published anonymously in *Tales of the Northwest: Or, Sketches of Indian Life and Character*.

JOHN STEINBECK (1902–1968)

Literary giant John Steinbeck also wrote stories about the Amerind, which were published in *The Long Valley* in 1938 (Viking).

LITTLE STEVEN

Little Steven is the publisher of *Native Peoples*, a magazine started in 1991 in response to the anniversary of Christopher Columbus's "discovery" of America.

CY WARMAN

Cy Warman, a turn-of-the-century author, was featured in a number of periodicals and anthologies, including *Frontier Stories* (Scribner's, 1918) and *Weiga of Temagami and Other Indian Tales* (McLeod and Allen, 1908).

His stories relate tales of Indians and their relations to French-Canadian settlers, often centering on half-breed characters.

FRANK WATERS (1902–   )

Frank Waters, born in 1902 in Colorado Springs, is the prolific author of very popular stories about American Indians. He wrote twenty-two books, including *Fever Pitch* (1930), *Masked Gods* (1950), *Book of the Hopi* (1963), *Pumpkin Seed Point* (1969), *Mexico Mystique: The Coming Sixth World of Consciousness* (1975), and *Flight from Fiesta*. His book *The Man Who Killed the Deer*, about a young Taos Indian caught between two cultures, was in print for more than forty years.

As Waters's father was part Indian, he spent some of his childhood at trading posts on Indian reservations. He was familiar with Utes who moved into his hometown and whom he visited with his father.

He attended Colorado College and majored in engineering, but dropped out to take a laborer's job in the Salt Creek, Wyoming, oil fields.

His most recent book, *Brave Are My People: Indian Heroes Not Forgotten*, published by Cedar Light Publishers in 1993, has been favorably reviewed and is destined to become a textbook in Native American studies. Saturday, June 26, 1993, was proclaimed Frank Waters Day by Governor Bruce King of New Mexico in celebration of Mr. Waters's ninety-first birthday.

CRYING WIND

Crying Wind, a Navajo woman, achieved success with her first book, *Crying Wind*, and her second, *My Searching Heart*, a fictionalized biography of herself and her family.

She is an artist, freelance writer, and lecturer who has received the "Distinguished Christian Service in the Highest Tradition of the American Indian" award from the CHIEF organization.

Her paintings have been shown in museums and art shows.

BEVERLY HUNGRY WOLF

A Blackfoot woman, Beverly Hungry Wolf introduced her culture to readers through her book *The Ways of My Grandmothers*. That work brings people into Blackfoot life, explaining history, legends, myths, and skills such as moccasin making, tanning, quilling, beading, and cooking. The book is an essential history of the Blackfoot tribe.

PRICES

BOOKS

League of the Ho-De-No-Sau-Nee or Iroquois by Lewis H. Morgan, Dodd Mead & Co.; 1904; very good condition; $45–$70.

Life Among the Indians by Cranston and Curts, Cincinnati, Ohio; about Findley's personal experiences as an Indian missionary; 1857; good condition; $30–$50.

Primitive Industry or Illustrations of the Handwork in Stone, Bone and Clay of the Native Races of the North Atlantic Seaboard of America, George Bates, Salem; 1881; very good condition; $35–$55.

Recollections of Sheridan County Nebraska; pioneer and Indian (Wounded Knee) stories of Northwest Nebraska, which borders Pine Ridge Indian Reservation; 1976; very good condition; $75–$125.

Ephemera/Advertising, book, Indian Races of North and South America, *1883, first edition, good condition;* $150–$250. Courtesy of, and photo by, Dawn E. Reno (also photo of book opened to Black Hawk illustration).

Rinehart's Indians by F. A. Rinehart, Omaha, Nebraska; 1899; very good condition; $80–$125.

The American Indian in the United States 1850–1914 by W. K. Moorehead, Andover Press; 1914; very good condition; $30–$40.

The Blanket Indians of the Northwest by Col. G. O. Shields, Vechten Waring Co.; 1921; very good condition; $45–$70.

The North American Indian, Edward S. Curtis, Vol. 2, published 1916 by The Plimpton Press, Massachusetts; complete volume with text, vocabulary, Indian mythology, on Japan vellum with 75 photogravures, each with a tissue guard, leather- and cloth- bound; one of 272 completed and numbered sets (of a proposed 500 sets) of 20 volumes and accompanying portfolios. This volume, numbered 54, picturing the Haida and Nootka tribes of the Northwest Coast; particularly fine condition; $2,800–$4,000.

Who's Who in Indian Relics; very good condition; $20–$30.

Ephemera/Advertising, book; The North American Indian, *Edward S. Curtis, Vol. 2, published 1916 by The Plimpton Press, Massachusetts. Complete volume with text, vocabulary, Indian mythology, on Japan vellum with 75 photogravures, each with a tissue guard, leather- and cloth-bound; one of 272 completed and numbered sets (of a proposed 500 sets) of 20 volumes and accompanying portfolios. This volume, numbered 54, picturing the Haida and Nootka tribes of the Northwest Coast; particularly fine condition; $2,800–$4,000.* Courtesy of C. E. Guarino Auction Gallery, Denmark, Maine.

Two books; *Dictionary of American Indian* and *Voices from Wounded Knee*, ca. 1978; very good condition; $30–$40/set.

Three books; *"Totem Tales," Indians of Ohio* and a handmade bark book; ca. 1930; very good condition; $30–$40/set.

11 books and pamphlets; relating to American Indians; includes *Pawnee Bill's Trading Post Catalog*; very good condition; $50–$85/set.

Three books; *On the Border with Crook* (1891); *Heroes and Hunters of the West* (1858); *Life of Sitting Bull*; *History of the Indian War of 1890–1891*; very good condition; $55–$85/set.

Complete set of Henry R. Schoolcraft's *Information Respecting the History, Conditions, and Prospects of the Indian Tribes of the United States*, Philadelphia, Lippincott, Grambo and Co., 1853–1857; six volumes, large quarto, rebound in modern cloth, various degrees of water staining; many plates, maps, and engravings; two volumes inscribed by Commissioner of Indian Affairs, J. W. Denver; very good condition; $975–$1,150/set.

Crooked Beak of Heaven and *Indian Artifacts of Northwest Coast*; ca. 1975; very good condition; $50–$85.

Five North American Indian-related titles including Gladys A. Reichard, *Navajo Shephard and Weaver*, First Edition, November 1936; G. Moon, *Indian Legends in Rhyme*, 1917, illustrated by Karl Moon; Fr. J. K. Dixon, *The Vanishing Race*, plates by R. Wanamaker; H. Whitney, *Hunting with the Eskimos*, 1910, embossed frontice "Presentation Copy"; and L. Spence, *Myths and Legends of the North American Indians*, 1914; very good condition; $175–$230/set.

Lot of Northwest Coast Indian and Eskimo reference books; very good condition; $500–$575/set.

Nine American Indian-related books, nine volumes, includes Rev. J. G. Wood, *The Natural History of Man*, London, 1870; and George Mills, *Navajo Art and Culture*, Colorado, 1959; very good condition; $150–$200.

Two books; *The Tlingit Indians* and *Primitive Heritage*; ca. 1965; very good condition; $30–$60/set.

Two books; *The Washo* and *The Cheyenne*; ca. 1965; very good condition; $20–$35/set.

12 North American Indian-related books, including F. Dellenbaugh, *The North Americans of Yesterday*, New York, 1906; L. Frank and F. Harlow, *Historic Pottery of the Pueblo Indians*,

Boston, 1974; and G. Wharton James, *Indian Basketry*, Pasadena, 1902; very good condition; $175–$230/set.

MISCELLANEOUS

Calendar; dated 1950, December; months illustrated with Indian portraits and life scenes; nicely matted and framed; 27 x 37 inches overall aproximate framed size; excellent condition; $175–$200.

Indian Rock Ginger Ale pump dispenser (pump may not be original); ca. 1913–1919; very good condition; $4,150–$4,600.

Skookum dolls (four) made by Tammen Manufacturing Company of Colorado during 1910–1915 (used to promote Skookum apples); earliest are handmade dried apple heads; all in excellent condition; $30–$300/set.

Framed copy of a G. A. Custer letter sent to the agent at Fort Yates from Fort Lincoln about Custer's Indian scouts; very good condition; $25–$55.

Red Indian Cut Plug Tobacco lunch pail with black lettering on red background, with image of Indian with full headdress; 7¾ x 5¼ x 4¼ inches; good condition; $800–$1,200.

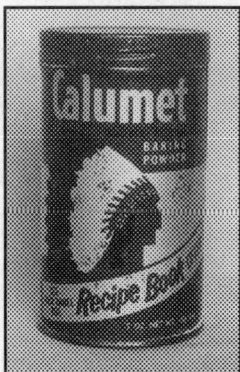

Ephemera/Advertising, can, Calumet Baking Powder, 7-ounce size; ca. 1950s; $15–$25. Courtesy of, and photo by, Dawn E. Reno.

Ephemera/Advertising, can, Merry-Mount Brand Tomatoes; color lithographed; packed for E. V. Fitts Co., Quincy, Massachusetts; excellent condition; $20–$30. Courtesy of, and photo by, Dawn E. Reno.

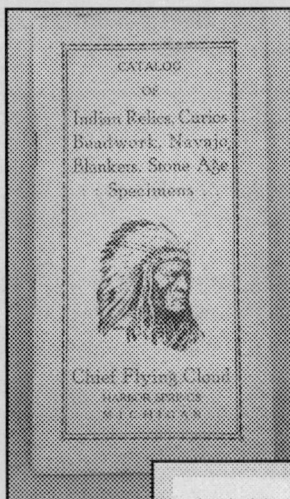

Ephemera/Advertising, Catalog of Indian Relics, Curios, Beadwork, Navajo Blankets, Stone Age Specimens; ca. 1920s; $15–$25. Courtesy of, and photo by, Dawn E. Reno (also photo of catalog opened to pages 24–25).

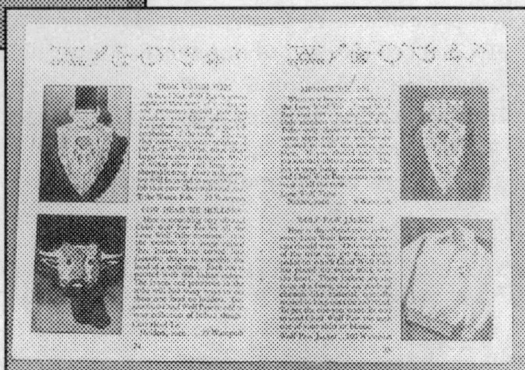

Tin Lunch Pail; Red Indian Cut Plug Tobacco tin has several Indian-type figural animals and people in the traditional red and black colors; manufactured by American Tobacco Co.; 8 x 5¼ x 4¼ inches; very good to excellent condition; $900–$1,500.

Black and red tin lunch pail for the American Tobacco Company with full-feathered Indian logo on sides; rare; 8 x 4¼ x 5¼ inches; good condition; $550–$850

Miscellaneous; lot of associated pieces for Chief Shunatona, director of the U.S. Indian Band; includes 8-x-10-inch photograph with lengthy inscription and signature; a piece of sheet music entitled "The Trail to Long Ago," with photograph of Chief Shunatona along with signature and inscription; several poems and letters dated 1930 from the "Land of the Ojibways, Minneapolis," another from a Pittsburgh hotel; very good condition; $35–$55/set.

Mug; Modoc embossed glass head of Indian chief on handled soda fountain glass mug; 3 x 5 inches; very good condition; $30–$100.

Old Axe advertisement; showing an Indian; ca. 1920; 9 x 6 inches; very good condition; $15–$50.

Peace medal; Brule; England's King Edward VII and Alexandra's Peace Medal inscribed "To a Good Indian Chief Red Shirt, from The Red Man Syndicate, 1909," probably given to Red Shirt when he was in England with Buffalo Bill's Wild West Show; very good condition; $2,500–$3,500.

PHOTOGRAPHS

"Buffalo Bill and Troup of Indians"; an important silver-print photo of William Cody with Iron Tail at his right and some 10 or more Indian chiefs and leaders who participated in Buffalo Bill's epic, which he produced as a movie in 1913 at Warbonnet Creek and Pine Ridge, North Dakota; photos probably taken by Conrad Luperti and D. T. Hargan; crop marks for newspaper release, reverse side indicates a possible Tuesday publication; 4½ x 8½ inches; very good condition; $250–$400.

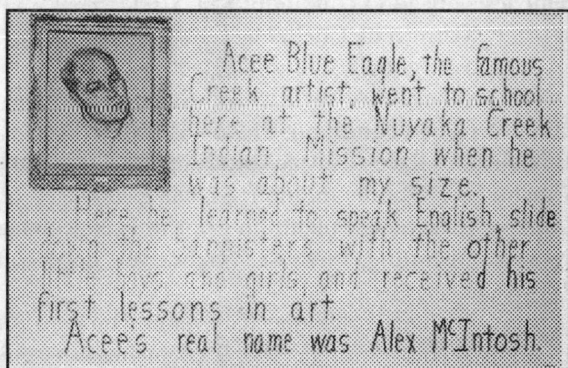

Ephemera/Advertising, photo; of artist Acee Blue Eagle and information about the Nuyaka Mission, where he grew up. Courtesy Bill and Oakla Spears/Nuyaka Mission. Photo by Donald Vogt.

Ephemera/Advertising, photo; the Nuyàka Mission. Courtesy Bill and Oakla Spears/Nuyaka Mission. Photo by Donald Vogt.

Photo of a nude Indian maiden from the back, signed "E. S. Curtis"; matted and framed; ca. 1910; image 10 x 8 inches; very good condition; $175–$230.

Photo of a nude Indian maiden from the back, signed "E. S. Curtis"; matted and framed; image 6 x 4 inches; ca. 1910; very good condition; $75–$100.

Matted sepia tone of "Old Person—Peigan" by E. S. Curtis; ca. 1911; 24 x 16 inches; very good condition; $140–$175.

Chief Many Tail Feathers, bust view, hand-tinted by William Bell; 6 x 8 inches; very good condition; $50–$100.

Platinum print; "Canyon de Chelly" by Edward S. Curtis; ca. 1904; 6 x 8 inches; very good condition; $1,600–$1,850.

"Portrait of an Indian Brave" by E. S. Curtis; ca. 1904; image 7 x 5 inches; very good condition; $1,725–$1,955.

Crotone; "Vanishing Race—Navajo" by Edward S. Curtis; ca. 1904; 9 x 7 inches; very good condition; $4,350–$5,000.

Broken Arm—Ogalla Sioux, platinum print by F. A. Rinehart, with original color tinting; 1898; 9 x 7 inches; very good condition; $160–$185.

Platinum print of Chief Wolf Robe (Cheyenne) by F. A. Rinehart, with original color tinting; 1898; 9 x 7 inches; very good condition; $150–$185.

Blackfoot; Chief Bird Rattler on card, bust view, hand-tinted by William Bell; 6 x 8 inches; very good condition; $50–$100.

Ephemera/Advertising, photo; Deaf Bull, a Crow Indian, vintage print by L. A. Hoffman, Niles City, Montana. Courtesy Larry Gottheim, Fine Early Photographs, Binghamton, New York.

Ephemera/Advertising, photo; Sioux Chief "Spotted Eagle"; vintage albumen print by L. A. Hoffman, ca. 1880. Courtesy Larry Gottheim, Fine Early Photographs, Binghamton, New York.

Curtis Goldtone photograph miniature; on glass in original frame; ca. 1910; 3 x 2½ inches; very good condition; $80–$150.

E. C. Watkins, S. F. Photo; Indian Camp; stereo on orange mount with portrait of an Indian squaw with papoose, woven basket; very good condition; $75–$125.

Photo of an Indian man signed by "E. S. Curtis"; matted and framed; ca. 1910; image 6 x 4 inches; very good condition; $70–$115.

Hand-tinted, framed picture of head and upper torso of male Indian wearing feathered headdress and hair-pipe bone breastplate; dated 9/23/27 on back; very good condition; $115–$175.

Hileman; original photograph of Two Guns White Calf, signed by both people; ca. 1927; 12 x 15 inches; very good condition; $100–$150.

Nez Perce; hand-tinted photograph of an Indian in a stand-up bonnet; ca. 1900; 7 x 4 inches; very good condition; $30–$45.

Nez Perce; cabinet view, "Steps" by Baily, Dix, and Meade, Fort Randall, DT; Cough Up Steps, a Nez Perce Indian, was so named because he yelled "Cough up, white man, cough up!" begging as people got off the trains in Pierre, South Dakota, after he lost both feet and a hand to frostbite; 1880s; very good condition; $115–$200.

Nez Perce; original photograph of a very well dressed Nez Perce lady with a Pendleton blanket; ca. 1910; 15 x 10 inches; very good condition; $50–$90.

Five portraits by C. W. Carter of Salt Lake City, Utah, and one by C. R. Savage: of Cheyenne and Shoshone warriors and squaws; very good condition; $775–$975/set.

Comanche; five photographs; stereopticon cards of Comanche Chiefs Horseback, Ho-Wear, Otter Belt, Tosh-A-Wah, and Horseback's Son; very good condition; $150–$200/set.

Two photographs; one titled "Sioux Appeal," the other "The Vanishing Race," by Edward S. Curtis, mounted on brown paper, with embossed copyright legend "L.L.A," both signed by the photographer ("Curtis") in ink; very good condition; $315–$400/set.

Five framed assorted Indian photographs; ca. 1935; very good condition; $25–$45/set.

Frame of three old Indian photos; ca. 1900; very good condition; $80–$100/set.

Large box full of black-and-white Indian artifact photographs; ca. 1985; very good condition; $20–$35/set.

Mohave; by Edward S. Curtis; three sepia photogravures, small octavo plates on Japanese paper: Mohave Mother, An Old Mohave, Sholya-Mohave Girl; 12 x 9 inches; all in very good condition; $125–$250/each.

Portraits of Ute chiefs, Dakota Sioux, Sioux, warriors, and children; very good condition; $625–$825.

Sioux; three photographs; two signed "J. C. H. Graybill": "Indian Council in Hostile Camp," Deadwood, South Dakota; "The Great Hostile Camp," Deadwood, South Dakota, and another

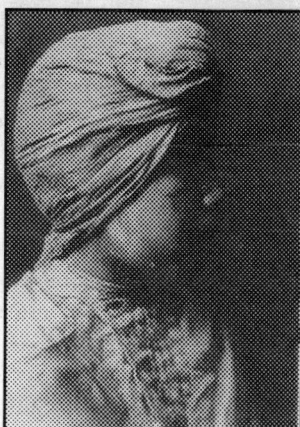

Ephemera/Advertising, photos, Edward S. Curtis; three sepia photogravures, small octavo plates on Japan paper, 12 x 9 inches; includes Mohave Mother; An Old Mohave; Sholya-Mohave Girl; all in very fine condition; $125–$250. Courtesy of C. E. Guarino Auction Gallery, Denmark, Maine.

camp picture; image size 9 x 6¼ inches (two), 7⅜ x 4¼ inches; very good condition; $500–$700/set.

Sioux; three photographs; Bigfoot's band, two signed "J. C. H. Graybill," "At the Dance" on the Cheyenne River; all signed on reverse: "Mrs. Cyrus J. Fry"; 1890; image size 6¼ x 9 inches (two), 7⅜ x 9¼ inches; very good condition; $650–$850/set.

Sioux; two photographs; one is a studio portrait of seven men including Cyrus J. Fry, U.S. marshal for South Dakota, and two Indians in handcuffs (image size, 66½ x 4 inches); and a portrait of "Plenty Horses," the slayer of Lieutenant Casey near Pine Ridge, with two soldiers (image size, 9 x 7½ inches), and American Heritage; very good condition; $750–$950/set.

Southwestern; stereo photo of Snake Priest with hand tinting, published by Montgomery Ward & Co., showing a Southwestern Indian with apparatus and hangings for Snake Ceremony; light soil on salmon mount; very good condition; $25–$55.

Three original photographs of different Indians; ca. 1900; very good condition; $35–$55/set.

Two American Indian Cabinet cartes de visite, 19th century, each inscribed on reverse; the first, 2½ x 3¼ inches, "A Victoria B.C. young Indian with his Hudson Bay blanket around him"; and the other, 4 x 8¼ inches, "Crowfoot, Chief of the Blackfeet, taken at Regina . . . when in route . . . July 7, 1884"; both in very good condition; $150–$175/set.

Three stereos on gray mounts by Keystone with photos of Village of Blackfeet Indians, Pueblo of Taos Indians, and Indian Squaw Making Pottery in Oraibi; all very good condition; $35–$55/set.

Two sepia photogravures by Edward S. Curtis; small octavo plates on Van Gelder: Havasupai Cliff Dwelling, Walalthoma-Havasupai (portrait); 12 x 9 inches; very good condition; $125–$250/set.

Photogravures by Edward S. Curtis, including A Holiday Lodge-Yakima, An Old Man of Waiyam, Piegan War-Bonnet, and Coup Stick (portrait), all small octavos on Japan paper; 12 x 9 inches; very good condition; $250–$500/set.

Lot of 45 or more stereos by T. W. Ingersol, printed in color from the original photographs in a numbered series, including View of El Paso, Los Angeles View, Yellowstone, Royal Gorge, California Street, Placer Mining, Wyoming scenes, A Chippewa Squaw; 1898; images fair to good condition; $45–$100/set.

Lot of 33 printed stereo views, most in full color, from photos taken of Indian tribes, scenes, portraits of Chippewas, Sioux, Cheyennes, Moki, and other tribes, buffalo herds, Custer Battlefield, Indian life, western views, etc., some original photo cards; good condition; $100–$225/set.

Ephemera/Advertising, photos, Edward S. Curtis, two sepia photogravures, small octavo plates on Van Gelder, 12 x 9 inches; includes: Havasupai Cliff Dwelling; Walalthoma-Havasupai (portrait); all in very fine condition; $125–$250. Courtesy of C. E. Guarino Auction Gallery, Denmark, Maine.

Ephemera/Advertising, photos, Edward S. Curtis; three sepia photogravures, small octavos on Japan, 12 x 9 inches; includes: A Holiday Lodge-Yakima; An Old Man of Waiyam; Piegan War-Bonnet, and Coup Stick (portrait); very good condition; $250–$500. Courtesy of C. E. Guarino Auction Gallery, Denmark, Maine.

Edward Curtis; large brown tone from the original folio "On the Shore at Nooka," plate no. 366; very good condition; $90–$115.

Edward Curtis; brown tone from the original photograph "The Piki Maker," plate no. 432; ca. 1906; 11 x 15 inches; very good condition; $100–$140.

Edward Curtis; brown tone from the original folio "Counting the Record," plate no. 413; ca. 1921; 11 x 15 inches; very good condition; $90–$115.

Edward Curtis; brown tone from the original folio "Yurok Drummer," plate no. 457; ca. 1923; 11 x 15 inches; very good condition; $115–$175.

Edward Curtis; brown tone from the original folio "Women's Dress—Tolowa," plate no. 464; ca. 1923; 11 x 15 inches; very good condition; $150–$175.

Edward Curtis; brown tone from the original folio "A Serrano Woman of Tejon," plate no. 512; ca. 1924; 11 x 15 inches; very good condition; $70–$90.

Edward Curtis; brown tone from the original folio "Fishing Platform—Hupa," plate no. 465; ca. 1923; 11 x 15 inches; very good condition; $70–$90.

Edward Curtis; brown tone (with onionskin) from the original folio "The Berry Picker—Clayoquat," plate no. 368; ca. 1915; 15 x 11 inches; very good condition; $60–$85.

Edward Curtis; brown tone (with onionskin) from the original folio "Ceremonial Bathing," plate no. 376; ca. 1924; 15 x 11 inches; very good condition; $90–$115.

Edward Curtis; brown tone (with onionskin) from the original folio "Wild Grapes," plate no. 480; ca. 1924; 15 x 11 inches; very good condition; $60–$85.

Edward Curtis; brown tone (with onionskin) from the original folio "The Fishing Pool—So. Miwok," plate no. 494; ca. 1924; 15 x 11 inches; very good condition; $150–$175.

Edward Curtis; brown tone (with onionskin) from the original folio "Depositing a Prayer Stick"; ca. 1924; 15 x 11 inches; very good condition; $80–$115.

Edward Curtis; brown tone (with onionskin) from the original folio "On the Shores of Clear Lake," plate no. 477; ca. 1924; 15 x 11 inches; very good condition; $90–$115.

Edward Curtis; brown tone from the original folio "Wife of Modoc Henry—Klamath," plate no. 445 (matted and framed); ca. 1923; 22 x 18 inches; very good condition; $85–$115.

Edward Curtis; brown tone from the original folio "Lucero-Santo Domingo," plate no. 557 (matted and framed); ca. 1925; 22 x 18 inches; very good condition; $85–$115.

Edward Curtis; large brown tone from the original folio "West Coast of Vancouver Island," plate no. 391; very good condition; $90–$115.

Edward Curtis; large brown tone from the original folio "Hupa Woman," plate no. 468; ca. 1923; very good condition; $70–$90.

Edward S. Curtis; Sepia (six); plate no. 232, "Flathead Camp on Jocko River," copyright 1910; plate no. 44, "The Pima Woman," copyright 1907; "A Piegan Dandy," copyright 1900; plate no. 187, "Tearing Lodge—Piegan," copyright 1910; all

Ephemera/Advertising, photos, Edward S. Curtis; three sepia photogravures; copy-right 1907 by E. S. Curtis from The North American Indian 1907–1930; *small octavo plates on Japan paper, 12 x 9 inches; includes: Yuma Girl; Yuma Maiden; Hapchach-Yuma (portrait of the same Yuma girl); all very fine condition; $175–$275/set.* Courtesy of C. E. Guarino Auction Gallery, Denmark, Maine.

marked "Photogravure John Andrew and Son"; also, plate no. 592, "Offering to the Sun—San Ildefonso," copyright 1925; and plate no. 426, "The Potter," copyright 1906, both marked "Photogravure; Suffolk Eng. Company, Cambridge, Mass"; very good condition; 20th century; $920–$1,100/set.

Edward S. Curtis; three sepia photogravures, small octavo plates on Japan paper; includes Mohave Mother, An Old Mohave, Sholya-Mohave Girl; 12 x 9 inches; all in very fine condition; $125–$250/set.

Edward S. Curtis; three sepia photogravures, small octavos on Japan paper; includes A Holiday Lodge—Yakima, An Old Man of Waiyam, Piegan War-Bonnet, and Coup Stick (portrait); 12 x 9 inches; very good condition; $250–$500/set.

Edward S. Curtis; three sepia photogravures; copyright 1907 by E. S. Curtis from *The North American Indian 1907–1930;* small octavo plates on Japan paper; includes Yuma Girl; Yuma Maiden; Hapchach-Yuma (portrait of the same Yuma Girl); 12 x 9 inches; all very fine condition; $175–$275/set.

Edward S. Curtis; three sepia photogravures, small octavo plates on Van Gelder; includes The Mohave, An Apache-Mohave

Woman, Kiho Carrier-Qahatika; 12 x 9 inches; all in very fine condition; $150–$300/set.

MISCELLANEOUS

Samoset chocolate plaster relief made by the Boston Sculpture Company displays the company's logo: a Samoset Indian in a canoe in 3-D; 19 x 25½ x 5 inches; good condition; $300–$650.

Postcards; fifty-six old Indian and old West-related; very good condition; $85–$125.

Five postcards with various views of Native American life; good condition; $25–$35/set.

L. Peterson; 14 postcards of Indians including Minnehaha, Chief Big Feather, Chief Yellow Hawk, Chief Sitting Bull, Chief Eagle Feather, Chief Geronimo, Chief High Horse, Starlight, Fighting Wolf, Red Cloud, Hiawatha, White Swan and papoose, Sunshine, Eagle Feather and squaw; very good condition; $85–$125.

Poster and armbands; poster is 20 x 30 inches, Indians of North America; two pairs Osage Indian engraved metal armbands; very good condition; $15–$20/set.

Eight lobby cards for an early Indian movie, each including photo prints with what appears to be tinted highlights; 14 x 11 inches; very good condition; $100–$350.

Paper movie poster for *Before the White Man Came* ("An All Indian Cast") with colorful full-headdress Indian chief on horseback; 26½ x 40½ inches; fair to good condition; $100–$225.

Report; Bureau of American Ethnology, Washington, 1889–1890 (1894), 11th Annual Report, with study of the culture and living customs of "The Sia," by M. Stevenson, report on ethnology of the (Eskimo) Ungara District, and comprehensive report on "Sioux Cults, Myths, Beliefs"; very good condition; $30–$40.

Report; Bureau of American Ethnology, Washington, 1888–1889 (1893), 10th Annual Report, with complete report on "Picture Writing of the American Indian," by G. Mallery; very good condition; $35–$40.

Report; Bureau of American Ethnology, Washington, 1890–1891 (1894), 12th Annual Report, including "U.S. Mound Explorations," by Cyrus Thomas, and report on mounds in Manitoba, Dakota, Minnesota, Wisconsin, Iowa, Illinois, Missouri, Arkansas, Louisiana, Mississippi, east and west Tennessee, Kentucky, Alabama, Georgia, South Carolina, Florida, West Virginia, Ohio, Pennsylvania, and New York; very good condition; $35–$45.

Report; Bureau of American Ethnology, Washington, 1878–1880 (1881), First Annual Report, with comprehensive report on "Evolution of Languages," by Powell, "Study of Mortuary Customs of North American Indians," "Central American Picture Writing," by E. S. Holden, "Cessions of Land by Indian Tribes to the United States," by C. C. Royce, "Sign Language among the North American Tribes," by Mallery; good condition except spine shaky; $35–$45.

Two reports; Bureau of American Ethnology, Washington, 1886–1887 (1891), Eighth Annual Report, on "Pueblo Architecture by Mindeleff"; "Ceremonial and Mythical Sand Painting of the Navajo Indians," by J. Stevenson; very good condition; $30–$40/set.

Two reports; Bureau of American Ethnology, Washington, 1898–1899 (1903); 20th Annual Report, very fine condition; report on the "Aboriginal Pottery of the Eastern United States," by W. Holmes, very good condition; $35–$60/set.

Two reports; Bureau of American Ethnology, Washington, 1885–1886 (1891); Seventh Annual Report, on "Grand

Medicine Society of the Ojibwa," good condtion; report on "Linguistic Families of North America," very good condition; $35–$45/set.

Two reports; Bureau of American Ethnology, Washington, 1887–1888 (1892), Ninth Annual Report, with detailed reports on the "Point Barrow Expedition," by J. Murdoch, very good condition; report on the "Medicine Men of the Apaches," by Capt. John Bourke, very good condition; $55–$85/set.

Mail Pouch Tobacco sign; thin cardboard lithograph under glass; extremely rare; shows Indian papoose hanging in pouch on tree; ca. 1905; 14½ x 19½ inches; very good condition; $1,850–$2,075.

Tin sign; Izaak Walton League of America embossed sign used to warn campers, hunters, and fishermen that the property is posted; 11½ x 18 inches (excluding frame); excellent condition; $150–$300.

H. B. Gardner Cigar sign; tin; rare and early Wells & Hope stone lithographed image of Chief Joseph Brant standing among tobacco plants in full dress and holding an opened box of cigars; reportedly, Chief Joseph Brant helped the Canadians repel the Americans at the Battle of Niagara and was honored by having Brantford, Ontario, named after him. 13¾ x 10 inches (excluding frame); excellent condition; $1,000–$3,500.

Iroquois Cigar paper sign, framed, displaying factory, interior, raw products, finished product, and logo; 18 x 22 inches; near mint condition; $350–$600.

Prince Albert Tobacco sign; tin; rare white background portrait of Chief Joseph with opened upright pocket tin; 19½ x 25½ inches (excluding frame); good condition; $1,500–$2,000.

Sleepy Eye Flour embossed tin sign; 19 inches high x 13½ inches wide; near mint condition; $1,000–$1,750.

Sign, lithographed on tin, self-framed, depicts "Old Sleepy Eye" Indian Chief; ca. 1895; 24¼ x 20 inches; very good condition; $430–$510.

Tin sign; Prince Albert Tobacco sign in frame; 28 inches high x 22 inches wide; very good condition; $2,000–$3,000.

Early Wells & Hope tin sign for Mandrake Pills and Seaweed Tonic, with Dr. Schenck on insert with Indian in the background; ca. 1880; 28 x 22 inches (excluding framing); fair to good condition; $700–$1,000.

Doe-Wah-Jak stove, embossed cardboard sign; unusual vertical full-standing image of Indian with peace pipe and beaded logo for "Round Oak" stove ad on this later photo-offset issue; 8¼ x 23½ inches; near mint condition; $200–$400.

Sitting Bull Durham Tobacco paper sign with defiant image of headdressed "Sitting Bull" with rifle aloft on poised pony; rare graphic western image; 9½ x 12½ inches; very good to excellent condition; $1,000–$2,000.

Steuben Brewing Company die-cut cardboard sign with full-head-dressed Indian chief in profile, with inclusion of real feathers on headdress; aproximately 12 x 18 inches; (excluding mat and frame); good condition; $400–$1,000.

11 stereopticon cards and 1 photograph; photo of Siwash home in Washington; stero cards show Sioux, tepees, and Winnebago; very good condition; $190–$250/set.

Stereo views (seven cards); Indians and the West: Feast Dance at Crow Reservation; Graves at Little Big Horn; Giant Ten Ox Team dragging Logs at Boulder Creek Camp; Unloading Reindeer at Seattle; Herd of Wild Buffalo near Flathead Lake; Ute Indian and Family; Cattle Roundup; very good condition; $60–$85.

Stereo views (three cards); The Southwest Indian tribes: Chief of Kachinas Dance at Moki Village; Moki Cliffs of the Middle Mesa, Arizona; Wolpi-a chief pueblo at the mysterious Moki race (Cliff Dwellers) Arizona; very good condition; $75–$100.

Ephemera/Advertising, stamps; first-day covers featuring Indian history; $15–$25.
Collection of Lahoma Haddock Goldsmith. Photo by Donald Vogt.

Store Display; colorful bust of full-feathered Indian chief in a contemporary frame stand for savings bank thrift account display; 22 x 34 x 8 inches; excellent condition; $75–$150.

Store Display; five-piece die-cut cardboard store display promoting Dr. Morse's Indian Root Pills for "constipation and biliousness"; images utilize Indians in nature scenes to promote the product; very good condition, although general soiling and horizontal crease to backdrop; approximately 42 x 27 inches; $250–$450.

Kennebec: Cigar Tin; depicts Indian in side view; ca. 1915; 2½ x 8½ x 4 inches; very good condition; $45–$70.

Portrait tin, lidded and hinged, with full-headdressed Indian chief in costume on large vertical wood-grained canister; 7 x 9 x 4½ inches; good condition; $100–$300.

Mohawk Chief Tobacco tin container; won best award at 1985 convention, Allentown, Pennsylvania; 4 x 6 inches; very good condition; $865–$1,265.

Prince Albert Tobacco paper advertisement in frame; 31 inches high x 24½ inches wide; very good condition; $1,700–$2,700.

Tobacco display boxes (two); colorful cardboard Red Indian Cut Plug five-pound box picturing full-headdressed Indian on two sides; and Honest Chewing Tobacco five-pound display box picturing two varieties of packets on opposite sides; both in good condition; $150–$300 each.

Sitting Bull Durham Tobacco Paper with image of rearing stallion surmounted with headdressed Indian defiantly raising rifle; "Defies the World"; approximately 7 x 10 inches; good condition; $300–$900.

Tobacco store bin; Indian with stretched bow is a "Sure Shot"; yellow, red, and blue; 15¼ x 7½ x 10¼ inches; good condition; $400–$650.

Chapter Eight

Jewelry

❦

BUYING INFORMATION

When considering the purchase of any antique item, it is always important to learn as much as you can about the field you're buying into. Since quite a bit of what is being sold as Indian jewelry is imported from the Philippines or Taiwan, "buyer beware" becomes an imperative. To educate those who are interested in building a collection of Indian jewelry, I have detailed a few ways to evaluate jewelry before buying.

HOLLOW SILVER BEADS   Silver beads were made three different ways: by hand, bench, or machine. Machine-made beads have no flaws and are all alike. Handmade beads may have flaws, and though they will be close to the same size, each will be a little different. Silver beads that are extremely shiny are not old. (Silver oxidizes with the passage of time.) Old silver beads should not be taken apart and polished.

PAWN   The practice of making pawn jewelry began in the 1870s when Indians traded at posts. They traded their jewelry during the season when they needed income to get through the winter and redeemed it when their sheep were sheared and payments for the wool gave the Navajo the cash they needed to feed and support themselves.

The pawned pieces were secondary, expendable pieces that the Navajo could afford to lose—they usually did not pawn their prized possessions.

Only if the Indian did not retrieve his jewelry within a specified time could the dealer sell it. Because of regulations imposed by the Bureau of Indian Affairs (that the jewelry could be sold for no more than what the dealer paid plus 10 percent), pawn jewelry that came on the market was a bargain.

Though there is still some pawn jewelry on the market, it is not as plentiful, nor as inexpensive, as it was before World War II.

Again, the buyer should beware. There are people making phony squash-blossom necklaces of 1941 dimes, and others who print pawn tickets to put on "junk" jewelry in order to sell it at true pawn prices.

SIGNATURES Most Indian jewelers do not sign their work or use hallmarks, though it is more common today than it was with the earlier work of the Navajo and Zuni smiths.

Before the white man influenced Indian style, a Native American artist could tell his work or the work of others by the style and the craftsmanship of the piece—it was not necessary to place another type of symbol like a signature on the work to announce its maker.

During the 1930s the Hopis began to regularly use hallmarks, and the Museum of Northern Arizona (Flagstaff) has a collection of these. Though the importance of marking one's work is supported by the museum and by the Hopi Silvercraft Guild, there are still those who do not think signing their work is important to their recognition as artists.

Books by Barton and Margaret Wright, and Mark Bahti, list some of the hallmarks well-known jewelry craftspeople use and may be of assistance in identifying your pieces.

STAMPING As with beads, the handmade stamps (indentations) will show slight variations, while the machine-stamped versions will be identical.

STONES Turquoise stones often have breaks and it is acceptable if you are buying a piece of jewelry for personal use. However, if you are buying for investment purposes, it is important to check the piece carefully. Do not replace a broken stone. Instead, have it mended by a reputable smith—preferably one familiar with turquoise and its markings.

Stones that have a hole plugged with a silver spike can be reliably dated as work made before 1900—when pieces were commonly repaired that way.

There are several tests you can use to determine whether or not you have a real piece of turquoise. Test a piece of turquoise by touching it with a hot needle—if it chars, you probably have a natural stone. If the turquoise melts, the stone is either stabilized with plasticizing ingredients or is not genuine at all. If you scratch the stone with a knife and it marks the stone with jagged edges (visible under a magnifying glass), the stone is real. If the edges of the stone are smooth, the stone has been stabilized. The final test involves the use of ultraviolet light: A plasticized piece of turquoise will look fluorescent.

WEAR MARKS   Wear marks will be noticeable on any jewelry that the previous owner wore regularly. Look for wear marks on items such as concha belts, which would receive abrasion from counters and chairs. Check rings and bracelets for that "too shiny" look. Look for dings or dents that prove the jewelry may have been struck against a hard object, and for the thinness of metal that has been worn in the same place for a long time.

WEIGHT   Quality of Navajo jewelry can often be judged by its weight. The Navajo silversmiths often used all (or much) of the silver they had available because of tribal preference for heavy silver.

After the 1800s, when trade and commercialism became more common, the silversmiths were given a certain amount of silver to work with and were paid per piece. During the period from 1870 to 1880, the Navajo jewelry was much lighter, though there are those who question whether that is the result of a shortage of silver or because there were so many beginners learning the craft at that time.

Don't be confused by weight. The Navajo silversmith, if allowed to make jewelry as he wishes, will opt for heavy jewelry with bold designs.

WORKMANSHIP   Machine-made pieces can be distinguished from handmade by telltale signs—which are often easy to spot. If a piece is handmade, you should be able to see filing marks or stress marks. If you are looking at a piece of jewelry that has repetitive units, such as a concha belt or squash-blossom necklace, the units will all be a little different if the piece is handmade. No matter how good the jeweler, the only way those pieces will be truly identical is if a machine has produced them.

THE MAKING OF INDIAN JEWELRY

Silver coins were the primary source of metal for jewelry made by the southwestern Indians. Before 1900, silversmiths melted down coins and cast them into ingots. They then hammered the ingot into a sheet and worked that into a finished piece.

The work was hammered down as smoothly as possible and then polished with sand or ashes. Old, unused jewelry dating from before 1900 often shows the marks left by polishing stones.

The following is a list of tribes and characteristics typical of their jewelry-making practices.

ANASAZI JEWELRY

The earliest jewelry makers, this tribe used shells and turquoise in their work. A hole was often punched through one end of the shell so that it could be strung to make a necklace or ornamental object.

Some pendants identified as Anasazi were carved from turquoise in the shape of frogs or other small animals. It is thought that the Cerrillos mines south of Santa Fe, New Mexico, were the source for much of the turquoise traded by these peoples.

HOPI JEWELRY

The Hopis learned the art of working silver after the Navajo and Zuni tribes. Lanyade, the Zuni silversmith who learned his trade from Atsidi Chon in 1872, taught a Hopi named Sikyatala ("Yellow Light") the trade in 1890. Early pieces mimicked those made by Navajo and Zuni smiths, but as time went on, the Hopi's distinctive style began to emerge.

The majority of Hopi jewelry, as we know it today, was produced after the 1930s when a conscious effort was made to get the tribe to produce more silverwork and to develop an overlay style. Dr. Harold Colton and Mary Russell Colton, his wife, began a project in 1938 at the Museum of Northern Arizona that encouraged Hopi jewelers to create their own style. These artisans used designs that had originated in Hopi basketry, pottery, and textiles.

After World War II, Hopi people who wanted to learn smithing were able to take classes on the GI bill. In 1949 the Hopi Silvercraft Guild was founded. It acted as both a workshop and commercial outlet for the jewelers.

The "overlay process" simply means that two sheets of silver are soldered together after designs are cut out of the top layer. The bottom layer is oxidized (blackened) and textured with chisel marks or stampwork. Afterward, the pieces are usually buffed to give the silver a soft matte finish.

Hopi work is of high quality, and designs are traditionally abstract. Though Hopi silversmiths generally do not use stones in their work, there are exceptions to the rule, and one should not attempt to identify a piece of jewelry as the work of another tribe on that basis. First, look at the style. Occasionally a Hopi jeweler will choose to include turquoise, red coral, or shells in his or her work.

IROQUOIS JEWELRY
Though the Navajo and Zuni are the best-known silversmiths of all Indian tribes, the Iroquois Indians were also known to work with silver. They began working silver around 1800. Their first work was produced by hammering coins and ingots into sheets and decorating them with stamped designs.

Brooches made of hearts were often called the Iroquois National Badge. A design that incorporated the much-used heart with a crown was called "Owl" or "Guardian of the Night." Brooches and dangling earrings were popular and were worn by both males and females.

GREAT LAKES AREA JEWELRY
The Lakes area tribes made silverwork that was less intricate than that of the Iroquois tribe.

The Menomini tribe made and wore hair decorations, earrings, bracelets, and combs of stamped or simple engraved designs.

MANDAN JEWELRY
The Mandan, as well as other Prairie tribes, used antlers to make bracelets. The antlers were made into strips, then engraved and soaked so that they could be bent into shape.

NAVAJO JEWELRY
It is said that Mexican silversmiths taught the Navajo Indians how to make jewelry, yet the Indians did not use the Mexican-style filigree. The stamped designs found on Navajo jewelry are similar to Mexican leatherwork designs, and even the swastika and arrow motifs are attributed to Mexican sources.

Atsidi Sani was the first Navajo silversmith. His teacher was a Mexican blacksmith named Nakai Tsosi who worked near Mount Taylor during the mid-1800s. Tsosi taught Sani ironworking and silversmithing techniques; however, neither made jewelry. The Navajo came up with the idea on their own and began making and wearing jewelry after their release from Bosque Redondo in 1868.

Atsidi Sani, the silversmith, taught at least nine other people his trade, including his son, Red Smith. His work training others provided a new way for the Navajo to boost their economy, and the sale of their jewelry soon provided a surplus income, as well as adornments for themselves.

Before 1850, the Navajo people acquired silver ornaments through trade or battles with neighboring Spanish or Mexican settlers. After 1850, the jewelers began using American coins as a source of silver, but after 1890, law stated they could no longer deface U.S. coins. While the Native jewelers stopped melting U.S. coins, they continued to use Mexican pesos up until 1930, at which point the coins were no longer exported to the States. By 1935, jewelers were buying their silver in sheets and wire forms. Today most jewelers use the same type of silver for their work.

Prior to 1880, decorations were applied by rocker engraving or cutting the design into the metal with a file. Previously, a cold chisel was used, and after 1885, stamping was common. To stamp a design onto metal, a piece of a worn-out file made of carbon was heated until it glowed, then was pulled from the fire and shaped with hammering. After the desired shape was formed, the piece was reheated and slowly cooled. The smith could then file final design details. The tool was cleaned and gently heated, and once more quenched. This process gave the piece the hardiness needed to keep it from bending, yet kept it soft enough to stop splitting or chipping when struck.

Navajos made silver pieces by pouring molten silver or by hammering down silver ingots directly into carved stone molds. It took time to carve a design into a mold, so the technique was not used often.

To make a good cast, a two-piece mold was necessary, with a spruce hole and air vents. It had to be coated with fine charcoal (or smoked) so that the hot metal would flow evenly into the design and not stick in the deeply carved spaces. The cooled piece was then filed and sanded until smooth.

This technique was used to produce buckles, bracelets, buttons, rings, *najas* (crescent-shaped pendants), and *ketohs* (bow-guards worn around the wrist, pronounced "gato").

Soldering is one of the hardest jewelry-making tasks to master, even for those jewelers of today who have modern torches and the help of chemical engineers who formulate fluxes. Indians had to make their own solder by combining silver filings with brass filings from old pans or cartridge cases. The mixture was placed at the soldering point, along with borax (used as a sedimentary flux). The pieces were put into the red-hot coals of a forge—just below the material's melting point. If the silversmith was lucky, the solder would melt and the pieces would hold together when cooled. Sometimes pieces weren't heated sufficiently and went back to the forge. If the pieces became oxidized, the process was begun over again.

Jewelry became so important to the Navajo that no Navajo Indian felt properly dressed without it. It became a sign of wealth. Navajo often exchanged jewelry for livestock, food, material, or medical services.

By the turn of the century, lighter pieces were being made by the Navajo for sale to tourists traveling to the Southwest. The era of tourist trade had begun.

Northwest Coast Jewelry

Northwest Coast Indians wore metal jewelry made of copper or silver. The Indians of this region had been metalworkers long before the arrival of the white man, and although they used stone hammers and anvils, the results they achieved were far from crude.

Tlingit silver bracelets were worn by shamans and incised with straight lines, geometric shapes, and the stylized animals instantly recognizable as Northwest Coast decoration.

In the early nineteenth century, silver and gold replaced copper as the metal of choice because they were easier to work and obtain.

At one time it was believed that Tlingits learned their jewelry-making techniques from Russians, but today it's generally recognized that the skills the Indians had were handed down from genration to generation long before the Russians' arrival. Tlingit history states that their first blacksmith was a Chilkat woman named Shukasaka. Her skill working metal had won her that name, which means "half man."

Tlingits used silver coins, brought to them by traders, to make nose and finger rings. Silver coins, the traders' money, had no value in their society, nor did any object without a practical use. The only thing they could think to do with such things was to present them to one another as gifts. The words in the Tlingit, Haida, and Kwakiutl languages that mean silver are all variations on the English word "dollar."

Though Tlingits received praise for their copper and iron-work, the Haida tribe was most proficient with silver. They produced silver articles such as rings, earrings, bracelets, spoons, and napkin rings. Of all the jewelry, Haida bracelets continue to be most popular. They are heavy and deeply carved, whereas Tlingit bracelets have bands of even width and are lighter in weight.

Northwestern tribes commonly wear nose rings and other jewelry as symbols of status.

Before the turn of the century, white influences/motifs were used as frequently as native designs. For example, the American eagle was an oft-used motif. Haida eagles are generally more geometric than the realistic forms of Tlingit eagles.

Whale designs of the Tlingits are distinctive and best recognized by the segmented, fingerlike flipper which reveals the skeletal structure beneath its skin.

A Haida silversmith who has received much attention is Charles Edenshaw. His career spanned fifty years, and his style moved from an early split representation of a dogfish to his "classic style" reached in 1880 and recognized by less angular form lines, more fluid junctures, and more carefully planned negative spaces.

PLAINS

There's no doubt that the Southern Plains tribes influenced southwestern jewelry. The concha belt, naja, and metal bridle were common adornments of the Plains Indians, and later adopted by southwestern tribes.

The Plains tribe wore their own metal decorative pieces by the beginning of the nineteenth century, using silver and brass until German silver was introduced in the 1860s. They worked with metal until the 1880s, when such ornaments were readily available and the need to produce them diminished.

Conchas were originally hair ornaments that were attached closely to the scalp, but the decoration grew until the hair plate grew to as long as six feet. When a man sat down, the hair plate was often pulled around his shoulder and across his lap, resembling a belt. Plains women often wore these ornaments as belts and let the extra length trail down one side.

The Navajo adopted the use of concha belts from the Plains but changed the material—from German silver to silver—and applied Mexican-style decorations to the discs.

Naja decoration was constantly used by the Plains Indian on ear pendants, headstalls, and other items. When the Navajo made bridles, the construction was almost identical to those used by the Plains Indians.

While the Navajo utilized some Plains ideas, it seems that the Plains Indians copied the Navajo idea of stamped designs on metalwork.

SEMINOLE AND CHOCTAW JEWELRY

Seminole and Choctaw silver jewelry is simple and consists mainly of brooches and pendants. The Seminole were also known to use watch chains as jewelry (though they seldom owned watches), but these chains were of European and not Indian manufacture.

Seminoles have also produced coin necklaces since before the Second Seminole War. They may have from one to nine coins on them; the number varied during the late nineteenth century. Most were placed in the front of the necklace, but in the early 1900s, the coins encircled the whole necklace, from front to back. Sometimes women wore more than one of these necklaces at a time. The coins used were usually Liberty quarters and Mercury dimes. In more recent years, necklaces seen at Seminole tribal fairs were made from dimes.

This tribe also wore pierced silverwork earrings and pendants during the 1920s and 1930s. Other earlier pieces have been identified as Seminole work.

ZUNI

This tribe learned to work with copper and brass in approximately 1830, though excavations by archaeologist F. W. Hodge proved that the Zuni peoples had been using pieces of turquoise in their jewelry long before this time.

Atsidi Sani, the Navajo smith, traded with the Zuni in the 1870s and eventually taught his trade to a Zuni man called Lanyade. As a result, Zuni forms and settings are very similar to those made by the Navajo jewelers.

Frank Hamilton Cushing, the explorer and historian who lived with the Zuni tribe from 1879 to 1881, told of the Zuni's jewelry-making techniques. He said that draw plates made from deer scapulae were used by the Zuni to form silver and copper wire from silver and copper rods. The thinning, bending, stamping, and drawing of wire was done when the metal was cold, as heating made the metal weak and crumbly.

The Zuni smith Keneshde was the first to use turquoise from the Cerrillos mines during the 1890s. It is believed that Zunis made their jewelry strictly for personal use up until the 1930s, when they began creating pieces for sale to tourists.

The Zuni have been carving stone and shells for hundreds of years and making jewelry from shell, jet, turquoise inlay, mosaic on shell, wood, stone, bone, and ceramics almost as long. Silver is merely a vehicle to hold turquoise, with very little ornamentation. They make light pieces, often by using twisted wire, raindrops, wire scallops, or stamping. Zuni earrings are often long and dangly with pieces of stone or silver hanging from the wire.

Zunis excel in mosaic work and incorporate jet, turquoise, coral, and shell in their designs. They are known to carve small figures in their jewelry. Needlepoint, made with tiny, oval, pointed-end stones, is a specialty of the Zuni jewelry makers. This practice began in the 1940s.

The Zuni jewelry decorations are lighter and finer than those of the Navajo, whose jewelry has a massive look and feel to it. The Zuni tribe also is well known for fetishes, often carving necklaces that consist of fetish animals and birds.

BIOGRAPHIES OF SOME INDIAN JEWELRY MAKERS

There is also information within the general information section of this chapter about the various jewelry makers of the tribes mentioned.

ANDY ABEITA

(also see Chapter One for additional biography info)

An artist well-known for his fetishes, Abeita also makes jewelry on occasion. His pieces include heart-line inlaid stones, which are all semiprecious stones; amber, sugilite, malachite, turquoise, jet, coral, pipestone, serpentine, mother-of-pearl, pink mussel.

FLORENCE AGUILAR

Of the Santo Domingo Pueblo, Aguilar works in a mosaic technique.

VIDAL ARAGON

He began making fine overlay silverwork in the 1940s and is one of the best known of the Santo Domingo silversmiths.

RALPH ATENCIO

The first Santo Domingo jeweler, he learned his craft from the Navajos in 1893.

ABRAHAM BEGAY

A contemporary Navajo jeweler, he is known as a master silversmith, who combines both traditional and modern jewelry techniques in his work. His designs are innovative and he uses some of the best materials available.

One of the galleries that handles his work is Long Ago and Far Away in Manchester Center, Vermont.

MIKE BIRD (1946–)

Of the San Juan Pueblo, self-taught Mike Bird comes from an artistic family. His grandmother (Luteria Atencio) was a potter. Some of her work is owned by the Smithsonian. A weaver and embroiderer, his mother, Pablita Velarde, still shows at the Indian market.

Bird, like other traditional jewelers, has studied the ancient ways and incorporates what he has learned into his work. That work is evident in a necklace of his in the Millicent Rogers Museum (Taos, New Mexico).

Bird uses the cross and heart symbols often in his work, but has also created pieces with carved animals or fish on them.

He has won prizes for his work at the Indian Market for petroglyph figural pins.

CIPPY CRAZY HORSE
(CIPRIANO QUINTANA) (1946–)

This Cochiti jeweler works in silver and is the son of Joe H. Quintana, a most productive and successful silversmith.

Crazy Horse, however, did not study silversmithing with his father. He did not learn his craft until an accident disabled him and, unable to do much else, he tried his hand at silversmithing. Now he uses his father's work as an example and makes traditional silver jewelry.

Crazy Horse has regularly won awards with his jewelry in the eight years he has been entering his pieces at the Indian Market. He researches traditional styles, which he uses in his necklaces, bracelets, concha belts, rings, and other pieces.

Crazy Horse uses homemade tools in his work, but also employs the use of an acetylene torch, buffing wheels, and an assortment of other more modern devices.

Cippy Crazy Horse has won many awards for the clean aesthetic designs of his work, including the 1987 Indian Market George C. West Memorial Award, and first place for his concha belt in the "Traditional Jewelry without Stones" category.

JOSEPH JOJOLLA

A contemporary jeweler, Jojolla makes custom-ordered jewelery for his customers. He has made buckles, watchbands, rings, necklaces, and an occasional squash-blossom necklace (which he says takes him a little longer to make).

His tools include both old and modern examples, some dentist's tools, a wooden baseball bat (used for a bracelet mandrel), and a plastic hammer. At one time he polished his works with a washing machine motor.

His work has been featured by the IACA.

JAKE LIVINGSTON

This 1988 IACA "Artist of the Year" was born of a Zuni father and Navajo mother. His father, Jacob Halso Su, taught Livingston how to work with silver.

In 1969 Livingston left the Marine Corps, where he had earned three Purple Hearts, and went to work as an operating engineer and heavy equipment mechanic for the state of Arizona. In 1972 he started selling his work and was awarded Best of Show at the Gallup Ceremonial in 1974 for a reversible concho belt. He followed that award with Best of Show in 1975 for a four-sided gold necklace that sold for $60,000.

Livingston has won top awards at the Santa Fe Indian Market, the Heard Museum Show, and the Museum of Northern Arizona, among others.

CHARLES LOLOMA

(for more info on this artist, see bio in Chapter One)
Loloma is credited with being the artist who created the first

modern (ultracontemporary) Indian jewelry. He, and the generation of artists who follow him, have used gold as well as semiprecious stones, other than turquoise and coral, in their jewelry.

A coral, lapis lazuli, and gold bracelet made by Loloma was featured on the cover of an auction booklet for the American Craft Museum and sold for $10,000 at that auction.

ANTHONY LOVATO

A contemporary Santo Domingo jeweler, Lovato plans to keep the traditional tufa and sand-casting techniques alive by passing them down to the next generation, as they were passed to him.

He was awarded the Salem Fellowship in 1992.

PRESTON MONONGYE (1927–1987)

Collectors have long praised this Hopi jeweler's work in silver and have rewarded his excellence with over seven hundred awards.

A jack-of-all-trades, Monongye spent most of his adult life promoting Indian art both in the United States and internationally. He learned how to work silver under his uncle in the village of Hotevilla when he was nine years old. Later, he took a variety of college courses and served in the army during the Korean War.

GIBSON NEZ (1944–   )

Nez, born a Navajo-Apache, grew up on the Jicarilla Apache Reservation at Dulce, New Mexico, then spent quite a few years in the rodeo as a bronc rider. He is listed in the Indian Cowboy Association Hall of Fame. He started teaching himself the art of jewelry making in 1973, after working with leather for a while.

Many of today's up-and-coming jewelers credit Nez, an award-winning contemporary jeweler, with teaching them the tricks of the trade. Many of his pieces are held in stellar collections owned by well-known Americans such as Dale Robertson and Hal Ketchum.

Nez's large and stunning pieces of jewelry, produced in both silver and gold, are accented with quality pieces of turquoise, coral, and lapis lazuli. His work is sold at the Hogan in the Hilton, Santa Fe, New Mexico, and at the Moondancer Gallery, Redondo Beach, California.

He has won many awards, including Best of Show at the Heard Museum's competition for Native American artists, and over seven hundred ribbons in ten years. He is known to exhibit at the Indian

Market in Santa Fe, the Gallup Ceremonial, and the Northern Pueblos show in San Ildefonso.

His signature is a small offsided *G*, large *Z*, and small *N*. His pieces can fetch as much as $20,000.

ANGIE REANO OWEN (1946–)

A Santo Domingo jeweler, Owen does contemporary work, mostly in mosaic on shell, yet adheres to the traditional methods of jewelry making. She was born at the Santo Domingo Pueblo and grew up making jewelry. Taught by her mother, she began making heishe jewelry at a very young age. Owen sold her first attempts at jewelry making on the Plaza in Santa Fe; her jewelry was later purchased by the Los Angeles County Museum Shop, as well as other museum shops.

Her jewelry-making heritage stretches back through many generations. Her parents, as well as five brothers and two sisters, all make jewelry. The family still has pieces made by her grandfather and great-grandfather. She has based her jewelry designs on the traditions of her Anasazi and Hohokam ancestors, using similar shells, but modern production equipment.

Angie married Don Owen in 1969. He was recently coordinator of the Southwestern Association on Indian Affairs–sponsored annual Indian Market. Owen encouraged his wife to research early Hohokam and Anasazi jewelry. Her earrings trace the Hohokam sunburst and pendant styles. Angie continues to study, since the warm reception her work has received.

Angie Reano Owen allows the natural shape of a shell or stone to design her jewelry. She adds the geometric mosaics that follow the curve and line of the piece.

The jeweler's work is in the Heard Museum in Phoenix, and in others. She has ensured her techniques are passed on to the next generation by teaching her son and daughter the art of jewelry making. Her work is sold in galleries throughout the West and in New York, as well as at the Eight Northern Indian Pueblos Artist and Craftsman Show and Santa Fe Indian Market each year. She has won many awards for her work.

JOSEPH AND JERRY QUINTANA

Cochiti silversmiths, Joseph and Jerry are well known for their jewelry work and have won many awards.

HOWARD J. SICE

Sice, a Hopi/Laguna, makes silver bowls and jewelry, incorporating many designs into his work. His pieces incorporate silver, gold, turquoise, coral, rare earth, exotic metals, and faceted stones. He makes engraved and inlaid earrings, pins, and bracelets renowned for their quality.

Howard Sice won the Pueblo Grande Museum Auxiliary Fellowship in 1992, as well as an impressive number of other awards.

ROBERT SORRELL

A contemporary jeweler, Sorrell is a Navajo who works in cast silver. He won the Dorothy and Robert Walker fellowship in 1992.

ALAN WALLACE

Wallace, a contemporary jeweler, uses mosaic work when designing his award-winning bracelets, necklaces, and rings. He is from Taos, New Mexico, and also paints.

....
PRICES
....

Armband, Chippewa: one only, loom-beaded with braided yarn ties; 3 x 13 inches; very good condition; $100–$150.

Armbands; German silver bands with well-done stamped designs; very good condition; $75–$150.

Barrette, Apache: beaded hide; long plum and white beads in eight-point star-flower designs; 2½ x 4½ inches; very good condition; $35–$60.

Barrette, Navajo: silver and turquoise; sterling set with three oval blue-green cabochons; 1½ inches wide x 3 inches long; total weight 1⁄10 ounces; very good condition; $25–$45.

Birthing beads, Navajo: traditional birthing beads in juniper seeds, jet, and crystal; made by a medicine woman; very good condition; $30–$40.

Belt, Cheyenne: German silver belt with etched designs and brass clips on old leather; 20th century; 42 inches long; excellent condition; $225–$325.

Belt buckles (three): silver; two oval with stylized flowers and turquoise centers, one triangle decorated with a bear claw set in jet; very good condition; $165–$265/set.

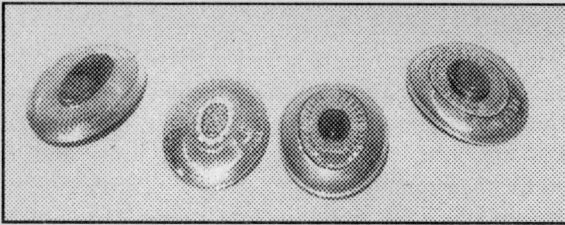

Jewelry, Gibson Nez, belt buckles, left to right—DeMoli turquoise from Nevada, $500; No. 8 turquoise from Nevada, $650; sugilite from Africa, $700; lapis inlay with pink coral, $900. All made in 1993. Courtesy of Gibson Nez. Photo by Robert Reno.

Belt buckles, Gibson Nez: DeMoli turquoise from Nevada, $500; No. 8 turquoise from Nevada, $650; sugilite from Africa, $700; lapis inlay with pink coral, $900; all made in 1993 and in mint condition.

Belt buckle, Hopi: sterling silver with scroll and humpbacked flute player design; 2¼ x 3⅜ inches; weight 2¾ ounces; very good condition; $95–$150.

Belt buckle, Jake Livingston: eagle with trees on both sides and mountain in background; turquoise, 14 carat gold, craw shell, malachite, pin shell, melon shell, mother-of-pearl; 1993; mint condition; $1,000.

Belt buckle, Navajo: man's; 6 x 8 inches; very good condition; $500–$700.

Belt buckle, Navajo: woman's; 5 x 6 inches; very good condition; $375–$525.

Buckle, Navajo: large rectangular turquoise, coral, and silver buckle; initials "J.C." in coral; ca. 1940; 3½ x 3 inches; very good condition; $30–$40.

Buckle, Navajo: "Old Pawn" sand-cast turquoise and silver buckle; ca. 1935; 3 x 3½ inches; very good condition; $60–$90.

Belt buckle, W. Begay: Zuni, sterling silver and petit point set with approximately 116 blue slivers; signed "W. Begay"; 2½ x 3½ inches; very good condition; $125–$200.

Bolo tie: silver with carved buffalo skull surrounded by silver; ca. 1965; 3 x 2 inches; very good condition; $85–$150.

Bolo tie: large silver, arrowhead-shaped, set with large turquoise stone; ca. 1970; 4 x 2 inches; very good condition; $85–$110.

Bolo tie: turquoise, silver, and coral "Eagle Dancer"; signed; ca. 1985; 4 x 5 inches; very good condition; $200–$230.

Bolo tie: turquoise, coral, and imitation bear claws; ca. 1986; 6 x 2 inches; very good condition; $70–$90.

Bolo and bracelet, Charlie Pratt: buffalo skull design; sterling silver with coral eyes; 1993; all in mint condition; bolo is $225; bracelet is $250.

Bolos, Gibson Nez: Nevada Blue, $1,200; sugilite, $900; lapis, $900; and Nevada Blue, $1,200; 1993; all in mint condition.

Bolo tie, Navajo: silver with turquoise chip inlay and ironwood center; ca. 1965; 1½ x 1 inch; very good condition; $20–$25.

Bolo tie, Navajo: unusual turquoise and silver with heishe trim; ca. 1965; 2 x 2 inches; very good condition; $40–$60.

Brass Bolo, Plains: with blue cotton which is probably a piece of a parasol; enclosed stereo card of Mow-way, a Comanche chief, wearing a similar object; 4½ inches diameter; good condition; $150–$200.

Bolo tie, Tommy Singer: Navajo, turquoise and silver and coral chip inlay peyote bird; signed "Tommy Singer"; ca. 1975; 2½ inches x 1 inch; very good condition; $40–$60.

Bolo tie, Zuni: "Old Pawn"; inlay, "Knife Wing" dancer; ca. 1935; 1½ x 1 inch; very good condition; $65–$85.

Bolo, two pins, and two tie bars, Zuni: silver inlaid with turquoise, abalone, coral, and jet; one pin represents the Zuni rain god;

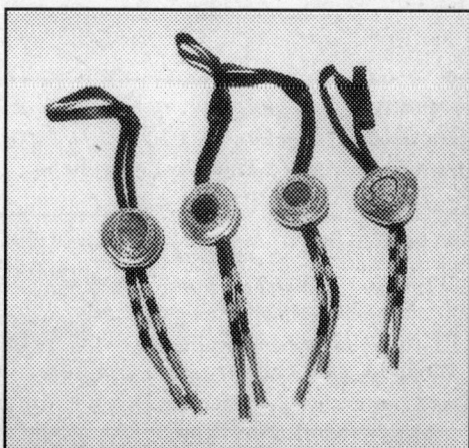

Jewelry, Gibson Nez, bolo, assortment, 1993, left to right— Nevada Blue, $1,200; sugilite, $900; lapis, $900; and Nevada Blue, $1,200. Courtesy of Gibson Nez. Photo by Robert Reno.

pins, 2 and 3 inches; tie bar, 1½ and 1¼ inches; good condition; $350–$450/set.

Bracelet, Alan Wallace: sterling with inlay of spiny oyster, turquoise, magnicite, sugilite; 1993, ⅜ inch wide by 3 inches; $1,200.

Bracelets, Alan Wallace: 14 carat and sterling with inlay of sugilite, turquoise, magnicite; 1993; ⅜ to ½ inch wide; $600, $950, and $2,100.

Bracelet: fully beaded wide bracelet with multicolored geometric designs; very good condition; $55–$110.

Bracelet: silver, decorated with village scene, signed "R. H. Begay"; very good condition; $40–$65.

Bracelet: silver, eagle and star motif; very good condition; $35–$50.

Bracelet: silver, leaf decoration inset with turquoise and red coral; very good condition; $40–$70.

Bracelet: silver-mounted mother-of-pearl, set with oval mother-of-pearl bead and stylized leaf decoration; very good condition; $90–$115.

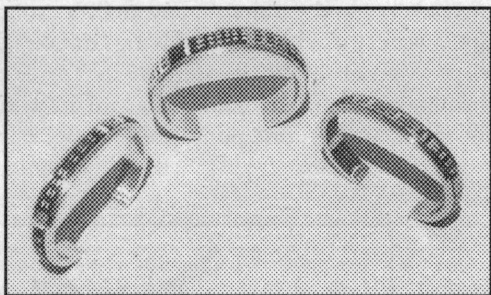

Jewelry, Alan Wallace, bracelets, ⅜ to ½ inch wide, 14 carat and sterling with inlay of sugilite, turquoise, magnicite; 1993; left to right; $600, $950, $2,100. Courtesy of Alan Wallace. Photo by Robert Reno.

Jewelry, Alan Wallace, bracelet, ⅜ inch wide x 3 inches, sterling with inlay of spiny oyster, turquoise, magnicite, sugilite; 1993; $1,200. Courtesy of Alan Wallace. Photo by Robert Reno.

Bracelet: silver-mounted turquoise set with three irregular-shaped turquoise, bead and leaf decoration; very good condition; $85–$115.

Bracelet: silver, set with small turquoise and red coral swirl decoration; very good condition; $30–$45.

Bracelet: silver, turquoise and red coral inlay; very good condition; $35–$45.

Bracelet: silver with recessed center in polished turquoise, scalloped border, stamped on reverse "J. W."; very good condition; $65–$100.

Bracelet: woman's or child's, silver with sculptured form and centered with a large, rich blue turquoise between two coral red pieces, the back of the silver band with hallmark initials "KJ"; early; very good condition; $100–$250.

Bracelets (two): silver, set with red coral leaf scroll decoration and pierced bands; very good condition; $60–$90 each.

Bracelet, Esther and Sammy Guardian: Zuni, lady's fancy silver, turquoise, and coral bracelet; sterling cuff with blue triangles surrounding other inlays of red, coral, and green malachite in a cardinal bird perched on a leafy branch and floral designs; signed "E & S Guardian (Esther and Sammy)"; 1 inch wide; very good condition; $175–$260.

Bracelet, Gibson Nez: "Kachina Maiden Bracelet"; sterling silver, inlay with clamshell background, lapis, coral, 14 carat gold, sugilite, turquoise (inlay is all facet-cut); 1986; near mint condition; $5,500.

Bracelets, Gibson Nez (two): sterling silver; left has one-facet inlaid lapis; right has coral and lapis; 1985; mint condition; $1,000 each.

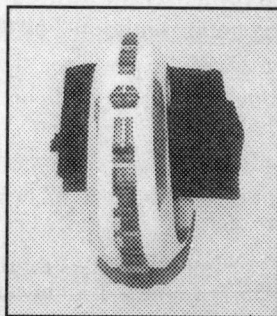

Jewelry, Gibson Nez, bracelet, "Kachina Maiden Bracelet," sterling silver, inlay with clamshell background, lapis, coral, 14 carat gold, sugilite, turquoise (inlay is all facet-cut); 1986; $5,500. Courtesy of Gibson Nez. Photo by Robert Reno.

Jewelry, Gibson Nez, sterling silver bracelets; left has one-facet inlaid lapis; right has coral and lapis; 1985; $1,000 each. Courtesy of Gibson Nez. Photo by Robert Reno.

Bracelet, Hopi: silver and multi-inlay bracelet; sterling cuff with bird (eagle-parrot) designs on either side of inlaid disc in Apache "Gan/Mt. Spirit" dancer; signed by the Hopi Crafts Guild; 1¾ inches; very good condition; $125–$200.

Bracelet, Jake Livingston: sterling silver, cardinal in center with flowers surrounding it; coral, turquoise, melon shell, abalone shell, pin shell; 1993; mint condition; $1,000.

Bracklet, Jake Livingston: sterling silver, with reverse center, eagle on one side and sun face on the other; side of the bracelet body—pottery design on one side and Navajo Yei on the other; inlay with turquoise, coral, lapis, 14 carat gold, melon shell, pin shell, sugilite, Nevada Blue Spiderweb turquoise; 1991; mint condition; $9,000.

Bracelet and necklace, Navajo: sterling silver and turquoise; very good condition; $350–$400/set.

Bracelet, Navajo: heavy silver bracelet set with a choice No. 8 Spiderweb stone; ca. 1935; 6 x 1½ inches; very good condition; $50–$80.

Bracelet, Navajo: crude sand-cast silver; ca. 1930; 6 inches x 1 inch; very good condition; $50–$70.

Bracelet, Navajo: early silver "tourist" set with an unusual reddish stone; ca. 1935; 6 inches x 1 inch; very good condition; $25–$45.

Bracelet, Navajo: early silver "tourist" set with an unusual turquoise stone; ca. 1935; 6 inches x 1 inch; very good condition; $35–$60.

Bracelet, Navajo: early turquoise and silver "tourist" bracelet; ca. 1935; 6 inches x 1 inch; very good condition; $35–$70.

Bracelet, Navajo: choice "Old Pawn" with large natural turquoise stone; ca. 1975; 6 x 2 inches; very good condition; $60–$85.

Bracelet, Navajo: heavy sand-cast silver bracelet in naja form and set with large turquoise stone; ca. 1970; 6 x 2 inches; very good condition; $75–$115.

Bracelet, Navajo: large, three-stone turquoise and silver bracelet; ca. 1970; 6 x 2 inches; very good condition; $85–$115.

Bracelet, Navajo: silver "slave" bracelet with attached ring and set with jet and mother-of-pearl stones; ca. 1986; 6 x 6 inches; very good condition; $50–$80.

Bracelet, Navajo: choice silver bracelet set with five very rare No. 8 Spiderweb turquoise stones; ca. 1965; 7¾ inches x ¾ inch; very good condition; $200–$260.

Bracelet, Navajo: lady's silver watch bracelet set with two turquoise stones; ca. 1965; 7 x 1½ inches; very good condition; $40–$60.

Bracelet, Navajo: "Old Pawn" Navajo single-stone turquoise and silver; ca. 1935; 7 inches x 1 inch; very good condition; $85–$115.

Bracelet, Navajo: "Old Pawn" turquoise and silver cluster bracelet; ca. 1935; 7 inches x 1 inch; very good condition; $30–$60.

Bracelet, Navajo: heavy sand-cast silver bracelet set with single turquoise stone; ca. 1940; very good condition; $70–$115.

Bracelet, Navajo: pawn silver, turquoise, and coral; triple triangle wire sterling shank set with two large blue spiderweb and one bloodred branch cabochon; signed DHG; very good condition; $60–$120.

Bracelet, Navajo: silver and turquoise ½-inch-wide sterling cuff with stamped and repoussé designs set with a single ¾-inch-long oval green cabochon; ca. 1930s; very good condition; $40–$75.

Bracelet, Navajo: silver and turquoise, sterling triangular three-wire shank set with gem-quality blue Persian cabochon; very good condition; $115–$155.

Bracelet, Navajo: silver and turquoise; heavy sterling wire shank set with large (2½ x 1⅞ inches) blue Morenci cabochon; very good condition; $300–$400.

Bracelet, Navajo: silver and turquoise; signed; very good condition; $110–$125.

Bracelet, Navajo: silver, turquoise, and coral; sterling shank with large leaf designs set with five carved blue-green cabochons

Jewelry, Preston Thompson (Winnebago), bracelet; contemporary sterling silver bracelet with natural high-grade turquoise spiderwebbed from Kingman mine in Arizona; won first place in art show at medical center in Houston; $1,500–$1,750. Courtesy of Naranjo's, Houston, Texas. Photo by Donald Vogt.

and one red branch; signed B.E.; very good condition; $175–$300.

Bracelet, Navajo: three-stone turquoise and silver bracelet; ca. 1960; very good condition; $60–$85.

Bracelets (three), Navajo: finely stamped sterling silver, one initialed "RA"; $100–$160 each.

Bracelets (three), Navajo: one silver with square stone initialed "F.B."; one silver with stamped geometric design; one sandcast with square turquoise stone; very good condition; $175–$225 each.

Bracelets (two), Navajo: sterling silver, handmade with solid inlay with turquoise, ivory, and wampum; one with wampum and stamped sterling; very good condition; $375–$475/set.

Watch bracelet, Navajo: silver and turquoise; heavy sterling bangle set with a single oval green cabochon on each side of the opening; attributed to Mark Chee; ca. 1930–1940; ⁹⁄₁₆ x ⁹⁄₁₆ inch; very good condition; $115–$160.

Bracelet, Preston Thompson: Winnebago, contemporary sterling silver bracelet with natural high-grade turquoise spiderwebbed from Kingman mine in Arizona; won first place in art show at medical center in Houston; very good condition; $1,500–$1,750.

Bracelet, Robert Ulibarri: Navajo, five-stone turquoise and silver bracelet, signed by Robert Ulibarri; ca. 1975; 6½ x 2 inches; very good condition; $120–$200.

Bracelet, Tlingit: hammered sterling silver carved totemic bracelet, marked Haines, Alaska; purchased during World War II; very good condition; $80–$175.

Bracelet, Tlingit: very old hammered-coin silver bracelet with a hand-carved American eagle design; ca. 1900; very good condition; $110–$185.

Bracelet, Zuni: woman's; silver band with incised decoration inset with 34 petite turquoise blue "gems"; old; very good condition; $175–$275.

Bracelet, Zuni: choice Zuni turquoise and silver channel inlay "row" bracelet; ca. 1935; 6 inches x ½ inch; very good condition; $35–$60.

Bracelet, Zuni: sand-cast sterling with openwork sunburst design and blue turquoise stone; very good condition; $140–$200.

Bracelet, Zuni: silver and turquoise three-wire sterling shank set "cluster" style with approximately 85 oval and round blue and blue-green cabochons; ca. mid-1940s; very good condition; $150–$230.

Bracelet, Zuni: fine inlay thunderbird bracelet with inlaid eagle designs; ca. 1965; 7 x 2 inches; very good condition; $60–$90.

Bracelet, Zuni: silver and turquoise; sterling with approximately 260 individual blue channel-style inlays, set in rosette designs; signed "RB"; very good condition; $125–$185.

Bracelet, Zuni: silver, coral, and shell; sterling bangle with inlays of red coral and gold mother-of-pearl in floral-like, foliate, and pie-wedge designs; signed "T.K.W."; very good condition; $85–$125.

Bracelet, Zuni: sterling silver and 50 turquoise stones, petit point; very good condition; $70–$90.

Bracelet, Zuni: stunning silver bracelet inset with 64 oval polished and graded turquoise stones of rich blue color set in a central sunburst with diamond forms at the sides with matched turquoise; very good condition; $100–$300.

Bracelet, Zuni: fancy silver, turquoise, coral, and shell inlay; lady's sterling "spinner"/reversible with red coral, jet, mother-of-pearl, and blue inlay cardinal on one side, and blue inlay, mother-of-pearl, and coral blue jay on reverse; weight 4½ ounces; very good condition; $200–$300.

Cast brass set, Charlie Pratt: ring, bracelet, and pendant (no chain); Hopi Kachina with semiprecious stones; mint condition; $495.

Chain, Navajo: heavy, handmade sterling silver chain; ca. 1940; 28 inches long; very good condition; $60–$80.

Collar tips, Hopi: fancy silver and turquoise; set with wedge-shaped inlay of mother-of-pearl and single green cabochon drilled bead; very good condition; $175–$225.

Combs and jewelry, Zuni: including petit point and needlepoint designs; very good condition; $85–$115/group.

Concha belt, Alan Wallace: "landscape" design, each concha is different, inlay with spiny oyster, lapis, sugilite, turquoise, magnicite, onyx, and sterling silver; 1992; $9,000.

Concha belt, Charlie Pratt: cast sterling silver with buffalo design; 1993; mint condition; $395.

Concha belt and pendant, Gibson Nez: Mediterranean coral, overlay hammered, stamped, with inlaid lapis; pendant inlay is pink and red coral, beads are inlaid as well; 1992; both in mint condition; $10,000 for belt; $2,200 for pendant.

Concha belt, Gibson Nez: Lone Mountain turquoise and sterling silver, turquoise insets; 1989; concha size 2½ x 3 inches; mint condition; $7,500.

Concha belt, Navajo: silver and turquoise concha; sand-cast; comprised of six spoked oval conchas, seven butterflies, a stamp-decorated buckle; all set with oval spiderweb turquoise stones; conchas 2¾ x 2⁵⁄₁₆ inches; butterflies 2 x 1½ inches; purchased in the early 1950s; 3 feet x 2¼ inches overall; very good condition; $950–$1,150.

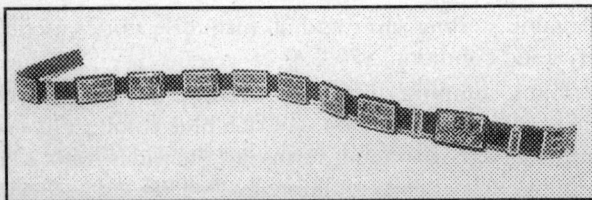

Jewelry, Alan Wallace, concha belt, "landscape" design, each concha is different, inlay with spiny oyster, lapis, sugilite, turquoise, magnicite, onyx, and sterling silver; 1992; $9,000. Courtesy of Alan Wallace. Photo by Robert Reno.

Jewelry, Gibson Nez, concha belt, Lone Mountain turquoise and sterling silver, concha size 2½ x 3 inches; turquoise insets; 1989; $7,500. Courtesy of Gibson Nez. Photo by Robert Reno.

Concha belt, Navajo: handmade silver concha belt with a turquoise stone in each concha; ca. 1885; 41 inches long; very good condition; $200–$300.

Concha belt, Navajo: comprised of seven stamped and engraved open-centered silver conchas (3⅜ x 4¼ inches), the open-centered buckle stamp- and repoussé-decorated (3¾ x 3 inches); purchased early 1950s; very good condition; $1,850–$2,300.

Concha belt, Navajo: nine stamped and repousséd silver conchas, the open-center buckle stamp- and repoussé-decorated; purchased early 1950s at Frost Curio, Cody, Wyoming; very good condition; $460–$700.

Concha belt, Navajo: embossed buckle, conchas and butterflies inlaid with turquoise; made by "B.Y."; 40 inches long; very good condition; $400–$500.

Concha belt, Navajo: silver inlaid with coral, jet, and turquoise, depicting twelve scenes of Navajo life, possibly the Begay family; initialed "BB"; 41 inches long; excellent condition; $700–$900.

Concha belt, Navajo: hand-stamped sterling silver, eight conchas and buckle; old style; 43 inches long; very good condition; $450–$650.

Concha belt, Zuni: concha-style/cluster, matched turquoise pieces; contemporary; very good condition; $2,300–$3,450.

Cross, H. Itule: Zuni, silver and coral cross won second-prize ribbon "Inter-Tribal Indian Ceremonial, Gallup, NM 1974"; very good condition; $160–$225.

Earrings, Hopi: two pairs of sterling silver in geometric designs in overlay style; very good condition; $35–$65/pair.

Earrings, Southwest: turquoise, shell, and coral; jaclas with contemporary silver and turquoise ear fasteners; very good condition; $115–$200.

Earrings, Zuni: choice silver earrings with a row of inlaid turquoise, lapis, and shell in each; ca. 1985; 1½ inches x ½ inch; very good condition; $30–$45.

Earrings, Zuni: unusual shape silver and shell inlay earrings; ca. 1986; 1½ x ¾ inch; very good condition; $20–$25.

Earrings, Zuni: unusual silver earrings with rows of turquoise inlays; ca. 1986; 1¾ x 1 inch; very good condition; $30–$60.

Earrings, Zuni: inlay "feather" earrings; ca. 1986; 1 inch diameter; very good condition; $25–$45.

Earrings, Zuni: choice silver earrings with rows of turquoise, jet, and shell heishe; ca. 1986; 2½ inches x ½ inch; very good condition; $30–$60.

Earrings, Zuni: choice turquoise and silver needlepoint earrings; ca. 1986; 2½ x ¾ inch; very good condition; $30–$60.

Earrings, Zuni: silver and turquoise channel work with turquoise-set suspensions; 2⅝ inches long; very good condition; $300–$400.

Earrings, Zuni: silver and turquoise; sterling "dangles" with an incised blue-green cabochon and silver drum attached to each; 3 inches long; very good condition; $45–$80.

Earrings, Zuni: turquoise and silver needlepoint earrings; ca. 1980; 3 inches x 1 inch; very good condition; $70–$90.

Earrings, Zuni: choice turquoise and silver needlepoint earrings; ca. 1986; very good condition; $30–$60.

Earrings, Zuni: fashioned from silver into seven pointed star forms with a central turquoise stone surrounded by seven petit point blue turquoise gems; screw ear holders; old; very good condition; $45–$70.

Necklace, Apache: beaded hide medallion, decorated with dark blue, red, sky blue, orange, clear lime, clear pink, and white beads in an eight-pointed star-flower design; very good condition; $30–$60.

Necklace, Blackfoot: fully beaded loop necklace in red, white, and blue; ca. 1890; 24 inches; very good condition; $70–$90.

Necklace, Cherokee: "tear" necklace (squash blossom) with matching bracelet, given to collector to be worn "when you have tears to shed that you are not able to shed"; very good condition; $175–$230.

Necklace, Cherokee: made of rattlesnake vertebrae and trade beads, especially for the collection; very good condition; $85–$115.

Necklace (choker): small Lone Mountain turquoise nugget choker on heishe; ca. 1965; very good condition; $20–$35.

Necklaces (chokers); three different Indian chokers; ca. 1975; very good condition; $15–$25.

Necklace, Don and V. Dewa: Zuni, silver and petit point turquoise, sterling with 48 blue silver and round shapes; signed "D. & V. Dewa (Don)"; very good condition; $85–$150.

Necklace, Gibson Nez: sterling silver hand-hammered and stamped, beaded; 1992; mint condition; $1,400.

Necklace, Jake Livingston: coral strands supporting 14 carat hand-tooled gold pendant with coral center; 1992; 18 inches long; mint condition; $7800.

Necklace, Jake Livingston: silver hand-stamped beads; won Best in Division for Traditional Jewelry in Santa Fe Indian Market 1992; pendant part has Nevada Blue Spiderweb turquoise stone in center; 18"; mint condition; $2,500.

Necklace (choker): malachite, beaded; ca. 1980; 18 inches; very good condition; $60–$90.

Necklace, Mary Marie: Zuni, silver and coral squash blossom; all sterling with six blossoms on each side interspersed with a central naja (horseshoelike pendant); all pieces set "cluster" style in matching bloodred color; signed "Mary Marie"; very good condition; $575–$920.

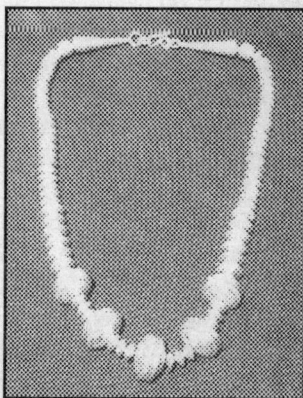

Jewelry, Gibson Nez, sterling silver hand-hammered and stamped beaded necklace; 1992; $1,400. Courtesy of Gibson Nez. Photo by Robert Reno.

Necklace, Navajo: made of silver with fine squash-blossom and featherwork, and blue turquoise with oxblood coral; 13 inches long; good condition; $225–$325.

Necklace, Navajo: sand-cast with silver squash blossoms and 48 silver beads; 15½ inches long; very good condition; $200–$300.

Necklace, bracelet, and earrings, Navajo: necklace of silver beads with ten squash blossoms in naja, with eight turquoise stones surmounted with silver blossoms, 15¼ inches; bracelet also silver with three large green turquoise stones; earrings of a small blossom; very good condition; $550–$750/set.

Necklace, Navajo: graduated size, handmade sterling with hand-stamped designs; 24 inches long; very good condition; $230–$285.

Necklace, Navajo: nine-strand shell heishe and turquoise nuggets; ca. 1940; 25 inches; very good condition; $300–$400.

Necklace, Navajo: six-strand shell heishe and turquoise necklace; ca. 1930; 26 inches; very good condition; $60–$90.

Necklace, Navajo: six-strand tubular coral and turquoise nuggets; ca. 1980; 26 inches; very good condition; $85–$175.

Necklace, Navajo: six strands of coral and turquoise beads; ca. 1986; 26 inches; very good condition; $115–$175.

Necklace, Navajo: unusual silver squash blossom with turquoise nuggets; ca. 1950; 28 x 2 inches; very good condition; $150–$200.

Necklace, Navajo: turquoise and silver squash-blossom necklace; ca. 1960; 28 inches; very good condition; $285–$350.

Necklace and earring set, Navajo: silver and jet set; signed; ca. 1986; 23 inches; very good condition; $40–$60/set.

Necklace and earring set, Navajo: turquoise and silver choker with leaf motif and matching earrings; ca. 1975; 18 inches; very good condition; $60–$100.

Necklace/Pendant, Navajo: silver, turquoise, and coral pendant; signed "Anson Joe A"; very good condition; $85–$135.

Necklace, Navajo: squash blossom with naja and single square-cut stone; handmade beads and squash blossoms; probably made for a man because of its large and heavy size; ca. 1920; very good condition; $3,600–$4,000.

Necklace, Navajo: silver and turquoise necklace, sand/tufa-cast sterling pendant with five geometric-shaped blue cabochons; signed "WB"; weight 4½ ounces; very good condition; $150–$225.

Necklace, Navajo: silver and turquoise squash-blossom necklace; ca. 1910; very good condition; $3,500–$4,600.

Necklaces (two), Navajo: silver and turquoise necklaces in squash-blossom style, each with turquoise-set naja; very good condition; $400–$525.

Necklaces (two), Navajo: silver and turquoise squash-blossom style chokers, each with turquoise-set naja; 13 inches and 13¼ inches; very good condition; $400–$575.

Necklace: elk teeth and claws with large blue glass beads strung on deerskin thong; ¼ inch wide; very good condition; $60–$85.

Necklace: finely carved and graduated lapis beads with four stamped, tubular-shaped silver beads probably a choker; 10 inches long; very good condition; $150–$250.

Necklace (Choker): short solid turquoise nugget necklace; ca. 1970; 16 inches; very good condition; $60–$85.

Necklace: shaman's style carved bond and beaded in red, white, and blue; 21½ inches long; very good condition; $200–$300.

Necklace: six-strand small turquoise nugget necklace on white heishe; ca. 1970; 31 inches; very good condition; $175–$230.

Necklace: carved dewclaw necklace; old; 15 inches; very good condition; $550–$750.

Necklace: beaded 30-strand coral-colored; ca. 1986; 28 inches; very good condition; $75–$110.

Necklace: five-strand coral, glass, and silver beads; ca. 1986; very good condition; $70–$110.

Necklace: three-strand tubular coral bead necklace; ca. 1930; 29 inches; very good condition; $50–$85.

Necklace, fetish: bone birds, fossilized water lily discs, witches' wampum, and coral cylinders; middle to late 1800s; very good condition; $200–$260.

Necklace, fetish: serpentine and soapstone fetish necklace with bears, foxes, and handmade silver beads with serpentine heishe work; ca. early 1900s; very good condition; $150–$175.

Necklace, fetish: serpentine, turquoise, abalone, pipestone, jet, mother-of-pearl, agate eagles, fish, various birds, squirrels, turtles, frogs, rabbits, bear, buffalo, and shell heishe; ca. 1980s; very good condition; $350–$460.

Necklace, fetish: squirrel fetish necklace made of serpentine; ca. 1960; very good condition; $115–$150.

Necklace: five-strand coral-colored glass bead necklace with silver beads and an old coin; ca. 1985; very good condition; $40–$60.

Necklace (group): including Job's tears (Cherokee), made of seed in light blue and gray; a Cherokee crinoids and raw turquoise stones; copper and shell bird necklace (Indians would cut telegraph wires in order to get copper to make necklaces); very good condition; $230–$575 each.

Necklace: ten strands of good-quality shell heishe with squaw wrap; ca. 1980; 30 inches; very good condition; $100–$115.

Necklace: graduated pipestone heishe discs; ca. 1970; very good condition; $115–$150.

Necklace: heishe, made of abalone, bone, jet, serpentine, and turquoise nuggets; ca. early 1900s; very good condition; $175–$200.

Necklace: turquoise, heishe, jacla, and coral beads in center; from Anadanko pawnshop; 20th century; very good condition; $350–$400.

Necklace/Pendant: silver and turquoise with pendant drop stylized leaf decoration; very good condition; $60–$80.

Necklace: silver, beaded with three turquoise drops; very good condition; $40–$60.

Necklace: silver, one of a kind, with hinged body and black jet stones; ca. 1986; very good condition; $60–$100.

Necklace: silver, two turquoise drops with leaf scroll drops; very good condition; $45–$65.

Necklace: turned bone and glass beads; ⅜-inch beads of clear green, blue, amber, white, and yellow with 3½-inch bone tubes; tipped with small brass cone bells; good condition; $50–$75.

Necklace (choker): turquoise nugget and coral choker with silver beads; ca. 1965; 16 inches; very good condition; $100–$125.

Necklaces (two): one Pueblo heishe, three-strand turquoise nuggets, 15½ inches long; and one two-strand Venetian trade beads; very good condition; $110–$150.

Necklaces: ten strands of Venetian red beads with white hearts; 11½ inches long; good condition; $75–$125/set.

Necklaces (chokers): three different pen shell heishe chokers; ca. 1965; very good condition; $25–$45.

Necklace (choker), Nez Perce: ca. 1870; very good condition; $575–$700.

Necklace, O. Crespin: heishe necklace made of turquoise, serpentine, and pipestone, by O. Crespin of the Santo Domingo Pueblo, New Mexico; contemporary; very good condition; $200–$250.

Necklace, Pima: rare rattlesnake vertebrae ceremonial necklace showing much use; ca. 1880; 29 inches; fair to good condition; $150–$185.

Necklace (choker), Plains: four rows of hair-pipe bones interspersed with leather dividers and red and blue trade beads; tin cone and horsehair suspensions attached to a shell disc; very good condition; $35–$70.

Necklace (choker), Plains: 15 bear claws with small faceted and large Russian cobalt beads; 15 inches long; very good condition; $500–$700.

Necklaces (three), Plains: a glass trade bead choker composed of numerous bead types, such as amber eight-sided wound press-faceted and clear wound melon, 15½ inches long; a Blackfoot fully beaded wrapped necklace over a trade cloth body with ermine and rawhide wrapping, bead colors are crystal green and white heart reds, 16 inches long; and a Crow bead wrapped necklace, over a braided red wool body with engraved German silver disc and dentalia shell suspensions, bead colors are white, crystal green and gold, black, sky blue, pink, and royal blue, 24 inches long; provenance: The Science Museum of Connecticut; very good condition; $700–$920 each.

Necklace, Pueblo: "Treasure Necklace"; appears to be made up of pieces from other jewelry, including a few crosses, fetishes, and old trade items; very good condition; $350–$400.

Necklace (choker), Pueblo: large strand, graduated turquoise nugget necklace with heishe spacers; 15½ inches long; very good condition; $75–$110.

Necklace (choker), Pueblo: interlocking coral with stamped designs on 14 silver beads; 15 inches long; very good condition; $350–$450.

Necklace (choker), Pueblo: three strands superfine ironwood and 14 carat gold heishe; ca. 1970; 16 inches; very good condition; $200–$250.

Necklace, Pueblo: made of turquoise and shell, "marriage/wedding" style; ca. 1900–1930; 25 inches long; very good condition; $460–$630.

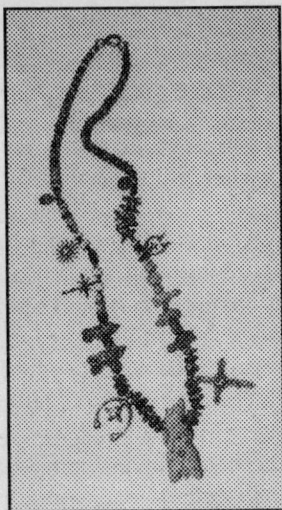

*Jewelry, Pueblo, necklace;
"Treasure Necklace"; appears to be
made up of pieces from other jewelry, including a few crosses, fetishes,
and old trade items; very good condition; $350–$400.* Courtesy of,
and photo by, Joyce Williams.

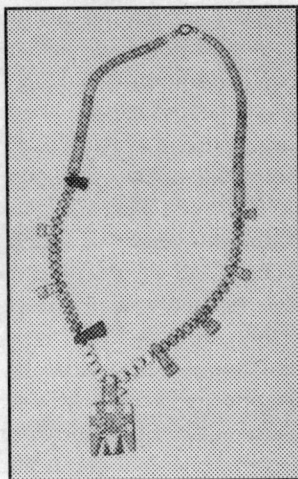

*Jewelry, Pueblo, necklace, "Old
Pawn"; inlay on battery casing
back; turquoise, coral, and shell;
eagle pendant; excellent condition;
$250–$300.* Courtesy of, and
photo by, Joyce Williams.

Necklace, fetish: Pueblo; coral and jet; single strand of eleven black
bears with red heart-line inlays interspersed with tube-type
heishe and finished off in sterling cones and clasp; very good
condition; $200–$300.

Necklace, Pueblo: "Old Pawn"; inlay on battery casing back;
turquoise, coral, and shell; eagle pendant; excellent condition; $250–300.

Necklace, fetish: Pueblo, single strand of hand-cut/carved serpentine, abalone, mother-of-pearl, and melon shell bears, birds of
various sizes, and squirrels, all with black jet inlay eyes interspersed with mother-of-pearl heishe beads; very good condition; $175–$320.

Necklace, Pueblo: turquoise nugget and shell; five strands of vertically drilled green Persian interspersed with light brown
heishe beads; "squaw-wrapped" neckband; very good condition; $150–$185.

Necklace (choker), Santo Domingo: turquoise and pipestone, graduated-size brown stone interspersed with green heishe and finished with sterling beads and clasp; very good condition; $30–$60.

Necklace, Santo Domingo: pawn Santo Domingo turquoise jacla; ca. 1910–1930; very good condition; $100–$150.

Necklace, Santo Domingo: turquoise heishe with silver beads; made in Santo Domingo Pueblo; contemporary (ca. 1980); very good condition; $350–$400.

Necklace, Santo Domingo: turquoise nugget; matching blue-green discs of irregular shapes with matching graduated-size heishe forming a portion of the neckpiece; very good condition; $350–$450.

Necklace, Santo Domingo: unisex mixed turquoise, serpentine, and pipestone heishe necklace; ca. 1950; 22 inches; very good condition; $25–$35.

Necklace and earrings (set), Santo Domingo: classic "T-Bird" tourist necklace with matching earrings; ca. 1935; 28 x 1½ inches; very good condition; $40–$60/set.

Warrior Society necklace, Sioux: Dakotas; constructed of quill-wrapped hide strips, otter skin, trade mirrors; used in the Grass Dance; ca. 1920s; $8,500.

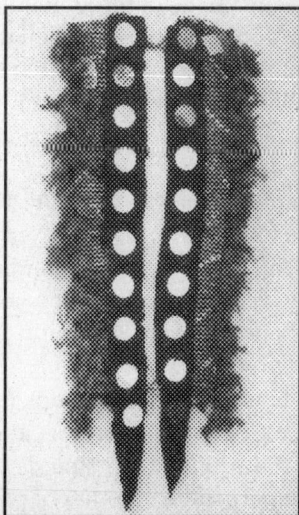

Jewelry, Sioux, Warrior Society necklace; Dakotas; ca. 1920s; constructed of quill- wrapped hide strips, otter skin, trade mirrors; used in the Grass Dance; $8,500. Courtesy of Canfield Gallery. Photo by Robert Reno.

Necklace, Southwest: loom-style decorated with cobalt blue, green, red, yellow, orange, sky blue, and lime-colored beads in geometric design; 1 inch wide; very good condition; $15–$20.

Necklace, Southwest: shell and turquoise; composed of seven strands of brownish white shell disc beads, interspersed coral-shaped red glass and turquoise disc beads and nuggets, pair of jaclas attached, each composed of graduated turquoise discs and white shell suspensions; attached pawn ticket: "no. 8504, 7–6–57, Louise James, Beeds, $98.00"; $18^{1/2}$ inches long; very good condition; $430–$500.

Rings and earrings, Southwest: silver and turquoise; Zuni, two cluster rings and a pair of turquoise and jet mosaic technique earrings; very good condition; $85–$130/set.

Necklace and bracelet, Southwest: Navajo necklace, silver and coral squash blossom, 16 inches long; Zuni bracelet, three-row, turquoise and silver, 1 inch wide; both very good condition; $400–$575.

Necklace and earring set, Wesley and Ella Gia: Zuni; fancy silver, turquoise, coral, and shell necklace and earring set; sterling inlays of blue turquoise, red coral, jet, white and gold mother-of-pearl, serpentine, melon shell, and abalone in bird and flower designs; signed "Wesley & Ella Gia, Zuni, NM"; very good condition; $575–$975/set.

Necklace, Zuni: made of turquoise nuggets with a pair of turquoise, coral, and red spondylus shell drops; turquoise probably from Lone Mountain; 20 inches long; good condition; $250–$350.

Necklace and earrings (set), Zuni: choice Zuni inlay "sun face" squash-blossom set; ca. 1986; 25 inches; very good condition; $220–$350/set.

Necklace and earrings (set), Zuni: turquoise, coral, and jet inlaid "pipe tomahawk"; ca. 1986; very good condition; $100–$115.

Necklace and ring set, Zuni: handmade sterling link chain with three rectangular plaques set with matching blue-green needlepoint slivers; sterling ring similar in design; very good condition; $200–$250.

Necklace, fetish, Zuni: ten strands with seventy hand-carved stone effigies; 14 inches long; very good condition; $300–$450.

Necklace, fetish, Zuni: two strands of hand-carved abalone, pipestone, serpentine, mother-of-pearl, and shell birds, bears, and foxes by Quam, interspersed with brown olive-shell heishe; finished with sterling beads, cones, and clasp; very good condition; $200–$300.

Necklace, fetish, Zuni: strung with selected turquoise forms interspersed with pieces of red coral and flying "birds" made of mother-of-pearl shell, each element spaced by tiny circular shell or bone discs; old; very good condition; $100–$300.

Necklace, Zuni: silver and turquoise bow squash blossom; ca. 1916; very good condition; $1,400–$1,800.

Necklace, Zuni: silver, turquoise, coral, and shell; sterling squash-blossom style with inlays of blue-green, red, mother-of-pearl, tortoiseshell, black jet, and abalone in individual horse-head design; ca. 1940–1960; very good condition; $375–$550.

Pendant, Andy Abeita: Pueblo, Baltic amber bear pendant, sterling silver wrap; 1½ x 1 inch; $60.

Pendant, Andy Abeita: Pueblo, jet bear pendant, sterling silver wrap; 1⅛ inch x ⅜ inch; $30.

Pendant, Andy Abeita: Pueblo, Picasso marble bear pendant, sterling silver wrap, 1½ x ¾ inch; $45.

Pendant, Charlie Pratt: sterling silver Hopi Kachina, with semi-precious stones; 1993; 18 inches long; mint condition; $395.

Pendant, Gibson Nez: "Corn Maiden"; 14 carat gold with Mediterranean coral and Bisbee turquoise; 23 inches long; 1984; mint condition; $14,000.

Jewelry, Gibson Nez, pendant, "Corn Maiden," 14 carat gold with Mediterranean coral and Bisbee turquoise; 1984; 23 inches length; $14,000. Courtesy of Gibson Nez. Photo by Robert Reno.

Pendant and chain, Hopi: sterling silver with overlay-style Kachina mask design with feather; signed (Jackson Seklestewa); 1½ inches diameter; very good condition; $35–$50.

Pendant and chain, Hopi: silver; perched eagle in overlay-style design; signed; hallmarked; very good condition; $45–$80.

Pendant, Jake and Irene Livingston: fancy silver and shell inlay multisided pendant; sterling paneled plumb boblike shape with inlays of blue, red, white, and gold mother-of-pearl, jet, abalone, and turtle shell in hummingbird, blue jay, robin, and cardinal designs; Yeibichai and flowers inlaid on the surfaces of the surrounding mounting, and more flowers and foliate designs above each bird; signed "Jake and Irene Livingston"; 3½ inches long x 2½ inches wide; very good condition; $800–$1,550.

Pendant, Jake Livingston: swivel back with cardinal and blue jay on other (two photos); coral, turquoise, melon shell, abalone, pin shell, light coral; 1993; mint condition; $900.

Pendant/Necklace, Navajo: silver, turquoise, and coral; sterling round, fluted, and melon beads and mounting set with two hand-carved blue and one bloodred cabochon; signed "E." with fleur-de-lis overhead; very good condition; $70–$140.

Pendant, Navajo: sterling silver and turquoise in overlay style, set with a round blue Persian cabochon; signed Mary B. Smith; very good condition; $35–$75.

Pin/Pendant, Navajo: silver and turquoise; sterling pinwheel with hand-stamped designs and set with oval green cabochon; very good condition; $25–$45.

Pendant/Earrings, Northwest Coast: pair of matched carved ivory animals used as pendants or earrings; ca. 1975; very good condition; $175–$230.

Pendant and chain, Northwest Coast: in form of Northwest Coast mask; marked "sterling, 1979, ss., 24/50, Beaverworks"; suspended on hand-wrought link chain; mask is 1½ inches; very good condition; $160–$215.

Pendant, Northwest Coast: ivory carved pendant with abalone inlay; ca. 1975; 3 x 2¾ inches; very good condition; $175–$200.

Pillboxes, Southwest Navajo: silver set with turquoise; very good condition; $40–$90.

Pin, Haida: carved argillite wolf pin, signed John York, Haida; ca. 1950; 3 x 1½ inches; very good condition; $60–$100.

Pin, Navajo: "Old Pawn" silver pin set with nine turquoise stones; ca. 1940; 4½ inches diameter; very good condition; $40–$65.

Pin, Navajo: roadrunner pin with turquoise eye, pin back, along with a silver earring with wire pierced ear holder; contemporary; very good condition; $40–$60.

Pin, Navajo: silver and coral, sterling naja (horseshoe-shaped) containing one oval red cabochon drop (pendant style); very good condition; $35–$70.

Pin, Navajo: silver and turquoise; cast openwork sterling flowerlike design set with a blue-green cabochon; very good condition; $30–$40.

Pin, Navajo: silver and turquoise; tufa sand-cast sterling, eight-pointed star-flower set with a blue cabochon; very good condition; $20–$45.

Pins (three), Navajo: finely stamped sterling silver with salamanders and butterfly; signed "H"; excellent condition; $25–$65 each.

Pins (three), Navajo: sterling silver, two grasshoppers and a lizard; one stamped "H"; very good condition; $50–$100 each.

Pins (two), Navajo: sterling silver with spider designs and teardrop-shaped bodies in turquoise and mother-of-pearl; very good condition; $50–$100 each.

Pin: bee pin with turquoise body from which the silver eyes and antenna protrude, with wings of silver engraved on the surface and which surround the bee's tail; pin clasp closing beneath the body; very good condition; $45–$65.

Pin, Zuni: large inlay turquoise, coral, jet, and shell "sun face" pin; ca. 1940; very good condition; $150–$175.

Pins (three), Zuni: "Old Pawn" silver and turquoise pins; very good condition; $150–$260 each.

Ring, George Toledo: Navajo; silver, turquoise, and coral; five-prong sterling shank with leaf designs set with one each blue-green and pinkish red cabochon; signed George Toledo; ca. 1940s-1950s; very good condition; $85–$150.

Ring, Navajo: fancy silver and turquoise, sterling set with single gem-quality oval; Bisbee (Lavender Pit Mine–type) cabochon; 1⅛ inches x ½ inch; man's size 10½; very good condition; $40–$75.

Ring, Navajo: Hopi-style sterling silver and turquoise full-bodied Kachina ring with round blue cabochon eyes; signed J.C.T. (J.C. Tso), Gallup, 6/5/78; very good condition; $30–$65.

Ring, Navajo: sterling silver and turquoise with hand-stamped designs containing single blue cabochon set "shadow box" style; lady's size 6; very good condition; $25–$50.

Ring, Navajo: fancy sterling silver and turquoise with large leaf design, containing a single gem-quality oval blue cabochon (1⅛ inches x ½ inch); lady's size 7; very good condition; $85–$115.

Ring, Navajo: men's; sterling silver and turquoise with gem-quality blue Persian cabochon; very good condition; $85–$115.

Ring, Patsy Spenser: Zuni; fancy silver, turquoise, and coral; sterling peacock with blue, red, and gold mother-of-pearl inlays; signed "Patsy Spenser"; very good condition; $125–$175.

Ring, Preston Thompson: Winnebago, stamped and etched work; very good condition; $460–$575.

Ring and earrings (set), Navajo: transitional coral and sterling silver; ring is shadow box design; earrings are needlepoint; very good condition; $230–$300/set.

Ring: silver, incised bear claw, set with turquoise; very good condition; $35–$40.

Ring: silver, set with turquoise; signed "A.B."; very good condition; $40–$50.

Ring: sterling silver, set with irregular-shaped turquoise; very good condition; $20–$25.

Ring, Victor Coochwytewa: Hopi, fancy silver and coral ring; sterling in overlay style set with large oval red cabochon; signed with rain cloud symbol (Victor Coochwytewa); very good condition; $85–$115.

Ring, Zuni: fancy silver and turquoise; sterling, set with blue and blue-green inlays in Indian dancer design; signed; very good condition; $115–$160.

Tie bar: silver, with an unusual large precious stone, ca. 1940; very good condition; $15–$25.

Tie bars (three); bag containing three old silver tie bars, one Zuni and two Navajo; ca. 1940; very good condition; $40–$60.

Trade beads, Crow: necklace made of mosaic glass beads, bear claws, strung on sinew; ca. late 1870s; very good condition; $700–$800.

Trade beads: assorted silver beads and red padre beads; ca. early 1900s; very good condition; $150–$200.

Trade beads: assorted silver beads; some Viennese and some mosaic beads; ca. early 1900s; very good condition; $175–$230.

Trade beads: glass foil beads; early 1900s; very good condition; $230–$350.

Trade bead collection; frame containing over 30 strands of rare Peking glass beads and other artifacts; ca. 1880; frame 37 x 23 inches; very good condition; $470–$750.

Trade beads: rare strand of round red yellow-core "chief" beads; ca. 1820; very good condition; $85–$175.

Trade beads: mixed-size faceted Russian cobalt blue trade beads; ca. 1820; very good condition; $100–$150.

Trade beads: ten strands of old blue tile or Crow trade beads; ca. 1880; very good condition; $260–$320/set.

Trade beads: very large cobalt blue Peking glass trade beads; ca. 1890; very good condition; $60–$85.

Trade beads: very rare greasy yellow "Crow beads" along with a few red; ca. 1840; very good condition; $115–$150.

Trade beads: very unusual strand of swirled striped disc-shape Venetian trade beads, ca. 1820; very good condition; $60–$115.

Trade beads: glassed frame (cracked) of very old Venetian trade beads; ca. 1880; frame 18 x 10 inches; very good condition; $375–$440.

Trade beads: large dark green Peking glass trade beads; ca. 1880; 22 inches; very good condition; $40–$60.

Trade beads: large dark green Peking glass trade beads; ca. 1880; 22 inches; very good condition; $40–$90.

Trade beads: rare blue "Padre" or Father Kino beads from Arizona; ca. 1800; 22 inches; very good condition; $40–$80.

Trade beads: rare, huge mixed-shape chevron trade beads; ca. 1800; 22 inches; very good condition; $315–$400.

Trade beads: rare medium-sized green chevron trade beads; ca. 1840; 22 inches; very good condition; $60–$85.

Trade beads: rare old yellow Venetian trade beads with multicolored inlays; ca. 1840; 22 inches; very good condition; $60–$85.

Trade beads: rare strand of old mixed black and blue Venetian trade beads; ca. 1840; 22 inches; very good condition; $60–$90.

Trade beads: strand of large mixed Venetian trade beads; ca. 1840; 22 inches; very good condition; $60–$85.

Trade beads: unusual faceted red Venetian trade beads; ca. 1900; 22 inches; very good condition; $45–$70.

Trade beads: unusual strand of mottled Venetian trade beads; ca. 1860; 22 inches; very good condition; $40–$70.

Trade beads: very large and unusual mixed Venetian trade beads; ca. 1880; 22 inches; very good condition; $50–$80.

Trade beads: very large cobalt blue Peking glass trade beads; ca. 1880; 22 inches; very good condition; $80–$115.

Trade beads: rare "dusty rose" Peking glass trade beads; ca. 1880; 24 x 3 inches; very good condition; $165–$200.

Trade beads: beautiful black Venetian trade beads with various- color inlays; ca. 1840; 24 inches; very good condition; $70–$90.

Trade beads: choice large cobalt blue Peking glass trade beads; ca. 1880; 24 inches; very good condition; $115–$175.

Trade beads: huge, rare long strand of cobalt blue Peking glass trade beads; ca. 1880; 24 inches; very good condition; $80–$115.

Trade beads: huge, rare Venetian chevron trade beads in various- color inlays; ca. 1820; 24 inches; very good condition; $175–$230.

Trade beads: huge strand of ancient faceted cobalt blue Russian trade beads; ca. 1880; 24 inches; very good condition; $100–$120.

Trade beads: huge tubular *cornaline de leppo* trade beads with yellow core called "chief beads"; ca. 1800; 24 inches; very good condition; $85–$150.

Trade beads: jade green Venetian glass disc trade beads; ca. 1880; 24 inches; very good condition; $60–$90.

Trade beads: large black Venetian trade beads with blue and white inlays; ca. 1820; 24 inches; very good condition; $85–$150.

Trade beads: large old Venetian cobalt blue trade beads showing much use; ca. 1880; 24 inches; very good condition; $45–$70.

Trade beads: mixed black and inlaid Venetian trade beads; ca. 1840; 24 inches; very good condition; $65–$100.

Trade beads: rare strand of large faceted Venetian vaseline glass trade beads; ca. 1860; 24 inches; very good condition; $55–$85.

Trade beads: strand of large mixed Venetian trade beads; ca. 1840; 24 inches; very good condition; $75–$100.

Trade beads: unusual deep red and other old Venetian trade beads; ca. 1880; 24 inches; very good condition; $40–$60.

Trade beads: unusual mixed-shape red Peking glass trade beads; ca. 1880; 24 inches; very good condition; $65–$90.

Trade beads: unusual shape and design mixed-color Venetian trade beads; ca. 1880; 24 inches; very good condition; $65–$90.

Trade beads: very large old oval cobalt blue trade beads; ca. 1820; 24 inches; very good condition; $60–$100.

Trade beads: very rare red and blue glass beads with beautiful white feather inlays; ca. 1840; 24 inches; very good condition; $70–$115.

Trade beads: huge and rare cobalt blue Peking glass trade beads; ca. 1880; 26 inches; very good condition; $200–$260.

Trade beads: huge tubular yellow-core red "chief" trade beads; ca. 1820; 26 inches; very good condition; $85–$175.

Trade beads: rare large, yellow-core *cornaline de leppo* "chief" beads; ca. 1840; 26 inches; very good condition; $85–$150.

Trade beads: strand of huge yellow trade beads with colored diamond designs; ca. 1920; 26 inches; very good condition; $85–$150.

Trade beads: strand of pristine faceted cobalt blue Russian trade beads and a few gold ones; ca. 1800; 26 inches; very good condition; $300–$400.

Trade beads: very large oval cobalt blue and light blue Dutch trade beads; ca. 1800; 26 inches; very good condition; $85–$150.

Trade beads: strand of beautiful cobalt blue Peking glass trade beads; ca. 1880; 28 inches; very good condition; $85–$115.

Trade beads: Venetian black trade beads with pink, white, and blue dot inlays; ca. 1820; 28 inches; very good condition; $85–$150.

Trade beads: very rare "dusty pink" Peking glass trade beads; ca. 1880; 28 inches; very good condition; $85–$100.

Trade beads: large cobalt blue Peking glass trade beads; ca. 1880; 29 inches; very good condition; $50–$85.

Trade beads: very unusual shape and color old trade beads; ca. 1880; 29 inches; very good condition; $60–$90.

Trade beads: jade green Peking glass trade beads; ca. 1880; 30 inches; very good condition; $110–$155.

Trade beads: rare strand of cobalt blue and clear Dutch glass trade beads; ca. 1800; 30 inches; very good condition; $115–$175.

Trade beads: strand of graduated chevron trade beads; ca. 1820; 30 inches; very good condition; $85–$175.

Trade beads: strand of huge cobalt blue Peking glass trade beads; ca. 1880; 30 inches; very good condition; $150–$200.

Trade beads: rare solid black Peking glass trade beads; ca. 1880; 32 inches; very good condition; $50–$85.

Trade beads: long strand of cobalt blue Peking glass trade beads; ca. 1880; 33 inches; very good condition; $60–$90.

Trade beads: strand of unusually long cobalt blue Peking glass trade beads; ca. 1890; 36 inches; very good condition; $40–$60.

Trade beads: strand of cobalt blue Peking glass trade beads; ca. 1920; 38 inches; very good condition; $170–$200.

Trade beads: large cobalt blue and clear Venetian trade beads; ca. 1840; very good condition; $50–$85.

Trade beads: rare strand of round red yellow-core "chief" beads; ca. 1820; very good condition; $85–$175.

Trade beads: Riker mount containing an assortment of 65 old trade beads; ca. 1860; very good condition; $30–$60.

Trade beads: Riker mount containing eight large old green chevron beads and one blue one; ca. 1840; very good condition; $25–$40.

Trade beads: strung on sinew; burnt orange and black glass; unusual; very good condition; $230–$300.

Trade beads: very unusual strand of swirled striped disc-shape Venetian trade beads; ca. 1820; very good condition; $60–$115.

Wampum: large strand of clamshell wampum; ca. 1900; 40 inches; very good condition; $40–$60.

Wampum, Plateau: rare strand of clamshell wampum beads; ca. 1850; 36 inches; very good condition; $40–$60.

Watchband, ring, earrings; Hopi: sterling silver; very good condition; $175–$230/set.

Watchband, Navajo: silver with coral and turquoise stones; very good condition; $50–$80.

Watchbands; four lady's turquoise and silver watchbands; ca. 1975; very good condition; $50–$80 each.

Watch tips, Hopi: sterling silver with large Kachina design in overlay style; signed; very good condition; $35–$65.

Wrist ornament, Navajo: sterling silver, leather-mounted tufa/sand-cast in X-like design; mid to late 20th century ; very good condition; $80–$115.

Chapter Nine

Leather

~

The North American Indians hunted animals to supply themselves with food, clothing, and shelter; they made use of every part of the animal's body. The skins of buffalo, deer, elk, caribou, bear, and moose were made into tepees, clothing, boats, shields, containers to hold food and medicines, and cradleboards for their infants.

To prepare skins for use required much time and effort, for the skins would become stiff and smelly if not treated promptly and correctly. Some Indians learned to treat the skins so skillfully that hides were transformed into soft buckskin; others treated them just enough to keep them from spoiling.

The men of the tribes in the Southwest and Northeast usually did this work, though in most other tribes, the women handled the treating, cleaning, and preparation of skins.

The hides were fleshed with tools resembling chisels, which were often made from buffalo leg bones or gun barrels. Scraping the hide was accomplished by pulling a bent antler tool over the skin to plane and thin it. If the animal had hair (like a deer), its hair was removed with a curved tool with a metal end or a blade of some sort. The scraping tool was used like a plane, pulled firmly until the piece was free of hair.

Rawhide is used for parfleches, holy bags, saddlebags, moccasin soles, drumheads, and rattles. The Plains Indians utilized rawhide better than most other tribes since they did little farming and were basically hunter/gatherers; they used hides for all purposes and virtually replaced pottery and wooden items with pieces made from hides.

To make other garments, such as tipis, bags, and moccasins, the rawhide is softened. Tanning the hide meant applying a paste of brains and liver onto the skin. A smooth stone is used to rub the mixture into all of the hide's pores. Then the hide is left to soak in water for a couple of days. It is dried and moistened again. Once more it dries and it is then scraped with a rough stone, which gives the hide an even, grainy appearance. The piece is stretched, wrung out, and dried; then it was softened by stretching again and often smoked so that it would remain soft.

In most tribes a woman was judged by her tanning skills—she was considered industrious if she tanned well, and lazy if she didn't.

Many people interested in Indian artifacts have collected articles made of leather or rawhide; two of the first Americans to bring home articles from the various "modern" (as opposed to prehistoric) Indian tribes were the explorers Lewis and Clark.

The two men left on their long voyage in 1804, after a hurried education in the natural sciences, and were instructed to bring back examples of the natural resources of the region. They distributed peace medals to the Indians, as well as goodwill. In return, the Indians gave them articles that included a Mandan buffalo robe later presented to President Thomas Jefferson. The robe was painted with scenes of the Mandan and Minnetaree tribes fighting the Sioux and Arikara.

SOME LEATHER/RAWHIDE ITEMS

ARTWORK Battle scenes and tales of a warrior's heroism were often painted on buffalo skins, tepees, tepee liners, and warrior shirts to acknowledge the warrior's deeds. The earliest version of such warrior art was collected during the Lewis and Clark expedition from the Mandan tribe in 1804. It is now the property of the Peabody Museum, Harvard University.

A tipi liner made by the Wahpeton Sioux depicts Appaloosas, a breed of horses kept by the Nez Perce. The scene is a battle between the Nez Perce (on horseback) and the Sioux on foot.

Other tribes, such as the Chiricahuas, used deerskin to celebrate an Apache girl's puberty rite. Symbols were painted on the piece, as well as the story of the rite itself.

BOATS The Mandan Indians made circular boats which were made of bison skin lashed to willow frames. These paddle bullboats were used by these Indians for travel or to fish along the Missouri River.

CASES A painted, cylindrical rawhide case was used to hold headdresses, feathers, whistles, and other ceremonial items. If the case belonged to a medicine man, it would hold herbs and fetishes.

Though most of these sacred cases were painted, some tribes (such as those along the Columbia River) incised the decorations on their work.

The western versions of these bags were painted with red paint mixed with wax as their final coating; eastern versions might be varnished with a transparent yellow mixture made from resin or buffalo gallstones.

Bows, bow cases, and quivers were made by the Hidatsa men and were often decorated with images of their conquests. Such scenes are virtually uninterpretable today because their meaning was known only to the maker. The small Hidatsa tribe made cases, as well as a variety of leather goods—parfleches, robes, pipe bags, moccasins, and shirts—typical of the other Northern Plains tribes.

DRUMS   Hand drums were often made of deerskin and painted with decorations by the Plains Indians. Larger drums were made for ceremonial purposes, were used in preparation for war, and to time the steps during dancing rituals.

The Northwest Coast Indians are known to make a disc-shaped drum of caribou skins which is beaten with a drumstick.

The Hopis use drums during the Kachina ceremony, providing a beat for the dancers to follow.

MEDICINE BUNDLES   Sacred to their owners, medicine bags often were filled with pieces of rock, feathers, a bit of trade cloth, animal bones, and other artifacts that held a special, mystical meaning to their owners.

The power of a medicine bundle was different for each Indian. For some, the bundles held healing medicines; others relied on the powers tied up in their bundles for love, spiritual belief, or strength in battle.

Bundles are almost always the property of men, yet women often made the container at the prospective owner's instructions.

Medicine bundles could be passed from one owner to another, with a great deal of ceremony, or could be kept within one family for generations.

Ceremonial bags and bundles were hung on tripods, usually placed at the back of the lodge. Sometimes the man's shield, lance, and pipe were also hung on the tripod. In inclement weather, the tripod was brought inside. Each bag, whether it was used in religious or medicinal rites, was the property of one individual who was instructed in the songs, ritual, and prayers associated with that bundle.

The Lakes area Indians (particularly the Winnebago tribe) made medicine bags from the whole skins of small animals, such as otter, bobcat, and squirrel.

MEDICINE/POSSIBLE BAG   The Navajo tribe is in danger of losing the medicine men and women who have practiced their art for untold generations. Most who are practicing today are over fifty years old and have no one in line to take their place when they retire.

Some of the ceremonies the Navajo medicine men and women perform take ten or more years to learn properly. Young Navajos are either employed or attend school, leaving them little time to apprentice with a medicine person.

Concern over losing the medicine men entirely has prompted plans to begin a program that will give stipends to those interested in studying their ways.

PARFLECHE   Light leather containers resembling small suitcases, parfleches, were made by the Plains Indians and decorated with brightly colored geometric designs. At first they were practical, easily carried satchels; later, they became status symbols. They were both traded and given as gifts.

The parfleche is a symbol of the mobility of Indians who were once confined to certain areas (near shelter and water) due to the absence of domesticated animals in their society. Once the horse was introduced to their environment, life for the Plains Indian became easier. He could easily travel to and from water and shelter to hunt and pursue other activities.

Early parfleches used fewer colors and geometric designs than later examples, which were elaborately styled and extremely colorful.

Plains Indian women used the stiff rawhide of buffalo to make ceremonial robes, dresses, moccasins, leggings, and parfleches, used to hold dried meat and personal belongings. They decorated the leather with a sharpened, porous buffalo bone that was dipped in natural dyes.

Parfleches were beautifully decorated with triangles and other repeating geometric designs. Sometimes these designs (handed down from mother to daughter) can be used to identify particular artists. Designs on the parfleche were outlined in black and filled in with bright, rich colors, replete with symbolic meaning.

Among the Lakotas, red was the color of the sun; blue, the color of the moving spirit, the sky; and green, the color of the spirit of the earth.

SADDLES AND MISCELLANEOUS HORSE TACK Though most Native American men rode bareback, some used a hackamore which was noosed around the horse's lower jaw and often included a blanket or small hide cushion upon which the rider would sit.

Martingales were H-shaped accoutrements which hung over the horse's head and were often highly decorated with bead or quillwork.

SHIELDS Thick rawhide was used as protection by the Indians. They discovered that rawhide formed into a shield could stop the thrust of a spear or arrow. Jemez, Crow, Hopi, and other tribes decorated their shields with protective spirit designs, or pictorial stories of the warrior who owned the shield.

The thick, strong shields were constructed of three or four layers of shrunken rawhide. Their makers, all men, fasted and received their instructions from guardian spirits before starting their work. Sometimes a medicine man would make the shield, as well as conduct the corresponding ritual. He would be paid an appropriate sum in horses, robes, or other goods. The shields were painted and decorated with feathers, animal skins, and/or red trade cloth.

The Plains groups used rawhide alone to create shields, while the Pueblo groups used rawhide along with a removable animal hide cover.

Many Plains shields had two covers, both painted and decorated to reveal what the warrior had seen in a dream or vision as his powers. Like those of the Jemez, Crow, and Hopi, shields of the Plains Indians were often painted, decorated with horsehair, eagle and other feathers, different colors of cloth, and sometimes even bells or tin cones. They all helped to identify members of warrior societies.

TEPEES Skin tepees were decorated both inside and out with the history of the proprietary family, the tribe's history, and often became associated with famous members of the clan. They were renewed at ceremonial feasts during which a group of men would copy the old design onto a new skin.

The spokes of the tepee point to solar and stellar alignments, a testament to Native American interest in astronomy and belief in the power of the stars, moon, and sun's alignment.

The Plains Indians' tepee were the most decorated of all the Indians who used skin tents. Fifteen to twenty buffalo skins were used to make an average-sized tepee (fifteen to twenty feet across), while a large lodge (thirty feet wide with forty-foot-long poles) required up to fifty skins. The paintings on the sides of tepee were often ceremonial designs, paintings of warrior's exploits, or symbols that designated a medicine man or family.

TOBACCO OR PIPE BAG   Pipe bags are leather containers designed to hold the pipe and tobacco Indians used during rituals and ceremonies. They were often highly decorated and reflected the artistic ability of their owners.

Plains Indian decoration of pipe bags included porcupine quillwork, beadwork, or fringe, and are highly representative of the artwork of those tribes.

Through study of tobacco or pipe bags, one can follow the changes the Plains Indians underwent in the nineteenth century. Some are decorated with the horse, some with battle scenes, and you can even find some decorated with the American flag.

BEADWORK

Because quite a few Native Americans did use beadwork as a way of decorating their leather items, it is often difficult to determine exactly the tribal origin of a particular piece. Though most tribes were relatively isolated, they were aware of designs favored by neighboring tribes, and often borrowed from each other. Some tribes even sent women members to learn what other tribes were doing with beadworking designs.

In order to determine the distinctive traits of the beadwork of various tribes, one must consider the type of materials used, the construction or pattern, the medium used to decorate the item, the technique, colors, and design.

Almost all of the tribes practicing beadwork design also created netted beadwork. In this variation beads were not sewn onto a backing material, but rather to each other, making a solid beaded surface. This type of beadwork was used to cover solid rounded surfaces or would stand on its own, for example, as a large cape collar, such as those worn by the Mohave tribe described in Chapter Five.

This type of decoration was used to identify everything from dresses and moccasins to bridles and gun holders. The following is a sampling of how the different tribes used beadwork as a decoration on their leather items (see more information about beadwork in Chapter Five.)

RECOGNIZING DIFFERENT TRIBAL BEADWORK
ASSINIBOIN, SARCEE, AND BLACKFOOT
Assiniboin, Sarcee, and Blackfoot beadwork designs were exclusively geometric.

BLACKFOOT AND CROW
The Blackfoot and Crow used geometric spot-stitching beadwork designs until floral motifs became popular (about 1870). Examples of Crow work were often triangular and sewn on red cloth. The Crow rarely made tobacco bags; however, they did make beautiful beaded gun cases.

(See more information on Blackfoot beadwork in Chapter Five.)

CHIPPEWA
The Chippewa's beadwork was created with a variety of techniques. A wood heddle separated the warps so that the beaded weft could be inserted. Other beadwork was made with a needle, producing either single- or double-weft weaving.

This sewing style was also used by the Winnebago tribe.

IROQUOIS
The Iroquois used a unique method to accentuate their beadwork—they crowded the beads together and padded their designs to create a raised, textural effect.

This type of beadwork was done mostly on velvet pieces, probably because velvet is so much easier to work with than tanned hides and made a nice background for the colorful beads these Indians used.

MICMACS
Micmacs used delicate, double-curving forms and, like other tribes, imitated European embroidery in their beadwork.

NEZ PERCE
The Nez Perce tribe made a distinctive four-tabbed beaded leather bag which was widely traded. A similar bag was made by the Athabascan tribes.

NORTHEAST, LAKES, AND NORTHERN PLAINS
These tribes created intricate designs by laying strung beads in a pattern, then sewing them into place. They also produced shaded floral designs which decorated all kinds of clothing, bags, moccasins, and turbans.

Northeastern beadwork has a lacy and stylized appearance. Floral work is common among tribes such as the Penobscot, Iroquois, and Micmac.

NORTHWEST COAST
Northwest Coast beadwork, though influenced by the styles of the Northern Plains, is distinguished by designs one often sees repeated in their painting, sculpture, and rugs—the geometric patterns drawn from their oceanic life featuring seals, whales, eagles, bears, and ravens.

PLAINS INDIANS
The Plains tribes used a method of affixing their beadwork called "lazy stitch" sewing. This simply means that the beads were strung together, then attached to the garment at the ends of short lengths of beads; in other words, each bead was *not* individually fastened to the material.

"Pony" beads were larger beads, used from about 1800 on. Seed beads became popular around 1840 and remained so.

SAUK AND CHIPPEWA

These two tribes used bilateral symmetry in their boldly styled beadwork.

QUILLWORK

Decorating with quills is a Native American art that predates beadwork. Quills were taken from the porcupine and dyed different colors, then flattened when pushed through the clenched teeth of the woman in the process of making the quillwork decoration. The effect of the decoration is one of flattened reeds that, when placed artistically, form a geometric or floral design.

Decorating with quills demanded great dexterity. The quills were dyed, split, flattened, and sewn with many different techniques.

In the Cheyenne tribe, the craft of quilling was taught amidst great ritual and ceremony. If men saw the work in progress, it was said they would be deafened or gored by a bull.

Symbols were common in quillwork, as in most other Indian arts. A star placed below the smoke hole of a tipi was a symbol of the sun, bringing blessing on all who entered the dwelling.

Quillwork was still in use after the white man brought beads to the Indian, but the Indians found it easier to work with the beads, and quills eventually lost favor.

Described below are some of the ways different tribes used quillwork.

RECOGNIZING DIFFERENT TRIBAL QUILLWORK

CREE

The Cree Indians are credited with doing the finest quillwork in North America. Quills were woven into the work and pushed tightly together so that their design gives one the impression of long, flattened beadwork.

HURON AND IROQUOIS

The Huron and Iroquois used an embroidery technique, probably taught to them by French settlers. Moose hair was used to embroider moccasins, robes, boxes, and other items.

NORTHEASTERN AND LAKES INDIANS

The Northeastern and Lakes region Indians applied quillwork to birch bark by pushing dyed quills through holes in the bark and bending the ends. Boxes of all kinds—rectangular, circular, oval, and square—were made by the Micmacs and other Northeastern tribes for sale to the Anglo traders.

PLAINS

Plains quillwork was geometric in design and was used primarily to adorn clothing. Moccasins, breastplates, cradleboards, leggings, quirts, belts, and anything else made of leather was decorated by the Plains Indians with their fanciful quillwork.

PRICES

APACHE

Apache, hatband: braided leather hatband with beaded holders; ca. 1986; 28 inches; very good condition; $25–$45.

Apache, pouch: beaded hide, of rectangular form, yellow ocher paint decoration, tin cone suspensions on bottom; bead colors royal blue, white, yellow, and white-heart reds; attached note reads: "medicine bag, made by Apache Indians in Arizona, 1898"; 6¾ inches long; good condition (minor bead loss); $185–$230.

Apache, pouch: beaded hide, decorated with concentric rosette motif on pink ground; fringed with tin cone suspensions; provenance: The Science Museum of Connecticut; 7 inches long; very good condition; $230–$460.

Kiowa-Apache, strike-a-lights (group): strike-a-light made of saddle leather, ca. 1860, very good condition, $1,900–$2,300; Apache strike-a-light, formerly of the Kober collection, very good condition, $1,750–$2,000; Apache (Chiricahua) strike-a-light, beaded, ca. 1870, very good condition, $1,430–$1,750; Apache skeletal bag, formerly of the Guy collection, ca. 1890, very good condition, $950–$1,150.

ARAPAHO

Arapaho, cradleboard cover: quill-wrapped parfleche decoration on a canvas body over a bentwood frame, quilled suspensions with

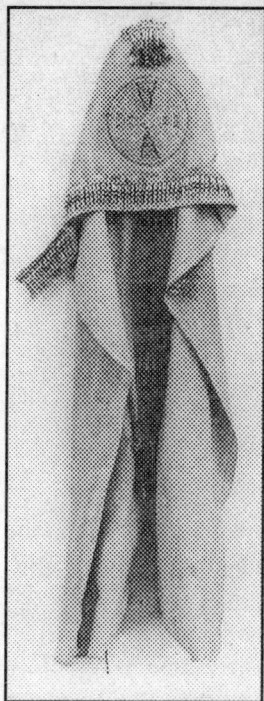

Leather, Arapaho, cradleboard cover; quill-wrapped parfleche decoration on a canvas body over a bentwood frame; quilled suspensions with deer toe attachments at crown; frame is 34 inches long; provenance: a Massachusetts historical society; $3,565–$4,000. Courtesy Robert W. Skinner, Inc., Bolton/Boston, Massachusetts.

Leather, Arapaho, possible bag; ca. 1875; made of beaded buckskin; 13 x 23 inches; $4,000–$5,200. Courtesy of Canfield Gallery. Photo by Donald Vogt.

deer toe attachments at crown; provenance: a Massachusetts historical society; frame 34 inches long; fair/good condition (extensive quill damage and fading); $3,565–$4,000.

Arapaho, knife case: rectangular with geometric beadwork and containing an old knife; 9 x 3 inches; very good condition; $150–$230.

Arapaho, lidded box, parfleche: rectangular, rawhide, with painted geometric designs; ca. 1985; 40 x 22 inches; very good condition; $110–$175.

Arapaho, parfleches (pair): beautiful matched rawhide cases with geometric designs painted on both sides; ca. 1980; 24 x 15 inches each; very good condition; $350–$700 each.

Arapaho, possible bag: made of beaded buckskin; ca. 1875; 13 x 23 inches; very good condition; $4,000–$5,200.

Arapaho, quiver: hide quiver containing two old arrows; ca. 1880; 30 x 5 inches; very good condition; $115–$175.

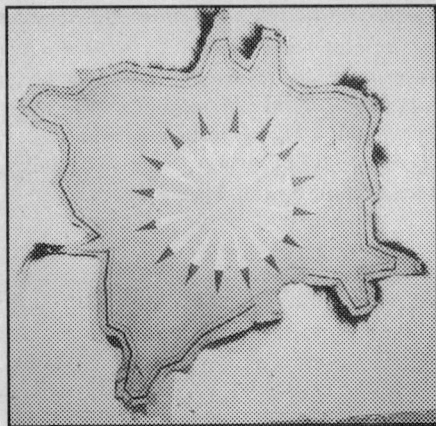

Leather, Assiniboin, bison robe; painted sunburst featherlike design outlined in red and black lines; 75 inches high x 75 inches wide; excellent condition; $950–$1,100. Courtesy of Willis Henry Auctions, Inc.

ASSINIBOIN

Assiniboin, bison robe: painted sunburst featherlike design outlined in red and black lines; 75 inches high x 75 inches wide; excellent condition; $950–$1,100.

ATHABASCAN

Athabascan, gun case: large hide gun case with fine floral embroidered designs and fringe; ca. 1920; 50 x 7 inches; very good condition; $230–$575.

BLACKFOOT

Blackfoot, parfleche: rare old black-outline rawhide medicine case with long fringe; ca. 1880; 15 x 9 inches; very good condition; $550–$650.

Blackfoot, pipe bag: fully beaded background in white with geometric designs in blue, greasy yellow, green, light brown, and red; top tabs with beaded borders of translucent green; 28 inches long; very good condition; $1,450–$1,650.

Blackfoot, pipe bag and small bag: beadwork in blue, red, orange, etc.; very good condition; $180–$280.

Blackfoot, pouch: fully beaded on painted parfleche in geometric blocks of cobalt, salmon, green, greasy yellow, and blue beads with attached twisted fringe and black button closure; 12 inches long; very good condition; $1,700–$2,100.

Blackfoot, quirt: braided rawhide with wood handle; some wear; old; very good condition; $550–$750.

Blackfoot, rattle: very rare painted hide Medicine Society ceremonial rattle; very good condition; $100–$175.

Blackfoot, shield: painted, rawhide shield with trade cloth and feather drops; ca. 1980; 30 x 17 inches; very good condition; $60–$115.

CHEYENNE

Cheyenne, knife sheath: hide with beaded decoration in alternating red and white bar designs with greasy yellow background and hide fringe; 10 inches long; very good condition; $600–$800.

Cheyenne, knife case: choice full-beaded sinew-sewn knife case with geometric designs; 9 x 2 inches; very good condition; $200–$260.

Cheyenne, parfleche: rectangular rawhide case with handle and geometric designs; ca. 1986; 12 x 9 inches; very good condition; $150–$200.

Cheyenne, pipe bag: beaded and fringed hide pipe bag, with remains of yellow and blue pigment, stitched in pink and light and dark blue against a white beaded ground with narrow strips around the top and down each side, broad panels containing checkered columns flanked by triangles on the front

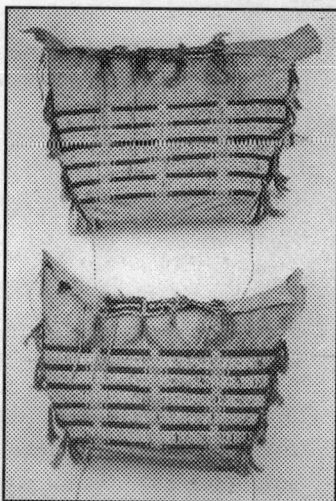

Miscellaneous, possible bags, Cheyenne (pair); late 19th century; soft buckskin pouches decorated with beadwork panels in dramatic colors; red-dyed horsehair attachments inserted in tin cones; the name "possible bag" was adopted by traders from a Lakota word meaning a container for any possible thing; provenance: from an old Missouri collection; $11,000–$11,500/set. Courtesy of Canfield Gallery. Photo by Robert Reno.

and back, the openwork section below with a pair of crosses in blue and (faded) yellow porcupine quillwork against a pale red ground, the hide fringe twisted; 39½ inches long; very good condition; $2,875–$3,450.

Cheyenne, possible bags (pair): soft buckskin pouches decorated with beadwork panels in dramatic colors; red-dyed horsehair attachments inserted in tin cones; the name "possible bag" was adopted by traders from a Lakota word meaning a container for any possible thing; provenance: from an old Missouri collection; late 19th century; $11,000–$11,500/set.

Cheyenne, pouch: rare buffalo hide "peace medal" pouch with circular green and white beadwork; ca. 1880; 4 x 3½ inches; very good condition; $70–$115.

Cheyenne, pouch: rare rectangular rawhide pouch with bead and quill decoration and tin cones; ca. 1800; 7 x 5 inches; very good condition; $85–$115.

CHIPPEWA

Chippewa, bandolier bag: beaded floral design with bird in gold, pink, red, green, blue, and black on translucent bead background, blue and green fringe with wool tassels; 46 inches overall length; very good condition; $1,000–$1,400.

Chippewa, bandolier bag: floral design in pink, red, green, blue, yellow, and black on white beaded background, trimmed in pony beads and wool tassels; 48 inches overall length; very good condition; $650–$850.

Chippewa, shield: Bear Society shield by Alfred Sky; very good condition; $350–$460.

Chippewa, two bandolier bags: beaded floral designs in green, blue, red, pink, yellow, and brown on white beaded background; 35 inches x 38 inches overall; good condition; $1,000–$1,400 each.

COMANCHE

Comanche, cradleboard (doll size): beaded deerskin on painted wooden frame, bound by buckskin strings; homemade cloth doll included; the picket-top vertical boards are loose; sinew-sewn lazy stitching, traces of yellow paint; 24 inches long; good condition; $260–$350.

CREE

Cree, bag: rectangular fringed Plains Cree hide bag with beaded floral designs; ca. 1920; 14 x 7 inches; very good condition; $125–$150.

Cree, pouch: small moose-hide pouch with a beaded star on one side and a flower on the other; ca. 1920; 3 x 3 inches; very good condition; $25–$35.

CROW

Crow, buffalo robe: painted robe, native tanned multicolored depictions on a subtle yellow pigment field of exploits such as hunting bear and buffalo and a variety of battles; details from scenes include dancer wearing otter-skin turban with roach and German silver ornamentation, wounded warrior with scalp locks, split-horn warbonnets, and two riders attacking a Crow warrior on foot; 56 x 79 inches; very good condition; $7,200–$8,100.

Crow, knife case: choice hide case with sinew-sewn geometric beaded designs; 9 x 3 inches; very good condition; $210–$250.

Crow, parfleche: rectangular rawhide container with fringe and with red and green painted designs; 13 x 12 inches; very good condition; $240–$350.

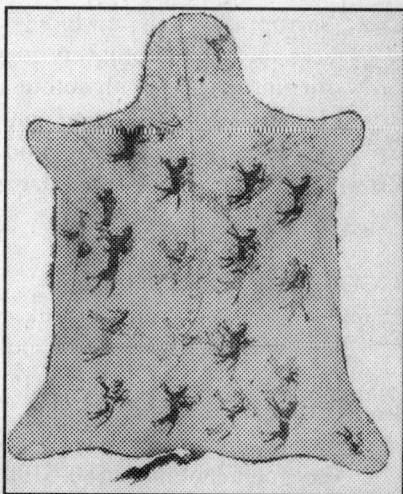

Leather, Crow, buffalo robe; painted robe, native tanned multicolored depictions on a subtle yellow pigment field of exploits such as hunting bear and buffalo and a variety of battles; details from scenes include dancer wearing otter-skin turban with roach and German silver ornamentation, wounded warrior with scalp locks, split-horn warbonnets, and two riders attacking a Crow warrior on foot; 56 x 79 inches; $7,200–$8,100. Courtesy Robert W. Skinner, Inc., Bolton/Boston, Massachusetts.

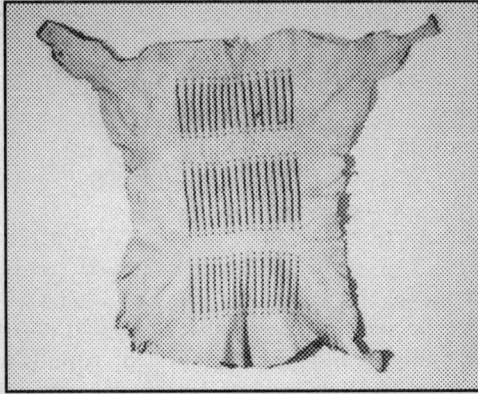

Leather, Crow, puberty robe; calfskin, beaded in strips of cobalt, greasy yellow, translucent red and white; ca. 1890–1910; 48 inches high x 37 inches wide; very good condition; $550–$750. Courtesy of Willis Henry Auctions, Inc.

Crow, parfleches (pair): matched pair of blue-outlined elk-hide parfleche cases; ca. 1880; 28 x 12 inches; very good condition; $800–$1,150 each.

Crow, pouch: rare hide medicine pouch with geometric beaded design; ca. 1880; 3 x 2½ inches; very good condition; $150–$175.

Crow, puberty robe: calfskin, beaded in strips of cobalt, greasy yellow, translucent red, and white; ca. 1890–1910; 48 inches high x 37 inches wide; very good condition; $550–$750.

Crow, stirrup: one only; rawhide over wood with beading, brass tacks, and trade cloth; very good condition; $200–$400.

Crow, stirrups: rawhide with cutout and beaded designs over wood form; ca. 1870s; very good condition; $800–$1,000.

Crow, tepee bag; ca. 1880; very good condition; $775–$875.

Crow/Ute, mirror bag: beaded bag; ca. 1860; very good condition; $7,500–$8,625.

IROQUOIS

Iroquois, bag: green, yellow, pink, blue, and red floral design in seed beads, and attached handle trimmed in seed beads; 19th century; 12 inches to handle; very good condition; $90–$110.

Iroquois, bag: green, yellow, pink, blue, and red floral design in seed beads on black velvet; 19th century; 15½ inches to handle; very good condition; $80–$100.

Iroquois, purse: beaded polychrome flowers and date "1929"; 3¾ inches long; very good condition; $100–$175.

Iroquois, purse: beaded polychrome flowers, birds; 6 inches long; very good condition; $100–$175.

Iroquois, two bags: seed beading in blue, red, green, and yellow on black with red trim; 6 inches; very good condition; $200–$300 each.

Iroquois, two bags: floral designs front and back with red trade cloth edging; red, green, white, pink, and yellow beading; 19th century; 7 inches x 4½ inches; very good condition; $100–$180 each.

Iroquois, two purses: one with intricate beading, unusual shape, and beaded dangles; the other with large beaded dangles and metal rickrack; 8 inches; very good condition; $100–$200 each.

KUTENAI

Kutenai, parfleche: choice rawhide case with long fringe and painted designs; ca. 1985; 12 x 11 inches; very good condition; $150–$200.

LAKOTA

Lakota Sioux, pipe bag: an elaborately decorated beaded hide tobacco bag with effigy of an equestrian warrior in beadwork embroidery on front and back; early 1900s; $9,000.

MANDAN

Mandan, pouch: unusual medicine pouch with pony bead decoration; ca. 1870; 4 x 4 inches; very good condition; $85–$115.

NEZ PERCE

Nez Perce, bag: large classic rectangular twined corn-husk bag with different geometric designs on each side; ca. 1890; 18 x 12 inches; very good condition; $315–$375.

Nez Perce, bag: classic rectangular twined corn-husk bag with crisp geometric designs; ca. 1900; 18 x 15 inches; very good condition; $800–$1,050.

Nez Perce, bag: rare small twined corn-husk belt pouch with geometric designs; ca. 1890; 3 x 3¼ inches; very good condition; $85–$110.

Nez Perce, corn-husk bag: stepped pyramid designs with clouds, rose, greens, purples, with three rows of triangles and bars on reverse side; 19½ x 20 inches; very good condition; $600–$800.

Nez Perce, parfleche: choice rectangular rawhide container with long fringe and painted decoration; ca. 1985; 16 x 8 inches; very good condition; $110–$185.

Nez Perce, pipe bag: body woven in Germantown yarn in geometric pattern in green, red, yellow, black, and burgundy, with a series of tin buttons on both sides; length 20 inches plus 6-inch fringe; fair condition; $175–$400.

Nez Perce, pouch: old fold-over corn-husk belt pouch with subtle geometric designs; ca. 1890; 5 x 5 inches; very good condition; $110–$150.

Nez Perce, pouch: beaded; ca. 1880; 7 x 6 inches; very good condition; $110–$175.

Nez Perce, sheath: large hide knife case with beaded floral design, containing an old Sheffield knife; ca. 1920; very good condition; $185–$230.

Nez Perce, three corn-husk bags: one with arrow and diamond designs, one with arrowhead designs, one with interlocking diamond design; 7½ to 13 inches long, 7¼ to 10 inches wide; good condition; $825–$1,025/set.

NORTHERN PLAINS

Northern Plains, bridles: sinew-sewn, beads on deerskin; poor/fair condition (extremely dry and brittle); $25–$45.

Northern Plains, knife sheath: fully beaded with white background and geometric designs in green, yellow, red, and cobalt on painted parfleche; 15 inches long; very good condition; $150–$200.

Northern Plains, medicine pouch: quillwork in red, yellow, and turquoise, fully beaded in salmon, cobalt, and red with hawk-bells; 11 inches long; very good condition; $400–$600.

Northern Plains, moccasins: fully beaded in light blue, green, white, translucent gold, greasy yellow, cobalt, and translucent red beads with painted parfleche soles; 9½ inches long; very good condition; $400–$600.

Northern Plains, pair of possible bags: early 1900s; combining quillwork embroidery and beadwork; $7,800.

Leather, Northern Plains, pair of possible bags; early 1900s; combining quillwork embroidery and beadwork; $7,800. Courtesy of Canfield Gallery. Photo by Robert Reno.

Northern Plains, parfleches, three; three-dimensional rawhide containers; ca. 1875; very good condition; $1,150–$3,500/group.

Northern Plains/Plateau, shirt: beaded and fringed hide shirt, decorated on the sleeves and on the front and back with four elongated panels containing geometric devices in green, translucent blue, red, and pink beadwork on a white ground, a circular medallion on the front decorated with four tiny crosses in black, white, translucent red, and clear glass beads on a translucent green and white ground; ermine pelts and trade cloth suspensions on the sleeves; 27 inches long; very good condition; $4,600–$5,700.

Northern Plains, pouch for tobacco: rawhide with blue, red, yellow, and white beading; 20 inches long plus fringe; very good condition; $1,000–$1,500.

Northern Plains, pouch: geometric beaded medicine pouch; ca. 1890; 4½ inches; very good condition; $70–$90.

Northern Plains, pouch: beaded peace medal pouch; ca. 1906; 4 inches diameter; very good condition; $50–$110.

Northern Plains, quirt: wooden handle with red paint and brass tack decoration, some beadwork on straps; 31 inches long; very good condition; $700–$900.

Northern Plains, two pipe bags: fully beaded in white background and multicolored geometrics and fully quilled slats; 32 and 36 inches long; very good condition; $650–$850.

NORTHERN PLATEAU

Northern Plateau, belt: sinew-sewn and decorated with red and white centers and yellow beads in connected square designs on a blue beaded background; 43 inches long and 1¾ inches wide; very good condition; $115–$150.

Northern Plateau, parfleche: red, dark blue, and yellow; older; 20 x 28 inches; very good condition; $150–$225.

NORTHWEST COAST

Northwest Coast, gloves: brown caribou fur, bound in cotton binding; ca. 1900–1920; 16 inches long; very good condition; $30–$50.

Northwest Coast, hand drum: polychromed; hide stretched and nailed to bentwood frame, interior decorated with stylized human face in red and black; provenance: estate of Dr. Samuel W. Fernberger, collected in Alaska prior to 1910; 11¼ inches diameter; very good condition; $250–$400.

Northwest Coast, mask: highly unusual hide-covered mask with hair, paint, and abalone inlay; 10 x 7 inches; very good condition; $230–$350.

Northwest Coast/Salish, drum: ca. 1890; very good condition; $6,300–$7,500.

PEYOTE

Peyote, fan: dyed feather fan with beaded handle and twisted fringe; 14 inches; very good condition; $110–$175.

PLAINS

Plains, awl case and awl: native tanned hide with multicolored bead decoration and two brass beads; includes a metal awl with deer-antler handle; 16 inches long including fringe; very good condition; $140–$200.

Plains, awl case: fully beaded in light blue, green, greasy yellow, translucent salmon, and cobalt on painted parfleche with horsehair suspensions; 24 inches long; very good condition; $400–$600.

Plains, bag: otter-skin bag, possibly an arrow quiver, with quill decoration over old painted parfleche; gold and red ribbon decoration with an aluminum mirror and one tin cone with a red feather; 33 inches long; very good condition; $750–$950.

Plains, bag: buckskin, beaded and fringed; very good condition; $120–$220.

Plains, bag: elk leg dewclaw bag with hair on and buckskin fringe; old; very good condition; $100–$300.

Plains, belt: fully beaded; light blue field with floral and geometric designs in green, brown, red, pink, and dark blue; sinew-sewn; beads missing in several places; 28 inches overall; good condition; $15–$20.

Plains, belt: men's; fully beaded; blue, white, and red diagonal lazy-stitched designs; line of ¼-inch brass spots runs down the center; metal buckle; 41 inches overall; good condition; $30–$45.

Plains, belt: leather backed with geometric designs in multicolored beads, cobalt and tassel ties with metal beads; 44 inches long; good condition; $125–$175.

Plains, belt pouch: military leather, beaded in cobalt, yellow, blue, green, red, black, and pink on a background of white, with brass closure and twisted fringe; 6 inches overall; very good condition; $900–$1,300.

Plains (Cheyenne or Sioux), bag: soft leather with diamond motif in green, blue, and yellow beading on a beaded white background; side panels beaded in linear designs with tin cone and orange horsehair; 12 inches wide x 18 inches long; good condition; $800–$1,000.

Plains, deerskin panel: decorated with band of quilled fringe, tipped with hawkbells and dyed horsehair tassels; edged with ½-inch band of blue, white, red, and green beadwork and four rows of red quillwork; sinew-sewn; 7 x 23 inches; very good condition; $35–$65.

Plains, deerskin: panel decorated with beads, porcupine quillwork, and feathers; sinew-sewn; 9 x 15 inches; very good condition; $35–$60.

Plains, drum: painted with designs of birds, animals, and snakes, and marked "Pawnee Bill's Tom Tom"; 4 x 13 inches; very good condition; $70–$90.

Plains, drum: painted hand-held buffalo medicine drum with painted designs in red and black and buffalo horns on edge; old; 16 inches; very good condition; $1,250–$3,250.

Plains, drum: round hand drum with faded paint decoration; ca. 1890; 10 x 2 inches; good condition; $100–$150.

Plains, drum: round hide-covered hand drum and stick; drum has a painted eagle; ca. 1965; 15 x 3 inches; very good condition; $45–$80.

Plains, elk-antler quirt: brass tack decoration; early; 17 inches long; very good condition; $975–$1,275.

Plains, five bags: beaded in geometric motifs with drawstring closures; two with fringe; 3 to 6 inches; very good condition; $230–$290 each.

Plains, flat bag: fully beaded in hourglass geometrics in green, red, cobalt, yellow, salmon, and black with light blue background; 12 inches long; very good condition; $250–$350.

Plains, flat bag: fully beaded, rounded bottom, with four winds symbol in salmon and light blue background, with beaded fringe suspensions; 16 inches overall; very good condition; $250–$350.

Plains, gloves: pair, buckskin, beaded in red horse design; very good condition; $100–$200.

Plains, knife case and knife: beaded case, fine old handmade knife; ca. 1920; 10 x 3½ inches; very good condition; $85–$150.

Plains, knife sheath: hide with beaded decoration in red and blue with greasy yellow background and hide fringe; 8 inches long; very good condition; $400–$600.

Plains, mirror knife sheath: blue, green, orange, and white beadwork on hide; very good condition; $50–$70.

Plains, moccasins and blanket strip: moccasins are hard-soled; both very good condition; $350–$460.

Plains, net bag: rare, rawhide with deerskin rim; decorated with light beadwork; pink and yellow beads; 7 inches overall; good condition; $15–$20.

Plains or Plateau, pouch bag: with three loom-beaded tabs; old; very good condition; $100–$250.

Plains, parfleche: rectangular folded rawhide container with painted designs; ca. 1900; 25 x 11 inches; very good condition; $350–$460.

Plains, parfleche: rectangular rawhide box with geometric painted designs; ca. 1885; 6 x 3½ inches; very good condition; $125–$160.

Plains, pipe bag: beaded vertical design in green, light blue, black, and gold; sinew-sewn; quilled slats in white, red, and purple; hide fringe and attached beaded drop with tin cones and horsehair; 27 inches overall; very good condition; $500–$700.

Plains, pipe bag: geometric designs on blue background in white, red, green, and metallic; quilled slats, fringed; 34 inches long; very good condition; $450–$600.

Plains, pipe bag: supple, finely beaded deerskin with many tin cones and horsehair drops, pony-beaded drop panel, long fringe; beaded in translucent green, cobalt, light blue, light rose, greasy yellow, and white; ex-collection of the Minnesota Museum; 39 inches long; excellent condition; $9,000–$10,000.

Plains, pipe bag: beaded, hide; stitched on both sides and along edges with sinew-sewn beaded decoration on a yellow and red painted hide body, four forked tabs at opening, remnant twisted fringe; bead colors are sky blue, white, black, mustard and

Leather, Plains pipe bags, from left to right: Plains pipe bag, geometric designs on blue background in white, red, green, and metallic, quilled slats, fringed, 34 inches long, very good condition, $450–$600; Plains pipe bag, 19th-century quillwork bag with quilled slats, lacks fringe, early form, 25 inches long, good condition; Plains pipe bag, geometric designs in cobalt, red, orange, light blue, and green on white, quilled slats, fringe, 43 inches long. Courtesy of Willis Henry Auctions, Inc.

Leather, pipe bags, left to right: Plains pipe bag, supple, finely beaded deerskin with many tin cones and horsehair drops, pony-beaded drop panel, long fringe, beaded in translucent green, cobalt, light blue, light rose, greasy yellow, and white, ex-collection of the Minnesota Museum, 39 inches long, excellent condition, $9,000–$10,000; Plateau pipe bag, 19th century, with fingered top, beaded floral and bird motifs in light blue, cobalt, green, red, and white, fringed, 31½ inches long, very good condition, $900–$1,200. Courtesy of Willis Henry Auctions, Inc.

clear green, red, and sapphire blue; body length 12 inches; very good condition; $575–$800.

Plains, possible bag: beaded and quilled, trimmed with tin cones and red horsehair suspensions; 36 x 26 inches; very good condition; $2,000–$2,300.

Plains, pouch: fully beaded in floral geometrics of black, light blue, translucent salmon, light brown, greasy yellow, and cobalt on a white background; 7 inches; very good condition; $125–$175.

Plains, pouch: beaded, white with blue, red, and green; tin cone dangles on beaded strips; reservation period; 4½ x 5 inches plus dangles; good condition; $600–$700.

Plains, pouch: beaded hide; painted overall in yellow ocher, bead-edged tab mouth, tin-cone-decorated suspensions on body and at bottom; bead colors are white, clear gold, white-heart reds, cobalt, and pea green; 10¾ inches long; very good condition; $320–$375.

Plains, pouch: beaded hide, decorated with paint, beads, and tin cone suspensions; brass button closure; 17½ inches long; very good condition; $250–$320.

Plains, pouches (five); bead- and quill-decorated hide; most fringed; tribes represented include Shoshone, Santee Sioux, and Cheyenne; very good condition; $320–$430 each.

Plains, pouches (six): beaded hide pouches, including three "strike-a-lights" trimmed with tin cones and three small oval pouches; provenance: collected by Henry H. Wright, second lieutenant, 9th Cavalry, December 12, 1872, on frontier duty, commander of detachment of Companies C and E, and Navajo Indian scouts; 4¼ to 5½ inches long; very good condition, $1,750–$2,100/set.

Plains, quirts, miscellaneous group: Cheyenne, wooden tacked handle, ca. 1870, very good condition, $2,900–$3,450; Northern Plains, ca. 1880, very good condition, $850–$950; Crow, with tacked decoration, ca. 1870, very good condition; $2,100–$2,300.

Plains, tobacco bag: beaded with blue, white, yellow, and red beadwork points, decorated with tin cones and feathers; 6½ x 14 inches; very good condition (fairly brittle); $35–$60.

Plains, tobacco bag: beaded with blue, white, yellow, and red beadwork points, decorated with tin cones and feathers; fairly brittle; 6½ x 14 inches; very good condition; $35–$60.

Plains, two knife sheaths: with sinew beadwork, small; one beaded in green, cobalt, red, and yellow, with beaded drop; other has green and white beadwork; 19th century; very good condition; $200–$300/set.

Plains, warbonnet case: painted rawhide; late; 8 x 24 inches; very good condition; $100–$200.

PLATEAU

Plateau, bag: flat bag with floral design with small beads; early; 7 x 9 inches; very good condition; $150–$300.

Plateau, beaded bag: floral motif with birds, blue, red, black, mauve, green, and light blue on white background; 13 inches high x 11 inches wide, excellent condition; $1,250–$1,500.

Plateau, beaded bag: floral motif in red, light blue, and blue on white background; 11 inches high x 9½ inches wide; excellent condition; $700–$900.

Plateau, beaded bag: flowers in cobalt, yellow, green, and brown on white background; 13 inches high x 11½ inches wide; excellent condition; $450–$600.

Leather, Plateau, beaded pieces—from left to right: Plateau beaded bag, flowers cobalt, yellow, green, and brown on white background, 13 inches high x 11½ inches wide, excellent condition, $450–$600; Plateau beaded bag, floral motif with birds, blue, red, black, mauve, green, and light blue on white background, 13 inches high x 11 inches wide, excellent condition, $1,250–$1,500; Plateau beaded bag, floral motif, red, light blue, and blue on white background, 11 inches high x 9½ inches wide, excellent condition, $700–$900. Courtesy of Willis Henry Auctions, Inc.

Plateau, belt: black leather with goldenrod and red beading; 36 inches long; very good condition; $20–$50.

Plateau, gauntlets: decoration of floral cut beads in light blue, white, greasy yellow, salmon, and cobalt; 12½ inches long; very good condition; $50–$100.

Plateau, pipe bag: fringed, with fingered top, beaded floral and bird motifs in light blue, cobalt, green, red, and white; 31½ inches long; very good condition; $900–$1,200.

Plateau, two bags: geometric designs in green, yellow, light blue, cobalt, and translucent beads on native tanned hide; 2¾ x 3 inches and 4½ x 3¼ inches; very good condition; $80–$110 each.

Plateau, two pairs of gauntlets: one with beaded geometric design, and the other with silk thread designs on hide; 12 and 13 inches long; excellent condition; $150–$225 each.

Plateau, possibles bag: beaded deerskin, 5½-inch wide sinew-sewn beaded panel, geometric design in blue, white, red, and pink on a green field; matching design on flap; black cut-glass beadwork loop trim; further decorated with yellow horsehair tassels in tin cone bells; 10 x 14 inches; good condition; $800–$1,050.

POTAWATOMI

Potawatomi, bag: fine little net beaded hide "puzzle" pouch; ca. 1920; 5 x 3 inches; very good condition; $15–$20.

Potawatomi or Tlingit, gun scabbard: open multicolored appliqué beadwork on red trade cloth with two double-decorated tabs at the bottom, made from native tanned hide; mid to late 19th century; very good condition; $550–$750.

PUEBLO

Pueblo, belt: full-length with beaded border and nickel conchas; very old and rather fragile; framed; very good condition; $375–$475.

SAN FELIPE

San Felipe, shield: ca. 1860; very good condition; $10,950–$11,500.

SANTEE SIOUX

Santee Sioux, bag: beaded and fringed with floral design; ca. 1900; 8 x 8 inches; very good condition; $100–$250.

Santee Sioux, pipe bag: three-sided buckskin, Santee designs; 8 inches; very good condition; $225–$325.

Santee Sioux, pouch: round hide pouch with Santee Sioux stylized floral beadwork; ca. 1920; 8 x 4 inches; very good condition; $65–$85.

SARCEE PLAINS

Sarcee Plains, shoulder bag: beaded; ca. 1860; very good condition; $4,300–$4,600.

SHOSHONE

Shoshone, parfleche: ca. 1880; 13 x 28 inches; very good condition; $4,600–$5,750.

Shoshone, pipe bag: well-beaded with long fringe, commercial hide; 29 inches; very good condition; $600–$700.

SIOUX

Eastern Sioux, bag: beaded buckskin telescope bag with old brass military telescope; very good condition; $300–$400.

Leather, Sioux, possible bag; late 19th century; made of tanned hide; its end panels and top flap decorated with bands of sinew-sewn bead embroidery in geometric designs; a panel of stripes across the face of the bag in porcupine quill embroidery in red and yellow; ornamental details include feathers and tassels of yellow horsehair in tin cones; $4,500. Courtesy of Canfield Gallery. Photo by Robert Reno.

Sioux, possible bag: made of tanned hide, its end panels and top flap decorated with bands of sinew-sewn bead embroidery in geometric designs; a panel of stripes across the face of the bag in porcupine quill embroidery in red and yellow; ornamental details include feathers and tassels of yellow horsehair in tin cones; late 19th century; $4,500.

Sioux, awl case: beaded with flap; 6½ inches; very good condition; $90–$165.

Sioux, bag: beaded buckskin bag; ca. 1900; 3½ x 5 inches; very good condition; $75–$135.

Sioux, bag: buckskin with horse and rider on front; 7 x 8 inches; very good condition; $400–$600.

Sioux, belt bag: beaded; old; 3 x 4 inches; very good condition; $300–$400.

Sioux, bow case and quiver: buckskin with porcupine quill trim and fringe; ca. 1890; 38 x 6 inches; very good condition; $230–$275.

Sioux, box: rawhide with painted parfleche designs and good color; ca. turn of the century; 6 x 6 x 12 inches; very good condition; $375–$575.

Sioux, case: beaded in stepped pyramid design in greasy yellow, blue, red, and cobalt, and edged in pink; containing bone-handled knife and fork; 7 x 2¼ inches; very good condition; $250–$350.

Sioux, drum: rawhide hand-held drum, cover with red and blue circle design; very good condition; $100–$300.

Sioux, hatband: quilled on buckskin; old; very good condition; $100–$200.

Sioux, knife case: choice, fully beaded hide with classic sinew-sewn geometric designs; 7½ x 7½ inches; very good condition; $175–$230.

Sioux, knife case: painted rawhide with lightning design; very good condition; $40–$50.

Sioux, knife sheath: beaded in geometric designs and cross in cobalt, red, yellow, and green; sinew-sewn with tin cones, and beaded drop with tin cones and dyed horsehair; 19 inches overall; very good condition; $650–$850.

Sioux, knife sheath and dagger: sheath beaded with red, blue, and green beads on white ground, waistband of tin cone dangles, 8 inches; the bone-handled dagger is made from an old file and has a short stag grip, 10½ inches overall length; ca. 1850–1860; very good condition; $850–$1,150.

Sioux or Blackfoot, awl case: beaded and colorful; ca. 1870; very good condition; $750–$920.

Sioux, paint pouch: beaded bar design in red, pink, and blue on white ground; the original catalog label reads "Paint Pouch taken from Crazy Horse, Pine Ridge Reservation, South Dakota, 1878 from D.C. Blanchard," an Episcopal missionary; 10½ inches long (without fringe) x 3¼ inches wide; very good condition; $2,800–$3,500.

Sioux, parfleche: rare rectangular lidded rawhide box with painted black-outline geometric designs; ca. 1890; 18 x 10 inches; very good condition; $575–$800.

Sioux, parfleche: rectangular folded rawhide case with geometric painted designs; ca. 1890; 25 x 10 inches; very good condition; $230–$350.

Sioux, parfleche: rectangular rawhide container with geometric painted designs in red, green, blue, and yellow; ca. 1890; very good condition; $400–$575.

Sioux, parfleches (pair): ca. 1875; 12 x 22 inches; very good condition; $3,500–$4,600 pair.

Sioux, pipe bag: geometric designs in light blue, cobalt, greasy yellow, and white-heart red with white background on painted yellow hide; ca. 1880, with history inside the bag; 21 inches overall; very good condition; $600–$800.

Sioux, pipe bag: quilled front and reverse in geometric designs in red, yellow, and lavender; quilled slats in turquoise, red, and white; fringed beaded edge in gold, blue, and white; sinew-sewn with quilled drops with tin cones; 25 inches overall; $650–$850.

Sioux, pipe bag: rawhide, beaded in two shades of blue and red on white, with red, green, and orange quillwork; 26 inches plus fringe; good condition; $1,100–$3,000.

Sioux, pipe bag: porcupine quill decoration in yellow, purple, red, and white, with tin cones and red feathers and beaded side panel, hide painted yellow, quilled drop with tin cones; 27 inches long; very good condition; $1,600–$2,000.

Sioux, pipe bag: background in beaded white with red and white quilled strips and twisted fringe, yellow painted hide; 35 inches long; very good condition; $1,800–$2,200.

Sioux, pipe bag: beaded buckskin with quilled slats, long fringe, good colors and beads; early 1890s; very good condition; $1,500–$2,900.

Sioux, pipe bag: beaded and fringed; stitched in dark blue, lime green, greasy yellow, and white-heart red on a white beaded ground with geometric motifs on both sides, beaded linear pattern at mouth and down both sides; sinew-sewn; traces of green paint; 22½ inches long (excluding fringe); good/very good condition (minor fringe loss); $800–$1,100.

Sioux, pipe bag: hide, beaded and fringed, with small beaded and fringed knife sheath on the front; bag stitched on both sides and along edges with geometric devices against a white ground; bead colors are apple green, bright blue, yellow, and white-heart reds; the lower dyed quill-wrapped hide openwork in a butterfly motif, hide fringe, dyed red horsehair, and tin cone suspensions; quill-wrapped hide suspension from bead-edged mouth; sinew-sewn; 23¼ inches long (excluding fringe); very good condition; $1,750–$2,300.

Sioux, pipe bag: hide, quilled and fringed, decorated on the front and back with bright red quillwork panels containing geometric motifs in purple, yellow, and (faded) green, the short openwork section below wrapped in orange-red dyed quill-work and decorated with a row of small tin cones and red feather suspensions; remains of ocher, beaded trim along the sides; 26½ inches long; very good condition; $2,300–$2,375.

Sioux, pipe bag: quillwork is red and yellow; beaded buckskin; background is white with green triangles trimmed in blue, and blue crosses trimmed in red; ca. 1885; 33 inches long; very good condition; $2,900–$3,500.

Sioux, pipe bag: hide, beaded and fringed, stitched on the front and back with white beaded panels containing angular and arrow-feather motifs in green, light and dark blue, yellow, translucent red, and metallic beadwork, the lower openwork section bound in red, purple, and cream-colored porcupine quillwork (varnished?); collected by Dr. Edgar I. Bradley at the Fort Belknap Indian Reservation, Montana; 42 inches long; very good condition; $1,750–$2,075.

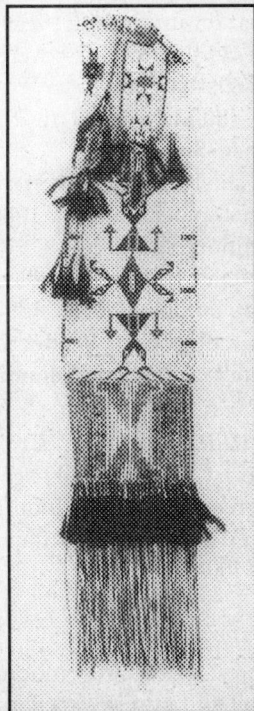

Leather, Sioux, pipe bag; beaded and fringed hide pipe bag; with small beaded and fringed knife sheath on the front, bag stitched on both sides and along edges with geometric devices against a white ground; bead colors are apple green, bright blue, yellow, and white-heart reds; the lower dyed quill-wrapped hide openwork in a butterfly motif, hide fringe, dyed red horsehair, and tin cone suspensions; quill-wrapped hide suspension from bead-edged mouth; sinew-sewn; length excluding fringe 23¼ inches; $2,000–$2,500. Courtesy Robert W. Skinner, Inc., Bolton/Boston, Massachusetts.

Sioux, pipe bag: quilled slats and fringe, buckskin body, beaded panels; early 20th century; very good condition; $1,000–$2,000.

Sioux, purse: German silver top; green, cobalt, greasy yellow, and white-heart red on a white background; very good condition; $200–$300.

Sioux, pouch: beaded in geometric designs and crosses of blue, red, yellow, and green on a white background; fringed; sinew-sewn; 31 inches overall; excellent condition; $2,400–$3,000.

Sioux, pouch: round beaded hide pouch with other bead suspensions; ca. 1920; 9 x 3 inches; very good condition; $30–$55.

Sioux, quirt: beaded, wood; good condition; $475–$675.

Sioux, rattle: painted, rawhide; old; very good condition; $100–$200.

Sioux, rifle case: beaded on hide in geometric designs with crosses and beaded initial, in blue, red, green, and yellow on a background of white; sinew-sewn; fringed; beaded on front and reverse; signed "C. J. Fry"; 48 inches long; $3,000–$3,500.

Sioux, saddle: rawhide, with stirrups, tree of elk horn and wood covered with rawhide; very good condition; $900–$1,300.

Sioux, saddle: rawhide-covered with stirrups, rare; good condition; $800–$1,200.

Sioux, shield: painted rawhide; 10 inches; very good condition; $40–$50.

Sioux, shield: rawhide, contemporary, with painted decoration and turkey feathers; ca. 1980; 16 inches diameter; very good condition; $30–$55.

Sioux, tepee bag: large; quilled bar design with beaded ends and flap, on buffalo hide; ca. 1880; very good condition; $3,000–$4,000.

Sioux, wall pocket: beaded buckskin; ca. turn of the century; 16 inches; very good condition; $375–$475.

SOUTHERN CHEYENNE

Southern Cheyenne, tail bag: beaded in white-heart red, translucent green and yellow, blue, and light blue on a white background; red ocher-painted flap; 9½ inches long; excellent condition; $400–$600.

SOUTHWEST

Southwest, bridle: woven horsehair bridle in natural white with iron bit and tassels; excellent condition; $100–$200.

Southwest, drum: cottonwood with sunburst design, painted stretched; 23 inches diameter; very good condition; $150–$200.

Southwest, parfleche: cottonwood with floral and sunburst design, painted stretched; 12 inches diameter; very good condition; $125–$175.

TLINGIT

Tlingit, bag: sealskin bag with fur and with beaded flowers; ca. 1920; 10 x 6 inches; very good condition; $35–$60.

UTE

Ute, awl case: beaded with three beaded thongs; ca. 1870; 21 inches long; very good condition; $400–$500.

Ute, bag: strike-a-light bag with yellow background and blue and white geometric designs and tin cone dangles; old; very good condition; $650–$750.

Ute, rifle scabbard: hide, beaded and fringed, decorated on the butt and point with light blue beaded panels of terraced triangle and rectangle decoration in yellow, blue, and translucent red and green; remains of red trade cloth and purple quilled trim, a leather shoulder strap, cloth bundle, and small animal's horn attached; 49½ inches long; very good condition; $4,600–$5,200.

WASCO

Wasco, bag: rare net-beaded hide with openwork diamond beaded designs and white bead fringe; ca. 1860; 6 x 3 inches; very good condition; $65–$90.

Wasco, sally bag: rare, with "water bug" designs; ca. 1840; 5 x 5½ inches; very good condition; $175–$230.

WOODLANDS

Woodlands, bag: velvet bag with cut-glass beads in floral and American flag design; old; 5 x 8 inches; very good condition; $75–$150.

Woodlands, gloves: pair, buckskin, beaded in floral design; very good condition; $80–$180.

Woodlands, pouch: white, blue, red, and green beadwork on front panel (6½ x 6½ inches), deer hide with thong draw, fringe at bottom; ca. 1950s; 15 inches long plus fringe; good condition; $185–$385.

Woodlands, purse: beaded snap purse with horse and "1908" in design; combination latch; old; very good condition; $125–$200.

YAKIMA

Yakima, bag: rectangular, floral beaded, with fringe; ca. 1975; 11 x 12 inches; very good condition; $80–$100.

Yakima, bag: fully beaded with old-time contour floral beadwork; 15 x 13 inches; very good condition; ca. 1910; $350–$575.

Yakima, bag: hide, rectangular, fringe and floral designs; ca. 1930; 9½ x 4 inches; very good condition; $60–$85.

Yakima, gauntlets: large high-top buckskin gauntlets with beaded elk and foliate motifs; ca. 1920; 14 x 9 inches; very good condition; $110–$300.

Yakima, parfleche: ca. 1890; 14 x 28 inches; very good condition; $4,600–$5,750.

Chapter Ten

Miscellaneous Categories

≈

Some collective pieces just never seem to fit into neat categories, so we lump them together—whether or not they are related—into a category entitled "miscellaneous." However, listing them as such does not mean these items are unimportant, nor are they the rare, one-of-a-kind items that most avid collectors only see once or twice in a lifetime.

We hope that we have at least touched upon most items collected by the Native American aficionado. If not, perhaps you'll find your favorite item, or at least an interesting piece of information, in this chapter.

Most tribes and characteristics of their work and culture have been covered in the other chapters of this book; however, there is certain information pertaining to miscellaneous items that I feel should be briefly mentioned.

The Blackfoot men's societies, for example, are called All-Friends Society. Of the old groups encompassed by the All-Friends Society, only the Horns and the Brave Dogs are still in existence. They are the policemen of the tribe, enforcing tribal law, as well as orders from the chief. Motokiks is the women's secret society. Four is their sacred number, and corresponds to the four directions (North, East, South, and West) and the four seasons.

I should also mention again here that the items that are considered ceremonial or sacred should not be in the hands of people uneducated about Native American traditions. Some museums and collectors have held items that tribal members consider to have special meaning for them. During the past decade, researchers and Native Americans have urged dealers and collectors to return sacred items to the tribes to whom they once belonged. They have declared, and rightly so, that digging in ancient burial sites is akin to grave robbing. Sadly, during the research for this new edition, I saw sacred masks and ceremonial bundles for sale in shops throughout the Southwest. It is my sincere hope that one day the Native American people of this country will have their sacred items returned to them and that those of us who have some knowledge of tribal history will encourage others to respect the tribal members' wishes.

Miscellaneous Items

AMULETS Certain tribes made amulets to hold the umbilical cords of newborns. The amulet was pinned to the cradleboard and the infant's clothing, to keep him or her safe. Lizard amulets, made from one of the toughest, most difficult creatures to kill, were used to protect boys; turtles for girls. The turtle, credited with the world's creation, symbolized life—thus guarded over girls, who would later in life bring new life to the tribe.

BREASTPLATES Early breastplates were made from dentalium shells, while later ones were made from bones. They were worn by men, women, and children in tribes west of the Rockies. Some were decorated with feathers, fetishes, pieces of colored cloth, or animal claws.

BUSTLES Bustles made of brightly colored feathers collected during the year were worn by "fancy dancers" during tribal ceremonies. The bustle, often made of eagle and hawk feathers dyed brilliant oranges and reds, was attached to the back of a dancer's outfit. Bustles are still used by dancers in today's intertribal ceremonials and meetings. They are more ornamental today than they were a century ago—and often are made from synthetic feathers rather than those of the endangered eagle.

CRADLEBOARDS Cradleboards were used by the working women to carry their babies. The mother was able to use her hands while the baby, wrapped in a soft cloth or hide and put into a moss bag, would sleep, lulled by his or her mother's warmth, closeness, and rhythmic movements.

When traveling, the strap on the back of the cradleboard was hooked over the saddle horn. The cradleboard could also be hung from the branch of a tree while a mother worked.

Early Blackfoot cradleboard frames were made of willow branches. Later examples were sawed out of a board in the desired shape. Once the frame was made, it was covered with buckskin and beaded. The baby was kept in a bag with a hood attached to it, which served as protection from the elements.

Some cradleboards were made with a lining of fur; other times shells were sewn on for the baby's amusement; some were made out of cloth. All have straps on the back from which to hang the cradleboard. Some tribes, such as the Mission Basket Maker tribes, made their cradleboards out of basketry materials. These cradleboards resembled their wooden and leather counterparts, though some may be slightly curved instead of flat (see Chapter Three for further information).

Almost all of the tribes of North America made some form of cradleboard. Each differed according to the materials available. Some were decorated with beadwork, some with quills, some with shells.

The Flatheads (Chinook, Salish, and some prehistoric tribes) used a cradleboard that forced the soft infantile head to become flattened on top. One painting of a woman with an infant in a cradleboard shows the infant strapped against a flat piece of bark. Against the infant's head is another piece of flat wood, which is attached to the foot end of the cradleboard with sinew. It appears that the mother could adjust the piece, which would flatten the child's head, making the piece tighter or looser as the child grew.

CALUMET (SACRED PIPE) (also see Pipes and Medicine Pipe) The American Indian always used the calumet, a sacred pipe, in important transactions. An age-old traditional ceremony, as graceful and meaningful as Japanese tea ceremonies, was held whenever the calumet was used.

The pipes were usually made of red, black, or white marble, their heads finely polished, and the quill, usually 2½ feet long, was made of a strong reed or cane and decorated with colorful feathers and locks of female hair.

The calumet is considered a symbol of peace and always respected as such. The Indian people believed strongly that if the pipe wasn't held in reverence, they would suffer great misfortune as a result.

The calumet of war was distinguished by red feathers. It was presented and smoked when its owners were trying to determine what the weather should be, what to plant or eat; it was used to strengthen peace, or to call for war.

As with other possessions, the calumet was decorated and designed by the craftspeople of the tribe. Carving and painting decorated the pipe, along with hair, quillwork, and feathers. Once trade beads, coins, and tinklers came into use, they, too, were used to decorate the pipes.

The Plains Indians (Sioux especially) used catlinite to make pipe bowls, while the Comanche and Shoshone tribes used a greenish material. The Iroquois used a brownish black soapstone, and the Pueblos developed pottery or clay pipes with reed stems.

EFFIGIES/DANCE STICKS Animal or human effigies were forms that the Indian tribes believed to *represent* the spiritual powers in which they believe. Effigies are not "idols" as some have believed, but instead are tangible representations of "God."

Effigies were used as hunting medicine (e.g., buffalo effigies for hunting the same) as well as for war or for curing illnesses. The effigies used for hunting could be as simple as a piece of stone shaped in the form of a buffalo or could be more elaborately carved to show details such as the buffalo's bulging eyes and protruding tongue.

War medicines/effigies vary greatly. They can be feathers used to adorn war shirts or headdresses, or carved human figures worn on necklaces, or war pipes decorated with human hair or feathers or carved with human figures or animals.

At victory dances, war effigies are used to reenact pivotal moments. One such dance stick (Hunkpapa) was sold in 1987 at the Willis Henry Auction in Dedham, Massachusetts, for a world-record amount. (Others like it are pictured in *Plains Indian Sculpture* by John C. Ewers.) Most dance sticks are now owned by museums.

Crow officials who participated in a ceremony called the Hot Dance (which the Hidatsa tribe introduced to the Crow in 1875) carried a stick carved in the shape of a crane. The crane's beak, long and slender, was partially open, and its neck decorated with a circlet of quill-decorated fringes which ended in tin cones and feathers.

Horse effigy batons used in dances were carved by Plains warriors in remembrance of horses lost in battle. They were approximately three feet long, painted or decorated with animal hair, and marked with triangles that distinguished the animal's battle wounds.

The warring tribes often made effigy clubs carved from wood, decorated or painted, and carried during victory dances. One such club made by the Hunkpapa Lakota tribe around 1890 is carved in the shape of a man's face. Feathers adorn the back of his head, and he appears to hold a studded shield.

Medicine effigies include carved wooden bowls, spoons, human figurals, and stomach kneaders. The effigies were carved with figures used to portray their strong medicine.

Feasts gave the Indians another occasion to carve effigy items such as spoons and bowls. Ceremonial, witchcraft, and courting effigies were also produced (e.g., the courting flutes).

Ceremonial effigies include the Mandan evil spirit, Mandan and Hidatsa corn ceremony effigies, the snake effigy of the Hidatsa rain ceremony, the Thunder ceremonial effigies of the nomadic tribes, and Sun Dance dolls of Crow, Shoshone, and Ute tribes.

MEDICINE AND PIPE BUNDLES AND THE SUN DANCE CEREMONY (see more information on medicine bundles and pipes in the item information listed in this chapter)

The Beaver Bundle ceremony is performed by women—and in the old days lasted a month or more as each society went through its particular version of the ceremony.

Often there would be a few medicine bags transferred during the ceremonies or some owners would open their bags to have a dance and give out tobacco. Beaver bundles were transferred and cherished like medicine pipe bundles. A man in the tribe would be designated as main beaver man. He and his wife (or wives, depending on the tribe's customs) would have learned the names of all the birds and animals held in the bundle, all the songs needed for ceremonies associated with the beaver bundle, and all the legends. Beaver men knew how the seasons changed and could predict the weather. They kept track of time and the changing moon with sticks kept in their bundles, and they were responsible for the Sun Dance and Holy Smoke ceremonies.

The Beaver Bundle Dance was last performed in 1967. Today the knowledge of the ceremony is almost lost.

The Sun Dance traditionally lasted approximately five days. People who participated in the ceremony pledged to go without food or water while they danced, prayed, and performed rituals that signified they gave part of themselves to "The One Above."

In the Blackfoot tribe, the medicine pipe bundle was owned by a man and wife; a child, the third owner, wore the special top-knot wrapping and fur headband that accompanied the bundle. Each time a bundle of this kind was opened, a ceremony was held with corresponding ceremonial songs.

The bundles came with a great deal of responsibility as they were sometimes passed from generation to generation. The owners had to take special care that nothing happened to the precious object and that the sacred ceremonies were followed carefully. If one family took over a sacred bundle from another, the family taking on the responsibility often gave up their best and most valued property (horses, cattle, money, etc.) to show their sincerity in taking on the responsibility.

The bundles were hung from tripods during the days when the families lived in tepees. When Indians began living in houses, bundles were hung by a nail on the outside of the house during the daytime and brought in again at night. Each time the bundle was moved, incense was lit and prayers said.

NATOAS BUNDLE Holy women wear a Natoas bonnet, considered sacred, during the Sun Dance. A rawhide band holds large plumes and feathers. Generally the Natoas is kept in a bundle and taken out only for ceremonies. Though there are very few bundles still held by Indians, there are, unfortunately, several that are held by museums or private collectors. Since these items are sacred, the American Indian people consider it sacrilegious when a Natoas bundle is opened up for display.

PIPES Effigy pipes were made by Plains Indians during the prehistoric era out of wood or catlinite. (Catlinite was most common.) They were carved or adorned with sculptured figures.

Stones were polished to a fine sheen with the tools available and were chosen for their ability to endure heat without cracking. Pipestone (called catlinite in honor of George Catlin) was found near the place known today as Pipestone, Minnesota.

Pipes took many different shapes and sizes—some with the smoking hole on an end, others with the hole in the middle. Most of the pipes we see today were made during the period from 1830 to 1910, with the majority of those being made in the 1880s. Examples of animal effigy pipes are available in finely carved and primitive styles.

The Plains Indians took the art a step further and carved portrait pipes. As early as 1829, pipes carved to portray an individual's likeness were found. The Plains Indians carved their own likenesses, as well as those of white men they admired, onto pipes.

One such pipe has a portrait of the civil chief of the Winnebagos cut into the front. The pipe was given to Caleb Atwater (a negotiator at Prairie du Chien in 1829) and forwarded to the president; the chief requested that the president put it under his looking glass.

Most medicine pipes are held in museums or private collections; the few that are still owned by the tribes are relied upon to conquer illness or to give their people strength and are considered sacred objects.

ROACHES   Native Americans often wore a head decoration called a *roach* during special occasions. The roach, made of animal hair, trailed from the front of the head down the back, standing up straight like a skunk's stripe. Sometimes roaches were dyed a bright color. They were worn by the eastern tribes and sometimes by the Plateau and Plains tribes.

TWINED BAGS   Women in Great Lakes tribes (as well as Pacific Coast tribes) made bags out of twine and used them for storage and for carrying various items. Fibers used to make the bags were from the bark of a basswood tree and brown buffalo hair. The sacred thunderbird and great cat were legendary figures used as motifs on such bags.

PRICES

Ankle bells: large pair with five 2½-inch bells to the side; very good condition; $15–$25.

Amulet, Tlingit: old and interestingly carved fossil ivory or bone shaman's amulet with abalone inlay; ca. 1840; 2½ inches x 1 inch; very good condition; $275–$300.

Bag, beaded: unusual pony-beaded bag with beaded drops; ca. 1900; 9 x 3 inches; $50–$75.

Bag front, Yakima: large, rectangular beaded bag front with stylized floral beadwork; ca. 1920; 13 x 13 inches; very good condition; $200–$225.

Bag, Iroquois: fancy beaded and sequined cloth bag; decorated on both sides with lavender, clear dark red, sky blue, pony trader blue, green, yellow, orange, clear, and white beads in floral and foliate designs; ca. 1900; 7¼ inches long x 7½ inches wide; very good condition; $80–$120.

Bag, Iroquois: rounded beaded velvet bag with beaded floral design on both sides; ca. 1880; 7 x 6 inches; very good condition; $50–$75.

Bag, Nez Perce: old beaded cloth, decorated with clear dark green, cobalt blue, and waxy yellow beads in a large floral and foliate design on an opaque beaded background; 12 x 9 inches; very good condition; $195–$240.

Bag, Nez Perce: classic rectangular twined corn-husk bag with bright-colored geometrics and floral designs; ca. 1910; 7¼ x 7 inches; very good condition; $450–$600.

Bag, Nez Perce: huge rectangular twined corn-husk bag with crisp bright-colored geometric designs on each side; ca. 1880; 23 x 16 inches; very good condition; $700–$1,000.

Bag, Nez Perce: large rectangular twined corn-husk bag with different geometric designs on each side; ca. 1890; 18 x 14 inches; very good condition; $550–$600.

Bag, Nez Perce: large rectangular twined corn-husk bag with bright-colored geometrics on both sides; ca. 1900; 18 x 13 inches; very good condition; $225–$275.

Bag, Nez Perce: oval full-beaded bag with different cut bead geometrics on each side; ca. 1910; 11 x 8 inches; very good condition; $150–$200.

Bag, Nez Perce: rare round twined corn-husk Sally bag with red and blue geometric designs; ca. 1890; 7½ x 6 inches; very good condition; $150–$200.

Bag, Nez Perce: rectangular twined corn-husk bag with bright-colored geometric designs; ca. 1910; 10 x 8 inches; very good condition; $250–$300.

Bag, Nez Perce: unusual round twined corn-husk medicine bag with colorful geometric designs; ca. 1880; very good condition; $100–$150.

Bag, Tlingit: choice floral beaded "octopus" bag with bead and red wool suspensions; ca. 1920; 18 x 9 inches; very good condition; $500–$575.

Bag, Wasco: rare beaded Wasco wall pocket done in old beads; ca. 1860; 4½ x 8 inches; very good condition; $75–$100.

Bag, Yakima; Sally bag with colored geometric corn-husk decoration; ca. 1900; 10 x 7 inches; very good condition; $450–$500.

Bag, Yakima: large rectangular hop string bag; ca. 1920; 16 x 3 inches; very good condition; $80–$100.

Bag, Yakima: rare old double-sided contour floral beaded bag; ca. 1910; 9 x 7 inches; very good condition; $65–$85.

Bag, Yakima: rounded small rectangular cloth bag with a beautiful beaded flower; ca. 1920; 6 x 5 inches; very good condition; $75–$100.

Bag, Yakima: twined Yakima hop string belt pouch; ca. 1920; 8 x 7 inches; very good condition; $100–$125.

Bags (4), Nez Perce: made of corn husk, Indian hemp, cotton, and multicolored wool forming the decorations; 5½, 5½, 7¼, and 10 inches long; good condition; $550–$750.

Beaded bolo tie, Apache: blue opaque and opalescent colors in barber polelike and ten-pointed star-flower designs; very good condition; $25–$40.

Beaded set, Yakima: hair holder, bolo tie, and two buckles, all with cut bead floral designs; ca. 1975; excellent condition; $100–$150.

Beadwork, Athabascan: rectangular floral beaded pincushion; ca. 1920; 4 x 2 inches; very good condition; $700–$800.

Beadwork, Chippewa: beaded black velvet pillow cover with floral designs; ca. 1910; 17 x 18 inches; very good condition; $100–$125.

Beadwork, Paiute: pair of red and white beaded salt and pepper shakers; ca. 1940; 3 x 2 inches; excellent condition; $65–$85.

Beadwork vase, Paiute: geometric designs; ca. 1940; very good condition; $50–$75.

Beadwork, Navajo: group of contemporary beaded pieces; includes belt, key chain, pen earrings, large earrings are porcupine quills; very colorful; excellent condition; $300–$350 group.

Belt: large sterling silver and turquoise concha with five oval conchas; six butterflies and 3-x-4¼-inch buckle; set with large (average ¾ inch) turquoise stones; two in buckle; all set on black leather belt; all hand silverwork; 3 inches wide, 41 inches long; excellent condition; $400–$500.

Belt: silver and turquoise concha; nine cast-silver conchas, including buckle, set with ¾- x ½-inch blue spiderweb stones on black leather belt; 36 inches long; excellent condition; $400–$475.

Bookends: pair of cast-iron "Indian chief" bookends; ca. 1930; 6½ x 5 inches; excellent condition; $50–$75.

Bows (two): one Mohave, one Pomo, both polychrome-decorated; very good condition; $175–$250 each.

Bowl, Tlingit: rare large ceremonial "seal" bowl with shell and white bead inlay; ca. 1900; 15 x 8 inches; very good condition; $1,500–$2,000.

Box, Eastern Woodlands: beaver box, birch-bark circular with sweet-grass-wrapped edge bands, the cover decorated with beaver in porcupine quillwork, sides with quillwork in natural white and red geometrics; 4½ inches diameter, 2¼ inches high; very good condition; $100–$300.

Box, Passamaquoddy: quillworked birch-bark box, circular with sweet grass bindings at rims, the cover with a seven-leaved tree floral in natural porcupine quills, the sides with a band of joined "X" forms in quill; ca. 1920s; good to very good condition; $150–$275.

Brass Bells, Plains: antique pair of leather-mounted dance-type bells; 25 inches long; fair condition (shows use, age, and tarnish); $50–$100.

Breastplate, Crow: long hair-pipe bones with leather spacers and green faceted trade beads along with dark blue trade beads; ca. 1880; $600–$800.

Breastplate, Sioux: child's breastplate; heavy silver conchas with stamped designs on leather, with silver beads, colored trade glass beads, and bone cylinders; out of Oklahoma; ca. 1940; very good condition; $1,800–$2,000.

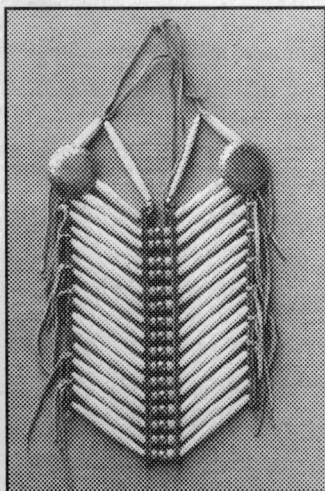

Miscellaneous, breastplate, Sioux; child's breastplate; heavy silver conchas with stamped designs on leather with silver beads, colored trade glass beads and bone cylinders; ca. 1940; out of Oklahoma; $1,800–$2,000. Collection of N. A. McKinney. Photo by Donald Vogt.

Breastplate, Sioux: large real bone breastplate with Crow bead spacers and tin cones; ca. 1960; 40 x 9 inches; very good condition; $200–$250.

Breastplate: 92 hair-pipe bones with central row of brass beads; also, brass beads and hair-pipe bones in the neck suspension; fringe on sides; a row of ten eagle claws divided by shell and brass beads is draped across the bottom of the breastplate; 29 inches tall; excellent condition; $1,750–$2,000.

Breastplate: young girl's bone and bead breastplate; ca. 1965; 24 x 2 inches; excellent condition; $35–$60.

Bride's suitcase, Hopi: called *Songo Sivu*; it is made of the stems of the sungo tala; suitcase is used by the Hopi bride to hold a part of the wedding costume when she leaves the home of her groom's mother to return to her own mother's home; width 28 inches; excellent condition; $1,500–$2,000.

Buttons, Navajo: pair of large sterling silver and turquoise buttons, each set with one round blue-green cabochon; 1⅛ inches diameter; excellent condition; $60–$80.

Miscellaneous, brush and comb holder; belonged to Quanah Parker's wife, Topai; Cecil Horse, son of Hunting Horse (Kiowa), brought it to the museum about 30 years ago. Courtesy of Jack Glover, Sunset, Texas. Photo by Donald Vogt (two views—open and closed).

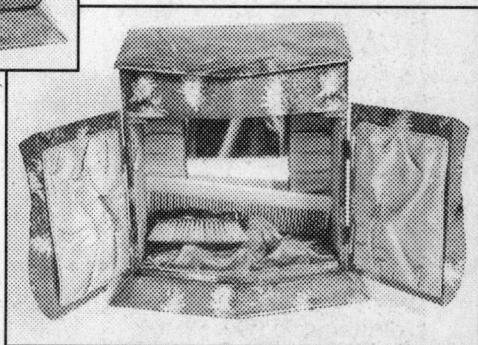

Canteen, Hopi: polychrome, Kachina design; stubs for carrying strings are chipped; 6¼ inches; good condition; $125–$150.

Canteen, Navajo: rare early hand-hammered silver tobacco canteen with etched deer design on one side and triangles indicating the four directions on the opposite side; the silver stopper is attached by small link chain; 5 x 3 inches; very good condition; $600–$800.

Chess set, made by Charlie Pratt: Koshare and mudheads, cast bronze with paint; unlimited edition; chessboard is walnut and birch; cast in 1992; each figure is 4¼ inches tall; $4,500.

Chest, Kwakiutl: very rare blanket chest from an old Alert Bay collection; decorated with totem poles on each end and a stylized eagle carved into the center of the front panel; ca. 1880; 20 x 11½ inches; very good condition; $450–$550.

Cigarette case: unusual pre–World War II fully beaded Lucky Strike cigarette case; ca. 1935; 3¼ x 2½ inches; $150–$200.

Coins: Indian-head pennies; bag containing 100 old Indian-head pennies; ca. 1900; very good condition; $30–$50.

Coins: roll of fifty mixed-date U.S. Indian-head pennies; ca. 1900; excellent condition; $40–$50.

Coins: bag containing 100 old assorted-date Indian-head pennies; excellent condition; $45–$65.

Corn-husk bag, Nez Perce: twined, geometric polychromed decoration; very good condition; $150–$200.

Corn-husk bag, Nez Perce: beautiful twined corn-husk bag with very colorful floral designs on one side and geometrics on the other; ca. 1900; 11 x 11 inches; very good condition; $400–$600.

Cradle face, Nez Perce: fully beaded in floral design and geometric border in blue, red, green, salmon, and greasy yellow; 18½ inches long x 15 inches wide; very good condition; $1,300–$1,700.

Cradle, Hupa: classic twined baby carrier with dentalium shell suspensions; ca. 1880; 22 x 7 inches; very good condition; $200–$275.

Cradle, Nez Perce: miniature baby carrier with beaded floral designs; ca. 1890; 10 x 4 inches; very good condition; $400–$600.

Cradle, Nez Perce: rare full-size baby carrier with contour beaded top and original board; ca. 1890; 40 x 12 inches; very good condition; $1,500–$2,000.

Cradleboard, Apache: yellow-painted wood with yellow cloth and red, white, and blue rickrack; ca. 1950; 35 inches high; very good condition; $35–$75.

Cradleboard, Paiute: woven for a new baby girl with imbricated design, attached dyed fabric; excellent condition; 20½ inches long; $300–$500.

Dance ankle bells: two pairs with large 1½-inch bells (six to a strap) and a pair of children's one-bell set; excellent condition; $40–$60/set.

Dance harness, Sioux: Warrior Society; a cape or bandolier worn over the shoulders and draping front and back; constructed of

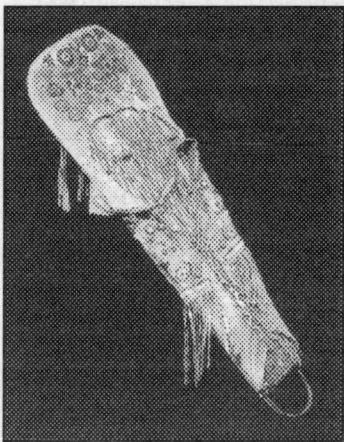

Miscellaneous, cradleboard, Plains; basketry rod construction covered with hide, adorned with beadwork with floral motifs; beads are white, pink, blue, red, and green; hide hood is missing; ca. 1880s; 10 x 31½ inches; very good condition; $2,000–$3,000. Courtesy of W. E. Channing & Co., Inc.

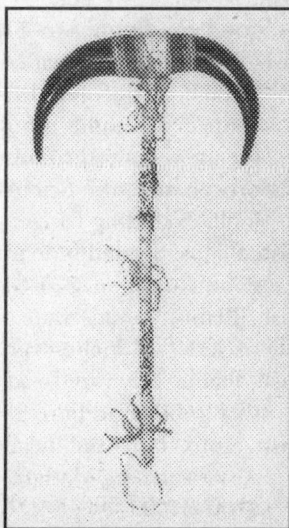

Miscellaneous, ceremonial buffalo horns on wand, Osage; ca. 1900; excellent condition. Courtesy of, and photo by, Joyce Williams.

panels of quill-wrapped rawhide strips edged with tin cone and dyed feather tassels, a whitetail deer tail attached at the center; ca. 1900; $9,500–$10,000.

Dance strap, Sioux: hide with carved deer hoof painted red, with brass beads and a strip of purple-painted horsehair; 46 inches long; good condition; $250–$350.

Dance wand, Sioux: beaded cow-horn dance wand; old; 17 inches handle; good condition; $200–$350.

Decoy: prehistoric decoy of petrified ivory with four hand-drilled holes for varied suspension underwater; very good condition; $300–$500.

Decoy: small fish decoy by Timothy Idlout, Northwest Territories; carved whalebone, movable bone fins, lead weight; very good condition; $300–$500.

Dish, Northwest Coast: carved and painted cedar grease dish in beaver form with abalone inlay; signed LaValle; ca. 1980; 4 x 3 inches; excellent condition; $150–$225.

Dish, Tlingit: small carved wooden seal dish with abalone inlay; ca. 1920; 6 x 1½ inches; very good condition; $75–$100.

Drum, Taos: classic Taos tourist drum with Eagle Dancer painted on it; ca. 1950; 6 x 5 inches; excellent condition; $20–$35.

Effigy piece: rare flint thunderbird ceremonial point; prehistoric; very good condition; $75–$100.

Fetish, Kiowa: early beaded umbilical cord fetish; ca. 1890; very good condition; $75–$150.

Fetish, Pawnee: pony-beaded hide fetish of triangular form with trade-bead-decorated fringe, net-beaded body woven in concentric diamond motif; pony bead colors are violet-blue, greasy yellow, turquoise, pink, Venetian glass trade beads; provenance: the Science Museum of Connecticut; 3½ inches long, excluding fringe; excellent condition; $1,000–$1,500.

Fetish, Plains: beaded hide umbilical cord fetish; 46 x 9 inches; very good condition; $75–$100.

Fetish, Plains: round trade fetish in turtle form with full-beaded back; 5½ x 4 inches; very good condition; $100–$135.

Fetish, Plains: very rare bead hide horse effigy fetish; 5 x 5 inches; very good condition; $350–$400.

Fetish, Sioux: hide umbilical cord fetish in turtle form with beaded American flag design; 6 x 3 inches; very good condition; $300–$400.

Fetish, Sioux: rare umbilical cord fetish with fully quilled back in lizard form; ca. 1870; 7 x 2 inches; very good condition; $300–$500.

Fetish, Sioux: umbilical fetish; beaded hide; turtle in green, dark blue, and white; ca. late 1800s; very good condition; $500–$750.

Fetish, Zuni: black grizzly bear with turqoise eyes, red coral tongue, mother-of-pearl teeth, and holding mother-of-pearl fish in one paw; 6½ inches high; very good condition; $200–$250.

Fetish, Zuni: brown serpentine carved Zuni bear fetish; ca. 1975; 2 inches x 1 inch; excellent condition; $20–$30.

Fetish, Zuni: carved-antler bear fetish with turquoise eyes; ca. 1970; 4 x 2 inches; very good condition; $75–$100.

Fetish, Zuni: carved brown serpentine Zuni bear fetish; ca. 1975; very good condition; $40–$60.

Fetish, Zuni: carved brown serpentine bear fetish; ca. 1940; 2 x 1½ inches; very good condition; $50–$75.

Fetish, Zuni: carved-stone bear fetish; ca. 1940; 2 x 1½ inches; very good condition; $20–$30.

Fetish, Zuni: hand-carved turquoise badger fetish with fine detail; ca. 1970; 21½ inches x 1 inch; excellent condition; $100–$125.

Hair feathers: cut legal feather hair drops; excellent condition; $30–$50.

Headstall, Navajo: silver horse headdress; ca. 1885; 18 inches long; $3,500–$4,500.

Headdress: roach type with tie strings; contemporary; excellent condition; $40–$60.

Miscellaneous, Headstall, Navajo; silver horse head-dress; ca. 1885; 18 inches long; $3,500–$4,500. Courtesy of Canfield Gallery, Santa Fe. Photo by Donald Vogt.

Horn spoon, Northwest Coast: in two sections; tenoned and horn-pegged, elongated oval bowl tapering to a carved and incised totemic handle, abalone inlay accents; 10⅛ inches long; good condition (minor bowl loss); $900–$1,000.

Indian wedding post: excellent condition; $20–$25.

Ivory pipe, Tlingit: carved ivory pipe in bird and shaman form, with abalone inlays; ca. 1975; 3 inches x ½ inch; excellent condition; $200–$300.

Ivory, Tlingit: carved and painted four-figure ivory totem pole; ca. 1935; 6 inches x 1 inch; excellent condition; $60–$80.

Ivory, Tlingit: rare carving depicting a blanketed shaman with abalone inlay on a wooden base; ca. 1900; 4 x 2 inches; excellent condition; $300–$500.

Loom model, Navajo: very good condition; $200–$250.

Martingale, Crow: beaded geometric designs in white, light blue, greasy yellow, salmon, cobalt, and green, with dyed horsehair suspensions and many brass bells; on trade cloth with selvage edge showing; early; 46 inches overall; very good condition; $600–$800.

Martingale, Crow: made of buffalo hide, beadwork and red trade cloth ornamentation; collected on the Crow reservation in Montana; ca. 1860s; $15,000.

Martingale, Plains: bridle and reins and matching martingale; beaded design in red, white, and blue; very good condition; $700–$900.

Mask, Northwest Coast: rare and unusual hide-covered mask with abalone inlay and real hair; 10 x 7 inches; very good condition; $300–$400.

Navajo miniature rug, loom, and doll: handmade tree-branch loom containing a partially finished red, gold, black, and brown eye dazzler and a traditionally dressed seated figure; 17 x 13 inches; excellent condition; $75–$100.

Needlepoint: needlepoint pictures that use Navajo symbolism; made for collector as gifts; excellent condition; $75–$100.

Northwest Coast clan crest: polychrome decorated, carved, and incised wood raven's head, concave base on tapering neck, abalone inlaid nostrils, beak, and eyes; traces of deep turquoise pigment over beak and eye grounds, crimson beak edge, and dark brownish black pigment over crown and neck, which is drilled for attachment and ornamentation; good pati-

Miscellaneous, martingale or horse collar, Crow; ca. 1860s; made of buffalo hide, beadwork and red trade cloth ornamentation; collected on the Crow reservation in Montana; $15,000. Courtesy of Canfield Gallery. Photo by Robert Reno.

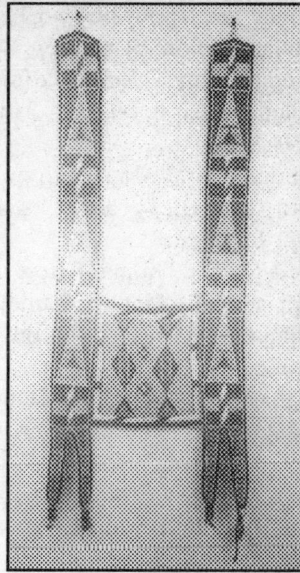

Miscellaneous, miniatures; group of miniature fetishes by Lance Chema and Dan Quam are poised on miniature Indian rugs; $150–$300 each. Courtesy of Miniatures at the Kiva/Steve Cowgill. Photo by Donald Vogt.

nation; 5¼ inches high, 4⅞ inches long; excellent condition; $8,000–$10,000.

Paint: native red and white painted stones and two small jars of trade vermilion; excellent condition; $10–$15.

Painted skull: painted and decorated prairie-bleached buffalo skull with feathers; ca. 1985; 10 x 20 inches; excellent condition; $100–$125.

Peace medal case: pony-beaded peace medal case; ca. 1900; very good condition; $100–$150.

Peace medal: John Tyler peace medal in silver and with a hole drilled to wear it; ca. 1841; 3 inches diameter; good condition; $250–$325.

Peace medal: round silver Andrew Jackson peace medal on bone bead choker; ca. 1865; 11 x 5 inches; very good condition; $300–$350.

Peace medal: silver Thomas Jefferson peace medal with hole drilled in it; ca. 1801; 3 inches diameter; good condition; $350–$450.

Pelt: Indian tanned beaver pelt on willow hoop stretcher; old; very good condition; $50–$100.

Pillow, Athabascan: round moose-hide pillow with floral beadwork and "Alaska" in beading; ca. 1935; 15 inches diameter; very good condition; $60–$80.

Pincushion, Whimsy, Iroquois: large ornately beaded pincushion with horse and floral designs; ca. 1880; 10 x 8 inches; very good condition; $125–$175.

Pipe: German-manufactured wooden calumet pipe with carved Indian bust; ca. 1890s; 22 inches; very good condition; $50–$100.

Pipe: carved frog pipe in black stone; small repair; 3½ x 1¾ inches; very good condition; $120–$200.

Pipe and stem, Plains: catlinite with a wooden stem, deaccessioned from a Maine museum; ca. 1880; 22¼ inches long; excellent patina; $250–$350.

Pipe and stem, Plains: catlinite with a wooden stem, square-type bowl, deaccessioned from a Maine museum; ca. 1880; 23½ inches long; excellent patina; $350–$450.

Pipe and stem, Plains: catlinite, stem with ribbonwork in blue and gold, and quillwork in purple and aqua; deaccessioned from a Maine museum; pre-1800; 34 inches long; excellent patina; $1,600–$2,000.

Pipe bowl: small, catlinite; very good condition; $50–$75.

Pipe, Eastern Sioux: catlinite pipe with quilled wood stem; ca. 1880s; excellent condition; $2,700–$3,700.

Pipe, Haida: steatite pipe bowl in double bird form; rare; ca. 1870; 2 x 2 inches; very good condition; $100–$150.

Pipe: made to honor a Shawnee chief who was instrumental in establishing the Indian school at Chilocco; made from birch poles; stem 62 inches, bowl 7 inches; very good condition; $125–$150.

Pipe, Plains: catlinite bowl; quill-wrapped stem; $6,500.

Pipe, Plains: wood and stone pipe, composed of red catlinite elbow pipe head with deeply grooved panels on the shaft and tall, cylindrical bowl, the wood stem of rectangular section carved in high relief with a splayed turtle and three deer heads, inscribed in ink on the underside "Purchased from Crazy Horse, Oelrichs, S.D. Nov. 24th–92"; total length 35¼ inches; very good condition; $6,500–$7,500.

Pipe, Sioux: catlinite pipe with catlinite stem wrapped in rawhide; old; good condition; $200–$400.

Pipe, Sioux: black stone "T" bowl with red stone and pewter inlay and a tacked "corkscrew" stem; 31 x 5 inches; very good condition; $400–$475.

Miscellaneous, pipe, Plains; catlinite bowl; quill-wrapped stem; $6,500. Courtesy of Canfield Gallery. Photo by Robert Reno.

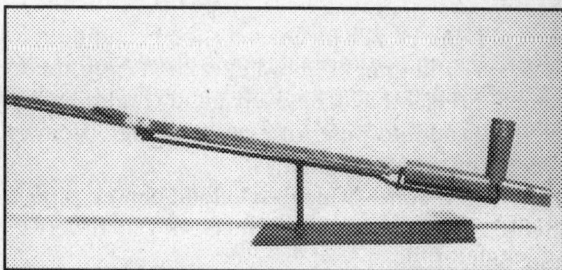

Miscellaneous, pipe, Sioux; catlinite; stem is file-branded, green and yellow stripes with red horsehair strip, catlinite bowl with raised ridges; ca. 1870–1880; 31¾ inches long; ex. Robert Riggs Collection. Courtesy of Willis Henry Auctions, Inc.

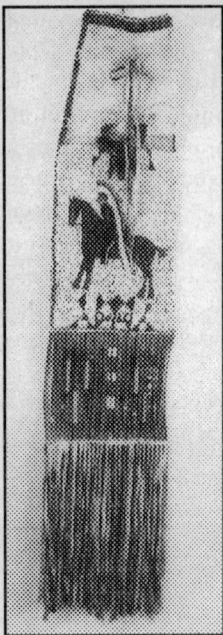

Miscellaneous, pipe bag, Lakota Sioux; early 1900s; an elaborately decorated beaded hide tobacco bag with effigy of an equestrian warrior in beadwork embroidery on front and back; $9,000. Courtesy of Canfield Gallery. Photo by Robert Reno.

Pipe, Sioux: red catlinite "T" bowl with a rectangular red catlinite stem; ca. 1890; 21 x 4 inches; very good condition; $275–$325.

Pipe stem: catlinite with four carved linear bands and two carved arrow designs; 15 inches long; very good condition; $60–$100.

Pipe, Tlingit: carved ivory pipe with abalone inlay eyes; ca. 1850; 4½ inches x ½ inch; very good condition; $125–$200.

Pipe, Wasco: excavated gray stone "L" pipe bowl from the Columbia River; ca. 1800; 1¾ x 2½ inches; very good condition; $75–$100.

Pipe, Wasco: rare old gray "T" bowl excavated from the Columbia River; ca. 1700; 4 x 3 inches; very good condition; $100–$150.

Pipe: eagle-claw catlinite pipe with catlinite angle stem; pre-1850; good condition; $200–$350.

Pipe: small carved stone "wineglass" cloud-blower pipe from the Columbia River; prehistoric; 3 inches x 1 inch; very good condition; $80–$120.

Pipe bag, Ute: side panel of beaded crosses in geometric design in red, blue, greasy yellow, and cobalt with beaded white background, with red quilled slats and fringe; 31 inches overall; very good condition; $350–$400.

Plaque: porcelain, hand-painted plaque made by KPM Porcelains; of Indian attacking stagecoach; excellent condition; $600–$800.

Pouch, Tlingit: round seal fur pouch with beaded designs all around; ca. 1920; 3½ x 4 inches; very good condition; $80–$100.

Purse, Navajo: handmade woven purse in gray, black, and maroon; contemporary; excellent condition; $75–$100.

Purse, Yurok: rare carved elk antler dentalium money container from the lower Klamath River; ca. 1800; 4 inches x 1 inch; very good condition; $175–$225.

Quillwork pillows (two), Cheyenne: backed with canvas and decorated with bands of red and yellow quillwork on hide; pillows stuffed with sweet grass were a common element of Cheyenne Indian tepee furniture, but are now extremely rare; provenance: Reese Kincaide, Mohonk Lodge Trading Post, Colony, Indian Territory (Oklahoma); ca. late 1800s; each pillow approximately 10 x 16 inches; $4,600/set.

Rattle, Iroquois: turtle shell; provenance: estate of Dr. Samuel W. Fernberger; 16½ inches long; good condition (minor shell loss); $300–$500.

Roach, Plains: porcupine hair dyed in red, blue, yellow, white, green, and natural; 13¼ inches long; very good condition; $225–$325.

Roach, Plains: porcupine hair and dyed rose deer hair, woven on reverse; 17 inches overall length; very good condition; $175–$225.

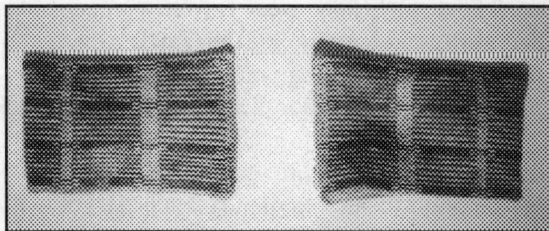

Miscellaneous, quillwork pillows (two), Cheyenne; late 1800s; backed with canvas and decorated with bands of red and yellow quillwork on hide; each pillow approximately 10 x 16 inches; pillows stuffed with sweet grass were a common element of Cheyenne Indian tepee furniture, but are now extremely rare; provenance: Reese Kincaide, Mohonk Lodge Trading Post, Colony, Indian Territory (Oklahoma); $4,600/set. Courtesy of Canfield Gallery. Photo by Robert Reno.

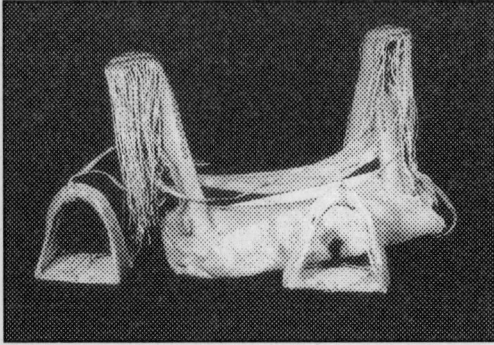

Miscellaneous, saddle, Plains; wood-frame saddle, wrapped with rawhide, with deer hide covered; beaded panel drop in geometric design of navy blue, light blue, and lavender beads with red stroud cloth edging; 17 x 24 inches; very good condition; $1,800–$2,500. Courtesy of W. E. Channing & Co., Inc.

Roach, Sioux: hair center head roach; old; very good condition; $275–$450.

Sally bag, Wasco: rare old twined Sally bag with bead and button decoration; ca. 1840; 4 x 4½ inches; very good condition; $80–$100.

Silver medal; George Washington silver medal on real bone bead necklace; ca. 1780; 24 x 1¼ inches; very good condition; $250–$300.

Slave killer: large classic greenish slate slave killer weapon from the Columbia River; ca. 1800; very good condition; $500–$600.

Soul catcher, Tlingit: rare fossil ivory carved totemic soul catcher; ca. 1870; very good condition; $150–$200.

Spoon, Haida: large bent-horn spoon with totemic carved handle and abalone inlays; ca. 1900; 11 x 3½ inches; very good condition; $600–$700.

Spoon, Haida: large carved mountain goat horn spoon with many totemic carvings on the handle; ca. 1900; 11 x 2 inches; very good condition; $500–$700.

Spoon, Haida: rare old ladle of carved mountain sheep horn; ca. 1870; very good condition; $125–$175.

Spoon, Northwest Coast: large spoon of mountain sheep horn with simple circular designs on the handle; ca. 1880; very good condition; $125–$200.

Spoon, Plains: bent-horn spoon decorated with geometric beadwork on the border; 9 x 2 inches; very good condition; $175–$225.

Spoon, Tlingit: black spoon of carved mountain goat horn with totemic designs and with abalone inlay and native copper reinforcement; ca. 1900; 8 x ½ x 3 inches; very good condition; $450–$550.

Sterling silver tray, Navajo: hand-stamped; 18 inches long x 5¾ inches wide; very good condition; $375–$475.

Stone fetish, Zuni: green serpentine badger with rawhide-wrapped mother-of-pearl arrowhead, olive-shell heishe, red coral, and blue turquoise on its back; 1⅜ x 3½ inches; very good condition; $100–$125.

Tableta: Pueblo tableta from Rio Grande area; ca. 1910; 8 x 9 inches; very good condition; $2,800–$3,200.

Tomahawk: "U.S. Indian scout" government issue; wood handle finished with stag antler end, embossed "U.S.I.S." between crossed arrows; 17½ inches long; very good condition; $500–$700.

Totem, Haida: argillite totem; approximately 8 inches tall; very good condition; $1,000–$1,250.

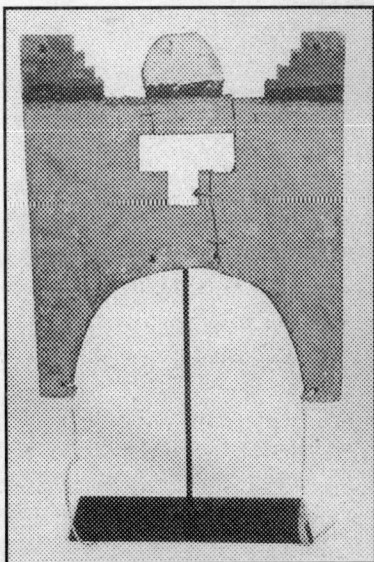

Miscellaneous, tableta; Pueblo tableta from Rio Grande area; ca. 1910; 8 x 9 inches; $2,800–$3,200. Courtesy of Canfield Gallery, Santa Fe. Photo by Donald Vogt.

Totem, Tlingit: carved and painted bone or ivory totem pole from Alaska; ca. 1940; 6½ x 1 inch; very good condition; $80–$100.

Trade pipe: rare old white clay Hudson Bay trade pipe; ca. 1870; 5 inches x 2 inches x 1 inch; very good condition; $50–$75.

Wedding pillow case, Chippewa or Eastern Sioux; buckskin, beaded in floral designs and "Good Luck"; fringed; very good condition; $100–$200.

Whistle: Ghost Dance bone whistle with quillwork streamer tipped with tin cones and dyed horsehair tassels; very good condition; $150–$200.

Chapter Eleven

Pottery

❧

There is nothing more beautiful than a well-made piece of Indian pottery, and though there are many throughout the United States, the best-known potters come from the Southwest. The women and men involved in this age-old art learned their trade from members of the family, or from other members of the village where they lived. Theirs are not skills learned at a school, and I know of no place that teaches the art of making Indian pottery.

I believe that is why Indian pottery is so innovative, yet at the same time so steeped in tradition that designs used centuries ago are still being used today. The art of pottery-making combines Native Americans' love of the earth with their need to express themselves and produces a utilitarian bowl, pot, or dish. What could be more fulfilling?

What has amazed me during my research on the subject is that examples of ancient pottery bring less on the antiques market than the modern pottery. In fact, at many sales of Indian art, interest in prehistoric pottery is light and many pieces are passed by, while more recent "historic and later pottery" pieces sell well.

New potters are winning awards at annual crafts markets and exhibitions on a yearly basis, and their work, as I said before, combines the old techniques with new ideas. Their biographies are included in this chapter; however, there are new faces at the markets every year. In order to keep up with them, one must attend the southwestern markets.

Modern New Mexico and Arizona-area Indian women still hand-throw pottery, without the benefit of a wheel. They use a yucca-leaf brush, with one end chewed into fibers. Acoma, San Ildefonso, Zuni, and Hopi mesas are still painting deer, birds, flowers, geometric designs, and identifiable symbols of their villages. Modern potters also use new techniques, like selective firing, in which the black carbon is burned away to reveal red clay.

Though there are few collectors today who can interpret them properly, there was much symbolism built into the decorative elements used in the early pottery created by the Zuni, Hopi, and San Ildefonso Indians, among others.

For example, turkey tracks built into a Zuni design could indicate a wish for the return of wild turkeys (their feathers were used to decorate dance sticks); a design that resembles bats' wings can be symbolic of two rainbows. Each stroke of decoration held meaning; no decoration was made by chance.

For those collectors wishing to expand their knowledge of these symbols, there are many wonderful books that devote themselves exclusively to identifying each sign and explaining its meaning. They are too numerous for this writer to explain in this chapter (see the Bibliography).

The Making of Pottery

The process of preparing the clay for making Indian pottery begins long before the potter's hands knead the clay and form it. First, the potter travels to gather clay from deposits in the area. (Sometimes he or she must travel a great distance to find desirable clay.) Next, the clay is pulverized to a fine powder and cleaned (by sifting or tossing in a winnowing basket) to get out all the lumps and small rocks. After the cleaning is complete, the clay is stored until the potter is ready to use it.

The final step, before use, is for the clay to be moistened and tempered. The clay is kneaded on a dry, flat surface. While kneading, the potter tempers the clay with shells, sand, limestone, or plant fibers. The right amount prevents the clay from cracking during firing and drying. Before using the wet clay, modern potters often sift or cleanse it through nylon mesh or stockings.

The two pottery techniques used by the American Indian include coiling, and modeling and paddling. Sometimes the two techniques are combined. Once the pot is "built," the drying, polishing, decorating, and firing techniques are basically the same.

After the pot has been sun-dried for a couple of days, it is smoothed (or sanded) with a flint chip or piece of bone. (Today's potters use a kitchen knife or scraper.) Then the pot is wiped with a wet cloth.

If the pot will be decorated, it is necessary to apply a slip to the piece. This creamy mixture of colored clay and water is applied with a rag or rabbit's tail and is allowed to dry before the piece is polished with a small, smooth stone.

Firing is the trickiest part of the pottery-making process. It is during the firing process that a piece is either "finished" or broken. The great potter Maria Martinez used the firing process to create the black-on-black surface distinctive of her work. During this process, the fire is smothered with manure, giving the pottery a shiny black finish. (The manure is generally a powdered or pulverized horse manure, which, when burned, creates a reduction reaction—or oxygen—and forces the heat and smoke inward, into the clay, blackening it.) If the fire is not smothered, but allowed to burn openly, the pottery will be red. The pot is decorated, after polishing, with a paint, which, *in firing*, turns matte black. (That is, the black-on-black effect is the result of both the firing, which will turn any pot black, and the painted decorations.) After firing, the pottery is wiped clean of soot.

Different types of decoration are applied by various tribes, and these techniques have changed little over the centuries. Southwest potters (such as the Papago, who use sticks) paint their pottery. Corrugated pottery was produced in the prehistoric Southwest, though some of the contemporary potters are rediscovering the necessary techniques and enhancing the traditional forms with their own variations. Other types of decorating include impressing, incising, or scratching designs in an unfired pot or engraving the designs after firing.

Basic pottery forms of the Native American can be divided into five regional types: the North, stretching from west of the Great Lakes to the East Coast; Central, stretching from Georgia in the South to Michigan in the North, and from Illinois in the West to the eastern border of Pennsylvania; the Southeast, encompassing all of Florida and north along the Atlantic coast to Delaware; the Gulf region of Louisiana, Mississippi, Alabama, part of Georgia, and the eastern border of Texas; and the Southwest—Arizona, New Mexico, part of Texas, Oklahoma, and the southern halves of Utah and Colorado.

The northern region potters (from tribes such as the Iroquois, Fox, Mandan, and Shoshone) used angular incisions as designs in most of their pieces. The pottery was mostly a gray-blue color, mixed with beige. Cord marks, or cord-impressed designs, are commonly found on pottery made in this region.

In the southeastern region, the pottery is lighter, and the decoration stamped or brushed. Tribes who were known to make pottery in this region include Cherokee, Creek, Apalachee, and Seminole.

The central region (tribes such as Quapaw, Shawnee, and Winnebago) produced reddish pottery in various shapes and designs—such as the "head pots" of the middle Mississippi culture of Arkansas and the hunchback female effigy bottles made by the same culture.

The Choctaw, Caddo, Chickasaw, and Natchez tribes of the Gulf region produced pottery with incised or engraved designs.

The southwestern potters are many, and it is important for those who want to understand the pottery of that region to familiarize themselves with as many examples as possible. Pottery is still made in the traditional way in the Southwest, and one can find potters, taught by their mothers, sisters, aunts, or grandmothers, who are well worth collecting. The pottery culture in the Southwest is so strong that it can be divided into periods.

The first, the Modified Basket Maker period (A.D. 400–700), saw pottery like the Lino Black-on-Gray (unslipped) and the Abajo Red-on-Orange, while the Developmental-Pueblo Period (700–1050) consisted of black-on-white pottery with painted designs. The Great Pueblo Period (1050–1300) gave us hard, thin, highly polished pottery and the introduction of polychrome pottery. During the period from 1300 to 1700, the Regressive Pueblo Period, polychrome pottery was developed further and mineral glaze paints were being used.

Today's pottery ("modern" is from 1800 to the present) is made chiefly in the pueblo villages, with each area producing its own distinctive pottery products (e.g., Santa Clara's red and black pottery with impressed designs; San Ildefonso's black-on-black; Acoma potter's, white to yellow-brown slip and geometric and parrot-like bird patterns.)

EXAMPLES OF POTTERY-MAKING TRIBES

Prehistoric pottery of the Amerind is more artistic than one would expect. Pottery effigies are almost abstract in form, highly polished pieces made out of whatever minerals (jasper, terra-cotta, or hematite, for example) the people had available to them.

Bowls and other vessels were sometimes footed and, more often than not, decorated. Their exteriors were incised by broad, curvilinear lines, sometimes creating designs of birds and other animals, sometimes forming a series of lines and circles.

Beakers and bowls were adorned with bird, animal, and human effigies, and designs varied from region to region.

ACOMA

This pueblo's pottery-making artists usually paint fine-lined geometric designs on their pieces. They typically decorate pots with birds and often make corrugated white pottery.

Pots are sold in front of the visitors' center at the Sky City. The Pueblo Pottery store on the road into Acoma sells traditional pieces, and other examples are available at the Laguna grocery store and Indian Pueblo Mart. (Note: Ask to see pieces not on display, as the nicer pots are often kept in back.)

ANASAZI

Anasazi Indians of the Southwest were cliff dwellers who populated the area around A.D. 1000 and created black-on-white, thin-line geometric abstractions on their pottery.

(See information on Anasazi Indians in Chapter Two.)

HOPI

The Hopi potters' earliest pieces were black-on-white, gray, and sometimes orange. They began trading yellow ware during the fourteenth and fifteenth centuries. After the Spanish built missions in the Hopi area in 1625, Hopi potters developed other shapes and designs, and these post–mission period examples are called Polacca Yellow Ware. By the end of the nineteenth century, trading began to be an important part of the Hopi's economic system, and the Hopi-Tewa potter Nampeyo began copying some of the designs on prehistoric vessels. She combined new and old shapes and patterns, creating her own style (see more about her in the biographies section of this chapter).

Hopi pottery techniques have changed little since those early days. They still build vessels by hand, using the coil-and-scrape method, then polish the pots by using a rounded stone. The pots are then painted with yucca and grass brushes and fired in an open fire. Coal fires are also used, since they produce higher temperatures than wood fires, and during later centuries, sheep dung became a popular fuel.

During the 1800s the Hopi slip method was one similar to that used by Zuni and Acoma potters. The descendants of Paqua Naha (Frog Woman) utilize a rare fine, white firing clay as their slip.

Hopi pottery had practical uses for cooking, carrying and storing water, and serving and storing food. A water jar is called *kuysivu,* and the dipper used to get the water out of the jar is a *kuyapi.* A shallow, open bowl was used for serving, while a water jar had a narrow opening to keep the water from splashing out. The Hopi kept food warm with a *shoe pot,* which had one open end where the food was inserted, and a closed end that was shoved into hot coals.

Hopi potters often decorated their pieces with macaws, large wild parrots that never lived anywhere in Hopiland; their images and feathers were introduced by Mesoamerican traders. Contemporary Hopi ceremonial outfits are still decorated with macaw feathers. During the late 1300s, Hopi potters began creating polychrome designs on their pottery that depicted people, animals, and birds. Some of the humanlike designs are said to have depicted Kachinas; other designs told of Hopi myths.

Though the Hopi potters incorporated some Spanish designs into their work after the Spanish founded missions in Hopiland during the 1500s, the Hopi people banished the Spanish (as well as all of their designs) after the 1680 Pueblo Revolt. During the same period, the Hopis welcomed Rio Grande refugees into their homeland and began incorporating Rio Grande motifs and shapes into their own work. History again affected the Hopi style of pottery during the droughts and epidemics in the 1700s and 1800s when many Hopi people fled to their Zuni neighbors' pueblo. There they learned Zuni designs (such as the fleur-de-lis and pomegranate designs), which they incorporated into their own designs when they returned to their own land.

Today's pottery-making is based on the First Mesa, with some men joining in what was traditionally a female occupation (e.g., Tom Polacca, Fannie Nampeyo's son; then Polacca's sons, Gary Nampeyo Polacca and Loren Hamilton Nampeyo).

A list of the most important Hopi potters includes Nampeyo; Roberta Silas; Tom Polacca; Fannie, Elva, Daisy, Nellie, and Leah Nampeyo; Elizabeth White; Lawrence Namoki; Sadie Adams; and Garnet Pavateya.

MISSISSIPPIAN CULTURE

This culture, located in the area of the Mississippi River, is an ancient one, dating from A.D. 1000–1650. They created polychrome, engraved, punctated, incised, and appliquéd pottery. For more information see *Ancient Indian Pottery of the Mississippi River Valley,* by Roy Hathcock.

MOGOLLAN

The Mogollan peoples lived at approximately the same time as the Anasazi in the eastern part of southern New Mexico.

Though the Hohokam were their neighbors in the west and the Anasazi were their northern neighbors, the Mogollan created their own type of pottery, which we now recognize by the Mimbres art used as decoration.

Only five generations (between A.D. 1000 and 1150) produced black-on-white and polychrome pottery from the Mimbres Valley in New Mexico; most examples had geometric decoration, but many portrayed human and animal figures that depicted life during that 150-year period. The stories told through the decorations on this type of pottery reveal how the people felt about birth, death, love, and even human sacrifice.

Funerary pottery made by these people was placed over the deceased's face, and then a hole was punched through the pot (as though the pot, too, were dead).

Archaeologists have studied this fascinating culture, and are often frustrated by the fact that nearly every Mimbres site has been destroyed by looters, a distressing matter for the contemporary generations whose ancestors were Anasazi or Hohokam.

SAN ILDEFONSO

San Ildefonso was the northernmost village of those pueblos using the Rain Bird design, and its pottery is also noted for its distinct black-on-white wares, as well as red ware. The potters of San Ildefonso have made pottery in essentially the same fashion for over seven hundred years. They chose not to follow the trends in design technique adopted by other pottery-makers, and instead adhered to their richly formal heritage.

Perhaps this unchanging atmosphere was in part a result of their language (Tewa), which was markedly different from others in the region. Though they had a rather slow beginning, San Ildefonso potters are some of the best in North America.

SANTA CLARA

Though pottery-making goes on year-round, the heavy season is May to October, when potters beef up their stock for summer fairs, markets, and the tourist season. Sometimes a potter will work at his or her craft for eight to ten hours per day.

Men such as Ernest Tapia, Camilio Tafoya, Luther Gutierrez, Joe Tafoya, and Joseph Lonewolf have made their living making pottery and have done as well as the more notable female potters.

Potters believe that their clay has a soul and that, treated properly, it will in turn honor its maker. When a Santa Clara potter gathers clay for his or her work, it is often a family expedition. Clay pits are found on or near the reservation where the potters work. Clay gathered from different locations produces a variety of colors in finished pieces.

Santa Clara potters use clay, tempering materials, and red paint for their creations. They gather clay from a place called *Na Pi' i we*, about a mile west of the pueblo. The tempering material comes from a place about seven to eight miles northwest of the village called *Makawa oky*.

After the clay dries in the sun for a couple of days, it is put in a washtub and covered with water. The clay soaks for two to four days, during which time the potter periodically draws off the excess water and adds clean water, repeating the process until the runoff water is clear.

The potter then stirs the clay until the lumps are removed and the mixture is passed through a sieve. Rocks and lumps are sorted out and discarded.

Next the potter sets aside the amount of clay that will be needed over the next several days. In a day or two, it is ready and mixed with tuff or "sand." Broken pieces of unfired pottery may be added to the mixture in order to absorb some of the excess water.

Temper or filler is usually volcanic tuff, which, when combined with the clay mixture, acts as a binder to strengthen the body. It also serves to counteract shrinkage and facilitate uniform drying. Mixing the clay with the tuff is hard and tiring work, usually done on the floor in the house. It is kneaded like bread dough and, if wet, dried until it is the proper consistency for modeling.

Tools such as modeling spoons (or gourds), shaping and scraping tools, a mold, some water, and a lapboard are a few of the things a potter will gather when he or she is ready to mold. The key item, on which the clay base is first formed, is called the *puki* (pookie). As the potter rotates the puki (by hand), he or she has access to the whole pot.

Most vessels begin in the same manner—as a lump of clay, a little larger than a fist, that the potter models into the shape of a cone. The clay is held with the left hand and rotated. With the right fist, the potter punches a depression into the center, then enlarges the opening of that depression with the fingers of the right hand. The base is laid on the lapboard, depression side up, and the potter takes a shaping spoon *(kajape)* and shapes the piece, making strokes parallel to the rim.

Scraping and thinning from the bottom of the base to the top, the potter finishes one area, then turns the piece and performs the process again on the next. Rotating the vessel, he or she moves the wooden stick diagonally, removing small amounts of clay from the exterior of the vessel and working the entire surface until it is smoothed. The tools are kept moist by constantly dipping them into the water basin the potter keeps handy.

The vessel is built by adding successive rolls of clay to the piece, working as before, until the vessel is the desired shape and size. It takes approximately two days for a piece to dry—depending on the size of the piece and the weather. Then it is time for smoothing and sanding. Sanding thins the walls, removing any gouges or lines, then reduces the walls again. So much dust is created by this step that it must be done outside the house. In the past, pieces of bone or a sharp stone were used to smooth the surface.

Once the exterior and interior are smooth, slipping is done and polishing begins. Polishing is done with smooth polishing stones, and the process takes precision and patience. Once the polishing is complete, the firing begins. Santa Clara potters vigilantly keep a fire going under the pieces of pottery being fired. The heat must be kept even; it is a job that takes the diligence of one who knows the importance of this final process. When the fire cools, the pottery is carefully removed and the potter decorates the piece.

Santa Clara potters, both contemporary and historical, are well known in today's Indian collectibles market. Some of the families who are active in this art are the Gutierrez family—Catherine,

Denaria, Dolorita, Faustina, Laurencia, Luther, Margaret, Petra, and Pula—as well as Luther's daughter, Pauline Naranjo. The Naranjo family also includes Barbarita, Veronica, Candelaria, Belah, Celestina, Christina, Elizabeth, Everesta, Flora (and her family), Isabele, Madeline, and Teresita. (Note: Christina Naranjo was a Tafoya, Camilio "Sunflower" Tafoya's sister, and also sister to Margaret Tafoya). There are also a number of children coming through the ranks who show great promise.

Helen Shupla (deceased since 1987) and her husband, Kenneth, were as well-known as the talented Tafoya family, and notable potters include Camilio "Sunflower" Tafoya, his daughter, Grace Medicine Flower, and his son, Joseph Lonewolf, whose miniatures are among the finest made by the modern potters. Joseph's daughter, Susan Snowflake Romero, is also producing pots at this time. Her father's miniatures command prices from $1,000 to $3,000, and hers are available from $300 to $500. Helen Shupla's son-in-law Alton Komelestewa is carrying on her style. One should not overlook Margaret, Madeline, and Mida Tafoya and their families, as well (see biographies in this chapter).

TAOS

Pottery made in this pueblo traditionally incorporates flecks of mica in the clay (see individual potters for more information).

TESUQUE

Tesuque potters seemed to better comprehend the changes in pottery-making and concentrated on small decorative details, incorporating designs like the Rain Bird into a secondary design. Tesuque pottery reached its peak at the end of the nineteenth century and rapidly declined after that.

ZUNI

The Rain Bird design is one of the most frequently used and easily recognized of all Zuni pottery designs. Birdlike figures have been found on their pottery dating back to the classical Mesa Verde pottery (approximately the thirteenth century) and was, at that time, a very geometric figure.

The figure was used by other pottery-making people of that region, with practically no change in the motif. It continued to be used in the Tularosa region on black-on-white wares. The red ware that succeeded the early black-on-white (Four-Mile Polychrome) also used birdlike figures on the outsides of bowls, as did the Jeddito black-on-yellow pottery.

Though Four-Mile Polychrome wares were produced until the fifteenth century, they disappeared shortly after that. The Hopi yellow wares were clearly influenced by the Jeddito black-on-yellow.

Before the conquest by the Spaniards, Sikyatki Polychrome pottery came into popularity and spread over the whole Pueblo region.

Zuni pottery underwent a change in glaze types by approximately 1700, when the potters favored a dull and flat look to their pots. The Rain Bird design first came into evidence at this time and is divisible into several distinct features. The center of the design is a single coil, representing the bird's head and beak, and below this coil is its crest. On either side of this design is a stepped outline that encloses two solid figures—the body and the wings.

Through the study of Pueblo pottery design, one can discern many minute changes in this design, yet the basics are the same whether one calls the design a bird, a chicken, a turkey, or its rightful name, the Rain Bird.

The symbolism of designs found on Indian pottery may be disputed, but anyone who has studied the Native American cultures must come to the conclusion that all decoration had meaning for the decorator—the Indian myths and stories were an integral part of life—thus, the Rain Bird figure, which existed on so much of the pottery made in the Southwest, was a significant one.

Other pottery-making groups, such as the Hopi, Acoma, Laguna, Santa Ana, San Ildefonso, Tesuque, Cochiti, Zia, and Santo Domingo peoples, all used a form of the Rain Bird design. Most made very small, if any, changes in the design.

SPECIAL POTTERY

EFFIGY POTTERY   Effigy pottery pieces, most of which were made by women, were only a small portion of the articles Indian men used in religious ceremonies. They were traded to other tribes, sometimes carried great distances, and were highly prized by their owners (see references to effigy pieces in other chapters).

OLLAS   Large water jars (ollas) were used in the Southwest to carry liquids. Indian women would balance these large jars on their heads and carry them to the spring or well and back. The potters often competed to see who could make the thinnest, finest, largest, and most beautifully decorated ollas.

STORYTELLERS   Storyteller figurines, made famous through the work of potter Helen Cordero (1915–   ) and well publicized by knowledgeable southwestern galleries—such as the Adobe Gallery in Albuquerque, New Mexico, owned by Alexander Anthony, Jr.— have become an integral part of Pueblo pottery. These figures, originally modeled after Cordero's grandfather and his storytelling techniques, have shown up at major auctions, galleries, and Indian markets, winning prizes and commanding four- and five-figure prices. They are folk art in the purest Native American form.

Though figurative pottery has been a part of Indian pottery since the beginning of their history, storytellers are a "new" form initiated by Cordero, but derived from Cochiti figural pottery. Figures such as the "portraits" of Anglo professionals developed by Cochiti potters in the late 1800s were made to "tease" the white man, and their forms often took the shape of sheriffs, cowboys, priests, circus entertainers, and even Italian opera singers. Louis Naranjo and Ivan Lewis reproduced such caricatures in recent years, and have updated their humorous versions of Anglos to include bikini-clad women and tourists in shorts, carrying cameras.

Cordero began making her storytellers in the 1950s, combining the ancient seated figure, with outstretched legs, head thrown back, and mouth wide open, with tiny figures seated or climbing on the figure, their faces showing either rapture or fear (depending on the story she was depicting). Cordero was forty-five years old at the time, her children grown, and she needed to make extra money. She never realized what an impact she would make on the art of pottery.

When asked by a folk art collector to make larger examples of the figures, she modeled one after Santiago Quintana, her grandfather, a storyteller of such expertise that he always had children begging him for a new tale. Quintana was well-known—both in the Cochiti Pueblo and to historians who had listened to the old man when they wanted to make sure they "got it right." He is quoted in many volumes of ethnographic works and was photographed and quoted by Edward S. Curtis in *The North American Indian* (1926).

Almost instantly Cordero's storytellers won prizes at the New Mexico State Fair and the Santa Fe Indian Market. She was asked to give demonstrations at universities and national monuments, and has been included in exhibits both in the United States and abroad. Her work has been displayed at major Indian art shops and galleries throughout the country. Her work has even appeared on the cover of *National Geographic* (November 1982).

Her business exploded and Cordero produced many different kinds of storytellers, including a kneeling version inspired by one of her customers who got down on his hands and knees and begged her to make him a storyteller. She did—and the storyteller was on his knees, as was her collector.

Originally potters who made storytellers were from the Cochiti Pueblo. Now the number of artisans making these figures has risen to above a hundred, and they come from many other pueblos (e.g., Jemez, Acoma, Nambe, Isleta, and San Felipe). Each pueblo has an unmistakable style of pottery, and their storytellers are as unique as other examples of their pottery.

Other storyteller potters—We have included only a handful of biographies of storytellers to highlight innovative or award-winning craftspeople. As with other types of pottery, there are many more who follow in the tradition of master storyteller potter Helen Cordero, and we believe it is a folk art collectors of Indian art should watch carefully.

CORDERO FAMILY

Helen's family has followed her lead, and nowadays her son, George (1944–), daughter, Tony, and grandchildren Tim (1963–), Buffy (1969–), and Kevin Peshalakai (1964–) also make storytellers. We were fortunate enough to see an example of both Helen's and Buffy's storytellers at the Adobe Gallery in Albuquerque, and have heard that the younger children are also picking up their grandmother's technique.

TONY DALLAS (1956–   )

Mudhead storytellers are the trademark of Hopi potter Tony Dallas. His mother-in-law, Lucy Suina (1921–), another storyteller potter, introduced him to the art of making pottery in 1982. His clown storytellers are unique in that Cochiti potters are enjoined from making and selling clown and Kachina figures. Dallas's mudhead storytellers usually hold a bowl, and the little mudheads that crawl all over the larger figure are very "active."

LOUIS AND VIRGINIA NARANJO

Naranjo is a well-known name in pottery, but the Cochiti pottery husband-and-wife team of Louis and Virginia are well known for their nativities and storyteller figures. Their highly original work includes animal figures in the storyteller style. Virginia won an award for one of her turtle storytellers in 1973, and both she and Louis have won many other awards since that time.

ROSE PECOS (1956–   ) AND SUN RHODES

The husband-and-wife team of Rose Pecos and Sun Rhodes are Jemez storyteller makers whose figures are made in the Navajo style. The boys who listen to the storyteller wear cowboy hats and are more realistic in size compared to the adult around whom they gather. The girls often hold Navajo wedding baskets or cradleboards, and detailing on their clothing is in the Navajo style.

MARGARET QUINTANA

This contemporary potter is of Cheyenne/Arapaho heritage and grew up in a southern Cheyenne community of Watonga. She works with micaceous clay to form Cochita-style storytellers. She learned the art form after marrying her husband, Paul, and moving to the Cochiti Pueblo. Quintana began learning how to work with red Cochiti clay in the early 1980s. Her interest in mica arose when she saw it in the Sangre de Cristo Mountains in Taos. Her work is featured in the Millicent Rogers Museum and in many Taos galleries.

ADA SUINA (1930–)

Also of the Cochiti Pueblo, Ada has won prizes for her storytellers, nativities, and drummers since she began making them in 1976. Her work is extremely fine, and the faces on her figures large and distinctive. Ada has passed her talent on to her four daughters, who have also begun to win prizes with their pottery figures.

MARY E. TOYA (1934–   )

Toya is of the Jemez Pueblo and has earned the distinction of making the largest storyteller, which holds 115 children. The children hold pots, baskets, bags, dolls, balls, and drums, and the figure stands eighteen inches high. It took Mary Toya six months to make this masterpiece. Toya also is known for her seven daughters who follow in the storyteller pottery-making tradition. She has won prizes for almost every kind of pottery and has also made some of the smallest examples of this pottery type.

BIOGRAPHIES OF INDIAN POTTERS

KAREN ABEITA (1961–)

Abeita, a Hopi, left her reservation when she was in her late teens to study in Albuquerque, New Mexico. She became an optical technician, working for a while in Arizona and Kansas. In 1984 her mother died and Abeita returned home to Polacca to care for her younger siblings.

Pottery became a way to earn a living, and having come from a distinguished line of potters (her grandmother's first cousins, Sadie Adams, Joy Navasie, and Beth Sakeva, are known and well respected), she learned quickly. She didn't learn the trade from family members; rather, she turned to people her own age such as Fawn Garcia, James Garcia Nampeyo's wife. Mark Tahbo also exchanges ideas with her.

Abeita's pottery is traditional Hopi/Tewa design made of native materials that she and her husband, Darryl Daw (a Navajo), collect. Her decorations are often inspired by prehistoric pots from the Sikyatki ruins.

Work done by Karen Abeita can be seen at the Robert F. Nichols Gallery in Santa Fe.

DELORES ARAGON (1969–)

Aragon learned her pottery style from her mother, Marie Juanico, an Acoma potter (see information about her later in this chapter). She began creating small animals from clay at the very early age of five. She also has had the help of Wanda Aragon, her mother-in-law and respected Acoma potter, who encouraged her to continue using traditional techniques and materials. Her husband, Marvis Aragon, Jr., also receives some of the credit for teaching Delores the traditions of pottery, as well as about life, "[how] everything has a meaning" (*Focus Santa Fe*, April/May 1993). Delores has begun to teach her young son, five-year-old Marvis III, how to make his pottery special.

Aragon works in miniature and has earned a respectable reputation for her fine-line work, as well as for combining modern elements (lizards) with the ancient (flute players).

Her work can be found at the Robert F. Nichols Gallery in Santa Fe.

KAREN KAHE CHARLEY (HOPI)

As a child, Charley was allowed to play with clay while her mother modeled pottery, but she didn't begin taking the art seriously until returning to the reservation in 1983, after living and working elsewhere for almost ten years. She and her husband, Jim, traveled around the Midwest while he worked as an ironworker. Charley's mother, Marcella Kahe, taught her daughter in the same manner that Marcella's mother had taught her. The orange-red color in Charley's pottery is a family secret that other Hopi potters have not yet imitated.

Charley has shown her work at the Santa Fe Indian Market, Pueblo Grande in Phoenix, and at the Tulsa Indian Arts Festival.

TONY DA (SAN ILDEFONSO)

One of the few male traditional potters, Da was well known for his innovative work in the field of pottery. He is the grandson of the grande dame of pottery, Maria Martinez. Since his untimely accident, Da no longer pots; he does paint, however. Considered by

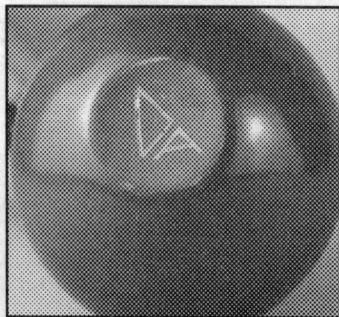

Pottery, small red jar with feather design made by Tony Da; design is repeated three times with three turquoise nugget insets; 3¾ inches tall, 5 inches diameter; ca. 1960; signed Da—never signed Tony Da; $4,500. Courtesy of Alexander Anthony/Adobe Gallery. Photo by Robert Reno.

some to be the greatest innovator of all, he is still copied by many currently well-known potters. Prices for Da's pottery have skyrocketed, and his work looks to become increasingly collectible.

Marie Juanico

An Acoma Pueblo potter, Juanico first learned her craft at the age of four by watching her mother, Delores Sanchez. Her mother's pottery was often exhibited at the Heard Museum in Phoenix. Juanico incorporates traditional and complex Mimbres designs into her pots, a style she attempted to teach her daughter, Delores Aragon (see biography earlier in this chapter).

Juanico digs and mixes her own clay and colors and makes her pots by hand, often building the pot with no distinct image of how the shape will turn out.

Marie Juanico is of the opinion that more Acoma potters should return to traditional methods, and to their traditional language (Tewa).

Her work is shown at the Robert F. Nichols Gallery in Santa Fe.

Lucy Lewis

Born at Acoma Sky City during the 1890s, Lewis did not go to school, but instead grew up on the mesa in the Indian way. Her pottery was influenced by her great-aunt, Helice Vallo. Lewis married Toribio Luis (or Haskaya) in the late 1910s and is the mother of nine children. The oldest son, Ivan, is a Cochiti storyteller potter. His wife, Rita, and children Dolores, Emma, and Andrew also make pottery.

Dr. Kenneth Chapman, artistic director of the New Mexico Museum, showed Lucy ancient pottery when Laura Gilpin took Lewis to Santa Fe in 1958. Chapman had also influenced Maria and Julian. Lucy received the Indian Arts Foundation award, as well as the Maria Martinez award for her fine-line decorated pottery. She was the first at the Acoma Pueblo to show her work. She has won numerous other awards and received world recognition for the Mimbres designs that are so popular in Acoma pottery. Her pieces are highly collectible.

Charles Loloma

See Loloma's biography in Chapter One.

MARIA MONTOYA MARTINEZ (1887–1980) (93yr)

Born at the San Ildefonso Pueblo, this great, unassuming artist lived there until her death when she was well into her nineties. Because of the lack of well-kept records, her birth date is not exact, but believed to be approximately 1887. She died in 1980.

Her aunt Nicolasa taught Maria at a young age to make cookware and everyday ceremonial vessels. From those early lessons, Maria learned how to find the clay, mix it with ash, and construct the vessel's walls by pinching clay coils onto its base in a puki saucer. Then the pot would be sun-dried, and its sides scraped with gourds or tobacco can lids. The piece was then dipped in slip and polished with river stones until it was ready to be fired. Almost as important as the making of the pot was the ceremony and thanks given to each part of the process.

Maria's pottery debut took place at the 1904 World's Fair, the same year she married her husband, Julian. Together they attended an archaeological dig on the two Anasazi sites nearby. It is said that Maria found four ancient polishing stones in the dig that fit perfectly in her hand. She asked, and received, permission to keep the stones. Later during the dig, some potsherds were uncovered, and the head of the dig, Edgar Hewett, asked if Maria could re-create the pots. Maria made the forms, and Julian duplicated the designs, but neither of them knew how to blacken the pots. Julian experimented with a number of firing methods and finally discovered that using smothered dung in the firing process produced the desired effect. Together, Maria and Julian also discovered that the pots were made of black volcanic dust from the Pojoaque area.

A decade of trial and error passed by before Julian finally perfected the technique of painting the pots with a matte black to create the black-on-black pots that are today recognized as their trademark. In 1919 Julian first painted on a polished pottery surface with a chewed end of a yucca plant, producing the earliest examples of the matte black-on-black pieces; their firing process with dried manure had already been discovered. The stylized *puname* feather patterns and the *avanyu*, which have become signatures of San Ildefonso pottery, were also Julian's discoveries.

Julian worked at the Museum of New Mexico as a janitor, and the couple spent a great deal of time there, studying the ancient ceramics held in the storerooms of the museum. Maria made and polished the pottery forms, while Julian painted the designs. Maria's sister, Clara, also worked with them, doing most of the polishing.

In 1923 Maria began signing her pots. Julian added his own signature to the pots in 1925, and there were a total of seven variations on her signature that she used throughout her career.

When they returned to the San Ildefonso Pueblo, Maria passed on some of her skills to the other women of the village and began selling her pottery. Julian and Maria were excited, at that time, to get $.75 to $1.25 per piece! As their pottery skills improved, so did the pueblo's economy. In 1924 they bought the first car in the pueblo. It was a black car that Julian apparently couldn't resist decorating with his pottery designs. By the 1930s, they received $2 for a medium-sized pot and had become celebrities.

After Julian's death in 1943, Maria's daughter-in-law (her son Adam's wife, Santana) worked with her, decorating pottery. From 1953 to 1971 (when he died), Maria's son Popovi Da did decorative work for her pottery. He was also responsible for assembling a collection of her pottery, now on display at the Popovi Da Studio of Indian Art at San Ildefonso. Her grandson Tony Da held the promise of a brilliant career, but stopped potting after an auto accident. In 1971 Popovi died, and Maria's sight began to fail. By that time, her days of creating pottery had ended.

Maria's sisters, Maximiliana and Desidera, as well as Barbara Gonzales, Maria's great-granddaughter, were potters and creators of valuable works. Maria outlived her husband and three of her four sons.

She traveled with her pottery, meeting presidents, movie stars, and other celebrities, yet she lived like any other pueblo woman, wearing traditional clothes and understating her many accomplishments. Her concerns were always for her people and her pueblo.

Maria's works have been shown all over the world, and her techniques were demonstrated in almost every world's fair from 1904 to her death. In the 1930s she toured the country under the auspices of the U.S. government. She was awarded numerous prizes and awards for her accomplishments, including two honorary doctorates—one from New Mexico State University in 1971, the other from Columbia College in 1977. Her pottery is held by museums all over the world.

Maria's pottery is one of the best drawing cards an auctioneer has when holding a sale of Indian items.

NAMPEYO (1856–1942)

Nampeyo was also called the "Old Lady." She lived on the Hopi First Mesa in Northern Arizona. When archaeologists uncovered the prehistoric village of Sikyatki, three miles away from where Nampeyo lived, her husband (a worker at the archaeological site) brought home some pottery pieces. Nampeyo sought, and received, permission to re-create some of the ancient designs on her own pottery. Soon she was experimenting with variations and is credited with creating a new form of artistic expression with her work.

She taught her daughters, granddaughters, and great-granddaughters her art. They have a hard time meeting the demand for their work today.

CHRISTINA NARANJO

Daughter of Serafina Tafoya, Christina continues the Tafoya family's potting traditions. She created some of the pots she made in the 1970s with the help of her daughter, Mary Cain, and those pieces are signed by both of them. Mary's daughter, Linda, is also a potter; her work is featured at many galleries.

Her daughter, Teresita, creates carved polished black pieces. Her large bowls sell for approximately $6,000 at shows and in galleries. The family traditions continue as Teresita's daughter, Stella Chavarria, learns the trade.

JOY NAVASIE

Also known as the "Frog Woman," Navasie uses the ancient Sikyatki style of decorations on her pots and paints them on almost pure white slip.

DEXTRA QUOTSKUYVA (1928–)

A Hopi potter who learned her trade from her mother, Dextra did not make her first pot until she was thirty-nine years old (1967). She uses organic and mineral paints, yucca leaf brushes, and polishing stones, just as her great-grandmother, Nampeyo, did.

CAMILIO TAFOYA

As mentioned earlier in this chapter, the Tafoya family is extremely well-known for their pottery. Camilio, the son of Serafina, has been making miniature pottery in a contemporary style for years. His children, Grace Medicine Flower and Joseph Lonewolf, are also recognized for the innovations they have contributed to the field. Lonewolf's daughter Rosemary also pots, as do his three other children.

SERAFINA TAFOYA (1863–1949)

This well-known potter started a tradition of potters within the Tafoya family. Her three children, Camilio Tafoya, Margaret Tafoya, and Christina Naranjo, all became potters, and many of the children and grandchildren of this family have also followed in their famous relatives' footsteps (see other biograhies in this listing).

MARGARET TAFOYA

A Santa Clara potter whose trademark is polished blackware, Tafoya uses bear paws frequently in her work and believes that they are good luck because "the bear always knows where the water is."

In 1991 *National Geographic* declared Tafoya a "Master of Traditional Arts." Tafoya digs clay from nearby areas, as many other potters do, and offers thanks to Mother Clay as well as to Mother Earth as she is about to create a new piece. She forms pots coil by coil, and her pieces are inspired by ancient myths that she heard from parents and grandparents. Her pots are decorated with rain clouds, bear paws, buffalo horns, water serpents—Santa Clara symbols of survival. She makes deeply carved large blackware and redware vessels which are highly valued for their excellence.

Tafoya swears the secret of her work is in the polishing, and she retains polishing stones passed down through several generations of her family. Four generations of the Tafoya family have left their mark on what is now considered classic pottery. Her children, Virginia Ebelacker, Mela Youngblood, Toni Roller, and Esther Archuleta, have carried on the pottery-making tradition.

YELLOWBIRD

A San Ildefonso native, Yellowbird creates animals out of clay. He works with his hands, shaping the pieces until the body of an animal, such as a bear, is recognizable. Once the piece is created, he will dry the piece, paint it with slip, then polish it with a stone and fire the piece.

His pieces currently bring from $100 to $200.

ACOMA

Acoma, bowl: geometric designs in dark brown and orange on a white slip; shows crack; 5 inches high x 5½ inches diameter; $150–$200.

Acoma, canteen: bird motif; ca. 1940s; 7½ inches; very good condition; $200–$250.

Acoma, group by Dorothy Torivio from Acoma Pueblo: seed pot, 4 inches diameter x 1¾ inches, $460; seed jar, 3 inches tall, $350; and seed pot, 3½ inches diameter x 1½ inches, $345.

Acoma, jar: water jar with finely painted birds in the style of Maria Poncho, in shades of orange on a white slip background, concave bottle bottom; ca. 1930; 12½ inches diameter x 10⅝ inches high; good condition; $2,200–$3,200.

Acoma, jar: pottery jar, umber and ocher on white slip; 4⅝ inches diameter x 3¼ inches high; good to better condition; $25–$75.

Acoma, jar: geometric designs, polychrome decorated in brown, white, and red; 5 inches high x 7 inches diameter; very good condition; $250–$300.

Acoma, olla: 11 inches high x 12 inches diameter; very good color and condition; $1,600–$2,000.

Acoma, pot: polychrome with cream white base, floral designs in earth red and brown; old; 7 inches high, 7 inches diameter at center; good condition; $150–$350.

Pottery, Acoma, group by Dorothy Torivio from Acoma Pueblo; left to right—seed pot, 4 inches diamter x 1¾ inches, $460; seed jar, 3 inches tall, $350; and seed pot, 3½ inches diameter x 1½ inches, $345. Courtesy of Alexander Anthony/Adobe Gallery. Photo by Robert Reno.

Pottery, Acoma, pot; with deer figurine designs; made by M. Antonio; 8 inches; $600–$800. Collection of Donna McMenamin. Photo by Donald Vogt.

Pottery, Acoma, seed pot; brown, orange, gold, and yellow design; designed and made by Charmac Shields Matseway; 7½ inches wide x 3½ inches deep; excellent condition; $600–$800. Courtesy of, and photo by, Joyce Williams.

Acoma, pottery vessel: water pitcher with bird and floral effigies in orange on a cream slip with black geometric design; 8 inches high x 8 inches diameter; very good condition; $200–$300.

Acoma, seed pot: decorated with three humanoid/insect motifs; signed "S . . . Garcia"; 5 inches high, 6 inches diameter; very good condition; $350–$450.

Acoma, seed pot: brown, orange, gold, and yellow design; designed and made by Charmac Shields Matseway; 7½ inches wide x 3½ inches deep; excellent condition; $600–$800.

ANASAZI

Anasazi, Cibola Province, black-on-white pitcher: ca. A.D. 950–1200; 5 inches high x 5¼ inches diameter, $275–$375.

Anasazi, Cibola Province Puerco/Escavada, black-on-white pitcher: ca. A.D. 950–1000; 5½ inches high x 5½ inches diameter; $450–$600.

Anasazi, pitcher: black and white geometric design; ca. A.D. 1000–1100; 6¼ inches diameter at body, 6½ inches high; very good condition for so historic a vessel; $300–$600.

Anasazi, pot: bird effigy pot with incised lines on handle forming the tail of the bird, the bird's body extending from the side of the bowl with incised eyes; patina ranges from blackened fire areas to encrusted brown and warm terra-cotta tones; no restoration; ca. prehistoric; 7 x 5 inches; $200–$400.

Anasazi, Cibola Province Puerco/Escavada, black-on-white pitcher: ca. A.D. 950–1200; 5 inches high x 5¼ inches diameter; $300–$500.

COCHITI

Cochiti (possibly), pot: basketry pot with handled top, double bulbous body form with white (graying tone) background slip, with black geometric and floral decoration on body and handle; ca. 1900 or earlier; 6½ inches high, 5 inches diameter at middle base; good condition; $50–$250.

Cochiti, bowl: ceramic with deep brown/black geometric design on a beige cream slip; signed "Cochiti, New Mexico" at base; old; 6 inches wide at top, 2½ inches high; very good condition; $50–$175.

Cochiti, canteen: decorated with a tree with two applied frogs on white background; signed on bottom "Laurensita Herrera"; 3½ inches high, 4½ inches long; very good condition; $275–$375.

Cochiti, figurines: set of three males in bondage positions; made by Virgil Ortiz, who got the idea from Madonna's book *Sex*; 1993; 5¾ inches (tallest) x 7½ inches (longest); $1,500/set.

HOHOKAM

Hohokam, scoops: adult's, 6 x 9 inches; and child's, 3 x 5 inches; both plain ware; ca. prehistoric; $40–$180.

HOPI

Hopi/Anasazi, bowl: in a yellow slip with geometric step designs in black; ca. prehistoric; 7 inches diameter; good condition; $130–$180/set.

Hopi, bowl: Kachina bowl (possibly Nampeyo) in red and dark brown with beige background, with a full figure covering entire circumference; two holes drilled later for hanging purposes; 13 inches diameter; excellent condition; $2,900–$3,300.

Hopi, bowl: Polacca polychrome bowl with red, brown, and red-brown design on white slip; ca. 1880s or earlier; 9½ inches diameter; some restoration; $200–$400.

Pottery, Hopi, canteen; ceramic, polychrome decorated with orange and deep brown feather design on cream slip base; ca. 1930s; 5½ inches high; good color and condition; $250–$500. Courtesy of C. E. Guarino Auction Gallery, Denmark, Maine.

Hopi, bowl; polychrome leaf design; unsigned; ca. 1910; 7½ inches diameter x 3¼ inches tall; very good condition; $600–$700.

Hopi, canteen: ceramic, polychrome decorated with orange and deep brown feather design on a cream slip base; ca. 1930s; 5½ inches high; good color and condition; $250–$500.

Hopi, canteen: stylized thunderbird design; 5½ inches; good conditin; #175–$225.

Hopi, Kachina and pre-Columbian pot: 2-inch high Kachina made of cottonwood, in black and yellow; 3¾-inch-high pottery jar with two figures with arms on their knees; both very good condition; $90–$150/set.

Hopi, olla: Hopi Tesuque polychrome decorated in geometric and rain god designs in orange and black; ca. 1900–1920; 9 inches high, 12 inches diameter; very good condition; $5,600–$6,600.

Hopi, olla: small; geometric designs in red, black, and brown; very good condition; $185–$265.

Hopi, pot: "Frog Lady" pot with polychrome decoration in brown and orange on a cream base; wonderful tonal quality shows its age and the artistry of the potter; signed on the base "PAQUA" with a drawing of a frog in brown; 7½ inches wide, 3½ inches high; generally good condition; $375–$500.

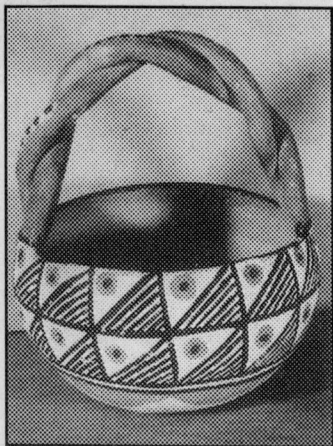

Pottery, Hopi, pot; "Frog Lady" pot with polychrome decoration in deep brown and orange on warm cream base; shows age and artistry of potter; signed on base "PAQUA" with drawing of frog in brown; 7½ inches wide, 3½ inches high; generally good condition; $375–$500. Courtesy of C. E. Guarino Auction Gallery, Denmark,

Pottery, Hopi, pot; large polychrome pot with gently sloping sides that curve inward at neck; cream slip decorated in deep brown and orange in various abstract geometrics; ca. 1920–1940; approximately 9 inches diameter, 6½ inches high; base of pot inscribed "Nampeyo" in pencil, but not proven to be original; $325–$650. Courtesy of C. E. Guarino Auction Gallery, Denmark, Maine.

Hopi, pot: gently sloping sides that curve inward at the neck, the cream slip decorated in deep brown and orange in various abstract geometrics; the base is inscribed "Nampeyo" in pencil; ca. 1920–1940; about 9 inches wide at the center, 6½ inches high; very good condition; $325–$650.

Hopi, storytellers: two made by Tony Dallas, a Hopi who lived with a Cochiti family and learned how to make storytellers there (Cochiti potters are not allowed to make mudheads or Koshares, but since Tony is a Hopi, he can); the Koshare is 9 x 3½ inches, $1,050; the mudhead is 6 x 3 inches, $795.

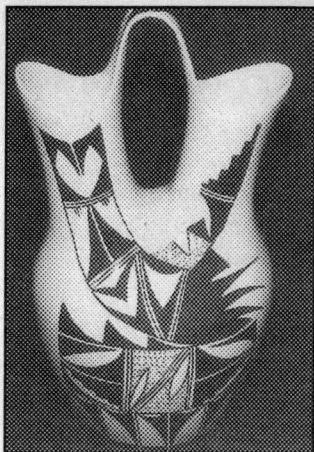

Pottery, Hopi, wedding vase; cream, brown, and burnt sienna design; 10½ inches tall; made by "Frog Woman"; excellent condition; $600–$700. Courtesy of, and photo by, Joyce Williams.

Pottery, Isleta, storytellers made by Stella Teller of Isleta Pueblo; left to right—boy holding two children and lamb, 4¾ inches tall, $800; polar bear holding six baby bears, 6 inches tall, $1,100; girl holding a baby, a mudhead, corn doll, and Kachina, 5½ inches, $1,200. Courtesy of Alexander Anthony/Adobe Gallery. Photo by Robert Reno.

Hopi, wedding vase: cream, brown, and burnt sienna design; made by "Frog Woman"; 10½ inches tall; excellent condition; $600–$700.

ISLETA

Isleta, three storytellers made by Stella Teller: boy holding two children and lamb, 4¾ inches tall, $800; polar bear holding six baby bears, 6 inches tall, $1,100; girl holding a baby, a mudhead, corn doll, and Kachina, 5½ inches; $1,200.

Isleta, pot: braided handle, polychrome decorated with red and black geometric forms typical of the Isletas; ca. 1900; 4½ x 5½ inches; good condition; $100–$300.

LAGUNA

Laguna, olla: geometric and floral designs in brown and red on white slip on red clay; 9½ inches high x 10 inches diameter; very good condition; $400–$600.

MARICOPA

Maricopa or Pima, bowl: tan clay with black paint of four panels of circular designs; late 19th century; 5 inches high; good condition; $100–$150.

MIMBRES

Mimbres, bowl: geometric design; ca. A.D. 1000–1150; 4 inches high x 9 inches diameter, $150–$300.

Pottery, canteens, group; rear—Maricopa pottery canteen, ca. 1880, $1,750–$2,000; left—Maricopa pottery canteen, ca. 1870, 7 x 6½ inches, $1,800–$2,000; right—Maricopa pottery canteen, ca. 1890, 6½ x 6½ inches, $1,500–$1,750. Courtesy of Morning Star Gallery, Santa Fe. Photo by Donald Vogt.

PUEBLO

Pueblo, bowl: with Koshare figures around edge; made by Margaret Gutierrez (formerly Margaret and Luther, he's deceased); serpent design encircles body of pot; 4½ x 5½ inches diameter; $1,000.

Pueblo, jar and wedding jar: good condition; $85–$135.

Pueblo, seed jar: black polished glaze (darker at the top), low profile; 6½ inches high x 11 inches diameter; very good condition; $115–$165.

Pueblo, two pieces: small olla made by Lucy Lewis, polychrome parrot design, ca. 1970, 4 inches tall x 4 inches diameter, $900; turkey figurine in polychrome; ca. 1960; 3 inches wide x 2½ inches tall; $600.

Pueblo, storyteller (front and back) made by Helen Cordero: has 14 children, male storyteller; 1985; 11 inches; $8,500.

Pottery, Mojave, effigy pot; 6½ inches high; clay effigy pot of female with beaded earrings; very good condition. Collection of, and photo by, Evelyn Ackerman.

Pottery, Pueblo, bowl with Koshare figures around edge, made by Margaret Gutierrez (formerly Margaret and Luther, he's deceased); 4½ x 5½ inches diameter; serpent design encircles body of pot; $1,000. Courtesy of Alexander Anthony/Adobe Gallery. Photo by Robert Reno.

Pottery, prehistoric pieces; from left to right—Cibola Province Puerco/Excavada, black-on-white pitcher, ca. A.D. *950–1200, 5 inches high x 5¼ inches diameter, $300–$500; Anasazi culture, Cibola Province, black-on-white pitcher, ca.* A.D. *950–1200, 5 inches high x 5¼ inches diameter, $275–$375; Cibola Province Puerco/Escavada black-on-white pitcher, Anasazi culture, ca.* A.D. *950–1000, 5½ inches high x 5½ inches diameter, $450–$600; Mimbres culture, geometric design bowl, ca.* A.D. *1000–1150, 4 inches high x 9 inches diameter, $150–$300.* Courtesy of Willis Henry Auctions, Inc.

Pottery, Pueblo; left—small olla made by <u>Lucy Lewis</u>, *4 inches tall x 4 inches diameter, polychrome parrot design, ca. 1970, $900; right—turkey figurine in polychrome, 3 inches wide by 2½ inches tall, ca. 1960, $600.* Courtesy of Alexander Anthony/Adobe Gallery. Photo by Robert Reno.

Pueblo, storyteller made by Helen Cordero: male storyteller with one child on lap and one to the side; ca. 1970s; 9½-inch-tall storyteller and 2-inch-tall child; $7,500.

Pueblo, storyteller made by Louis and Virginia Naranjo: female storyteller and girls, the girls wearing tabletas (Louis was the first to use tabletas in his storytellers); 1993; 7 inches tall x 6½ inches wide; $1,350.

QUHATIKA

Quhatika, canteen: 19th century; very good condition; $250–$300.

San Ildefonso, bowl: blue corn with simple diamond rim design; signed; deaccessioned from a Maine museum; 2½ inches high, 4½ inches diameter; excellent condition; $150–$250.

San Ildefonso, bowl: geometric design; signed "Santana & Adam"; 2½ inches high, 4¾ inches diameter; excellent condition; $200–$300.

San Ildefonso, bowl: 12-point floral design in black and red, polychrome; possibly Juanita and Maximiliana or Marie; ca. 1920–1930; 3¾ inches high, 10½ inches diameter; good condition; $175–$225.

San Ildefonso, bowl: stylized bird design; deaccessioned from a Maine museum; signed "Marie"; 4¼ inches high, 6¼ inches diameter; excellent condition; $450–$650.

San Ildefonso, bowl: San Ildefonso blackware shallow bowl; incised "Marie" (famous Maria); has paper label from 1930s World Exhibit; 4¾ inches diameter x 1½ inches high; very good condition; $700–$900.

San Ildefonso, bowl: blackware; incised "Marie" with tag for 1930s World Exhibit on bottom; 7⅝ inches diameter x 2⅝ inches high; very good condition; $575–$775.

San Ildefonso, candlesticks by Rose Gonzales: black-on-black; 3¾ inches tall x 3¼ inches diameter; ca. 1980; $700.

San Ildefonso, jar: San Ildefonso blackware, attributed to Maria; 1930s era, exhibit sticker on bottom; 2⅛ inches diameter x 1¾ inches high; very good condition; $125–$300.

Pottery, San Ildefonso, candlesticks by Rose Gonzales, black-on-black, 3¾ inches tall x 3¼ inches diameter; ca. 1980; $700. Courtesy of Alexander Anthony/Adobe Gallery. Photo by Robert Reno.

San Ildefonso, jar: globular, black-on-black, feather design; signed "Marie & Julian"; 5 inches high, 5 inches diameter; very good condition; $400–$500.

San Ildefonso, jar: blackware; incised signature of "Maria Popovi"; avanyu figure design; ca. 1950; 6¼ inches diameter x 4½ inches high; good condition; $500–$700.

San Ildefonso, large jar made by Marie and Julian: has the avanyu (serpent) design. When Marie and Julian first started black-on-black, the process was to paint the whole pot and polish the serpent—later, the process was reversed. Julian found this process to be so difficult for Marie, he came up with a different process. This is one of six or seven known to be in existence. None of the early pieces are signed; ca. 1918–1919; 13 inches diameter x 8¾ inches; $25,000.

San Ildefonso, olla made by Carmilita Dunlap: black-on-black design; 11 inches deep; excellent condition; $2,500–$3,000.

San Ildefonso, two pieces: plate made by Marie and Julian Martinez, feather design, ca. 1930s, 14 inches diameter x 2½ inches deep, $11,000; lamp base shape signed Marie (one of the earlier pieces made by Maria, decorated by Julian, but before he started signing them in 1923, so this is 1920s), 12¼ x 8½ inches diameter; $10,000.

San Ildefonso, plate made by Maria and her son Popovi (and signed that way): dated July 1963; diameter 11½ inches x 2 inches deep; $10,500.

San Ildefonso, small jar-shape pot with avanyu design: signed Marie and Santana (Adam's wife—Marie and Julian's eldest son); ca. 1960; 5 x 7½ inches diameter; $4,000.

Pottery, San Ildefonso, olla; black-on-black design; 11 inches deep; made by Carmilita Dunlap; excellent condition; $2,500–$3,000. Courtesy of, and photo by, Joyce Williams.

Pottery, San Ildefonso; plate made by Marie and Julian Martinez, ca. 1930s, feather design, 14 inches diameter x 2½ inches deep, $11,000; lamp base shape, signed Marie (one of the earlier pieces made by Maria, decorated by Julian, but before he started signing them in 1923, so this is 1920s), 12¼ x 8½ inches diameter, $10,000. Courtesy of Alexander Anthony/Adobe Gallery. Photo by Robert Reno.

Pottery, San Ildefonso, plate made by Maria and her son Popovi, and signed that way; dated July 1963; diameter 11½ inches x 2 inches deep; $10,500. Courtesy of Alexander Anthony/Adobe Gallery. Photo by Robert Reno.

Pottery, San Ildefonso, small jar-shape pot with avanyu design; signed Marie and Santana (Adam's wife—Maria and Julian's eldest son); ca. 1960; 5 x 7½ inches diameter; $4,000. Courtesy of Alexander Anthony/Adobe Gallery. Photo by Robert Reno.

San Ildefonso, jar made by Tony Da: small red jar with feather design, repeated three times with three turquoise nugget insets; signed "Da"—never signed Tony Da (see photo of signature); ca. 1960; 3¾ inches tall, 5 inches diameter; $4,500.

San Ildefonso, vase: black-on-black with bold geometric designs and crimped lip; 14 inches high x 6½ inches diameter at shoulder; good condition; $150–$200.

San Ildefonso, vase and jar: blackware vase and blackware two-handled jar; good condition; $50–$90/set.

SAN JUAN

San Juan, redware (group): made by Alvin Curran of the San Juan Pueblo; 1993; 4½ inches tall x 5 inches diameter, $850; 2¾ inches tall x 4 inches diameter, $500; 4 inches x 5 inches diameter, $650.

San Juan, storage jar: wire reinforcement around rim; piñon pitch to seal crack (both are native repairs); ca. 1870s; 17 inches diameter x 11 inches tall; $15,000.

Pottery, San Juan, group of redware made in 1993 by Alvin Curran of the San Juan Pueblo; left to right—4½ inches tall x 5 inches diameter, $850; 2¾ inches tall x 4 inches diameter, $500; 4 x 5 inches diameter, $650. Courtesy of Alexander Anthony/Adobe Gallery. Photo by Robert Reno.

Pottery, San Juan, storage jar; 17 inch diameter x 11 inches tall; wire reinforcement around rim; piñon pitch to seal crack (both are native repairs); ca. 1870s; $15,000. Courtesy of Alexander Anthony/Adobe Gallery. Photo by Robert Reno.

Pottery, Santo Domingo jar; polychrome bird and flower design; 8½ inches deep; made by Robert Tenorio; excellent condition; $1,200–$1,500. Courtesy of, and photo by, Joyce Williams.

Pottery, Tony and Patty Padella, sculptures; unique sculpted pottery figures; buffalo dancer, buffalo maiden, and buffalo figure entitled "Plains Laziness"; the Padellas are from Santa Clara Pueblo; values range from $400 to $2,000. Courtesy of Wanda Campbell, Indian Art Unlimited.

SANTO DOMINGO

Santo Domingo, double-spout jar by Monica Silva: black paneled design on buff slip with red ocher beneath, concave bottom; placed first in 1976 Indian Arts and Crafts Show; ca. 1925; 10½ inches x 14 inches high; good condition; $800–$1,200.

Santo Domingo, jar made by Robert Tenorio: polychrome bird and flower design; 8½ inches deep; excellent condition; $1,200–$1,500.

TESUQUE

Tesuque, figurine: clay figure with original tag, "Tesuqui Pueblo"; old; 9½ inches; very good condition; $175–$250.

ZIA

Zia, dough bowl: polychrome; typical Zia geometric design with birds; ca. 1890; 18 inches diameter x 10 inches deep; $8,500.

Zia, olla: Zia bird and double rainbow design; ca. 1910–1920; 10 x 10 inches; $4,500.

Zia, storage jar: four-color polychrome with rainbow and bird design; ca. 1910; 19½ inches diameter by 17 inches tall; $28,000.

Pottery, Zia, olla; Zia bird and double rainbow design; ca. 1910–1920; 10 x 10 inches; $4,500. Courtesy of Alexander Anthony/Adobe Gallery. Photo by Robert Reno.

Pottery, Zia, olla; finely executed pottery olla; polychrome design with rim band of black-on-white; three parrots around body, each with central checkerboard motif, three stylized human figures incorporated in the design; 3½-inch band of black-on-white at base; ca. 1900–1920; opening 11¼ inches, 17 inches high, 17 inches diameter; excellent condition. Courtesy of Willis Henry Auctions, Inc.

Pottery, Zia, storage jar; four-color polychrome with rainbow and bird design; ca. 1910; 19½ inches diameter x 17 inches tall; $28,000. Courtesy of Alexander Anthony/Adobe Gallery. Photo by Robert Reno.

ZUNI

Zuni, jar: bands of heart-line deer and birds with sunflowers in orange and amber on white slip, concave bottom; late 19th century—possibly an 1885 Laguna copy of a Zuni piece; 12¾ inches diameter x 10½ inches high; good condition; $900–$2,000.

Zuni, olla, nursing fawn design: ca. 1890s, 13 inches diameter x 9½ inches tall; $15,000.

Zuni, olla: with two frogs in relief, a heart-line deer design; unsigned; ca. 1910; 7½ inches tall x 10 inches diameter; $3,000.

Zuni, pottery fetish bowl: turquoise surface with feathers and eight white, yellow, red, black, and green stone beak fetishes; contemporary; 7½ inches high x 9½ inches diameter; very good condition; $50–$90.

Zuni, seed pot: designed by Randy Nahohai; 7½ inches tall x 12 inches diameter; mint condition; $1,475–$1,575.

Pottery, Zuni, olla; nursing fawn design; ca. 1890s; 13 inches diameter x 9½ inches tall; $15,000. Courtesy of Alexander Anthony/Adobe Gallery. Photo by Robert Reno.

Pottery, Zuni, olla; with two frogs in relief, a heart-line deer design; unsigned; ca. 1910; 7½ inches tall x 10 inches diameter; $3,000. Courtesy of Alexander Anthony/Adobe Gallery. Photo by Robert Reno.

Pottery, Zuni, seed pot; designed by Randy Nahohai; 7½ inches tall x 12 inches diameter; mint condition; $1,475–$1,575. Courtesy of Wanda Campbell/Indian Art Unlimited.

MISCELLANEOUS

Miscellaneous, three pieces: Santo Domingo bowl, black on cream, San Ildefonso vase, 5½ inches high; and pottery pipe with yellow, light blue, and red designs, 3 inches high; all very good condition; $150–$200/set.

Miscellaneous, two jars: one Hopi, with bird designs in orange and dark brown, 7½ inches high x 6 inches diameter; the other Acoma, with geometric designs in brown on white slip on red clay; 4 inches high x 5 inches diameter; very good condition; $175–$275/set.

Pottery, miscellaneous, group; left rear—damaged Hopi vase, $50–$70; middle rear, Zia, ca. 1920s, $300–$400; right rear, Santo Domingo basket, ca. 1920s, $70–$90; front left, Jemez pot, $55–$75; front right, contemporary Jemez bowl, $75–$100. Courtesy of Old Town Antiques, Albuquerque, New Mexico. Photo by Donald Vogt.

Chapter Twelve

Tools and Weapons

∿

All Indian tribes made the most of whatever Mother Earth made available to them, whether it be wildlife, plants, or certain types of soil. When a large animal was killed, primarily for food, its hide was used for clothing, organs such as bladders were often used as vessels for liquids, and the bones were made into tools.

Pointed pieces of bone made awls, daggers, or engravers for pottery. Indian women used slimmer pieces of bone to make needles which they used to draw sinew through leather, or to poke holes in rawhide or fur in order to sew the pieces together. Needles made by Lakes and Northeast tribes were used for webbing snowshoes. Pins were even made from the penis bones of small animals, such as the raccoon. The Southwest tribes used bone pieces to make weaving tools. Some have serrated edges, while others are notched near the end.

Coastal tribes and those near other bodies of water used bones to make harpoons or projectile points for fishing. Some, like the Ingalik tribe, barbed their bone points to make pronged fish spears.

The larger animal bones, such as buffalo shoulder blades, were used to make hoes by the Plains tribes. That bone could also be used to make a knife. The Menomini, and other tribes, made deer and bear scapulae into scoops or spoons of varying sizes. The scrapers the women used to take the flesh off a hide were often made from the toe bones of a bear or dog, which were easily held by placing one's fingers in the joints. Other scrapers, made from deer legs by the southwestern tribes, were engraved and decorated.

Deer, elk, or caribou antlers were used to make spear throwers, harpoons, clubs, celts, wedges, spoons, purses, figurines, jewelry, combs, effigy figures, and handles. The Northwest Coast tribes made use of the bones of whales and were able to fashion a wide range of tools and objects from their large bones.

As the white man invaded the North American Indian's territory, weapons began to change. Indians began to make arrowheads and knife blades from iron and brass. Tomahawks were formed from a piece of hot strap iron hammered around a rod to form an eye. They were often used as a hand ax and carried in battle, because once fired, a musket was worthless until reloaded; a tomahawk could be used at will at close range.

In general, the shape, size, and material of tools and weapons changed drastically with the advent of colonial European civilization. North American Indians are proud of their heritage, and hold on to the old ways. You will still find artisans, leatherworkers, potters, jewelers, and basket makers who continue to use the tools of their ancestors.

TOOLS AND THEIR MAKERS

COOKING UTENSILS   Kettles date back to the Tetons' earliest contact with the white man. The Brulés were noted by Prince Maximilian to have used iron kettles as early as 1834. These iron pots were often ordered from trading posts or captured from army camps the Indians raided. All of the round-bottomed cast-iron kettles used by the Tetons were similar, varying in size from one to five gallons. Pots either were supported by three short legs or had none. Factory-made sheet-iron kettles were commonly traded and collected by such tribes as the Oglala, as were skillets. The Indians seem to have preferred those with a long handle because they were easier to use when cooking over an open fire. Old skillets were often cut up and used for arrowheads.

CRAFTWORK TOOLS   All craftwork tools were made by hand. Flint knives and sharp-edged stones were used for cutting, pointed pieces of bone became awls (used to make holes for stitching), and sinew was used as thread.

GARDENING TOOLS   In the Southeast, it was common for Indian tribes to make tools from shells. Whole conch shells were hafted as picks and hoes. Eastern Indians' hoes were made of chipped stone, as were projectile points. Spades and posthole diggers were hoes made with a straight edge instead of a rounded one.

A corn planter, which was a long, pointed stick or a long, shaped rock or shell that was attached to a wooden pole, was used by the New England tribes to help them plant their staple crop.

To fertilize the soil, fish were buried in each hill. Especially nutritious for the soil was the horseshoe crab, which was chopped and used as fertilizer. The corn first introduced to New England grew to three times its previous size with this fertilizer.

LEATHERWORKING/SEWING TOOLS As with other tools, the early leatherworking and sewing tools of the Plains Indians were soon replaced with more modern versions once trading was firmly established in the West.

Awls were used since Indians first worked on leather and are still in use today. Specialty awls with two ninety-degree bends in the shank's center were made exclusively for Indian trade during the 1800s. This strangely shaped tool was proven to be more functional than straight varieties. Floridian tribes made needles from thin pieces of shells. They also used plentiful shells to make chisels and plummets.

Hide scrapers were made from elk horn or antler by the Plains Indians until about 1880, when elk became extinct in that area. Fleshing tools were made from old gun barrels by the Tetons. They cut off the barrel and hammered the end flat. Nearly all the Plains Indian women used scissors similar to what we might buy in a store today. Needles were also commonly traded and used to sew beads onto cloth or to stitch the cloth itself. Some needles were even packaged as "beading needles" by such companies as the Brabant Needle Company of England.

Another tool developed solely for Indian use was the quill flattener. In the old days, when an Indian woman prepared to decorate with quills, she used a smooth object to flatten them. The nineteenth century brought about the advent of a tool to flatten quills that was deeply curved at both ends and forged around the middle.

Pottery and silver thimbles came into use as craftspeople realized that they did indeed help to push the needle through heavy materials. Potters and silversmiths recognized the appeal of such a product and began to make them for friends and relatives. They were soon sold, like just about every other Indian craft, to the white man.

MEAT-CARVING TOOLS Carving a cow on the Blood Reserve in the 1920s was done much the same way the Indians carved buffalo years before. The woman to whom this task fell began by sharpening the ax and knives. The first cut was made by bringing the ax down into the backbone, and by chopping away, she would bring the carcass away from the spine. She then cut a one-piece loin that was about four feet long. This tender cut was a favorite. The shoulder ribs were considered a special man's meal, which, cooked over an open fire in the tipi, were eaten right away. The other ribs were often smoked so they could be saved for later.

METALWORKING TOOLS   The earliest metalwork tools were made of copper by the Lakes area tribes (ca. 3000 B.C.). The Lake Superior region supplied those tribes with pure copper nuggets or copper veins found in rocky areas. Tools and weapons, such as spears, arrows, knives, and celts, were made from copper long ago by the Indians of the Old World Copper Culture (ca. 3000 B.C.)

MORTARS AND PESTLES   New England tribes made mortars and pestles from soapstone obtained from nearby quarries.

SPOONS   The Yurok and Hupa tribes made spoons from antlers, which only the men and guests were allowed to use for eating a corn-meal mush. The women of those tribes used mussel shells as their spoons. The spoons were a distinctive style, with jagged-edged handles.

WEAVING TOOLS   Weaving tools used by the Navajo include wood battens, pins, combs, and sacking needles.

WOODWORKING TOOLS   Woodworking tools such as the ax, pick, whetstone, hatchet, and celt were used by New England Indians to make house poles, bed planks, platforms, and other wooden items.

WEAPONS

ARMOR   The Northwest Coast tribes made suits of armor from tiny wooden slats which they pieced together and decorated with a variety of colorful geometric designs favored by different tribes. With these suits the Indians would wear wonderfully carved and painted wooden helmets.

BLOWGUNS AND DARTS   Cherokee and Iroquois Indians used blowguns and darts against their enemies. These items are rarely found today.

BOWS   The bows made by the Mohave tribe were wooden and were often decorated. Bows used in New England were characteristically five to six feet long and made of ash, oak, witch hazel, and hickory.

CLUBS War clubs of the New England tribes included the hatchet club. Made of a chipped stone, such as granite, quartz, basalt, or pegmatite, the head was attached to a piece of wood with sinew. A ball-headed club (rare) was made from a glacial cobble, attached to a bent piece of wood wrapped about the center. Pronged war clubs, wooden with a rounded knob, had a triangle of stone imbedded in the ball. War clubs could be made from small birch trees by cutting them about thirty inches from the ground and sharpening the roots into lethal prongs. Seal clubs, made of yew on the Northwest Coast, were used to kill seals, otters, halibut, and salmon. As with all other wooden implements made by Indians of the Northwest Coast, carving and other work decorated each piece, a favorite subject being the efficient hunter, the sea lion.

DAGGERS Northwest Coast weapons were often elaborately and beautifully crafted, and often became family heirlooms. Daggers made by Tlingits in the late eighteenth century were skillfully made from iron and copper and so beautifully decorated that Europeans were impressed with the Indian's ability to produce them.

Artists such as Kuch-Kee-Ees (Black Wolf of Klukwan) made daggers or swords and gave them names, such as Killer Whale Dagger. The carving on these pieces is bold and almost geometric, and historians are still baffled by the techniques used to create these pieces. Tlingit warriors were customarily the owners of such weapons.

FIREARMS Weapon-making was very important to the Sioux. That being the case, it's easy to understand why the use of iron caught their attention before 1840. Iron was far superior to the flint and bone they had used for weapon-making in the past, and they quickly replaced their lithic blades with those made of iron.

Most of the iron weapons the Indians used were commercially produced by the white man, though they did fashion some weapons using tools bought from traders. Indian agencies and trading posts during that period all had blacksmiths on or near the premises, and they all worked with the Indians, repairing pieces, shodding horses, making items such as traps, axes, fish and muskrat spears, and hoes.

The Tetons first traded for guns during the winters between 1799 and 1802, and by 1804, were well acquainted with guns.

Zebulon Pike, the explorer, estimated in 1804 that there were approximately one hundred guns owned by the Tetons, who, at that time, numbered approximately two thousand.

Fur-trading companies, both American and Canadian, sold what came to be known as the "Northwest gun." They were made in a standard pattern from 1750 to approximately 1900. The gun featured a light, smooth bore, fusil stocked to the muzzle. The Barnett Northwest gun, manufactured in England, was typical of those being purchased by the Tetons. The Smithsonian holds a Hudson's Bay Company Northwest gun that was dated 1876 and taken from Sitting Bull's band in 1881 at Fort Buford when they surrendered.

After the turn of the century, traders freely brought firearms up the Missouri River and sold guns such as the Jacot and Lacy rifles. The Plains tribes soon began using "trade" rifles, which had deadly accuracy, though they were double the weight of a Northwest gun. Companies selling trade rifles to the Indians from approximately 1836 to 1880 were the Pierre Chouteau, Jr., Company, the Edward K. Tryon Co. of Philadelphia, and the Henry E. Leman Co. (also of Pennsylvania).

When the Indian Wars began, Indians were using all types of rifles, acquired in many different ways. Sitting Bull surrendered a Winchester Model 1866 carbine when he returned to the United States in 1881. Indian police carried Whitney-Kennedy lever-action rifles in the late 1870s, which were marked "USID," as well as some Model 1877 Remington-Keene bolt-action carbines. The Oglala chief Young-Man-Afraid-of-his-Horse carried a .45–70 carbine, while the Oglala warrior Red Dog carried a Sharps buffalo rifle. Revolvers came into Indian hands after the Civil War. More than two hundred Colt single-action .45-caliber revolvers were captured by the Tetons at Little Big Horn in 1876. The Indian police were issued the last revolvers used by the Tetons.

The Northwest Coast tribes began receiving guns in trade when mariners began asking for the sea otter robes and elegant tanned elk hides of the Chinook people. Though it was generally regarded as unwise to trade guns to the Indians during that period, few seafaring traders let that stand in the way of accumulating skins and novelty foods. In return for hides and other items, the Native Americans received iron to make tools and weapons. Unfortunately, by introducing the gun to these tribes, the seafaring traders also introduced a more dangerous type of warfare.

FISHING TOOLS   Author's note: During the past five years, interest has skyrocketed in collecting items made for the fishing trade. Fishing tools made by Native Americans are in great demand, and prices have gone up considerably.

Early Archaic fishing tools were plummets with spears attached to the end of the weight. Harpoons were also common. They were made of bone and primarily used to catch larger fish (e.g., sea bass, bluefish, sturgeon, and seal). The Northwest Coast Indians decorated their harpoons and clubs with abalone inlay and engraving. Poles, halibut hooks, and lures were all made of wood. The halibut hooks made by Northwest Coast Indians were often so decorative that one wonders whether the maker grieved when the hook was lost with the fish. A tool made of two pieces of wood and a bone barb lashed together was extremely efficient in hooking the halibut, though its appearance belied the fact. Halibut hooks are often decoratively carved with birds, especially ravens, or animals such as bears.

Fishing for salmon, the most abundant fish in the Northwest, was of extreme importance to the tribes located on the Northwest Coast. To catch salmon during their fight upstream, the North Pacific Coast tribes used several kinds of harpoons, traps, and nets. Openwork fences (weirs) were built that allowed the water to flow through, but easily trapped the fish.

The most commonly used harpoon consisted of "two barbs of bone or horn fitted together to form a socket at their base and usually to hold a cutting tip or blade" (*Cultures of the North Pacific Coast*, by Philip Drucker). Other harpoons used the basic structure with minor changes, such as a single point and foreshaft. Nets used to fish for salmon ranged from dip nets to bags. Seine and gill net types were used only occasionally.

A herring rake was used to fish for the great schools that often swam inshore. The rake was an oar-shaped device with a row of sharp bone spikes along one edge. One person paddled the canoe while his partner swept the rake edgewise throughout the water, impaling herring on the spikes and then shaking them off into the canoe.

The whale-hunting Northwest Coast tribes used harpoons to strike the whale as it rose to the water's surface. Rituals were also performed by the tribal chiefs that encouraged dead whales to beach themselves close to the tribe's home.

Native Americans were the first fishermen to use decoys, though few are found intact today.

KNIVES Green River knives were named for the Green River in Massachusetts, and manufactured by the John Russell Factory (founded in 1832) in Greenfield, Massachusetts. Green River butcher and carving knives were sold wholesale to trading posts throughout the West for $1.50 to $3.50 per dozen. The trading posts, in turn, retailed the knives for $.50 to $1.50 each. The John Russell Company filled a void in American marketing with their knives because most blades that had been sold in this country up to that time were shipped to this continent from Sheffield, England.

The long butcher knives that backwoodsmen in the early West carried and considered necessary equipment impressed the Shawnee Indians so much that they called the frontiersmen the "Long Knives."

Though the knives made by the Green River factory were mainly used for skinning, the user of the blade would often sharpen and shape it to his liking. Sometimes its original shape was completely altered, and often the "Green River" name, which was hand-stamped on the blade, was obliterated. The Plains Indians sometimes took the blades out of their knives and fastened them to the end of a lance or on their gunstock war clubs. Collectors can find a number of examples of Green River knives that were used in this fashion.

Green River knives became so well known by trappers, frontiersmen, and Indians that phrases were coined using the manufacturer's name (e.g., "Up to the Green River" could mean stabbing someone with the knife by plunging it so far into the body that the blade went in up to the "Green River" name stamped on it). After 1836, approximately sixty thousand of these knives were sent west each year, and by 1840, the American-made knives dominated a market once held by the English factories in Sheffield.

The Russell-Harrington Cutlery Company, the result of a 1935 merge between the original John Russell Company and the John Harrington Company of Southbridge, Massachusetts, still produces butcher knives and other kitchen cutlery.

QUIVERS New England quivers were made of leather, bark, or wood, and bowstrings were often made of moose (or deer or buffalo) sinew, depending upon the maker's location and availability of animals. Plains Indians also used quivers and decorated them with paint, beads, or quills.

SPEARS   Spearing fish or lobster was often the easiest way to bring fish home for supper for New England Indians. Lobsters were speared with a two- to three-foot-long shaft. During the summer, when the water was low, a stone wall would be built in a drop in the stream bed, and a sieve of sticks made, onto which the fish would tumble. They also used nets made of hemp and other fibers and attached to a long, split stick.

Plains and Plateau Indians used spears for hunting land animals; Northwest Coast Indians used them for fishing.

PRICES

Ax: stone ax with rawhide haft; old; 19-inch haft; very good condition; $300–$400.

Ball war club: made from natural tree growth with patina on handle; old; good condition; $200–$300.

Bow case and quiver: fringed buckskin without other decoration; very rare; very old; fair to good condition; $2,000–$2,400.

Cheyenne, knife and sheath: beaded hide with traditional Cheyenne design; chain suspensions; trade knife with hilt wrapped in copper wire; ca. 1860s; $5,000.

Fork: three-tine fork with beaded handle; old; very good condition; $50 -$100.

Iroquois, two ladles: wooden, one with crosshatched chip carving on handle, the other a hardwood with wide bowl and turned tip end to latch on to a kettle's rim; old; 13 x 16 inches; very good condition; $25–$75/sct.

Jicarilla Apache, basketry fishing creel: aniline-dyed sumac design, leather strap; lid ties replaced; 15½ inches long x 7 inches high; good condition; $450–$700.

Knife: catlinite ceremonial knife, fetish attachments with arrowpoint and turquoise, with buffalo hair and braided sinew in the form of a snake's rattle; 10½ inches long; very good condition; $125–$225.

Knife and sheath: porcupine quilled decoration in orange, green, and white; knife with quilled handle; contemporary; 11 inches long; good condition; $200–$275.

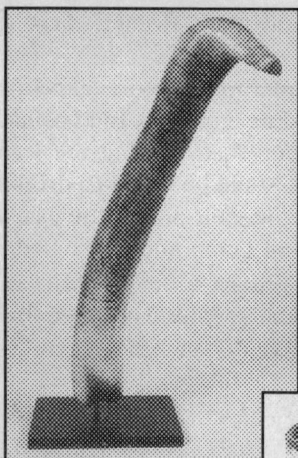

Tools/Weapons, hide scraper, Northern Plains; ca. 1850s; made of elk antler, incised decorations; 14 inches long; $2,000–$2,800. Courtesy of Canfield Gallery. Photo by Donald Vogt.

Tools/Weapons, Ketoh, Navajo; bow guards; left is ca. 1920, $900–$1,200; center is ca. 1940, $800–$1,000; right is sand-cast Navajo, ca. 1940, $1,000–$1,250. Courtesy of Morning Star Gallery, Santa Fe. Photo by Donald Vogt.

Tools/Weapons, Sioux, knife sheath; beaded hide knife sheath with bone-handled dagger; sheath has a waistband of tin cone dangles with red, blue, and green beads on white ground; the dagger made from an old file and has a short stag grip; ca. 1850–1860; 10 ½ inches long in 8-inch sheath; $1,000–$1,250. Courtesy of William R. Nash Collection. Photo by Donald Vogt.

Sword: iron hilt; from old Indian collection; 19-inch blade; good condition; $300–$400.

Northwest Coast, four spoons: made of goat horn, undecorated; 7 inches, 7¼ inches, and two 6 inches each; very good condition; $70–$90.

Northwest Coast, halibut hook: representing a carved bird design, with cedar rope and attached wooden hook; 9 inches long; very good condition; $90–$140.

Northwest Coast, halibut hook: unusual motif of fish with a shaman/human head in its mouth; deaccessioned from a Maine museum; late 19th century; 11½ inches long; well used; $150–$200.

Northwest Coast, spoon: mountain goat horn handle carved with totem designs of hawk, sea creature, beaver, and others, attached to the spoon with three copper rivets; 10 inches long; good condition; $550–$700.

Northwest Coast, spoon: carved with totemic carvings on handle; back marked "Sitka"; 5¼ inches long; very good condition; $45–$65.

Northwest Coast, spoon: horn, handle with detailed carving of a floral geometric design with "1902"; 7 inches long; good condition; $25–$45.

Northwest Coast, three ladles: made of mountain sheep horns; 11, 12, and 14 inches long; good condition; $50–$70 each.

Plains (possibly), war club: fully beaded floppy-head war club; 19 inches; very good condition; $375–$425.

Plains, bow: carved wood with notched ends, painted partially in dark pigment; 48 inches long; very good condition; $85–$125.

Plains, bow and three arrows: feathered arrows with carved horn ends, bird stunners; 2 feet 10 inches; very good condition; $140–$180.

Plains, gun: large-caliber rifle made by Tryon & Co., with saddle ring bar attached; old; very good condition; $2,000–$3,000.

Plains, knife sheath: hide surface covered with dirty white and red small beads in a geometric design, fringed at the bottom and with a side fringe tuft; early 1900s; very good condition; $150–$300.

Plains, pipe tomahawk: notched head with brass tack designs on a wooden stem; deaccessioned from Museum of American

Tools/Weapons, Plains, beaded knife sheath. Courtesy of Willis Henry Auctions.

Indian Heye Foundation, numbers on handle; 19¾ inches long; good condition; $1,300–$1,700.

Plains, pipe tomahawk: brass with steel insert, tacked handle with beaded horsetail drop; old; good condition; $1,000–$1,500.

Plains, skull cracker: stone head with wrapped handle beaded in indigo blue, greasy yellow, and red; 18 inches long; very good condition; $150–$250.

Plains; skull cracker, arrow, and lariat: skull cracker, red-dyed goat horn with beaded shank in cobalt on white, zigzag design, fabric-wrapped, sinew-sewn, 23½ inches long; arrow, forged tip and paint-decorated, sinew-wrapped, 24¼ inches long; lariat, braided with elliptical wooden tip, 136 inches long; very good condition; $500–$700/set.

Plains, spoon: carved of steer horn; handle wrapped in plaited quillwork; $1,200.

Plains, tomahawk: wood handle wrapped with braided twine, pitch tar or gum filling, several feathers attached; old; 16 inches long; good condition; $100–$300.

Pueblo: bow, arrows, case, and quiver: bow case painted with red, blue, green, and white pigments; six arrows with steel and flint points, sewn with sinew; 47 inches long; 19th century; very good condition; $2,300–$2,700/set.

Sioux, horn spoon: beaded cow-horn spoon; very good condition; $50–$100.

Sioux, maul: rawhide-wrapped granite maul, used to break the buffalo bones to obtain the marrow; early to mid 1800s; 17-inch handle; very good condition; $350–$550.

Sioux, spoon: buffalo-horn spoon; very old; very good condition; $200–$300.

Sioux, tomahawk: stone with carvings on head of buffalo, turtle, horse, and tipi; 19 inches; very good condition; $75–$125.

Sioux, war club: rawhide-wrapped stone with horsehair drop; 18 inches; very good condition; $75–$125.

Sioux, war club: salt-and-pepper beading with egg-shaped head; old; 19 inches; very good condition; $100–$200.

Sioux, war club: stone war club with red-painted rawhide handle and quartzite egg-shaped head; rare; early 1800s; 28-inch handle; very good condition; $1,000–$1,400.

Sioux, war club: rawhide-wrapped with egg-shaped head; 28 inches; very good condition; $300–$400.

Sioux, war club: black pipestone head is carved in the shape of a bighorn sheep ram; long-handled with quillwork decorations; very good condition; $300–$500.

Upper Missouri, knife: Hudson Bay–style stabber knife with bone handle; with leather case; 1880s; $800–$1,200.

Winchester rifle: .32-caliber with wooden butt; painted buffalo on one side and painted tipi and sun on the other; slash marks for buffalo kills on one side and diamonds on the other; 43¼ inches long; very good condition; $500–$700.

Wood bow with sinew string: old; good patina and very good condition; $400–$500.

Woodlands, knife: crooked spiral-carved handle of an animal figure, with inlaid diamond and circle designs and lead inlay near the metal blade; 11 inches long; very good condition; $150–$200.

Woodlands, tomahawk: iron spike tomahawk with 18-inch carved, striped maple handle; Revolutionary War era; very good condition; $575–$775.

Chapter Thirteen

Wooden Items

❧

The Native Americans are artists who utilize everything Mother Earth gives them. They used grasses to weave blankets and clothing. The animals provided food, clothing, and shelter. The sea gave them food, and the shells were transformed into utensils, tools, and ornamentation. The trees gave them shade on sunny days, and the cut wood was used to build shelter, ornamental items, and transporting devices. Indians used the bark from trees in sometimes ingenious, always useful, ways, and, was often used to create art by those tribes on the Northwest Coast.

In this chapter we describe a small portion of those items made with wood by the American Indian tribes.

EXAMPLES OF WOODEN ITEMS

BACKRESTS   Backrests made by the Plains tribes were constructed of horizontal slats of wood wound into an inverted cone shape and attached to a tripod, made of poles, by a loop at the top of the backrest. Furs were often thrown over backrests to make them more comfortable.

BARK ART   The Chippewa tribe perfected the decorative art of drawing pictures on bark. These drawings told the story of a ceremony or birth, and became a way of recording and preserving the history of the tribe. Birch-bark designs known as "transparencies" are formed by the Chippewa woman's teeth—she bites her design into the wood. The design is shown clearly when held up to the light.

The Midewiwin's (the Grand Medicine Society) information was recorded on a scroll-like piece of bark. Designs were pressed into the bark with the point of a bone, then rubbed with vermilion (a natural red dye) so that the impressions could be clearly seen.

BABY CARRIERS   Each tribe had its own style of baby carrier. The Northwest Coast made coffinlike boxes, which the parents sometimes chose to decorate. Wooden slats made up the "bed" of

Apache baby carriers. At the crown was a wooden hoop that acted as a shield against the elements. One would imagine that that wooden hoop, which made a half circle over the baby's head, also acted as a safety device. If the carrier were dropped, the hoop would protect the baby's head. Eastern tribes made their baby carriers of flat boards, with a footrest at the base and face guards on the sides.

BOWLS Bent-corner bowls made by the Northwest tribes were used for serving food. Early examples were made from birch bark, but later (nineteenth-century) pieces are usually made of yellow or red cedar. Characteristic of these bowls was an undulating rim—high at the ends with dipping sides. These bowls come in all sizes, from individual containers to great feast dishes, which can be up to twenty feet long. They are decorated, painted, carved, or embellished with shells, and their sides are joined in any number of ways—with pegs, lacing, lashing, or even fitted with tenons and scarfs. The sides of these bowls were bent by steaming the wood until it became flexible. Once carved with an adze and shaped with a knife to form the high-ended form, the sides were joined to a red cedar base. Brass tacks and shells were a popular form of decoration used around the rims of these bowls.

BOXES The Northwest Coast tribes made boxes used for storage, in cooking, and as coffins. Some were painted and carved, some trimmed with shellwork, and others simply painted. The sides were connected to the box in a rather unique way—they were sewn with spruce root. The ends of thicker wood boxes were joined with small wooden pegs.

The wood used by the Northwest Coast tribes to make these boxes was straight-grained red and yellow cedar, spruce, and yew, among others. They were split with a wooden or antler edge, adzed to a particular thickness or thinness, and shaved with a knife to achieve a flat surface.

Other tribes, such as the Cherokee, made boxes out of cedar wood. The boxes were small, designed to hold fetishes or other trinkets of significance to the owner. Often the boxes were painted with decoration.

CANOES AND BOATS The Chippewa tribe, the largest and strongest of the Great Plains, developed the birch-bark canoe, which became a major means of transportation at that time. Dugout canoes, made from one piece of wood, were popular forms of transportation for New England Indians.

Canoes and paddles made by the Northwest Coast Indians are as decorative as they are useful. The early models are characterized by a low bow, while later ones have an upswept bow. Detail in the geometric painting of these canoes is extremely important and mimics the work done on Northwest Indian masks. The animal's head is painted toward the front, or bow, of the canoe, and its hindquarters are depicted on the stern. The paddles are decorated as well. Black and red pigments were favored for this kind of decorative work.

The eastern forest Indians made birch-bark canoes by stripping the bark off the birch trees that grew in the Great Lakes region. First a tree was felled. Great care was taken to choose a tree that was tall and straight, with no knots and a tough, firm bark. Then the tree was examined for flaws, and if it was, indeed, perfect, the tree length was marked off at approximately eighteen feet and an incision was made lengthwise so that the bark could be stripped from the tree. Once the bark was properly stripped, it was flattened by use of a torch, which was carefully applied to the surface of the bark. If the bark was discovered to be too small, another tree's bark could be easily sewn and patched to the first.

When the framework was prepared and had the proper shape, it was covered with the bark. The framework for the canoe was usually cedar, but any other straight-grained green wood could be used as long pieces were split out. The gunwales, ribs, and sheathing were made from these long pieces, and the interior sheathing was thin and three or four fingers broad. Ribs, 1½ inches thick, were bent outside (the *natural* outside of the wood) to prevent splitting and breaking.

It was necessary to boil wood in a large steaming box to shape it, and once bent, pieces had to be tied in place. The canoe's shape is formed by the gunwales, which are made carefully and turn upward at each end. Crossbars divided the canoe into four equal sections.

Indians then formed a framework by driving stakes into the ground. The spot was made even and smooth before the bark was placed in the framework and the gunwales and end pieces attached. Then the V-shaped rear and bow boards were squeezed in to fit the gunwale angle. Once they were in place, the shape of the canoe was defined. Basket splints were then placed, edge to edge, in the canoe to line the inside and protect the exterior bark from abrasion.

After the ribs and thwarts were secure, the canoe was taken from the frame, turned over, and the seams sealed with pitch. Once the pitch was dry, the canoe could be personalized with decoration.

Wooden dugouts and bark canoes made by the Indians of old are not much different from the modern versions.

HEADDRESSES AND MASKS   Northwest Coast Indians were masters when it came to carved and decorated wooden objects, such as headdresses and masks. Dance headdresses were made of a cylindrical frame. Down the back hung a long panel of ermine skins, while the front was an incredible plaque of hardwood, painted and decorated (usually with abalone). The frontlet (or plaque) is said to represent a mystical creature, and on Haida and Tlingit headdresses it is often framed by rows of orange and black feathers with a band of iridescent green and black mallard head skin across the forehead.

The dance the headdress is made for is performed on many different occasions (e.g., to welcome visitors). In the Kwakiutl tribes, the dance is done before a figure appears and is masked with a crest indicating he is the headdress dancer. This figure becomes possessed, then flees the house.

Other masks made by the Northwest Coast tribes vary in form, shape, and purpose and may be used to celebrate times of change (e.g., birth, death, or marriage). The Skhwaikhwey mask is owned by one person and is passed on to that person's descendants. It is used in the cleaning ritual of the Salish. The Kwakiutl tribe uses a Goomokwey mask, made of wood and cedar bark. Goomokwey is the chief of the undersea world, and one who can gain his favor is rewarded with wealth and prestige. The Thunderbird, a favored subject of the Kwakiutl, is used in a dance that celebrates the power of ancestors who had contact with supernatural beings.

BARK HOUSES   East of the Mississippi, most Indians lived in wooden houses rather than the leather/rawhide tipis of other Indians. Iroquois and many Algonquian tribes made "great houses" of bark and poles. These buildings were very long (more than a hundred feet) and narrow (fifteen to twenty feet). Holes were made in the ceilings to let smoke from fireplaces escape.

In the early days, before the advent of the ax, the Indians harvested wood for their houses by burning down what they needed. Before proceeding to build, the "construction crew" would decide how big the house was to be, then proceed to collect corner posts, supporting poles, rafters, and bark (usually elm), which would be applied to the outside of the building.

Bunks were built on the inside of the building to comfortably house its inhabitants, and storage platforms built above these beds, to be used for storing corn and other foods.

Doors to the lodge were usually made of a tanned bearskin pelt attached to the jamb posts by thongs.

Indian settlements in the East were made up of a number of these buildings, sometimes stockaded to ensure the safety of the inhabitants.

MAPLE SUGARING ITEMS   One of the many foods introduced to white colonists by the Native American was maple syrup. To harvest sap from maple trees, the Northeast Indians made sap dishes which were placed under each tree. These dishes, usually made from elm or birch bark, would be scraped smooth and bound with strips at each end. Sometimes a bark "cone" would be filled with snow and topped with maple syrup as a treat for the children. Bark containers were made from white birch, elm, chestnut, basswood, ash, cedar, fir, and spruce.

In the spring, when the sap was flowing, the tree would be stripped by making two circular cuts on the trunk, and a third cut connecting the two others lengthwise. A sturdy stick was used to pry the bark from the tree.

Indians made water pails from this bark. Soaking it in hot water made it easier to fold. Sometimes these "pails" were even used for boiling.

MORTARS   Wooden mortars made by New England Indians were often up to twenty-five inches long. Logs were hollowed out to create mortars. The Mohegans were known to carve their mortars on the outside. The interior would be burned hollow, and the mortar scraped from the sides. When it was used to crush kernels, the force of the pestle would push the smaller pieces to the top of the mortar, while the larger ones stayed on the bottom.

SPOONS   Wooden spoons of the Northwest Coast Indians were usually made of alder, maple, or yew, and they resembled ladles. Though most are plain and practical, other spoons are decorated or embellished with carving, painting, and inlay.

Northeastern tribes used wooden spoons and bowls made from the burls of trees, burnt and scraped until they were just a thin shell. These serving vessels were often used by everyone in the tribe.

Though many were produced, few still exist because wood does not hold up well when buried in cold New England soil.

TOTEM POLES Totem poles are the work of Northwest Coast Indians, whose wood carvings were truly the best and most dramatic of any of the North American Indian tribes. The Haida tribe was unequaled as totem pole carvers. Sadly, hundreds of different types of poles have crumbled beyond salvaging. The Haida culture itself began to collapse in the mid 1870s when its people died by the thousands after contracting European diseases that they had not previously been exposed to.

Totem poles were made hundreds of years before European contact, yet the art of pole carving grew slowly because only the wealthiest and most powerful families in the village could afford to have them made. Once the tools used to make these poles were more modernized, production was greatly facilitated and the poles became more common. Totem pole carving was also encouraged by the unexpected flow of material goods into small villages.

Two distinct types of poles were carved: memorial poles, to honor past leaders, and house poles, decorative posts installed within the house itself. Some villages raised many poles, creating the appearance of a forest of poles, while others raised only a few or none at all. The oldest memorial poles were simple, uncarved shafts topped by a single carved figure.

House poles used in supporting the house roof probably developed after memorial poles. They display the lineage crests of the homeowners. They were not erected to memorialize the dead, but rather to record the family history. Their carvings are more detailed and complex, and they are physically broader than memorial posts.

Heraldic poles, or true totem poles, are freestanding storytelling poles. The poles tell of mythical and historical pasts by carving one figure on top of another and painting them brilliantly. They are public displays of important tales of renowned ancestors.

Characters most commonly depicted on totem poles are the raven, portrayed as a male; the eagle, with its curved beak turning back to the face; the thunderbird, a larger eagle with outstretched wings, and ears resembling horns; the grizzly, with a large open mouth and long, narrow tongue (sometimes biting a frog, which it holds in its hands); a wolf, similar to a grizzly, but thinner, with a more narrow snout and more pointed teeth; a beaver, always upright with its paws holding a stick; frogs (used as space fillers), with broad, toothless mouths and big eyes; a whale, with a flat face, rounded teeth, and circular blowhole above the forehead; and numerous others. Human beings are also depicted on totem poles and may have animal or bird characteristics.

Some well-known Kwakiutl totem pole carvers include Mungo Martin, Charles James, Bill Reid, Douglas Cranmer, and Robert Davidson. The totem pole carvers were well-respected members of the community, and their "signatures" were often carved into the strippling on the pole.

PRICES

Blackfoot: cradleboard made of peeled willow, sinew-strung, edged in black wool; attached painted fabric headrest with geometric hourglass designs in lavender, yellow, and green; fringed; 52 inches overall; very good condition; $200–$300.

Wooden items, Cree, decoy; bundled-stick goose decoy; James Bay, Ontario; $150– $300. Collection of Phyllis Ellison. Photo by Gene Kangas.

Wooden items, Cree, decoy; field goose decoy; not intended to float, but were stuck in snow or mud; made in James Bay, Ontario; $350–$550. Collection of Gene and Linda Kangas. Photo by Gene Kangas.

Eastern Woodlands, box: circular beaver box; made of birch bark with sweet-grass-wrapped edge bands; top cover decorated with beaver in porcupine quillwork; sides with quillwork in natural white and red geometrics; 4½ inches diameter, 2¼ inches high; generally very good condition throughout; $200–$400.

Iroquois, mask: false-face mask, carved from a living tree, stained and painted by "Sundown," an old Cattaragas artisan, about 1900. White face with black and ocher stain, red lips, indented teeth, black horsehair; life-size (10½ inches) mask worn by the practitioner of the family group that had multiple children to expunge fertility spirits; original instructive label attached; originally owned by Phillips Exeter museum collection; $1,200–$1,800.

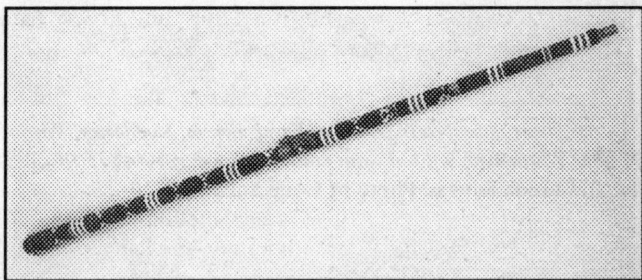

Wooden items, cane; belonged to Geronimo; beaded in blue background with white, green, and red designs; provenance stated in owner's papers. Courtesy of Jack Glover. Photo by Donald Vogt.

Wooden items, box; owned by Quanah Parker; heavily carved with eagles on both ends as well as on top; painted with white, blue, yellow, and red. Courtesy of Jack Glover. Photo by Donald Vogt.

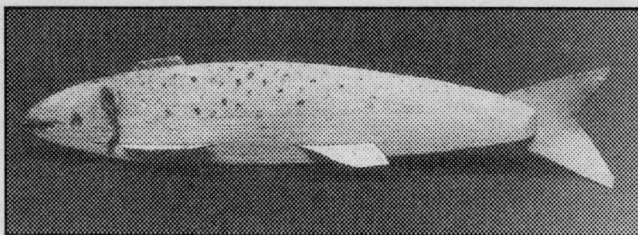

Wooden items, decoy; fish decoy from reservation near Lake Simcoe, Ontario; wood stained white with burned spots, gills, eyes, and mouth; metal fins and tail; $150–$300. Collection of Gene and Linda Kangas. Photo by Gene Kangas.

Wooden items, decoy; pike-spearing decoy by Frank Gensio, Stockbridge, Wisconsin; used on Lake Winnebago; natural cedar with copper fins; $500–$750. Collection of Gene and Linda Kangas. Photo by Gene Kangas.

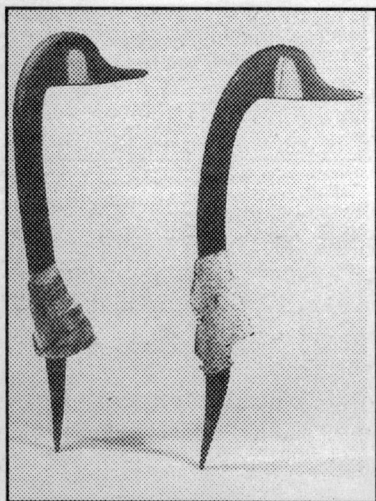

Wooden items, decoys; two stick-up Canadian goose heads; two-piece head and neck constructions; bottoms wrapped with natural birch bark to resemble the white chest of a goose; made in Prince Edward Island, Canada; $300–$500 each. Collection of Gene and Linda Kangas. Photo by Gene Kangas.

Wooden items, mask, Iroquois; false-face mask, carved from a living tree, stained and painted by "Sundown," an old Cattaragas artisan, about 1900. White face with black and ocher stain, red lips, indented teeth, black horsehair; 10½-inch life-size mask worn by the practitioner of the family group that had multiple children to expunge fertility spirits; original instructive label attached; originally owned by Phillips Exeter museum collection; $1,200–$1,800. Courtesy of C. E. Guarino Auction Gallery, Denmark, Maine.

Iroquois, mask: old spoon-mouth false-face mask; Seneca-Iroquois, Allegheny reservation; carved by an unidentified craftsman from basswood; stained with vegetal red, with incised markings, eyes, ocher-rubbed surface, long horsehair; originally owned by Phillips Exeter museum; ca. 1870s; life-size (11 inches long); $1,600–$2,000.

Northwest Coast, mask: red cedar, white pigment, black over the eyes; fitted with a headband and cut nails for holding in mouth; old split; from a sea captain's home in New Jersey; 17 inches high x 14 inches wide; $1,700–$2,000.

Northwest Coast, totem pole: polychrome decorated clan totem with orca, raven, bear holding a human figure, and frog; shows old breaks; old patina; from a sea captain's home in New Jersey; 48 inches high; very good condition; $800–$1,200.

Passamaquoddy, box: quillworked birch-bark box; circular form with sweet grass bindings at rims; cover decorated with a seven-leaved tree floral in natural porcupine quills; sides decorated with a band of joined X forms in quill; ca. 1920s; few quills missing, some loose, but generally in good condition; $200–$400.

Plains, dance cane: carved horse-head crook with brass nailhead designs at horse's neck; painted and etched wooden shaft; attached rawhide bridle; 49 inches long; very good condition; $700–$900.

Wooden items, mask, Iroquois; old spoon-mouth false-face mask; Seneca-Iroquois, Allegheny reservation; carved by an unidentified craftsman from basswood; ca. 1870s; stained with vegetal red, with incised markings, eyes, ocher-rubbed surface, long horsehair; 11 inches long, life-size; originally owned by Phillips Exeter museum; $1,600–$2,000. Courtesy of C. E. Guarino Auction Gallery, Denmark, Maine.

Wooden items, Micmac, decoy; close-up of stick-up seagull. Collection of Gene and Linda Kangas. Photo by Gene Kangas.

Wooden items, Micmac, decoy; stick-up of sea gull; hollow construction; a large and rare decoy; 10,000–$13,000. Collection of Gene and Linda Kangas. Photo by Gene Kangas.

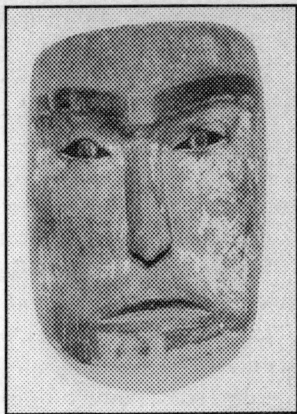

Wooden items, Northwest Coast, mask; red cedar, white pigment, black over the eyes; fitted with a headband and cut nails for holding in mouth; old split; from a sea captain's home in New Jersey; 17 inches high x 14 inches wide; $1,700–$2,000. Courtesy of Willis Henry Auctions, Inc.

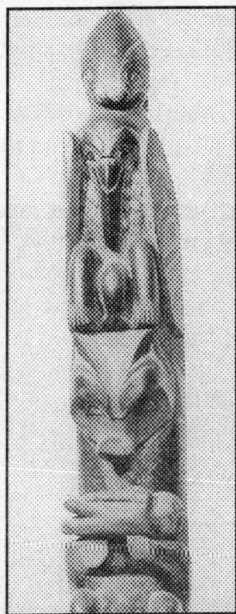

Wooden items, Northwest Coast, totem pole; polychrome decorated clan totem with orca, raven, bear holding a human figure, and frog; shows old breaks; old patina; from a sea captain's home in New Jersey; 48 inches high; very good condition; $800–$1,200. Courtesy of Willis Henry Auctions, Inc.

Haida, clan totem: carved wood with old dark finish, of a figure holding a seal upside down, with a bear cub on its head standing on a bear, standing on a human head, on small base; ca. 19th century; 21 inches high; very good condition; $500–$600.

Haida, spoon: made of horn, carved, with shell and bead inlay; 11½ inches; very good condition; $325–$425.

Haida, totem pole: raven over bear, worn dark patina with traces of red paint; ca. 1910; 13¾ inches high; good condition; $350–$550.

Haida, two spoons: both of horn with carved handles, one with provenance; ca. 1885; 7½ and 15 inches; very good condition; $350–$450/set.

Huron, quill case: birch bark with floral motifs in moose hair; deaccessioned from a Maine museum; 3¼ inches wide x 5¾ inches long; good condition; $125–$225.

Huron, sewing needlecase: birch bark with strawberry and floral decorations made with multicolored moose hair; 3¾ inches long; excellent condition; $100–$200.

Kwakiutl, figure: carved wood in the shape of a seal with inlay and shell eyes; 18½ inches long; very good condition; $200–$350.

Kwakiutl, two bowls: one a frog and one an otter, mother-of-pearl inlay, black-painted finish; both 20th century; 7½ and 20 inches; very good condition; $500–$700/set.

Kwakiutl, clan totem: carved wood with old dark varnish finish and frog, raven, and human forms, on platform; ca. 1920; 25½ inches high; very good condition; $500–$700.

Kwakiutl, complex face mask: beaver, raven, human face below beaver, cedar strips decoration; 20 inches high; very good condition; $3,000–$3,800.

Kwakiutl, dance staff: carved wood with abalone and mother-of-pearl inlay with horsehair; 6 feet long; very good condition; $80–$120.

Kwakiutl, totem pole: thunderbird, whale, and frog, polychrome painted with label "The Scenery Shop, Vancouver, B. C."; very good condition; $150–$250.

Wooden items, bowl, Northwest Coast; of flaring rectangular form, with stylized totemic face motif at each bowed end; linear incised decorations on sides; rim decorated with inset row of cowrie shells; subtle red and black pigment on end design; 14¹⁵⁄₁₆ inches; $1,500–$1,750. Courtesy Robert W. Skinner, Inc., Bolton/Boston, Massachusetts.

Kwakiutl, two clan totems: carved wood, polychrome decorated, winged eagle tops; signature on reverse side, "T. C. Smith"; 29½ inches high and 30 inches high; very good condition; $550–$650 each.

Kwakiutl, three whistles: one eagle whistle made of three pieces of wood bound with string, 9 inches long; one made of two pieces of wood with some red paint, sinew-bound, 9 inches long; one made of two separate whistles of four pieces of wood, sinew-bound, 9¼ inches long; late 19th century; good condition; $125–$175/set.

Micmac, box: birch bark with intricate floral design; deaccessioned from a Maine museum; late 18th or early 19th century; 6½ inches high x 11½ inches long; very good condition; $250–$300.

Northern Plains, dance wand: buffalo horn with beaded handle in light blue, red, white, and cobalt; 25 inches long; very good condition; $125–$175.

Northwest Coast, dance paddle: painted decoration on both sides; early; 28 inches long; good condition; $175–$275.

Northwest Coast, ladle: made of horn with stamped decoration on both sides of bowl; "R. D. 1786" initialed on back; probable Russian design influence; 17½ inches long; very good condition; $400–$500.

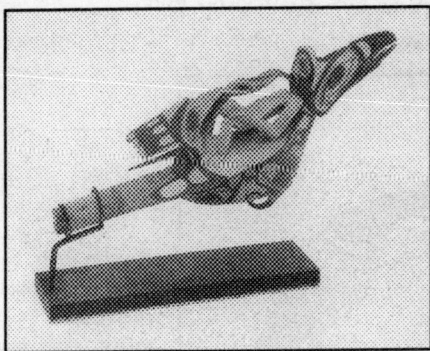

Wooden items, rattle, Northwest Coast; polychrome wood raven rattle; carved in two sections in the form of raven in flight with man reclining on his back with from being pulled from his mouth by kingfisher bird; the belly of the rattle-raven is decorated with a hawk with a sharply hooked nose; two-ply twined fiber-wrapped handle; 14 inches long; $5,000–$6,000. Courtesy of Robert W. Skinner, Inc., Bolton/Boston, Massachusetts.

Northwest Coast, mask: carved and painted wood with abalone inlay; signed "Lavalle"; contemporary; 9 x 7 inches; very good condition; $175–$400.

Northwest Coast, paddle: carved and painted wooden paddle; ca. 1900; 22 inches; very good condition; $200–$350.

Northwest Coast, totem pole: carved and polychromed; 9 inches high; very good condition; $75–$150.

Northwest Coast, totem pole: carved eagle and women on painted cedar; ca. 1940; 22 x 5 inches; very good condition; $65–$225.

Plains, box: painted, parfleche; late but looks old; 6 x 6 x 16 inches; very good condition; $100–$200.

Plains, drum holder: carved hardwood with green-pigmented finish; beaded top in white, cobalt, and white-heart reds with attached yellow-dyed horsehair; 43 inches long; very good condition; $200–$300.

Plains, pipe bowl: carved wooden bird with a bowl in its tail; 6 inches long; very good condition; $35–$65.

Sioux, backrest: finely crafted willow backrest; very good condition; $300–$400.

Sioux, cane: diamond willow cane with carved snake on staff; very good condition; $100–$200.

Sioux, cane: diamond willow cane carved with inlays, including picture of a girl; inscribed "Lucile Hegglund to P. F. McClure" (Dakota pioneer); 1912; $100–$200.

Wooden items, Shinnecock, decoy; heron decoy; Long Island, New York; relief-carved wings, two wooden legs; these large birds were hunted for food and feathers; $7,000–$11,000.
Collection of Gene and Linda Kangas. Photo by Gene Kangas.

Sioux, Eastern, bowl: made of burl wood, without decoration; rare; old; 9 inches; very good condition; $750–$950.

Sioux, mirror board: backboard, possibly from a shipping crate, has numbers and letters; old; 4 x 6 feet; very good condition; $300–$500.

Sioux, quirt: nice patina on hardwood handle; old; very good condition; $185–$300.

Woodlands: model canoe, and Northwest Coast paddle: canoe of birch-bark slat construction, 38 inches long; paddle carved on one side and painted on reverse side, 25½ inches; good condition; $275–$400/set.

Woodlands, box: birch bark with floral decorations, painted in red, with a lid and a double-curve motif design; late 18th or early 19th century; 4½ inches high x 10½ inches long; very good condition; $150–$250.

Woodlands, burl bowl: conical with dark marbleized surface; 15¼ inches diameter; very good condition; $400–$600.

Woodlands, ladle: carved wooden ladle; 12 inches long; very good condition; $85–$135.

Woodlands, spoon: carved wooden spoon, handle surmounted with a quail; 7¼ inches long; very good condition; $425–$625.

Woodlands, spoon: carved wooden spoon, handle carved with stylized heron's head; 18th century; 8¾ inches long; very good condition; $175–$275.

Woodlands, two ladles: two carved ladles, one made of tiger maple, and one with an early "make do" handle; 7½ and 11¾ inches long; good condition; $100–$130/set.

Zuni, Kachina mask: green, red, black, and gray painted leather, with nose and ears of green and red painted cottonwood; feathered topknot and lightning-strike decoration on back; hide appendages; tag reads "T. Dunn, Taos, N.M."; 9½ inches high x 13½ inches diameter; very good condition; $1,100–$1,300.

Appendix A

Tribes and Their Locations

≈

Alabama...............Chickasaw, Cherokee, Creek

Alaska...................Kwakiutl, Tlingit, Salish

Arizona.................Hopi, Hulapai, Mohave, Navajo, Yavapai, Pima,
Apache, Chemeheuvi, Maricopa, Chiricahua

Arkansas...............Quapaw, Caddo

California.............Wiyot, Modoc, Wintun, Patwin, Hupa, Yuki, Yana,
Maidu, Yanan, Yahi, Michoopoa, Pomo, Yuba,
Wappo, Yukian, Esalen, Chimarikan, Mono,
Salinan, Shoshone, Bankalachi, Tübatulabal,
Panamint, Yokut, Chumash, Pala, Cupeño,
Cahuilla, San Liuseno, Diegueño, Paiute,
Mohave, Papago, Pima

Colorado...............Cheyenne, Ute, Arapaho, Pueblo, Pagosa, Navajo

Connecticut...........Narragansett, Algonquian, Pequot

Delaware...............Iroquois

Florida..................Seminole, Tekesta, Salusa, Mikasuki, Calusa,
Timucua, Ais, Ocala

Georgia.................Cofitachiqui, Yamacraw, Creek, Seminole

Idaho....................Flathead, Sheepeater, Shoshone, Bannock

Illinois..................Algonquin, Illinois, Kickapoo, Michigamea

Indiana................Miami, Wea, Shawnee

Iowa.....................Arikara, Iowa, Sauk Fox, Otoe

Kansas.................Cheyenne, Osage, Sou, Otoe

Kentucky...............Shawnee, Wyandotte

Louisiana.............Coushatta, Tunica, Koroa, Yazoo, Quapaw,
Caddo

Maine	Adirondack, Malecite, Abnaki, Micmac, Penobscot
Maryland	Powhatan, Nanticoke
Massachusetts	Mohican, Souhegan, Mohawk
Michigan	Potawatomi, Chippewa, Ottawa
Minnesota	Arapaho, Ojibway, Arikara, Cheyenne, Winnebago, Sioux
Mississippi	Aquixo, Tunica, Chickasaw, Choctaw, Biloxi, Natchez
Missouri	Osage, Kaskaskia, Iowa, Arikara, Wyandotte
Montana	Flathead, Blackfeet, Piegan, Assiniboin, Cree, Crow, Sioux, Miniconjou, Cheyenne
Nebraska	Sioux, Omaha, Pawnee
New Hampshire	Abnaki, Nashua
New Jersey	Iroquois
New Mexico	Taos, Jumano, Apache, Pecos, Van Horne, Navajo, Zuni, Acoma, San Ildefonso, Keresan, Tiguex, Tiwa, Mimbreño, Piro, Tewa, Tampiro, Hueco, Pima, Jicarilla, Apache
New York	Oneida, Mohawk, Seneca, Onondaga, Iroquois, Adirondack
Nevada	Paiute, Gosiute, Mohave, Shoshone
North Carolina	Catawba, Waxhaw, Chitchiti, Crowatan, Tuscarora, Tutelo, Saponi, Chowanok
North Dakota	Bungi, Sioux, Arikara, Mandan, Minot
Ohio	Shawnee, Miami, Mingo, Iroquois, Shawano, Adena
Oklahoma	Wichita, Nadakao, Hasinai, Senis-Nasoni-Yscanis, Caddo, El Reno, Sioux, Cheyenne, Osage, Kichai, Creek
Oregon	Wallawalla, Wasco, Nor Paiute, Rouge, Yoncalla, Yumatilla, Molala
Pennsylvania	Erie, Delaware, Lock, Susquehanna
Rhode Island	Mohican, Shinnecock
South Carolina	Cherokee, Catawba, Waxhaw, Yamasee
South Dakota	Sioux, Sanarc, Two Kettle, Ponca

Tennessee ....Chickasaw, Chickamauga, Cherokee

Utah.....................Bannock, Shoshone, Ute, Paiute

Vermont................Abnaki, Iroquois, Mohawk, Mohican

Virginia................Potomac, Meherrin, Mataponi, Famunkey,
                      Chickahominy, Notoway, Tutelo

Washington..........Kyuquot, Clallam, Spokan, Wallawalla, Klickitat,
                      Yakima, Salish, Haida, Siletz, Tlingit, Kwakiutl

West Virginia........Shawnee, Iroquois, Fincastle

Wisconsin.............Tomahawk, Miami, Kickapoo, Chippewa, Tilini,
                      Ojibway, Fox, Winnebago

Wyoming..............Sioux, Kiowa, Shoshone, Arapaho, Blackfoot

Appendix B

Auctioneer Contributors

~

Colonel L. Doug Allard
P.O. Box 460
#1 Museum Lane
St. Ignatius, MT 59865
406-745-2951

Antiques and Art
James O. Aplan
HC 80 Box 793-25
Piedmont, SD 57769-9403
605-347-5016

W. E. Channing
53 Old Santa Fe Trail
Santa Fe, NM   87501
508-988-1078

Garth's Auctions, Inc.
2690 Stratford Road
P.O. Box 369
Delaware, OH   43015
614-362-4771
614-369-5085
614-548-6778

C. E. Guarino
Box 49—Berry Road
Denmark, ME 04022
207-452-2123

Frank C. Kaminski
Kaminski Auctioneers &
Appraisers
241 Main Street
Stoneham, MA   02180

Willis Henry Auctions, Inc.
Karel & Willis Henry
22 Main Street
Marshfield, MA   02050
617-834-7774

R. G. Munn
8625 Tumbleweed Terrace
Santee, CA   92071
619-596-7630

Skinner, Inc.
357 Main Street
Bolton, MA 01740
508-779-6241

Appendix C

Dealer Contributors

❧

Alexander E. Anthony, Jr.
Adobe Gallery
413 Romero NW
Albuquerque, NM 87104
505-243-8485

Wanda Campbell
Indian Art Unlimited
Route 1
Carmi, IL 62821
618-382-7702

Kenneth Canfield
Canfield Gallery
414 Canyon Road
Santa Fe, NM 87501
505-988-4199

William Corbett
Indian Museum
Southold, NY 11971

Von Hilliard
The Indian Shop
P.O. Box 246
Independence, KY 41051
606-428-2485

Long Ago and Far Away
Green Mountain Village Shops
Route 7A
Manchester Center, VT 05255
802-362-3435

Moondancer Gallery
Redondo Beach, CA
310-316-7220

Andrew Nagen
Dewey Galleries, Ltd.
74 E. San Francisco Street
Santa Fe, NM 87501
800-262-8256
and:
Andrew Nagen
P.O. Box 1306
Corrales, NM 87048
505-898-5058

Robert F. Nichols
419 Canyon Road
Santa Fe, NM 87501
505-982-2145

Silver Sun Traders
2042 So. Plaza
Historic Old Town
Albuquerque, NM 87104
505-242-8265
and:
Silver Sun Traders
656 Canyon Road
Santa Fe, NM 87501
505-983-8743

Collector Contributors

❧

Evelyn Ackerman
Culver City, California

Joe and Lee Dumas
Southgate, Michigan

Joyce Williams
Okmulgee, Oklahoma

Appendix E

Artist Contributors

❧

Andy P. Abeita
31 Saxon Road
Los Lunas, NM 87031
505-865-6156

Joseph R. Jojolla
202 Corporal
WSMR, NM 88002
505-678-6473

Jake Livingston
P.O. Box 252
Houck, AZ 26506
602-688-2768

Gibson Nez
Hogan in the Hilton
100 Sandoval Street
Santa Fe, NM 87501
505-984-0932

Charlie Pratt
2801 Rodeo Road, #B533
Santa Fe, NM 87501
505-982-8630

Alan Wallace
Jeweler and Painter
Box 2562
Taos, NM 87571
505-776-1325

SPECIAL THANKS TO THESE
FIRST EDITION CONTRIBUTORS

authors Gene and Linda Kangas
Ohio

auctioneer Jack Sellner, CAI
Scottsdale, Arizona

artist and museum owner Jack Glover
Sunset, Texas

collector Donna McMenamin
Houston, Texas

dealer Two Star Collection
Houston, Texas

dealer Naranjo's World of American Indian Art
Houston, Texas

collector David Atteberry
Dallas, Texas

collector William Nash
Tulsa, Oklahoma

collector Lahoma Haddock Goldsmith
Okmulgee, Oklahoma

dealer Old Town Antiques
Albuquerque, New Mexico

dealer Miniatures at the Kiva
Taos, New Mexico

dealer Larry Gottheim
Binghamton, New York

480

Bibliography

❧

The Antique Traveler, January 1988, 6, 13. "Indian Territory Sold at the Turn of the Century."

Antiques and the Arts Weekly, February 5, 1988, 1–3. "Lost and Found Traditions—Renwick Gallery Show on View Through March 6."

———. February 12, 1988, 100–101. "Ethnographic Art to be Sold at Hesse Galleries February 20."

———. February 12, 1988, 35. "Navajo Rug Exhibition Opening in Lexington."

———. September 25, 1987, 20. "It's Westward Ho at the Springfield Art Museums."

Appleton, LeRoy H. *American Indian Design and Decoration.* New York: Dover, 1971.

Arden, Harvey. "The Fire That Never Dies." *National Geographic,* September 1987, 375–403.

Arizona Highways, July 1972. "The Story of the Gallup Inter-Tribal Indian Ceremonial."

———. June, 1973. "Hopi Kachina Artist Alwin James Makya."

———. June, 1973. "Basket Making in Arizona by Don Dedera."

———. June, 1973. "Asmar—Interprets Southwestern Indian Ceremonies and Life."

Arnold, David L. "Pueblo Artistry in Clay." *National Geographic,* November 1982.

Art and Antiques, March 1988, 49–81. "America's Top 100 Collectors."

Babcock, Barbara A., and Monthan, Guy and Doris. *The Pueblo Storyteller.* Tucson, Arizona: The University of Arizona Press, 1986.

Barnett, Franklin. *Dictionary of Prehistoric Indian Artifacts of the American Southwest.* Flagstaff, Arizona: Northland Publishing Company, 1991.

Bataille, Gretchen M., and Sands, Kathleen Mullen. *American Indian Women: Telling Their Lives.* Omaha, Nebraska: University of Nebraska Press, 1984.

Beidler, Peter G., and Egge, Marion F. *The American Indian in Short Fiction,* an annotated bibliography. Metuchen, New Jersey, and London: The Scarecrow Press, Inc., 1979.

Bennett, Edna Mae and John F. *Turquoise Jewelry of the Indians of the Southwest.* Colorado: Turquoise Books, 1973.

Bennett, Kathleen Whittaker. "The Navajo Chief Blanket—A Trade Item Among Non-Navajo Groups." *American Indian Art Magazine,* winter 1981, 62–68.

Brose, David S.; Brown, James A.; and Penney, David W. *Ancient Art of the American Woodland Indians.* New York: Harry N. Abrams, Inc., 1985.

Brown, Dee. *Bury My Heart at Wounded Knee.* New York: Bantam Books, 1961.

Brownell, Charles De Wolf. *The Indian Races of North and South America.* Philadelphia: Hurlbut, Scranton and Company, 1865.

Bunzel, Ruth L. *The Pueblo Potter: A Study in Primitive Art.* New York: Dover Publications, 1972.

Canby, Thomas Y. "The Anasazi: Riddles in the Ruins." *National Geographic,* November 1982.

Catlin, George. *Letters and Notes on the Manners, Customs and Conditions of the North American Indian.* New York: Dover Publications, 1973.

Chavez, Denise. "Words of Wisdom." *New Mexico Magazine,* December 1987, 72–78.

Cirillo, Dexter. "Back to the Past: Tradition and Change in Contemporary Pueblo Jewelry." *American Indian Art,* spring 1988, 46–63.

Clark, Carol. "Charles Deas." *American History Illustrated,* 1992, 19–33.

Clark, Ella E. *Indian Legends of the Pacific Northwest.* California: University of California Press, 1953.

Clark, Jackson. "The 1988 IACA Artist of the Year." *The Indian Trader,* November 1987, 4–5.

Culin, Stewart. *Games of the North American Indians.* New York: Dover Publications, 1975.

Currier, William T. *Currier's Price Guide to American Artists 1645–1945 at Auction.* Brockton, Massachusetts: Currier Publications, 1987.

Dallas, Sandra. "Triumph on a Loom." *Americana,* June 1988, 54–57.

Densmore, Frances. *How Indians Use Wild Plants for Food, Medicine and Crafts.* New York: Dover Publications, 1974.

Discover Native America 1993, January 7–10, 1993. "Seminole Tribe of Florida, Orlando."

Dockstader, Dr. Frederick. "A Capsule View of the Hopi." *The Indian Trader,* March 1988.

Drimmer, Frederick, ed. *Captured by the Indians, 15 Firsthand Accounts, 1750–1870.* New York: Dover Publications, 1961.

Drucker, Philip. *Cultures of the North Pacific Coast.* San Francisco: Chandler Publishing Company, 1965.

Durrell, Pat. "Collecting Trade Beads." *The Indian Trader,* October 1987, 4–5.

Edler, Robert. *Early Archaic Indian Points & Knives,* Paducah, Kentucky: Collector Books, 1990.

Elliott, Malinda. "Collectors Find Hidden Gold." *New Mexico Magazine,* January 1988, 50–54.

Elliott, Mark. "Basic Techniques in Beading" and "Material and Techniques of Beadwork." *The Indian Trader,* October 1987, 14–15.

Erdoes, Richard, and Ortiz, Alfonso. *American Indian Myths and Legends.* New York: Pantheon Books, 1984.

Ewers, John C. *Plains Indian Sculpture—A Traditional Art from America's Heartland.* Washington, D.C.: Smithsonian Institution Press, 1986.

Falk, Peter Hastings. *Who was Who in American Art.* Madison, Connecticut: Sound View Press, 1985.

Fielding, Mantle. *Dictionary of American Painters, Sculptors and Engravers.* Connecticut: Modern Books & Crafts, Inc., 1974.

Fleming, Paula Richardson, and Luskey, Judith. *The North American Indians in Early Photographs*. New York: Harper & Row, 1986.

Frank, Larry. *Indian Silver Jewelry of the Southwest, 1868–1930*. Boston: New York Graphic Society, 1978.

Gillman, Carolyn. "The Way to Independence: An Exhibition at the Minnesota Historical Society." *American Indian Art,* spring 1988.

Gunn Allen, Paula. *Grandmothers of the Light—A Medicine Woman's Source Book*. Boston: Beacon Press, 1991.

Gustafson, Eleanor H. "Museum Accessions." *The Magazine Antiques,* October 1987.

Harsant, Wendy J. "The Otago Museum, Dunedin, New Zealand: The North American Indian Collection." *American Indian Art,* spring 1988.

Hassrick, Royal B. *The George Catlin Book of American Indians*. New York: Promontory Press, 1977.

———. *North American Indians*. Octopus Books, 1974.

Holm, Bill. "A Wooling Mantle Neatly Wrought: The Early Historic Record of Northwest Coast Pattern-Twined Textiles—1774–1850." *American Indian Art Magazine,* winter 1982, 34–47.

Hothem, Lar. *Collecting Indian Knives (Identifications and Values)*. Florence, Alabama: Books Americana, Inc., 1986.

———. *North American Indian Artifacts,* 3d ed. Florence, Alabama: Books Americana, Inc., 1984.

Hungry Wolf, Beverly. *The Ways of My Grandmothers*. New York: William Morrow and Company, 1982.

The Indian Trader, August 1987, 4. "The Folk Art Carvings of Johnson Antonio—The Making of a Bisti Carver."

———. October 1987. "The History of Glass Beads," 6—81. "Wampum—An Early Medium of Exchange," 10–11. "From Quillwork to Beadwork," 20.

———. December 1987. "The Plight of the Navajo Medicine- man," 4—5.

———. January 1988. "Indian Art Enjoying a Second Renaissance," 3–4. "The Meanings Behind Decorative Symbols Used in Indian Art," 6. "The Beauty of California Mission Basketry,"

7–9. "The Diamond Rattlesnake Basket," 9–11. "The Calumet: A Sacred Pipe Used for Rituals of Peace and War," 15, 18.

———. February 1988. "A Brief Description of the Pow-Wow and its Origins."

———. March 1988. "Southern Plains Museum Features Works by Tony Jojola," 21. "Wampanoag Historian Traces Forefather's Lives," 15. "Masayesva Selected Poster Artist for Festival of Native American Arts," 11. "Newlands Outline: A New Regional Style Rug," 3–4.

Jacka, Jerry D. "Innovations in Southwestern Indian Jewelry: Fine Art in the 1980s." *American Indian Art Magazine,* spring 1984, 28–37.

Jacka, Lois, and Tanner, Clara Lee. "Moments with Maria." *Native Peoples: The Journal of the Heard Museum,* winter 1988, 24–29.

Jacobsen, Anita. *Jacobsen's Sixth Painting and Bronze Price Guide,* vol. 6. Published by Anita Jacobsen, 1983.

James, George Wharton. *Indian Blankets and Their Makers.* New York; Dover Publications, 1974.

———. *Indian Basketry.* New York: Dover Publications, 1972.

James, H. L. *Rugs and Posts—The Story of Navajo Weaving and Indian Trading.* West Chester, Pennsylvania: Schiffer Publishing Ltd., 1988.

Kahn, Brenda Norrell. "Margaret Quintana, Mistress of the Storytellers." *The Indian Trader,* December 1987.

Kangas, Linda and Gene. *Decoys.* Paducah, Kentucky: Collector Books, 1992.

Kazin, Alfred. "Southwestward—The Great American Space." *American Heritage,* April 1987, 53–61.

Keating, Bern, and Harbutt, Charles. "Today Along the Nachez Trace Pathway Through History." *National Geographic,* November 1968.

Kent, Kate P. "Pueblo Weaving." *American Indian Art Magazine,* winter 1981, 32–45.

Kimball, Richard. "Up to the Green River—The Knife that Won the West." *The Indian Trader,* May 1988.

————. "The Great Tree of Peace." *The Indian Trader,* March 1988.

Kopper, Philip. *The Smithsonian Book of North American Indians Before the Coming of the Europeans.* Washington, D.C.: Smithsonian Institution Press, 1986.

Kramer, Fran. "Crystal Ball Gazing." *Antique Review,* February 1988, 27.

Kroeber, A. L. *Handbook of the Indians of California.* New York: Dover Publications, 1976.

Lamar, Howard R., ed. *The Reader's Encyclopedia of the American West.* New York: Harper & Row, 1977.

Laxalt, Robert, and Woolfitt, Adam. "New Mexico, the Golden Land." *National Geographic,* September 1970.

LeFree, Betty. *Santa Clara Pottery Today.* Albuquerque, New Mexico: University of New Mexico Press, 1975.

Looney, Ralph, and Dale, Bruce. "The Navajo Nation Looks Ahead." *National Geographic,* December 1972.

Mallery, Garrick. *Picture Writing of the American Indians,* vol. 1 and vol. 2. New York: Dover Publications, 1972.

Mariette, Kim Rosea. "Why Indians Painted Their Horses." *American West,* February 1988, 72–75.

Martin, Dolly, ed. *Seminole American Indian Magazine,* vol. 1 (1987). Official Publication of the Seminole Tribe of Florida, Inc.; Phyllis Finney Loconto, publisher; Hollywood, Florida.

McCoy, Ronald. "Apache Rawhide Playing Cards." *American Indian Art Magazine,* summer 1984, 52–59.

McCullough, David. "Frederic Remington." *American History Illustrated,* February 1988, 26–39.

McKay, Gary. "Connoisseurship—Consuming Interests." *Ultra, The Texas Lifestyle Magazine,* January 1988.

Meilach, Dona Z. *Ethnic Jewelry—Design and Inspiration for Collectors.* New York: Crown Publishers, 1981.

Mera, H. P. *Pueblo Designs.* New York: Dover Publications, 1970.

Meredith, Roy. *Mr. Lincoln's Camera Man: Matthew B. Brady.* New York: Dover Publications, 1946.

Miller, Pamela Stanley. *Authentic American Indian Beadwork and How to Do It.* New York: Dover Publications, 1984.

Moeser, Vikki. "Lost and Found Indian Traditions." *The Indian Trader,* December 1987.

Navajo School of Indian Basketry. *Indian Basket Weaving.* New York: Dover Publications, 1971.

Naylor, Maria, ed. *Authentic Indian Designs.* New York: Dover Publications, 1975.

Neihardt, John G. *Black Elk Speaks—Being the Life Story of a Holy Man of the Oglala Sioux.* Lincoln, Nebraska, and London: University of Nebraska Press, 1979.

New Mexico Magazine, November 1987, 43–49. "Santa Fe Creators."

O'Kane, Walter Collins. *The Hopis: Portrait of a Desert People.* Tulsa, Oklahoma: University of Oklahoma Press, 1953.

Overstreet, Robert M., and Peake, Howard. *Official Overstreet Price Guide—Indian Arrowheads,* 2d ed. New York: The House of Collectibles, 1991.

Page, Jake. "Inside the Sacred Hopi Homeland." *National Geographic,* November 1982.

Parker, Arthur C. *The Indian How Book.* New York: Dover Publications, 1975.

Perry, Erma. "Stephen Laurent: An Authority on the Abenaki Indian History." *Grit,* November 1987.

Plett, Nicole. "The Best of the Westerns." *Southwest Profile,* vol. 2, no. 2.

Raycraft, Don and Carol. *Collector's Guide to Country Store Antiques.* Paducah, Kentucky: Collector Books, 1987.

Reichard, Gladys A. *Weaving a Navajo Blanket.* New York: Dover Publications, 1974.

Rhodes, Lee. "Conceived in Beauty—Executed with Dignity." *Arizona Highways,* July 1972.

Ripp, Bart. "Eleven Indian Painters Created a Treasure at Maisel's." *Indian Trader,* March 1988.

Sagel, Jim. "Frank Waters." *New Mexico Magazine,* February 1988, 52–57.

Sayers, Robert. "Symbol and Meaning in Hopi Ritual Textile Design." *American Indian Art Magazine,* winter 1981, 70–77.

Schiffer, Nancy N. *Navajo Arts and Crafts*. West Chester, Pennsylvania: Schiffer Publishing Ltd., 1991.

————. *Pictorial Weavings of the Navajo*. West Chester, Pennsylvania: Schiffer Publishing Ltd., 1991.

————. *Miniature Arts of the Southwest*. West Chester, Pennsylvania: Schiffer Publishing Ltd., 1991.

Sides, Dorothy Smith. *Decorative Art of the Southwestern Indians*. New York: Dover Publications, 1961.

Smithsonian, August 1987. "At the Renwick, American Traditions."

Snodgrass, Jeanne O. *American Indian Painters—A Biographical Directory*. New York: Museum of American Indian, Heye Foundation, 1968.

Stafford, Kim R. "A Few Miles Short of Wisdom." *American West*, February 1988.

Starline, Marjorie. "Karen Charley, Traditional Hopi Potter." *The Indian Trader*, March 1988, 19.

Stuart, George E. "Mounds: Riddles from the Indian Past." *National Geographic*, December 1972.

Sturtevant, William C., ed. *A Seminole Sourcebook*. Garland Publishing, Inc., 1987.

Sutton, Jacqueline E. "Following the Santa Fe Trail." *Gift Reporter*, February 1988, 22–25.

Tanner, Clara Lee. *Indian Baskets of the Southwest*. Tucson, Arizona:University of Arizona Press, 1983.

Theran, Susan. *Official Price Guide to Fine Art*. New York: House of Collectibles, 1987.

Thompson, Laura, and Joseph, Alice. *The Hopi Way*. Washington, D.C.: United States Indian Service, 1944.

Titiev, Mischa. *The Hopi Indians of Old Oraibi: Change and Continuity*. Detroit: University of Michigan Press, 1972.

Tully, Lawrence N. Flints. *Blades and Projectile Points of the North American Indian*. Paducah, Kentucky: Collector Books, 1986.

Turano, Jane Van N. "Sotheby's Winter Sale of American Indian Art." *Maine Antique Digest*, February 1988.

Turnbaugh, William A,. and Turnbaugh, Sarah Peabody. *Indian Jewelry of the American Southwest.* West Chester, Pennsylvania: Schiffer Publishing Ltd., 1988.

———. *Indian Baskets.* West Chester, Pennsylvania: Schiffer Publishing Ltd., 1986.

Viola, Herman J. *Exploring the West.* Washington, D.C.: Smithsonian Books, 1987.

———. *After Columbus: The Smithsonian Chronicle of the North American Indians.* Washington, D.C.: Smithsonian Books, and New York: Orion Books, 1990.

Weatherford, Jack. *Indian Givers—How The Indians of the Americas Transformed the World.* New York: Crown Publishers, Inc., 1988.

Weinstein, Robert. "Silent Witnesses." *Photo Bulletin,* Ray Hawkins Gallery, Los Angeles.

Wheeler, George M. *Wheeler's Photographic Survey of the American West 1871–1873.* New York: Dover Publications, 1983.

Whiteford, Andrew Hunter. *North American Indian Arts.* New York; Golden Press, 1973.

Whitt, Jennie. "The Art of the Plains Indians." *The Indian Trader,* June 1983, 5–10.

Wild, Peter. "N. Scott Momaday: Gentle Maverick." *American West,* February 1988.

Wind, Crying. *My Searching Heart,* a biographical novel. Eugene, Oregon: Harvest House Publishers, 1980.

The World of the American Indian. Washington, D.C.: National Geographic Society, 1974.

Wright, Barton. "Kachina Carvings." *American Indian Art Magazine,* spring 1984, 38–45, 81.

———. *Kachinas: A Hopi Artist's Documentary.* Flagstaff, Arizona: Northland Press, with the Heard Museum, Phoenix, Arizona, 1973.

Wright, Robyn K. "The Burke Museum: Northwest Coast Collection." *American Indian Art,* spring 1988, 32–37.

Wright, Ronald. *Stolen Continents—The Americas Through Indian Eyes Since 1492.* A Peter Davison Book. Boston, New York, London: Houghton Mifflin Company, 1992.

Yenne, Bell. *The Encyclopedia of North American Indian Tribes.* Montana: Bison Books, 1986.

Zuend, Pat. "Michael Paul, Colville Indian Storypole Carver." *The Indian Trader,* November 1987, 9, 11, 13.

Index

Sure Shot Chewing Tobacco, 273
Susquehana
    clothing, 188
Sweezy, Carl, 29
Swords, 453

Tableta, 403
Tafoya, Camilio "Sunflower", 412,
    414, 424–425
Tafoya, Joe, 412
Tafoya, Madeline, 414
Tafoya, Margaret, 414, 425
Tafoya, Mida, 414
Tafoya, Serafina, 424, 425
Tahbo, Mark, 419
Tahoma, Quincy, 39, 48
Taiz, 246
Talahytewa, Stacy, 240
Talashoma, Lowell, 232
Tanner, Clara Lee, 9, 19
Taos Pueblo, 269–270, 278
    ephemera/advertising, 296
    miscellaneous, 394
    pottery, 414
Tapestry, 159
Teec Nos Pos
    blankets/rugs, 143, 165–166
Teepees, 347, 348, 352, 362, 378
Tejon, 88
Teller, Stella, 431
Tempera, 45–46
Terpning, Howard, 38
Tesuque, 414, 415, 439
Teton Sioux tribe, 14
Tetons, 236, 444, 445, 447–448
Tewa, 23, 409, 411, 419
Tewawina, Wilfred, 232
Thimbles, 445
Thompson, Preston, 326, 342
Thompson River
    baskets, 80, 133
Throws, 166, 174
Tie bars, 342

Tiger, Jerome, 28
Tillamook
    baskets, 133
Timucuan, 270
Tins, 290, 304
Tipi rest, 77–78
Tlingit, 288, 379
    art, 34, 50
    artifacts, 77
    baskets, 82, 99, 133–135
    blankets/rugs, 149, 175
    clothing, 192, 221
    jewelry, 311–312, 327
    leather, 373, 379
    miscellaneous, 387, 388, 390,
        395, 396, 400–404
    tools/weapons, 447
Toadlena, 268
Tobacco advertisement, 290, 304
Tobacco bags, 352, 371
Tobacco display boxes, 304
Tobacco paper, 304
Tobacco store bins, 304
Toboggans, 239
Toddy, Jimmy, 46
Toke, Lee Monette Tsa, 38
Toledo, George, 341
Tomahawk, 78, 403, 444, 454, 455
Tonkawa, 30
Tools, 78, 347
Torivio, Dorothy, 426
Tosque, 30
Totem poles, 50, 461–462, 465,
    467, 468–469, 470
Totems, 262, 403–404, 467, 468,
    469
Toya, Mary E., 418–419
Trade beads (see also Beads),
    342–346, 384
Trade pipe, 404
Trail of Tears, 267
Transitional, blankets/rugs,
    167–168